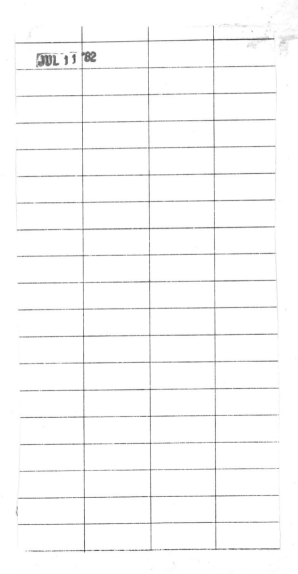

JUL 11 '82

The Work of the Catholic Church in the United States of America

The Work
of the Catholic Church
in the United States of America

by

ALFONSO ZARATTI, O. C. D.

Translated from the Italian

by

WILLIAM PACKER and JOHN HOBART

ROME, ITALY, MARCH 1956

Imprimi potest

Fr. CAROLUS A JESU MARIA
Provincialis

Romae, die 2 decembris 1955

The Nardini « Artistic » Publishing Company - **Rome, Italy**

CONTENTS

CHAPTER I

THE IDEAL ASPECT OF AMERICA

CHAPTER IV

JESUITS ON THE RED PATH OF GLORY — TWO LILIES AMONG THE NEGROES

CHAPTER V

GEORGE WASHINGTON AND CATHOLICISM

Chapter VI

CATHOLICS IN AMERICA DURING THE EPIC STRUGGLE FOR INDEPENDENCE

XV

CHAPTER XI

A STATISTICAL RECORD OF THE DEVELOPMENT
OF THE CATHOLIC CHURCH IN THE U.S.

BIBLIOGRAPHICAL NOTES

Introduction

Those who have written of the spirit of America and the history of the United States have almost invariably assumed that the architects of the American spirit and culture were Protestant. It is true that some of the first settlers in this Country were Puritans, who came to Plymouth, Massachusetts, in 1620. But Puritanism was then in the decline and most of that sect has long since died out. The Catholics who settled in Maryland stressed religious liberty from the outset and impressed their culture on their surroundings. The Faith and Church that they brought to the United States is the same as that which exists today. Thus the Catholic Church is the oldest organization in the United States and the only one that has retained the same life and form through each succeeding age. Yet Catholicism has received, although it is the strongest and most vigorous religious spirit in America, only perfunctory and even slighting notice in most studies.

It has been left, therefore, for Father Alfonso Zaratti, the eminent Carmelite historian, to point out the tremendous contribution that Catholicism has made to American culture. His monumental study on *The Work of the Catholic Church in the United States of America* is the fruit of long years of research and exhaustive travel throughout the length and breadth of this great Nation. It was my happy privilege to work with Father Zaratti during his stay in America, and I was impressed by his learning and diligence. He holds a doctorate in Church History from the Pontifical Gregorian University and degrees in Philosophy and Letters. In Rome they say that he was « born with a pen in his hand », for he has been writing books and contributing articles to scientific and religious publications since he was eighteen. He has founded three religious reviews and now directs the magazine « *Il Piccolo Fiore di Gesù* ». His diligence is no less remarkable and the voluminous correspondence that he carries on with writers and editors in all parts of the world is truly amazing. While with Father Zaratti I was struck by the fact that he was constantly making notes and checking correspondence.

It was indeed fortunate for the Catholics in the United States that the Carmelite Superiors in 1954 sent so industrious and talented a historian and journalist to visit us, study our history and institutions, and return to the center of Christendom and there write one of the most objective and factual studies on the Catholic Church in America. His work is a « must » for every student of Church History and for all Catholics who want to be thoroughly informed regarding their Faith and the United States.

Father Zaratti's book starts with an analysis of the ideals of our Country and goes on to show how many of the major events in our history were effected by Catholics. For example, whether you give credit for the discovery of America to Christopher Columbus or Leif Ericson, the feat was accomplished by a Catholic. Whether you start from the East Coast or the West Coast, you find innumerable communities settled by Catholics and the places named by them. From St. Augustine, Florida, to San Francisco, California; and from St. Paul, Minnesota, to San Antonio, Texas, you come across countless reminders of the Faith that baptized this land. « With a moment's reflection », Father Zaratti observes, « You will understand how all this inspires a sense of peace and serenity : an idyll of faith lived and experienced, like a guiding benediction ».

The result of Father Zaratti's study is that far from being an alien spirit in the United States, Catholicism is rather one of the greatest influences in the culture and genius of our Nation. With its emphasis on justice and truth and its support of liberty and equality, a stronger Catholicism will be one of the greatest bulwarks for the American way of life.

To get an over-all picture Father Alfonso Zaratti has felt obliged to reduce the accounts of the various missionary and colonizing efforts to a minimum. It is not that he regards their contributions as unimportant or their results ephemeral. On the contrary, it is because he finds the story so fascinating and so rich in detail that it must be drastically abbreviated for the sake of giving sharper clarity to the general pattern.

For the same reason he has arranged his material under general headings, rather than chronologically detailing the development of ecclesiastical provinces and dioceses. Institutions and religious Orders are treated only in a generic way, and a few typical figures are selected as representatives of the hundreds of explorers, politicians, philosophers, writers, ecclesiastics and religious who have labored for the good of the Church in America.

Too often Church historians have presented Catholicism as though it were something by itself. But Father Zaratti in his *Work of the Catholic Church in the United States of America* makes our Faith a part of the epic of

America. If one is to understand America properly, one must appreciate the role of the Church and that is why this book is so valuable. It gives a « bird's-eye view » of Catholic history in the United States in a highly readable style. The information is clear, to the point, and injected with some of Father Zaratti's own contagious enthusiasm for the spread of Christ's reign on earth. It is a distinct honor and delight, therefore, to recommend this work to the Catholics of America and lovers of Church History everywhere.

Rev. Godfrey Poage, C. P.

Immaculate Conception Monastery

Chicago, Illinois, U.S.A., 1955.

Preface

*M*any of my American Friends have repeatedly expressed their wish to read one of my books published in Italian. Instead of having any of them translated into English, I resolved to write one expressly for them on a subject concerning them more closely and which will show my acquaintance with their history and way of life.

This volume limits itself to generalities. Many volumes would be needed for a complete survey. My Friends must therefore content themselves for the present with what I have written, while I promise however, to publish further studies on America.

I wish to express my heartfelt gratitude to the Bishops and Priests and to all those who have contributed to the subject matter of this book.

The Author

THE IDEAL ASPECT OF AMERICA

A widespread prejudice, deeply rooted in many Europeans, obliges us to examine American idealism with impartiality so that we may judge it in its proper perspective.

Famous writers have declared that America is a nation with strong materialistic tendencies, a statement unfortunately repeated by innumerable amateur observers which continues to gain ground through automatic repetition. The late George Santayana, American poet-philosopher, tempered his judgment, it is true, by describing the American as « an idealist who works with matter... in terms of figures, of measurements, of discoveries, of economy and speed »; others, however, such as the Swiss Calvinist Henri Amiel, have not maintained such prudence. In the opinion of Amiel, « American life is reduced to a devouring, incessant activity. Americans must earn money, they must achieve predominance and power; they must crush their rivals and conquer Nature. They mistake existence for individual welfare and the expansion of the ego for happiness. This means that they do not live for the soul, they are unaware of what is immutable and eternal, and since they cannot penetrate into the heart of their own existence, they never advance beyond the edge of it ».

This evaluation seems the more serious when one considers that a similar one was recently expressed by the American writer Waldo Frank, according to whom America was born between the 16th and 17th centuries « out of the collapse of Catholic, Papal and Imperial Europe, of a united Europe ». The nation, then in its infancy, Frank continues, was to carry the problem of unity to another plane. America with its Puritanism and capitalism, which are practically the same thing, would thus be essentially an organism of power.

Briefly stated, many contend that America is dominated by the god of money, an allegation as ridiculous as the belief that « a man is worth as much as he possesses ». The significant titles of two widely popular sociological works by Andrew Carnegie ([1]) have become by-words mouthed by superficial observers who refer to America — without having taken the trouble to sound out its true national spirit — as the « empire of business », as a nation that only knows the « gospel of wealth », the « big stick policy » and « dollar diplomacy ».

Interpreting American statistics within the limited range of their vision, these observers draw the conclusion that the young Atlantis is divorce-ridden, that would-be divorcees look to California and Reno as their Meccas ([2]). Furthermore, they point out that gangsterism is rife in the metropolitan cities, that there are over 12,000 suicides every year, that alcoholism is rampant in all classes of American society ([3]), that Hollywood does not always produce films of instructive art or innocent comedy, and so on. It is not altogether surprising, therefore, that a journalist of Italian origin, basing his observation on such preconceived notions of American life and customs, should define America as « a puritan mind in a pagan body » ([4]).

4

The country's most authoritative clergymen, educators and moralists have consistently cried out against these excesses of judgment and often openly denounced unworthy attacks of this nature. A statement by Abraham Lincoln, which sounds almost like a sermon by Bossuet or Bordaloue, should be convincing enough for anyone. « We have grown in numbers, in wealth and in power as no other nation has ever grown; but we have forgotten God, » he said. « We have forgotten the Benign Hand that has preserved us in peace and has multiplied and enriched us... It is our duty to humble ourselves at the feet of Our Lord, to confess our national sins and ask for pardon and clemency » (⁵).

The Church, too, has raised its impartial voice. In his encyclical *Sertum laetitiae* of November 1, 1939, Pope Pius XII, far from closing his eyes to the less exalted aspects of America or trying to conceal them behind a veil of mercy, pointed out in accents worthy of St. Paul « the refusal to recognize the Divine Majesty; indifference towards the moral laws of supernatural origin; the detestable inconstancy which wavers between the licit and illicit, between justice and iniquity; spawning blind, excessive selfishness; the thirst for pleasure; alcoholism; extravagant and immodest fashions; crime that flourishes even among minors; the lust for power; neglect of the poor; the greed for ill-gotten riches; desertion of the farms; capricious matrimony; divorce; the disintegration of the family; the lack of mutual affection between parents and children; the falling birth rate; the weakening of the race; growing disrespect for authority; servility; rebellion and neglect of duty towards one's country and fellowmen ». Moreover, the Pontiff added, « we raise our paternal voice in lament that Christ is despised or ignored in so many schools, that the teachings of the universe and of mankind are limited to the spheres of naturalism and rationalism, and that new educational systems are being tried out, systems which can only bring dire consequences to the intellectual and moral life of the nation ».

This mirrors the negative and most obvious aspects of a slim minority of a race that finds itself in the critical phase of eruptive youth. Consumed by feverish activity, the American people have melted down the world's most adventurous spirits in its crucible to forge a new species of humanity, unlike any that has ever existed before it.

The student of a nation's ethical and religious problems cannot ignore these declared prejudices because if such criticisms reflected the truth, if the United States were a country basely materialistic and obtusely wanting in idealism, then any inquiry into the genuine religious vitality and decisive, creative influence of Catholic principles in the New World would likewise produce largely negative results. Therefore, we must go beyond those appearances that meet the eye and examine the truth closely and with wisdom — even in its ugliest aspects — before hurling stones against a people who have not yet been able to demonstrate the full measure of their idealism.

II — The noblest and most genuine heritage left to America by the Puritans was not a fanaticism automatically swept away with the Revolution, nor even that grim outlook on life appraised by Gilbert K. Chesterton more for love of coining a fine paradox than for accuracy. The Puritan heritage, which still today substantially influences the country's national and civic leadership, is above all a sense of personal responsibility and staunchness of character.

In his *History of the United States* (Chapter XXIV), Bancroft refers to two sayings of the Puritan Jonathan Edwards (1703-58). The first exults in the ethnic nobility of the American people : « When God removes one thing to make way for another, the new supersedes the old » (⁶). In the second quotation, theological in character, Edwards points out that the wheels of Providence do not turn by blind chance but, guided by the Spirit of God, go where the Spirit goes.

Emerson — and Stedman has commented that « every American has something of Emerson in him » — wrote that « America is the last opportunity offered by God to save the world ». Since the Sage of Concord, a Unitarian, minimized Christ the Saviour and reduced him to human status, his dictum, hardly original, is somewhat groundless.

Emerson's view, nevertheless, was echoed in an Allocution of June 14, 1946, by Pope Pius XII who, after qualifying as «unforgettable » his visit to the « great » nation ten years before, declared : « It is great in its immense industrial power, but even more in its spiritual power, in the great generosity of its people and in the high destiny that God has assigned to it, since well-being, power and virtue impose grave responsibilities of leadership ». Soaring words these, and all the more authoritative for having been pronounced by the best-informed observatory in the world, the Vatican.

The aristocracy of American authors, with Edwards and Emerson in the vanguard, foresaw the grandeur of the American destiny. From the moment the New World rose out of the voiceless, trackless sea before Columbus' enraptured eyes, it was meant to shine with the glory of a predestined world. This attitude (*per se*) instilled in America's literary leaders a sense of superior responsibility. « Either we live as free men or die by suicide », such was Lincoln's warning.

Self-styled experts find an easy answer in the more reserved comments of objective writers, such as Charles

Wagner (⁷), who either do not know America or else judge it by the play-boys, by the gangsters who haunt the cosmopolitan cabarets of Los Angeles and Chicago, and by the fashionable world of New York's Fifth Avenue.

The genuine American character is based first of all on self control, which the Puritans claim as their chief heritage. The greatness of this people lies in their superior traits, among them : a lofty, deeply rooted religious interpretation of life; a burning faith in individual and collective liberty; a credo as strong as their belief in God; a widespread optimism and profound respect for the given word; chivalry towards women; an inherited feeling for the patriarchal spirit and a simplicity that seems almost heroic; a restless dissatisfaction that continually spurs them to ever-greater achievements; a physical energy channeled into useful effort; a passion for adventure and risk, as exemplified by the pioneers; a positive concept of culture, but subordinated to action; and lastly, a perpetual eagerness to begin anew without resorting to chants and slogans for artificial stimulus.

Such gifts are second nature in the character of this young race, which takes them in its stride and makes the most of them (⁸).

The poet Russell was on the side of truth when in 1913 he defined America in his hymn *God of the Nations* as « the nation of the day at its dawn ». The same can be said for the poetess Miss Bates who saluted her country as « Beautiful for patriot dreams that see beyond the years », and still more realistically, Cross, who exalted the United States as a « temple of love of man and the home of human fraternity ».

American civilization is one apart and completely different from civilization as conceived in the Old World. Of America, founded on clearly defined principles of liberty which demand personal character and mature individual initiative, it may be said that the powers and functions of the Government aim chiefly at protecting freedom and providing security on a collective basis when the individual is unable to act for himself.

The British statesman Gladstone spoke his thoughts clearly when he pointed out that the secret of America's power lay in her love of liberty and respect for the law combined with the desire to preserve order; these are the elements of its national grandeur.

We are told that the great Leo XIII was deeply impressed by the happy solutions Gladstone found in America, in facing various individual and collective problems, as well as social and ecclesiastical problems. In 1877 Cardinal Gibbons traveled to Rome to receive the « red cap ». In a description left us by his biographer, we catch a glimpse of His Eminence speaking on the steps of the ancient Basilica of Santa Maria in Trastevere, his scarlet robes swollen by the wind. His words rang out like a message to Europe brought from beyond the Atlantic : in America there is liberty without license and authority without despotism, he told his listeners. While America is free, it is also strong; its power lies in its love for free institutions and its realism is based on an awareness of its own strength and its good will towards all. Do grave problems arise? « The calm justice and sound common sense of the Americans, you may be sure, will solve them without damage to the individual » [9].

The basic impulse of the individual American is to assert himself and progress materially and spiritually; thus he dedicates his life to a dynamic effort to advance in « the strenuous life », as Theodore Roosevelt termed it [10].

America was born out of the fortitude that enabled its settlers to wring a livelihood out of the savage solitude despite the hostility of barbaric Indians, and create an astounding new civilization. Echoing St. Paul who with his « He who works, eats » furnished a valid slogan to modern Russia, and following the example of industrious St. Francis of Assisi, the Pilgrims in the New World ruled that « no lazy wasp can live among us ». John Smith, the Father of Virginia, as if to discourage anyone who might still believe in the fable of easily found American gold, coined another maxim : « Here you need hope for nothing if not from your own labor ».

In his recent analysis of America, which he described as a « workers' society », Corrado Gini wrote that « the most notable difference (of the American character) lies in the psychology of work. In the Orient one works to live; in Europe one works to consume; in America one works to work. These are the three stages of a progressive evolution ». Who in Europe would ever imagine a revolt among lifetime prisoners because the prison administrators refused them the privilege to work ? And yet, in contrast to « the maximum penalty which in Europe consists in forced labor, is represented for Americans by forced idleness ».

With work, an American acquires money and this in turn multiplies a hundred fold his prospects for well-being and for ever more daring undertakings. From this point of view, the Faustian motto, « In the beginning is the deed », well suits the Yankee character and one can fully understand the rise of those crownless kings — oil kings, iron kings, copper kings, coal, rail, automobile kings, etc., answering to the names of Rockefeller, Morgan, Astor, Carnegie, Colgate, etc. The fact remains that here the way is open equally to all.

To follow Gini's analysis, numerous opportunities for success are available to everyone, opportunities not only to make something of one's self but also, in the light of Christian reality, to remake one's self in terms of self-rehabilitation. Even the prisons in America aim primarily at restoring human dignity to every inmate.

In the United States there is no phrase that touches the heart more than the plea, « Give me a chance ». Honest men as well as confessed criminals speak it almost like a prayer. At the same time, one finds here a profound sense of compassion and a will, especially among those who occupy responsible positions, to « shorten the way », to « move towards », to support worthy projects and develop the latent talents of others.

Among the various phrases applied to the United States such as « Land of Destiny », there is the well-merited term « Land of Opportunity ». Philanthropic, art-supporting America that discovered and moulded Enrico Caruso is capable of extending this sort of art patronage to an almost unlimited degree.

On the other hand, sound, practical thinking has skilfully guided the nation through dangerous political waters, on various occasions averting wars and the unnecessary spilling of human blood. Thus, the United States prefered, by means of clearly outlined international ententes, to purchase with hard cash various territories that were already moving within the orbit of the expanding Republic, as in the case of Louisiana, first a Spanish, then a French possession, Mexican Texas and Russian Alaska.

In 1803, Louisiana was ceded to the United States by Napoleon I for a compensation of $15,000,000. In 1850 Mexico yielded the territory of Texas for the sum of $10,000,000, while Alaska was acquired after paying Russia $7,200,000 in gold on the signing of the purchase treaty of March 30, 1867. Even in such financial transactions, those who reflect will see a flash of idealism.

III — The American tendency to do things on a grand scale, characteristic of a people in continuous ferment of development, is a symptom of that breathless constructive impulse that rests on imperishable spiritual values.

Appearances apart, if America is a land of vast and often disproportionate wealth, it is largely owing to the fact that it is rich in inexhaustible resources which still remain almost intact, although they are being exploited through practical, scientific methods. Hence we have the fabulous fortunes of some and along with them (and here is the point that closely touches the problem's idealistic aspect) the wholly American joy of art patronage and lavishing riches in all directions.

Some observers, such as the English Cardinal Manning, are alarmed — and not entirely without reason — at the danger of a North American plutocracy. Among the millionaires Cardinal Manning named was Andrew Carnegie, the philanthropist who gave away vast sums in the cause of human welfare. In his classic book, *The Gospel of Wealth,* Carnegie quieted such fears by giving assurance that they were wholly « imaginary », since in no other country in the world does wealth count for so little as in the Republic. Judging by the imperial munificence of the benefits he gave away, his word can well be taken seriously. In the year 1912 alone, this naturalized American citizen of Scottish origin donated around $131,000,000 towards the betterment of mankind. Among his gifts were : the University Fund of Scotland in 1901 ($10,000,000); the Carnegie Institute at Washington for scientific research in 1902 ($30,000,000); in 1904 a commission to recognize and reward acts of heroism ($5,000,000); the Pittsburgh Institute of Technology ($10,000,000); the Carnegie Foundation for the Advancement of Education ($15,000,000); the construction of 1,677 public libraries ($41,000,000); the Carnegie Corporation of New York for Anglo-Saxon

understanding ($135,000,000); the Carnegie Founda-
tion for International Peace in 1912, aiming at the abolition of war ($10,000,000). It is well to stop here as the
list threatens to become too long ([11]).

When J. Pierpont Morgan died, the people of the
City of New York read these moving words in the multi-
millionaire's testament : « I consign my soul to the hands
of my Saviour (and supplicate) my children to maintain
and defend... at the cost of any personal sacrifice the sacred
doctrine of redemption of sinners in the blood of Christ...».
When Col. John Jacob Astor left $450,000,000; Cornelius
Vanderbilt $350,000,000; Russell Sage and Cecil Gould
from $300 to $350,000,000 each and William L.
Vanderbilt $200,000,000, we must remember that they
all bequeathed a generous share of their fortunes to
welfare institutions.

The Hon. Luigi Luzzatti, one of Italy's unforgotten
statesmen and a financier of world renown, in a speech
before the Italo-American Association (July 24, 1922),
declared to an American audience : « As Minister of the
Italian Treasury, I have counted and distributed the
millions you have earned and accumulated... One senses
your remorse for too much wealth and your desire to ex-
piate for it, and while you pray to God, in your hearts
you dream of welfare works... You men of wealth *think*
of the miseries of humanity ».

The speaker was referring to the numerous free libraries for adults and children that Carnegie's millions
had brought into existence by the hundreds, and to the
Rockefeller Foundation established by the oil king —
one of the colossi of American finance — whose desire
for great wealth first awoke in him at the age of 18 when
he experienced the altruistic satisfaction of helping to pay
off the mortgage that hung over a small church in Cleveland, of which he was already a council member.

13

In his youthful memoirs, Rockefeller wrote that he intended to « earn honestly as much as possible, save as much as possible and give to others — but give well — as much as possible ».

With the establishment of the Rockefeller Foundation in 1913, there followed the International Health Commission, financed by the Foundation; the Institute of Medical Research; the International Fight Against Yellow Fever (1914), which waged a battle now concluded victoriously everywhere; the anti-malaria campaign (1916); the anti-tuberculosis campaign in France (1917); the financing of the Sanitary Service of the League of Nations (1920), and dozens of other fruitful initiatives. Although he was America's most renowned philanthropist, Rockefeller, whose son today follows in his footsteps, represents only one of rich America's innumerable altruists whose names are engraved on the tablets of church foundations, hospitals, parks, and institutions of every kind for culture and humanitarian works ([12]).

The most recent example of American maecenasism (May 6, 1945) is the generosity of a banker of Italian origin, Amedeo Pietro Giannini, founder of the Bank of Italy (in San Francisco, 1904), today called the Bank of America National Trust and Savings Association, second largest banking organization in North America. After having donated $1,500,000 to the University of California in 1928, on May 6, 1945, Giannini, already retired at the age of 75, declared his intention to contribute his entire personal patrimony to the establishment of the Giannini-Bank of America Foundation to distribute funds whereby young business men with particular banking aptitudes can learn this profession.

This Catholic (Giannini belonged to the Order of the Knights of Columbus) wholly assimilated that concept commonly defined as Puritan, according to which capital is held a social function, in that capital, created by the individual, goes — or, if you like, returns — to the society for which after all it was created. Does not American capitalism provide in the grand manner everything great and noble that constitutes the cultural and philanthropic prestige of America? About one-half of the country's universities and certainly the best of them, such as Harvard, Yale, Columbia, Johns Hopkins and even the Catholic University in Washington were founded and endowed by wealthy philanthropists, while the same is true of America's most noteworthy cultural works, libraries, museums, galleries, etc., as well as scientific laboratories of every kind and the finest hygiene and humantarian projects — hospitals, clinics, orphan asylums and rest homes. All were brought into being by private wealth.

Humanitarian romanticism? It hardly seems so in the strictest sense of the term. Following the line of reasoning traced by Pope Pius XII in his Encyclical *Sertum laetitiae,* this altruistic function of capital might be better defined as a fundamental Christian need — the opposite of communism — which, to continue quoting the Pope, demands « that goods created for all men should flow equally to all, according to the principles of justice and charity... Only in this way is it possible for property and the use of material goods to bring fertile peace and consistent vitality to society, that they may not precipitate dangerous conditions or constitute the basis of jealousy and warfare, once abandoned to a merciless game of force and weakness... ».

IV — American idealism is revealed by the deep admiration for simple and beautiful things : for nature, taken not only in the sense of its picturesque panoramas, but also in the green of a meadow, a garden, or a lawn, with which the American delights, whenever possible, to surround his vacation retreat or his own home.

An example of this highly developed appreciation of nature was the movement in America, which lasted for forty years, to choose a flower for each of the 48 States of the Union — an official flower characteristic of the territory. In many cases, these flowers were chosen by the State legislatures themselves.

The same is true of the official State « song » and State « bird », which in the separate areas serve a local esthetic purpose, as well as for the State flag and seal with a motto affixed.

Now we come to the theme of religion and the American system calling for separation of Church and State, unlike Western Europe, where the union between Church and State is held ideal. After the third Provincial Council of North American Catholicism, held in Baltimore in 1837, the Church dignitaries addressed a *Pastoral Letter to the Clergy and Laymen* in which the following words rang out like a noble challenge : « No religious chains bind us to any State in this Union nor to its central Government ».

The daring words — daring from the European point of view — clearly set forth the premise for the building of a strong, solid Christian civilization in the United States. This separatist policy gave American Catholicism a more powerful impulse than any other ethical-spiritual institution. America, youngest of the great family of nations that comprise world Catholicism, is also the most exuberant in its energy and zeal for missionary expansion. Cardinal Gibbons, in his discourse at the Basilica of Santa Maria in Trastevere, previously mentioned, said he was proud to belong to a nation « where the civil government holds over us the aegis of its protection, without interfering in the legitimate exercise of our sublime mission as ministers of the Gospel of Christ ».

On January 6, 1895, Pope Leo XIII echoed His Eminence Cardinal Gibbons in his Letter *Longinqua Oceani,* averring that the fortunate position of the Church in America was due to the fact that the Church « is not harried by civil laws; to the contrary, it is safeguarded from violence by virtue of common law and full justice of the Courts. Therefore, without any obstacles in its way, it enjoys full liberty of life and action ».

Cardinal Gibbons had manifest proof of this when in 1869 at the age of 35 he participated in the Vatican Council. He then noted the difference between the absolute freedom of the American bishops and the dependence of their European colleagues on higher authority. The Austrian, French and Spanish cardinals no more than dared to discuss the possibility of using their veto in the election of the Popes, whereas Cardinal Gibbons could draw satisfaction from the full independence granted the American delegates.

While Boissy d'Anglas at the Convention of February 21, 1795, called for the separation of Church and State in France in the hope of seeing the former perish so much the sooner, in the United States such a division was demanded by legislators representing the various denominations so that each believer might enjoy full liberty to worship God. The experiment proved an astounding success and has indeed operated to the advantage of the Church of Rome; to such a degree, it must be added, that after the moral bankruptcy of the Directory in France, writers and sociologists of the stature of Mme. de Staël, Benjamin Constant, Chateaubriand and De Tocqueville ([13]) referred to the American experiment in religious freedom as a model to encourage a Catholic renaissance in their own country.

On the theme of religious liberty in North America, it must be remembered that in the Declaration of Independence of the United States (1776), the Founding Fathers stated that the American people appealed « to the Supreme Judge of the world for the rectitude of our intentions » and placed « a firm reliance on the protection of Divine Providence ». Far from serving to screen a national indifference towards religion, freedom of worship, a sacred privilege to all Americans, has brought about a flowering of spiritual reverence shielded by the wisest tutelage, a devotion to customs and a tradition of supremely beautiful rituals.

The fact that the American Government abstains from any interference in Church affairs by no means signifies that the Government is agnostic or neutral by custom. James Bryce in his work on the American Republic points out that far from looking upon their country as atheistic, the Americans regard the general recognition of Christianity as « one of the principle sources of their national prosperity. »

Speaking to the French Chamber on the legal status of churches in the State of New York, Briand cited a celebrated American jurist who declared : « The authors of our Constitution recognized the close bond between the Christian religion and good government and the fact that religion is the most solid foundation of a sound morality ».

Ten Southern States exclude from every public function anyone who denies the existence of God. Pennsylvania and Tennessee declare any citizen ineligible to public magistrature who does not believe in God and refuses the sanctions of a future life. Thus, no one can justifiably draw the conclusion that religious liberty in America is synonymous with indifference, agnosticism or State intrusion. On the contrary, the individual is granted the full, free right to practise any doctrine or religious belief he chooses, provided he does not violate moral or civil laws and does not encroach on the private rights of others. In line with this policy there are also laws against blasphemy, polygamy and obscene literature, on the juridical basis that such things offend Christian sensibilities (14).

Some States legally forbid citizens to break the law of rest on Sunday, to hold public games, sell liquor or work in factories and offices on the Sabbath day, at the same time regulating and protecting religious gatherings and public processions, not overlooking the equal rights of all religious persuasions. Moreover, property belonging to all denominations and to the different church welfare organizations are exempt from taxes.

We quote a report from the register of the religious bodies in the United States taken in 1919 showing the value of ecclesiastic property controlled by the Catholic Church in that year as compared with the value of non-Catholic church property. Catholic real estate in the United States was estimated at $374,206,895 against $215,104,014 for Methodists, $164,990,150 for Episcopalians and $150,239,123 for Presbyterians. These figures reveal the active, generous fervor of Catholics, the majority of whom are not rich, and the faithfulness with which they contribute to the holy work, in accord with the slogan of American Statefree Christianity : « Church praying, Church paying ». This refers, of course, to the system whereby each religion is self-supporting.

Ten years later, in 1929, the same statistical sources gave these figures : Catholic property in the United States $648,091,000 against $535,924,000 for Methodists, $336,762,000 for Presbyterians, $326,620,000 for Baptists, and so on (15).

19

From the time of the American Revolution until today, religious manifestations have frequently been included in official ceremonies. Congress and the various State Legislatures maintain their own chaplains, paid out of public funds.

Catholic, Protestant and Jewish, are appointed by the State to officiate in the Army, the Navy, in prisons and in welfare institutions. Selection of chaplains is based on the number of the faithful representing the various denominations. In 1946 General Eisenhower, addressing a group of chaplains, remarked that a good chaplain is « worth more than his weight in gold ». One could hardly interpret this attitude as materialistic.

Going further into our investigation of the religious character of American public and official life, while it is true that the name of God appears nowhere in the Federal Constitution, nevertheless it figures in the oaths of office given in all government agencies, both State and Federal, in the national hymn and on all currency. God is mentioned in the State constitutions of Delaware, Oregon and Tennessee, while Iowa refers to the « Supreme Being », Maine to the « Sovereign Head of the Universe », North Carolina to the « Supreme Head of the Nation », and Colorado, Missouri and Washington to the « Supreme Head of the Universe ». Twenty-nine other States acknowledge their « gratitude to God for the liberties » which their constitutions provide.

The preamble to many State constitutions includes prayers and an outright act of faith in God, as in the case of Alabama, Georgia, Illinois, Kentucky, Mississippi, Oklahoma, Pennsylvania, Rhode Island, Texas, Virginia and Wyoming. Moreover, the constitutions of another 14 States specify freedom of worship which, for that matter, is confirmed by practically all the others ([16]).

An endearing passage in the Massachussetts constitution proclaims that « the public worship of God and instructions in piety, religion and morality promote the happiness and prosperity of a people and the security of a Republican government ».

In the introduction to Virginia's Bill of Rights, dictated by Thomas Jefferson in 1776, the proclamation of free worship is made in the name of the Omnipotent, who created the free mind and « did not choose to spread religious worship with coercive methods ». Adherence to God as the most valid tutelary guarantee of human freedom is the glowing golden thread that binds together the spiritual fabric of all American government documents.

Far from agreeing with a belief held in many countries that the spread of science is destined to kill religious faith, the Archbishop Ireland attested that the Americans bring to their thoughts and customs the spirit and morality of the Gospel. It is precisely for this reason that America punishes blasphemy, refusal to observe the Sabbath day of rest, polygamy and, generally speaking, every disturbance and affront to religion, morality and decency.

The two Houses of the United States Congress open their sessions with prayer and retain their own chaplains, as do the Army, the Navy and the Air Force. Respect for religious matters is so deeply rooted that in both World Wars, soldiers from all the Evangelical denominations willingly accepted the aid of Catholic chaplains when necessary ([17]).

The close accord between purely religious and ethical ideals which regulates the life of the American nation has determined this moral atmosphere. As the sociologist Fermin Roz put it, « Here the national spirit is religious and the religious spirit is national ». From De Tocqueville in 1835 until today, agreement on this point is universal. In 1903 Paul Adam stressed the power of the ideal centered on God. The Abbé Klein and the Rev. Charles Wagner, the latter a Huguenot, were similarly surprised by the wide currents of sympathy with which the American people responded to religion. Roz pointed out that in France the State is at once irreligious and interventionist while on the contrary, the United States Government, apparently neutral, is benevolent and favorable to healthy forms of worship.

The religious faith expressed in public manifestations finds a parallel on the individual level. It is wrong to draw the opposite conclusion from the census returns, even if many Americans profess to be non-religious. It must be pointed out that in a vast number of cases such admissions are purely anti-denominational and indicate a deep personal aversion to be classified in any one of the 300 different church families that comprise America's non-Catholic population. To the man who sought to enroll Abraham Lincoln in a certain Evangelist denomination, the great statesman, in whom some detected strong Catholic influences, replied that he would give his name to any group that did not swerve from sound Christian principles, and added : « Love your God with all your heart and your neighbor as yourself ». In his view, the division of the non-Catholic church into so many small sects did not reflect a corresponding differential of religious thought. Lincoln thus preferred to define himself as a « non-technical Christian » in the sense that he was exempt from any church affiliation.

V — Special consideration should be given to certain endearing traits that remind us of the pre-Reformist Christian character of a nation whose traditions derive directly from the glorious Anglo-Saxon Middle Ages before the withering shadow of the Tudor schism fell over it.

a) The first trait is that sense of faith and piety so prevalent in America, by which the individual and whole collective groups trust themselves devotedly to God and to Providence.

Divided by violent discord between Protestants and Catholics, the American nation seeks a basis of accord in the very fact of its birth. The Federal Constitution refers to religion in proclaiming freedom to all sects and in assuring that no one of them may acquire official status but this does not alter the fact that, as Bryce stated, Christianity is considered if not the legal religion, at least the national religion of the Republic.

The messages of President Washington astound us with their innumerable professions of reliance in God; and we note an echo to this faith in Providence in many speeches and documents of Thomas Jefferson. Even Lincoln trusted more in God's government than in his own ([18]), while Henry Wadsworth Longfellow, scorning those who maintained that Americans « have a figure in place of their hearts and a shining dollar on high », identified the representative citizen of this land of freedom as a man with a « heart within and God o'erhead ».

If you pick up a map of the United States, you will find that the names of many cities and counties allude to heavenly Providence. The word itself, in fact, recurs frequently. We find a Providence in Rhode Island, Kentucky, Maryland, Minnesota and South Carolina. Farther west in the magnificent State of California, the whole Providence Mountain chain exalts the hand of Providence. With a moment's reflection, one will understand how all this inspires a sense of peace and serenity : the idyll of a faith lived and experienced, like guiding benediction.

b) The Christian Flag.

A forerunner to « Old Glory », signifying national

unity and brotherhood in a terse symbol of the nation's history, will be found in the various standards that preceded it before the Continental Congress officially adopted the present-day national flag on June 14, 1777. Previously in 1747, when England was at war with Spain and France, Benjamin Franklin wisely pointed out the need for colonial flags and no doubt designed many of them himself, even choosing the mottoes. Some of them are quoted from the Bible : « Victory comes from God »; « God helps the strong »; « In God we trust »; « For the altar and the home »; « The Lord is our banner »; « In the name of God »; « Protect, O Lord, our crops » and others. An aura of ancient faith, expressed in the language of the Roman liturgy. Afterwards, as we have noted, came the present official flag.

There exists, however, another banner known as the Christian Flag — a blue cross on a white field. It is chiefly used during community prayers for the Army and Navy and in public gatherings of the faithful. Every warship has its own Christian Flag which on Sunday is hoisted over the stern where for one hour it waves above the Stars and Stripes.

c) The annual celebration of Thanksgiving Day.

Thanksgiving Day dates back to the year 1621, when the first crop struck the Pilgrims as an authentic miracle. Since then this rite has been more or less regularly observed. Over a century and a half later, on November 26, 1789, George Washington granted a request of Congress and of those American territories outside New England to extend the observance of this tradition to the entire nation as an act of gratitude for « the many and single favors of God Almighty ». Some Catholics, too, observed the celebration in their churches, particularly in the year 1789, so rich in significance did the event appear to them ([19]).

In 1864, President Lincoln officially fixed the date of this civil-religious festival on the last Thursday of November, at the close of the harvest season. The event is announced every year in the District of Columbia by a stirring presidential proclamation which invites the people to attend their respective churches for thanksgiving and prayer. With this gesture, the President assumes the role of a prophet who unites the nation around the altar and calls upon the people to prostrate themselves before the « God of every grace and power ». In turn, similar proclamations are made in the various States, especially in New England, by the State Governors.

An interesting note is the fact that today the entire Republic observes Thanksgiving Day except Utah, the Mormon State which gratuitously considers itself the only Christian State, whereas all the others are merely « Gentile » States.

Since 1911 the Catholic Church, too, has officially marked this solemn tradition which, in point of fact, harks back to a Biblical origin; for after the deluge, did not Noah build an altar to the Almighty on which he made his thanksgiving offerings? ([20]). In the national capitol, it is customary for government officials, members of the diplomatic corps and many citizens to attend the Holy Mass on this occasion.

In recent years it has also become customary for the President to address greetings to the nation also at Christmas time. Truman's Christmas message of 1945 was significant and amazingly prophetic. It was the Christmas of peace and with this in mind, the President said : « I do not believe that there is a single problem in this country or in the whole world that cannot be solved according to the teachings of the Sermon on the Mount. We must draw wisdom and inspiration from the past to guide us on our new path. Now that our enemies are conquered, we must unite to achieve the task that lies before us. We must not fail or lose heart... ». He concluded his speech with a prophecy of a world without wars : « On that day, near or far, this world will truly become the Kingdom of God ».

d) Still another presidential custom is that of swearing on the Bible when the supreme head of the State takes his oath of office. Tradition requires that he must himself choose the page on which he wishes to — how shall we say it? — register his promise. Moreover, he must read a short verse from the chosen page to adopt as a motto of government, much in the manner of the Roman Popes of the Middle Ages.

Let us recall some of the Biblical quotations selected by various American Presidents for their inaugural ceremonies. Garfield chose these words :

As the divisions of waters, so the heart of the King is in the hand of the Lord whithersoever he will, he shall turn it.

(Proverbs, XXI, 1)

McKinley took this thought as his own motto :

The learned in word shall find good things; and he that trusteth in the Lord is blessed.

(Proverbs, XVI, 20)

For his first official presentation he quoted these words of wisdom, which virtually constitute a prayer :

Give me wisdom and knowledge, that I may come in and go out before thy people.

(Paralipomenon I, 10)

26

Theodore Roosevelt, the unforgettable President who still lives in the hearts of Italians in America as well as in the hearts of his people, selected these incisive words of St. James in the Epistle (I, 22):

Be ye doers of the word, and not hearers only, deceiving your own selves.

(S. James I, 22)

President Taft repeated Solomon's wisdom:

Give therefore to thy servant an understanding heart, to judge Thy people, and discern between good and evil.

(I Kings, III, 9)

Harding turned for his inaugural quotation to the Prophet Micheas, inspired author of these immense words which through the ages have measured the value of practised religion:

I will shew thee, O man, what is good; and what the Lord requireth of thee, verily to do judgment, and to love mercy, and to walk solicitous with thy God.

(Micheas VI, 8)

The tight-lipped Coolidge, recalling his grandfather who used to read him the holy Gospel on the family farm in Vermont, chose the passage preferred by his beloved ancestor, the first 14 verses of the first chapter of the *Gospel of St. John,* which the ancient neo-Platonic philosophers would have liked to see engraved on gold plate.

Hoover demonstrated his acuteness with the appropriate Biblical quotation he chose, which reflects his idealism:

When prophecy shall fail the people shall be scattered abroad: but he that Keepeth the law is blessed.

(Proverbs XXIX, 18)

In 1932, Franklin D. Roosevelt swore his oath of faith to the Constitution on an ancient copy of the Bible brought to America from Holland by one of his ancestors. Architect of the New Deal, he had his Bible opened to the Pauline hymn of love (I Corinthians XIII, 1-13), in which Charity is crowned above Faith and Hope. An ideal program of government in miniature.

In 1945 it was the turn of Harry S. Truman, a Baptist. In his first message to Congress he recalled Solomon's prayer for « an understanding heart... that I may discern between good and bad ». To this theme, previously cited by Taft, he added humbly : « I only ask that I may be a good and faithful servant to my God and to my people ».

A witness of that unforgettable session recounts with journalistic objectivity : « Then I asked Mr. Truman what he believed in above everything else. Without hesitating he replied : « In the Sermon on the Mount, and that isn't just a religious answer ». He went on to say that no individuals, communities or nations have ever won anything without observing the Golden Rule (« Do unto others as you would have them do unto you »), and without maintaining a sense of decency towards individuals, groups and nations ([21]).

Guided by heavenly inspiration, the American people have reached the summit of their greatness. They have achieved unpredictable fortune and power through their breadth of vision almost like stars in the firmament of their still-brief history.

When Andrew Jackson, seventh President of the Republic, died in 1845 at Hermitage, Tenn., among his last words was the phrase : « Oh Lord, the Book and the Rock on which our Republic is founded ! »

This deep religious feeling shared by many American Presidents, calls to mind the solemn prayer that still introduces so many State constitutions : « In the name of God, so be it »; also the statement of George Washington, the Father of his Country, in his inaugural address when he said that no other people know and worship « the invisible Hand that guides the affairs of men » more than the Americans. Many succeeding Presidents followed his example by repeating his invocation for divine favors to the Government. Among them were John Adams and Thomas Jefferson, his two immediate successors, and the fourth President, James Madison who in his last annual message declared that his fellow-citizens should be grateful to God for a government that keeps close vigil over honest elections, freedom of speech and press, and trial by jury, a government, furthermore, that takes impartial action to maintain neutrality between religion and the State ([22]).

Certainly no better argument could be advanced to refute irresponsible accusations that the American people are lacking in spirituality.

VI — Not to be overlooked, surely, is the final proof to belie allegations of American anti-idealism : the nation's decision to intervene in the two World Wars — a decision that has joined for centuries to come the histories of the New and Old Worlds.

This intervention, as a result of which almost one million American youths darkened the soil of Europe with their blood, was part and parcel of the American destiny. Had not Catholic France of Louis XVI sent its own army overseas to consecrate the free nation? Had not Lafayette presented to George Washington the keys of the Bastille, now kept at Mt. Vernon? Had not the French tourist Moreau de Saint Méry who, in 1798, praised « the hospitable soil of this land of freedom », declared that « if its inhabitants were wise, they would

29

one day surprise the rest of the world with their power and perhaps even impose on it the law of their own felicity ? » (²³). Did not Walt Whitman, prophet of America's destiny, foresee the political evolution that would enable his country, once aware of its mission, to give liberty to the world ?

« *Sail, sail thy best, ship of Democracy* ».

Is this imperialism ? one asks in alarm. Is this wielding of the sword or dropping of atom bombs only to impose brutal violence arbitrarily ? Adverse propaganda, particularly during war times, has insinuated such aims. But these insinuations are lies.

In American religious and patriotic hymnology one encounters a wholly different vision of the ideal State, again and again represented in song as the nation's responsibility, especially in its most solemn hours and periods of deepest collective emotion. Katherine Lee Bates' song *America, the Beautiful,* for example, exalts the patriotic dream :

> « *Oh beautiful for patriot dream*
> *That sees beyond the years,*
> *Thine alabaster cities gleam*
> *Undimmed by human tears..* ».

In another popular patriotic hymn, *Not Alone for the Mighty Empire,* the author, William Pierson Merrill, turns to « unseen things » and, repudiating the passion for « battleships, fortresses and conquests by the sword », looks instead for « the conquest of the spirit ».

William Watson, in his song *Great and Fair Is She, Our Land* puts no trust in « riches, power and fame » but prays for a different aim, that,

« Our land may
Climb not to her goal
All forgetful of the soul ».

If America should enter another world war, one may be sure that her awareness of other people's sacred rights will guide her well-weighed decisions.

When the hour struck for the United States to intervene in the cause of world liberty, her armies assumed the role of mediaeval knights, striking chivalrously to bring freedom to the weak and oppressed. This altruism, achieved through sacrifice and blood, gives us a two-fold proof of idealism. Like the rest of the world, the Italians, when they were finally allowed to say what they thought, appreciated America's action to such a degree that they could hardly find words to express adequate praises.

After recalling that the United States with her intervention in the First World War « stalked like a giant to save Europe from military tyranny », Luigi Luzzatti extolled America in these words :

« At the dawn of their wondrous life shone like a halo
of sacrifice the freedom of God,
In the afternoon they reaped an immortal prize, the
freedom of the nations ».

In a black moment of wrath during his reckless adventure at Fiume, Gabriele D'Annunzio, unable to control his poetic temper, compared the destiny of young America with ancient Rome's and cried : « Rome fell when Rome forgot its ideals and turned to tangible things. America will fall because it worships the god of materialism, however much it may have masked this god in false idealism ».

31

In that moment, D'Annunzio was sincere only as impulsive natures can be in a moment of passion. Yet his outburst of rage could detract nothing from the verses he had written only three years before (July 4, 1918) in a wholly different vein of sincerity :

« *That immense heap of gold*
Does not beautify you, O Republic,
Nor the bottomless cup your wingless geniuses
Pour upon you from the darkness,

Nor the ax you speed
Whereby you transform your forests into shining cities,
Nor the impetus of air your houses
Which are your cathedrals,

Nor your numberless machines,
Slaves that serve your lucre and your leisure.
Nor the pride that heats your forge red-hot
And hammers out your progeny,

But a word
That comes from you, a Republican voice,
A word that renders you most fair.

And immediately your gold
And all your metals and all your smithies
And all your people
Are nothing if not shining light.

You are all light
That penetrates radiance even into the darkness of your
Thus, your black coals   (*mines,*
Seem to you like sparkling diamonds.

The solar springs
Are fixed in your eyes.
From your forehead to your heels
You are all light ».

Nor could Annie Vivanti, Anglo-Italian poetess converted to the Catholic Church, restrain her enthusiasm for America's idealistic intervention:

« *Hail, Sammy, brother of the West,*
You come to us with cheerful mien,
Wearing on your resplendent brow
The gift of the gods: youthfulness.

New and pure, you come from afar
Into this, our sanguine glory,
You come bearing Victory in your outstretched hand
As one carries a flower.

Your standard that yields to no one
Passes, waving, with solemn pride;
An immense tricolor flag that binds
The Atlantic, Pacific and the Piave.

As if by divine miracle
We contemplate the forty-eight stars
From beyond the sea rise and glitter
In the adamantine Italian sky ».

Another voice in our national chorus praising American idealism is that of Filippo Crispolti, a fine Italian Catholic writer, in an ode to the dream of peace among the peoples envisioned by President Woodrow Wilson:

« *He felt in his paternal heart*
All the laments of the afflicted,
And traced upon the Eternal Book
The rights of peoples.

Did you not seek the same well-spring,
You, in Your Credo, that differs only in part?
Thus involuntarily You were
His most powerful arm.

33

And the peace beloved by You,
That reassures and not oppresses,
Only that peace now turns sublime
Glory to God, for God dictated it ! ».

These four Italians — a Jew, a pagan writer, a Protestant who was to die a Catholic, and a 100 per cent Catholic — all evaluated similarly America's intervention in the First World War. Thus, despite their profound differences, these poets refute in their verses unwarranted accusations of American anti-idealism.

At the end of the Second World War, America confirmed, through a series of acts and declarations, the altruistic motives that once again inspired her participation in the world conflict. On September 2, 1945, the historic Stars and Stripes were hoisted over the United States Embassy in Tokyo and over the American battleship Missouri, where the Second World War came to its close with the signing of the Japanese surrender. President Truman pronounced this date « Victory Day » and asked that it be celebrated in prayer. In the opinion of the world's greatest democracy, he declared, victory was God's, to whom all glory was due.

In a radio message proclaiming September 2 « Victory Day », President Truman said : « God's aid guided us to this day of victory. With His help we will obtain peace and prosperity for ourselves and for the whole world in the coming years ». Again in a radio talk to the United States Armed Forces, he declared that America could only realize the fruits of victory « in a world free from the threat of war... Only through cooperation of all the nations can any one nation be completely secure... ». With the destructive force of war removed from the world, « we can now turn to the grave task of preserving the peace which our brave men and women have won ». On a third occasion in an address to 7,000 persons, President Truman said that another world war would be unsupportable; « it would signify the end of our civilization... Let us go forward to the mission which I believe God Almighty has reserved for us ».

Meanwhile, aboard the Missouri, General MacArthur opened the ceremony of the signing of the Nipponese surrender, first defeat suffered by Japan in its legendary history of 2,600 years, with a brief speech, offering this prayer : « It is my fervent hope, as it is the hope of all humanity, that a better world may be born from the blood and carnage of the past ».

In the National Cemetery at Arlington, Virginia, is buried in glory the Unknown Soldier who fell on the fields of Europe in the First World War. Twenty-seven years later, two more Unknown Soldiers were buried there, one brought home from the Pacific front, the other from the European front, more precisely from the area of Anzio and Cassino in Italy, two names that blaze gloriously in the history of the American Army and which have immortalized the idealism that underlies the American destiny.

CATHOLICISM : THE ORIGINAL AND DURABLE CONSECRATION

CHAPTER II

A history that traces America's religious development from its very beginning has not yet been written
— or, at any rate, has not yet come to light. Ordinarily,
Protestant historians choose to ignore how much took
place in the present area of the United States between
that Friday of October 12, 1492, when Columbus first
landed, and the 20th of December, 1620 — a lapse of
some 128 years! — when the ship with the spring-like
name of Mayflower anchored off the granite rock of Plymouth and set down the 120 Protestant pioneers, called
in Puritan annals « the Pilgrim Fathers » ([1]).

Diligent research by Catholic scholars over more than
a half-century has little by little gathered the materials
to fill this regrettable gap, making possible the reconstruction of a historical panorama that at the same time
reflects American Catholicism impartially ([2]). When this
work of detailed, wide-spread research by level-headed
historians is finished, it will be a genuine revelation.
Founded on historical sources — which for the New World
are predominantly those of missionaries and explorers —

39

it will bring to light the truth that the story of the United States is essentially a Catholic one.

II — Indeed America may be considered a Catholic land even in its pre-Columbian past.

It is not proposed here to delve deeply into the subject of the maritime incursions into America before 1492. Many reasonably sure indications would lead one to believe, that, between the eighth and tenth centuries, Christianity was brought to America by hardy Nordic seamen. Considering the understandably vague documentation at hand, it is difficult to say whether they were Icelandic or Danish, Irish or Swedish.

At the time of the wandering Apostle, St. Paul, the philosophic and cultured Seneca, in *Medea,* one of his last tragedies, described to perfection the future discovery of a New World located beyond the known seas :

« In time to come, the day will arrive when the Ocean will break the bonds of Nature and a majestic Land will be revealed to men. And to them Tethys will reveal new worlds, and no longer will Thule be the farthest point of inhabited regions ». (Act. II, Scene III).

Yet it is no less wonderful that centuries later this discovery was actually brought about — thanks to the courage of seamen, the prophetic guess-work of geniuses, the revelations of science and even pure chance. Modern studies have raised the hypothesis — or, if you will, the thesis — that there were communications between Europe and America by means of the ancients' lost continent of Atlantis ([3]). But this is mere conjecture.

In any case, the historical premises of Pietro d'Anghiera, Nicola Zeno and Gomara, as well as the conclusions of Father Lafitau, give some likelihood to such an assertion.

Traces of a knowledge of the incarnate God; the square cross found in Paraguay, which (according to Father Ruiz) was held almost in reverence for its magical properties; legends gathered from the lips of the aborigines that evoke an ancient man of prodigious renown, perhaps some primitive missionary — none of this can be wholly disregarded. And there are other indications that would seem to substantiate this theorizing — for example, the constant references in Nordic sagas to actual voyages, like that to Vinland attributed to Bishop John, or the notation affixed to Martin Behaim's map of 1492, according to which seven Portuguese bishops in the ninth century, fleeing from the Moors, repaired to a Western island called Antilia, where they founded seven cities.

Certainly these and similar documents do not offer enough authority or documentary proof to lead us very far. More valid historical evidence is offered by the Vikings' explorations of present-day Greenland (which up to the 16th century had its own diocese), the same Vikings who later pushed on to the American Continent. Testimonies such as those of Adam, canon of Bremen (1067), and Ari Thorgilsson (died 1148) may not be lightly dismissed, nor may those of Nicholas, abbot of Thingeyre (died 1159), or the surviving sagas of three intrepid Vikings — that of the Irish merchant Thorfinn Karlsefni (1305-35), which has come down to us in 28 manuscripts; that of King Olaf; and the third, either by Eric the Red or his son Lief, which survives in a manuscript from the beginning of the 15th century.

Today the concensus of scholars tends to favor this last one. On July 17, 1932, a statue of Leif Ericson, « the first white man to come to America », was dedicated at Reykjavik. It was a gift from America to the people of Iceland while that country was celebrating the thousandth anniversary of its Parliament. In the ecclesiastical field, the city of the ancient episcopate of Gardar in Greenland might, if its archives could be examined, reveal to us, at least in part, this enigma of history.

These Viking sagas, together with the commission given by the martyr-saint King Olaf II of Norway (1015-1030) to missionaries to preach the Catholic faith from Norway to Greenland, would seem to indicate that Europe came into contact first with the northernmost part of the American Continent. Other bits of evidence strengthen the theory even more — the Letter of Nicholas V, dated September 22, 1448, directed to the Icelandic bishops of Skalholt and Holar, in which the Pope urged them to undertake the spiritual care of the Greenlanders, who had repeatedly asked him or it ([4]); the appointment made by Innocent VIII (1484-92) of the Benedictine Mattio to the bishopric of Gardar; the Rescript (1492) in which Alexander VI congratulated Mattio on his good work and exempted him from the payment of some tributary obligation; and also the fact that these voyages figure in pre-Columbian maps, such as the one inserted into Claudius Ptolemaius' precious manuscript, belonging to Cardinal Filiaster (1427) and now in the library of Nancy. This map was devised by the noted Danish cartographer Swart (14th-15th centuries), and it indicated the daring northern voyages of a Viking hero in the direction of an island identified as *Viridis Insula*. This corresponds well with the *Illa Verde* noted in the Portulana map of the Catalan navigators and is perhaps none other than the island of Terranova, the present-day Newfoundland, which the ancient Norse heroes may have reached, perhaps, driven by storms or carried there by currents.

A rare and tangible relic of one such expedition has come to light. On a wide, flat millstone found by a Swedish farmer between Alexandria and Kensington, Minnesota, is this Viking inscription : « Hail Virgin Mary, save us from Hell, year 1362 ». The stone, now in the Alexandria Chamber of Commerce, thus bears the first Christian prayer to be found in this region and proves, furthermore, that these Vikings were Catholics and worshipped the Virgin Mary.

This relic is discussed in a learned work by Hjalmar R. Holand, *The Kensington Stone* (Privatdruck, Ephraim, Wis.; 1932). Measuring 2'3" by 1'4" by 6", it has 62 words, in 220 runic signs, engraved in it. Deciphered, they indicate that « eight Swedes and 22 Norwegians of Catholic persuasion must have made an expedition from Vinland toward the West ». As a result of the deciphering of the monolith, the Jesuit W. M. Peitz asserts that « ten of these were assassinated on the spot where the stone was found, while their companions set forth to find a place more to the north, a day's walking distance. Of these, ten proceeded on to the sea, a distance of some 14 days, to watch over the ships. Thus this is a question of a Viking voyage of 1362, which is indicated in the wording itself. The manner in which the explorers speak of Vinland indicates that they did not consider their enterprise as anything extraordinary ».

Other data, which Holand has gathered within the last ten years in northwest Minnesota, show at least the probability that the expedition of the Thirty in 1362 was neither the first nor the only one of its kind and that one may be certain the Norsemen founded a permanent colony at least in Nova Scotia.

« Knowledge of all these things », writes Peitz, « cannot have been in any case completely lost in the Nordic motherland. Indeed, in 1406, Norwegians landed on Greenland and established there a " colony of the East ", while the " colony of the West " vanished around 1363. When, at the time of the Union of Kalmarer in 1397, the Nordic countries were united under Danish rule, the fate of the Norwegians' " West colony " could neither have been ignored nor could it have been unknown » ([5]).

Within our times, many branches of science have made much progress toward the clarification of all this early history. The Jesuit father, Joseph Fischer, with his monumental edition of Claudius Ptolemaius' geographical works (published by the Vatican Library), has done important pioneer research in the field of geography and cartography. For his work the learned Jesuit was awarded the Silver Medal of Karl Richter, with the motto of *Pervestigatori Terrarum,* by the Geographical Society of Berlin in 1933. His work, in fact, has graphically documented the revival of interest in the Ptolemaic geography that spurred Columbus towards the West and has helped to explain the passion for intense exploratory activity of Columbus' day. By 1902, with his work, *The Discoveries of the Normans in America,* Father Fischer — jokingly called « the fisherman of maps » (*Kartenfischer*) — had recognized that the Normans, before Columbus, had set foot on the American Continent, having voyaged to Vinland before 1121 and to Markland (Newfoundland or Terranova) before 1347. And an American historian, the Jesuit Francis S. Betten, has emphasized that voyages to Vinland, three and a half centuries after Leif the Lucky's first discovery in 1000, were not unknown to the Normans.

Beyond this, details of those early explorations are lacking. Europe's contacts with « the inaccessible land of the North, unexplored because of the ice » — thus was it defined by Nicolaus Niger (Clavus Swart), the Danish cartographer — would have been have broken and the glorious Continent to the West would have been forgotten if Columbus' genius had not discovered it *ex novo* and revealed it to the world ([6]). For just as the Santa Maria waited at anchor for God to stir the wind in the harbor of Palos, so the extinct faith in far-away lands awaited anew « the divine sign to commence the voyage ».

From the viewpoint of historic-geographic research, all the voyages alluded to thus far, whether they were real or mythical, would have remained without consequence but for Columbus' discovery. Only after he announced his discovery did the historic-geographic study of the New World take its right direction (⁷).

The historian Bancroft (I, 1) summarized the difficult question when he wrote that the bands of intrepid mariners of pre-Columbian times whose voyages took them beyond Iceland and Sicily could easily have sailed from Greenland to Labrador. And yet, he adds, conclusive historical evidence is lacking to back up the natural probability that they actually made the crossings in question.

III — Christopher Columbus, that most noble and prophetic figure of the New Continent, was impelled to undertake his bold enterprise by a spirit of missionary zeal as fervent as any crusader's. *Hic noster est* was Leo XIII's verdict on him (⁸). Of Columbus, President Coolidge said that he brought with him the seed of republicanism and the promise of greater human liberty than in any voyager who ever crossed the oceans. And Pope Pius IX's characterization of him as a « messenger of health » suggests the rich psychological motives that sustained the Santa Maria's « Chief Pilot » across the dangerous waters. On June 8, 1912, under the auspices of the Catholic Knights of Columbus, a superb monument was dedicated in the capital of the United States to the Catholic discoverer of America. All Washington paid him homage in a civic celebration of the most solemn dignity.

The most striking element of Columbus' discovery was its providential timeliness, occurring as it did almost on the eve of the Protestant revolution that so grievously affected that Catholic faith which to Hilaire Belloc represented « Europe herself ». Columbus by his immense discovery fulfilled the prophecy of St. Hilary of Poitiers : « *Hoc enim Ecclesiae proprium est, ut vincar cum laeditur, tunc obtineat cum deseritur* » ([9]), because with it Catholicism was largely compensated for the losses it suffered on the Old Continent. When in the next generation the missionaries arrived to evangelize it, they were moulded in the spirit of the Catholic renaissance and revived the zeal of St. Teresa of Avila, of St. Ignatius Loyola and the reformer-popes.

A passionate scholar, mystically convinced of the prophecies that applied to him, Columbus felt himself divinely invested with a mission to expand the rule of Christ. Indeed, such a predestination he found in his very name of Christopher : « *Christum ferens sicut columba ramum olivae, genti americanae* » ([10]). Recalling later the high motive that sent him on his way, he was able to say with pride that it was a categorical imperative to become a missionary « *ut sacrum nomen Dei cognoscatur et praedicetur in hac altera mundi parte* ».

A precious document of the Columbian epoch, the polyglot psalter edited by Father Agostino Giustiniani, the learned Dominican orientalist (Genoa, 1516), has ample reference to Columbus. It tells us that he was deeply impressed by the fifth verse of the Eighteenth Psalm : « Through all the earth their voice resounds ». Among other things, Giustiniani says that Columbus « frequently stated that God had chosen him in order to fulfil this prophecy » ([11]) . When this was written, Columbus had been scarcely ten years in his first tomb at Valladolid, but first-hand testimony also exists from the time he was alive to prove that this was his attitude.

Columbus' missionary ideal was at once mystic and epical. According to the Franciscan, Juan Perez ([12]), he stated it to the « Catholic Rulers », Ferdinand and Isabella, in these terms : « To carry to remote lands the name and doctrine of Jesus Christ ». And he did so in the highest religious sense, which Joaquin Miller, the « Poet of the Sierras », has described as a mystical gesture of abandonment to the guidance of the Holy Ghost.

This great mystical ideal became sublime reality for the Discoverer on October 12, 1492, when he landed on the island which the natives called Guanahani, planted the cross on its soil and in a hymn of praise and gratitude consecrated it in the name of the Divine Saviour (San Salvador). Later, he gave the name of St. Mary of the Conception to the second island he discovered and to three other islands the names of the Catholic Spanish royalty who had financed the risky undertaking (Ferdinandina, Isabella, and Juana). To a sixth island he gave, out of gratitude, the name of « Little Spain » (Española), and finally — in nostalgic tenderness for the first victorious Christmas he spent in a land untouched by Christian culture — he bestowed on a seventh island the holy name of Nativity (Natividad) ([13]).

IV — On his second voyage to the New World — when the Admiral landed at Española on November 27, 1493 — there began the real evangelization of America. With three ships and three caravels, the expedition comprised 1,500 men of every social class.

On this expedition there were 12 missionary priests. At their head, as first Apostolic Vicar, was the much-discussed Catalan, Father Bernard Boyl, formerly confidential secretary to King Ferdinand the Catholic. He had been for some time a hermit at Montserrat under the Benedictines, and later, in France, he professed among the Minims under the ascetic Calabrian, St. Francis of Paola; many years later he reappears in history as abbot (a title that may have been purely commendatory) of a monastery of St. Michael. All of this whets the reader's appetite to know more about the protagonists of these solemn hours that gave birth to the faith in virgin America. One might say Father Boyl exercised the first apostolate of the New World ([14]).

Little is known of the other religious men in Father Boyl's party. According to authoritative writers, one can be sure of only a few names : Fray Roman Pene, of the hermitage of St. Jerome; Fray Jorge, commendatory of the Knightly Order of Santiago; and the Franciscans, Fray Juan de la Deule and Fray Juan Cosin, who were perhaps humble Lay Brothers. As to the celebrated Franciscan, Fray Juan Perez, there are some who claim he was among the group, but that is unlikely, at least on this voyage.

The name of Fray Pedro de Arenas is sometimes added to the list, but he was not a Franciscan. Frequent mention is also made of the great « Apostle of the Indies », Fray Bartolomeo Las Casas, as a member of Columbus' second expedition. This is a myth : it was Fray Bartolomeo's father who made the second crossing, as one of those who, without being adventurers, sought primarily to give « more than a purpose but a sense » to the expedition, by taking along domestic animals and seeds of European plants to introduce to the New World.

Instead, Bartolomeo Las Casas crossed the ocean in 1502 with Ovando, and then only as a layman, to look after the interests acquired in the meantime by his family. In 1510, moved by the sermon of a Dominican, he renounced everything to become a Dominican himself and an advocate for the oppressed Indians to whose terrible sufferings he bore witness.

The mission committed to Father Boyl and his associates was very precise. Alexander VI's Bull of May 4 enjoined the Catholic Rulers as follows : « We command, in virtue of your holy obedience, and since you have already promised to do so and, we have no doubt, will so do, considering your great devotion and royal magnanimity, that you send to said lands and islands men who are upright and God-fearing, learned, and expert in instructing the natives, and we charge you to appoint them to inculcate these peoples with the Catholic faith and good customs, bringing to this task a wholly proper diligence » ([15]).

As a result of this august command, which corresponded exactly to the aspirations of both the Catholic Rulers and Christopher Columbus, the latter received on the 29th of that same May, 1493, the following instructions : « ... Therefore Their Highnesses, wishing that our Holy Catholic Faith be augmented and increased, do command and charge said Admiral, Viceroy and Governor, with all the ways and means possible to him, to strive to induce the inhabitants of said lands and islands to embrace our Holy Catholic Faith; and to assist him, they do command the devoted Father Boyl to go with him with other religious persons » ([16]).

If the private life of Pope Alexander VI was not wholly in keeping with the dictates of the Gospel, at least « in matters of the Church he penetrated into its spirit ». Such is the verdict of history in his regard.

With the arrival of the first missionary-priests, there was initiated throughout the New World the sacramental life under the mystical effusion of the Holy Ghost. Incidentally, it may be observed that the American Con-

49

tinent was evangelized, almost from the very day it was discovered, by Catholic missionaries who gained ground by the most continuous and systematic preachings, and with such zeal that evangelization proceeded at the same rate as scientific exploration and political conquest. An historian has said with good reason that « for a hundred years the colonization and evangelization of America would be, in the strict sense of the term, Catholic and not Protestant » ([17]).

V — To whom was due the coveted honor of celebrating for the first time the holy sacrifice of the Mass on the new Continent?

The hypothesis that Columbus was accompanied on his first voyage by the secular priest, Don Pedro de Arenas, has not been supported by valid documentation; if it could be proved, the answer would be self-evident ([18]). On the other hand, a Franciscan tradition assumes that both Columbus and Queen Isabella belonged to the Third Franciscan Order and that Father Juan Perez, their counsellor and father superior of the Rabida monastery, not only helped implement the first Columbian trip but went along on the second. This tradition concedes to the distinguished Franciscan the honor of being first sacramental minister in the virgin land of « Little Spain », but it is without authentication and may have arisen like any popular legend.

A realistic sense of hierarchic observance, on one hand, and of Franciscan humility, on the other, would instead assign to the above-mentioned Father Bernardo Boyl, of the Order of the Minims, Apostolic Vicar and Secretary to Their Catholic Majesties, the privilege of celebrating the first Mass on American soil ([19]).

This could have taken place either on December 8,

1493, or on January 6, 1494, at Villa Isabella, on the island of San Domingo.

Yet others, basing their theory on documents no less provable, would grant this honor to Don Pedro de Arenas, not indeed on the first voyage but on the second. Between the two, we lean toward Father Boyl.

To the student of American history in general and North American history in particular, it becomes vividly apparent that the Holy Mass occupied a position of absolute supremacy in the grandiose life of the conquerors. When Ponce de Leon's galleon anchored off the southwestern beaches of Florida in 1521, that terrestrial paradise, redolent with the perfume of its exotic flowers, must have seemed crowned with incorruptible glory when the first Mass was celebrated on the soil of the present United States. On the Old Continent, already worn out by incessant outcroppings of paganism, they were demolishing Mass altars in the cathedrals of England, Scotland, Sweden, Norway, Holland, Germany and Switzerland. At the same time, other altars were rising on the New World's virgin soil, reflowering like sacred plants among the century-old oaks of California and the mango groves and banyan arbors of Florida.

In 1561, before the Catholic Queen Mary's arrival in Scotland, John Knox exultantly declared — to repeat his blasphemy — that the « Papists » would be so confounded by their adversaries that « not one would dare to hear or celebrate Mass any more than the thieves of Tiddisdale would dare to confess their crimes in the presence of an incorruptible judge ». Giving the lie to his statement, the Holy Mass, amid the joy of the choirs of the New World's Guardian Angels, and of the bold-hearted men who had come there, linked in a sacred embrace the sinful earth to the purifying heaven, in the precious Blood of the Mystic Lamb, just as in the mystical evocation of it by the brothers Hubert and Jan Van Eyck in Ghent cathedral.

It is pleasing to think that this Mass, in all probability, was celebrated on December 8, 1493, as already noted. For a temple there was no more than a humble little chapel made of interlaced tree-trunks and branches, but it ranked as first cathedral of the New World and first seat of the mission on the island of Española. Never was history more truthful than in the assertion that « the Catholic Church is the oldest institution of the United States ». Leo XIII, the poet-Pope, in an Encyclical to the Star-Spangled Republic, has nobly stated that « when America was only a new born child... it was taken to the very bosom of the Church that has maternally embraced it ».

Whoever surveys the epic of the Catholic Church on the new Continent will find that it derives its meaning from the celebration of the Mass, before the recreating sanctity of an altar. The souls of men are drawn to it as to a dynamo of erupting energy, to share in a grace that is like a young eagle spreading its wings toward the sublime heights, the closer to approach the light of God.

A contemporary American historian, Carlton J. H. Hayes, a Protestant turned Catholic, was once asked what represents the anchor of salvation that holds firm the morality of Catholicism in the United States in a shifting world like the present.

After considering the matter, he answered that this anchor is « the prop offered us by an unchanging sacramental system and by an unchanging Church that knows no alteration because it is God's. In thousands of churches scattered across the United States, the miraculous sacrifice of the Body and Blood of the Man-God is repeated daily, and from it derives the Church and its divine morality. The Mass, which nurtures virtue and inspires beauty, is the beneficent treasure that binds the gratitude of America » ([20]).

VI — Thus far we have seen that the new Continent was born under Catholic auspices, through the genius of a Catholic explorer, through the interest of a Catholic priest attached to two sovereigns — Ferdinand and Isabella — whom history defines as « Catholic ». Church money was behind Columbus' enterprise, too, for certain financial backers, together with the Spanish treasury, would have sponsored it but for the timely intervention of the Cardinal of Mendoza, one of the peers of Spain, who procured from the « Holy Brotherhood » 16,000 gold ducats, transmitted through Luis de Santangel, treasurer of ecclesiastic revenue in the Kingdom of Aragon.

A word or two might be said here to recall the various Catholic precursors and unwitting collaborators of Columbus in his historic expedition. Dante, to begin with, two centuries before, envisioned the New World, in the north, as the goal of Ulysses' fateful voyage :

« Ulysses' mad adventure I could mark past Cadiz... »

(Paradiso, XXVII, 82-83)

In 1459, in Venice, during the full splendor of the Renaissance, a white Camaldolese monk (of the same monastery of San Michele where his colleague Niccolo Malermi first translated the Scriptures into Italian) finished his famous World Map, now the treasure of the Marcian Library, which not only showed the Portuguese the way to the Cape of Good Hope but also marked off for Columbus the route to America. We allude to the famous Fra Mauro, *chosmographus incomparabilis*. Mention is made later of Paolo Toscanelli.

Another illustrious Church dignitary must be included in the company of those who paved the way for Columbus — the learned French cardinal, Pierre d'Ailly (1350-1420). In his work, *Imago Mundi,* he foresaw the possibility of reaching the Indies by a western route, citing the authority of Aristotle, Pliny and Seneca. The Columbian Library in Seville preserves a copy of it, annotated in the margins by Columbus himself, who also inserted many notes from the same source in his own work, *Libro de las Profecias.* With good reason Las Casas has emphasized the predominant influence of D'Ailly on Columbus ([21]).

Alexander VI was the first Pope to initiate an uninterrupted line of contact with the new Continent. It was he who promulgated, on behalf of Spain and Portugal, the famous Act of Arbitration that established the so-called « Vatican Line ».

The Dutchman Hugo Grotius — author of the first scientific work on international law — has criticized this intervention of the Pontiff in the name of law and the Gospel, but only because Grotius, in his militant Calvinism (though in his heart he still yearned for the Mother Church), failed to see that the Pope, a century and a half before his time, was considered « the supreme lord of the seas and the islands ». This same anti-papal sentiment is echoed in the 20th century by another sharp intellect, the Anglican Dean Inge, who in April, 1923 (cf. *Atlantic Monthly*), called the Roman Church « a militant autocratic empire that assumes for itself a militant sovereignty ».

But in 1493 no such scruples were even contemplated. It occurred to no one that the Pope's action was anything but just and proper. Since Martin V had granted the

King of Portugal as many lands as might be discovered
from the Bogiador Capes to the Indies, the discovery of
the New World immediately precipitated a quarrel between Portugal and Spain. The two appealed to the Pope's
judgment. To placate them, he traced the famous « line
of demarcation », 100 leagues from the Azores and Cape
Verde, giving Spain all the lands to the west of it and
Portugal all those to the east ([22]). The next year the
« Vatican Line » was fixed 270 leagues further west,
which is why Brazil, when it was discovered, fell into
Portugal's orbit.

Alexander VI personally designated this « line » on
the original map (1493) that is preserved in the Museo
Borgiano del Collegio Urbano. « How sublime », Cantù
has written, « to see the Pope, as in the Middle Ages,
sit down as arbiter between two great nations to prevent
a war and partition a new world for them! » ([23]).

The letter accompanying the Bull in question is
preserved in the archives of the Frari in Venice. It has
incalculable importance not only in the history of the
Missions but in the service of peace among peoples. In
it was confirmed the missionary principle that was to be
applied in America : « *ut fides catholica et christiana
religio nostris praesertim temporibus exaltetur ... ac
barbaras nationes deprimantur et ad fidem ipsam redu-
cantur* » ([24]).

The year after the Pope's decision, in 1494, Spain
and Portugal concluded the Treaty of Tordesillas, which
put into effect the papal « line of demarcation », which
crossed South America from the mouth of the Amazon
to the Bay of Santa Caterina. Through it Spain reserved
for herself an area that included Mexico and Peru,
New Granada and the Rio de la Plata, which she subsequently conquered, while Portugal deeded to herself

the southern Atlantic region, including Brazil, which Cobral discovered in 1509.

VII — In the pleiad of Catholic names, apart from those already encountered, that glitter in the Columbian constellation, one of the first is that of the learned Paolo Toscanelli (1397-1482), the Florentine buried in Santo Spirito, who was among other things the builder of the solstitial gnomon of the Duomo in Florence. He was a distinguished astronomer and cartographer who by 1474, developing the ideas of Eratosthenes and Seneca, had guessed the existence of a new continent. He was also a profound student of Ptolemy's geography.

Without entering into the Toscanelli - Columbus question ([25]), it seems certain that the feasibility of sailing to the Indies by a western route occurred to Toscanelli as well as to D'Ailly and that Toscanelli's map considerably influenced Columbus.

Toscanelli recalls another Florentine Catholic, Amerigo Vespucci, whose baptismal name has exalted him as nothing less than the perpetrator of Columbus' discovery. At the time of Columbus' death, Vespucci, then on the first of his four voyages to the New World, was elevated by the government to the rank of First Pilot, *Piloto-Major,* of Spain. He had hardly returned from his fourth — and last — transoceanic voyage, in September, 1504, when he wrote a letter about his trips to Lorenzo Pier Francesco de' Medici, whose Latin translation of it was published the following year under the title of *Mundus Novus.* A French translation was made from this, which eventually fell under the eyes of Martin Waldseemüller, an ecclesiastic and later a canon of St. Dié in Alsace, who included it in his *Cosmographiae Introductio* (1507), a great wall map of the world that has been called the « baptismal certificate » of America. Waldseemüller, together with the geographer and, it seems, poet Mathia Ringmann, prepared this map in the press-shop of St. Dié, founded by the canon Vautrin G. Lud ([26]). There, in lucid Latin, he proposed that the New World be called America : « *quasi Americi terra, ab Americo Vesputio sagacis ingenii viro inventa* ». Without further ado, when he published his map of the New World, he called it « America » ([27]).

One cannot say that Amerigo Vespucci was a usurper or even a plagiarist of Columbus' fame and glory. As Cantù has written, it was through one of those « accidents in which fate so capriciously distributes her favors » that Waldseemüller mistakenly believed the Tuscan had first touched the Continent on one of his four trips. The informative Las Casas — first priest ordained in the New World, whose father Francesco as we have seen, accompanied Columbus on his second voyage (1493) — protested against the name « America », calling it an impropriety as well as a belittlement of the legitimate discoverer's name. Just as the monarchs were ungrateful to Columbus, so too were the writers, and it was to vindicate him that Bolivar paid him tribute by naming one of the republics he created, Colombia.

On March 28, 1848, Tommaseo, writing in the name of the Venetian Republic to the United States government, to thank it for help given Venice by the consul W. A. Sparks, noted : « A citizen of an Italian republic was the first to discover your country, to which the citizen of another Italian republic gave his name, as if to seal it with the symbol of greatness » ([28]).

Thus, through an involuntary error, the New World became associated with the name of a saint of the ancient Mother Church — the Hungarian St. Emerico, or Americo in the purest speech of Florence, patron saint of

Ser Anastagio Vespucci's adventurous son. This name of St. Emerico is, in fact, most fitting, because it means « self-government or liberty ». Hence it well describes the country's innate sense of democracy. *Nomen-omen.*

Bancroft, on this point, did not miss another relevant aspect. « Italians », the historian reflects (I, 1), « had the glory of making the discoveries from which Italy gained nothing, neither in riches nor in power ».

VIII — Catholic priority in discovering and exploring the greater part of the New World was handed down — from Paolo Toscanelli, Christopher Columbus and Amerigo Vespucci — to a whole new dynasty of men who preceded the Englishmen Hudson and Cook.

John and Sebastian Cabot, father and son, were Catholic Venetians. In the summer of 1497 John coasted along the St. Lawrence River in Canada, and the next year with Sebastian he went as far as South Carolina, if not farther. The characteristic piety of Venetians distinguishes them. Their ship bore the name of an evangelist, St. Matthew, and they consecrated the lands they reached in the names of the saints of the Catholic liturgical calendar. Thus the capital of Terranova — the present-day Newfoundland — received the name of St. John, when John Cabot reached it on June 24, 1497 ([29]). The Catholic Cabots, who were the first to explore, for England, the waters later called Hudson's Bay, considered themselves « useless servants » and mere instruments in the hands of the Eternal for the realization of divine goals. When their mission was over, they retired into silence. Bancroft reflects (I, 1): « Sebastian Cabot gave England a Continent, and today no one knows where he is buried ! ».

The solidity of Catholic character (one might say

almost Franciscan character) is also shown in the confession Sebastian Cabot gave of the motive for his expeditions : « When the news came that Don Cristoforo Colon, the Genoese, had discovered the coasts of India, it caused great talk in the whole court of Henry VII, then reigning, and everyone spoke with great admiration of a feat that seemed more divine than human — to sail from the West to the East, where spices grow in a land hitherto unknown. For such fame and knowledge there spread in my heart an enflamed desire to attempt a like enterprise that would be worthy of note ».

Catholic also was Jacques Cartier (1491-1557), whom Sebastian Cabot chose to head another expedition to the Northeast coast of America. In 1554 Cartier sailed from his native St. Malo — first receiving the blessing of the diocesan bishop and taking with him priests the bishop had authorized — for his discoveries at Montreal and along the St. Lawrence ([30]).

In 1499, Alonso de Hojeada, the Spanish admiral, and Amerigo Vespucci sailed along the northern coast of South America and gave the name of « Little Venice » (Venezuela) to that country, where the houses are built on piles, as in Venice. Catholics also were Ponce de Leon, Magellan and Vincenzo Pinzon, who on January 10, 1500, touched the eastern tip of Brazil. Catholic, too, was Giovanni da Varezzano ([31]), a pure Tuscan from Val di Greve, who commanded the first French expedition to the New World, under Francis I. Aboard his caravel, the Delphine, in April, 1524, he first penetrated New York harbor, which he named after St. Margaret, and entered the river that is today named after Henry Hudson (who didn't get there till March, 1609, some 85 years later). A year after Verazzano, another Catholic seaman, Esteban Gomez, explored part of the

Hudson, which he named after St. Anthony, as Ribera's map of 1529 reveals.

After discovering the present New York area, Verazzano went north to Narragansett Bay — where Roger Williams later repaired when he was banished by the Puritans — and became the discoverer of Rhode Island. To him we owe the state's name. In a report to Francis I of France, he wrote that the land he had discovered was « as delightful and as large as the Island of Rhodes », the Mediterranean « island of roses » famous in the epic of Catholicism as the bulwark of the Crusades. Today some justice has been rendered Verazzano with the monument by the sculptor, Hector Ximenes, erected to him in Battery Park in New York in 1909.

The discoverers of the Pacific Ocean were Catholics. The very name Pacific was bestowed on it by the pious Portuguese, Magellan (1470-1521), for the mildness of its waters. With Pigafetta of Vicenza in 1520, Magellan sailed across it from Patagonia to the Philippines in that epical first trip around the world.

No less Catholic were the discoverers of the American interior and the explorers of its ways of communication. At their head stands Hernando de Soto, who in 1540, with the first priests, reached Georgia, the two Carolinas, Tennessee, Alabama, Missouri, Oklahoma and Mississippi by way of the Gulf of Mexico.

They were Catholics from first to last — from Diego Moriello, who in 1516 explored the coasts of Florida, to the above-mentioned Esteban Gomez, who in 1524 explored the eastern seaboard from Florida to Labrador; from Panfilo de Narvaez, who discovered the Mississippi from the Gulf coast in 1527, to Coronado, discoverer of New Mexico and Colorado in 1540. Also Catholics were the priests and missionaries, some of them Franciscans, some Jesuits, who explored the Great Lakes and the course of

the Mississippi, the « Father of Rivers », who went south
to Mexico and Peru and west to Arizona and California.

The Great Lakes are the five lakes of North America the conquest of which opened up the way to the interior and to the exploration of the Mississippi, and to the
gradual domination of the whole Continent. To five Catholics, in chronological succession and in the course of
53 years (1615-1668), goes the whole credit for their
discovery.

The first, Lake Huron, was found by the missionary
Father Caron, who anticipated by ten days the identical
discovery of Champlain (1615). This feat represented a
striking advance over the discoveries of Cartier (1535)
and others after him, whose progress had always been
impeded by the extremely strong rapids of the St. Lawrence. The second of the five Great Lakes, Lake Ontario,
was discovered in the same year, 1615, by the great
Champlain. The third, Lake Michigan, was discovered
19 years later (1634) by the Canadian explorer Jean Ni-
colet. The fourth, Lake Superior, another 25 years later
(1659), was mastered by the Catholic explorers, Radisson
and Grosseliers, who traveled along its southern
edges. And the last, Lake Erie, was claimed by Joliet,
pupil of the Jesuits, who discovered it in 1668 ([32]).

IX — The list of such Catholic priorities is so long
that it can hardly be exhausted.

The United States today is, as it were, set within
a four-sided frame of boundaries, which while serving
as practical frontiers also affirm, from all four sides, the
glorious ideal of the Catholics' scientific-missionary zeal.
The very place-names have their own eloquence : from
the St. Lawrence River in the north to the missionary
city of St. Augustine in the south, from the ancient

missions named for St. Louis, Santa Fé and San Antonio in the southwest to San Francisco, the « Golden Gate » washed by the Pacific.

The tangible geographical limits of the United States recall in their names the primeval poetry of faith, the Catholic influence that presided at their origins : « Sault Ste. Marie, Marquette and St. Paul are the patrons of the country at its nothern border; New Orleans, St. Augustine and San Antonio are its sentinels in the south; Baltimore (named after the converted nobleman), Boston (the town of the holy abbot Botulphus) and New York are its eastern bulwarks; and the cities of Sacramento, San Francisco and Los Angeles (The Angels) are the custodians of the western seas. Catholic providence often smiles... » ([33]).

The Catholicism that presided at the discovery of all these places is the same that has consecrated them with the sweetness of a blessing. Infinite are the names that bear witness to it — Trinidad, San Salvador, Concepcion, Natividad, all christened by Columbus; Sacramento, the present capital of California; Sangre de Cristo, as it is called, one of the Rocky Mountains' highest peaks; the various cities dedicated to the Immaculate Conception in Paraguay, Chile and the Philippines; San Domingo; Hollywood, which if it is identified today with the bright but evanescent splendors of the cinema still reveals in its name the Franciscan piety of the *padres* and their mystic devotion to the Cross of Calvary; the former Lake Sacramento, now Lake George, a Jesuit discovery; St. Joseph Lake, as it was baptized by Father Allouez, now Lake Michigan.

As we have seen, the place-names of California charmingly insert into the geography of America almost the whole litany of the Franciscan order. Stoddard's poem on the beauty of the *Angelus* was inspired not only by the gracious and silvery bells of the old missions but also by the mystical anthology of their saint-names sanctifying the shores of the Pacific.

X — Contemporary historians in America like to lay stress, and for the most valid and worthy reasons, on the practical achievements of Catholics in their country. They press their point by reminding us of the work of the missionaries and Catholic explorers and the large part they played in the discovery and development of the national wealth, such as petroleum and various mineral deposits. They boast, and with reason, of how they taught the rational exploitation of the land, introduced hydraulic irrigation, initiated reclamation projects and instilled that passion for agriculture that is the basis of today's prosperity.

The pioneer Catholics, whether missionaries or not, are praised for having imported the cultivation of oranges, lemons and vines, for having tended the forests and introduced reforestation. They are eulogized for having first exploited the nation's waterways, today harnessed to produce immense electrical power, for having discovered, in the present state of New York, the first salt mines and, in Pennsylvania, the inexhaustible oil-fields that were to bring titanic industries into being.

Praise, too is due the Catholics who published the first book in the New World (in Mexico City, 1544), the *Brief Doctrine,* printed at the expense of the Franciscan bishop Zumarraga of that see, which anticipated the first Protestant publication, the *Bay State Psalm Book* (1639) by 95 years ([34]), and to early Catholic achievements of every type — first books printed on presses, the first works on the American Indians' philology, grammar and vocabulary. The first railway in the Western Hemisphere was built 1827 by a Catholic, Charles Carroll, who also put his signature on the Declaration of Independence.

A Catholic — it is pointed out with legitimate pride — was the founder of the United States Navy; another was the father of the superb Military Academy at West Point; a third organized the United States Cavalry; a fourth established the equally renowned Naval Academy at Annapolis; a fifth, Thomas Lloyd, was the first secretary of Congress and published the first issue of the *Congressional Record*. He learned stenography in Flanders, in the Jesuit College of Sant'Omer and among his instructors was Father John Carroll, later Archbishop of Baltimore. Lloyd, elected secretary of the Assembly that elected Washington president, took the historic minutes of the occasion and published them in his own newspaper the next day.

To stray for a moment into the field of art, the very melody of Francis Scott Key's hymn, *The Star-Spangled Banner,* which was declared the national anthem on March 3, 1931, is said to be the composition of the Irishman, Tourbough O'Carolan (circa 1750), who is called the « Last of the Bards » ([35]).

Mention of the American flag recalls that its three heraldic colors — red, white and blue — are no less than the three mystic colors of early mediaeval heraldry, intended to symbolize and denote the Holy Trinity. The Cross, it is true, does not figure in the American flag, since the Puritans, as we shall see, intentionally eliminated it. Nevertheless — certainly without their knowledge — the heraldic colors remained the same that St. John de Matha, founder of the Order of the Most Holy Trinity, chose as his emblem in the Rome of Gregory VII. John Greenleaf Whittier, the Quaker poet of the Civil War, alluded to de Matha in his praise of the American flag :

« Is not your sail the banner
      Which God hath blest anew,
The mantle that De Matha wore,
      The red, the white, the blue ? »

This poet, with a sensibility that one could call Catholic, wrote thus of the mighty American Ship of State :

« Sail on, sail on, deep-freighted
      With blessings and with hopes;
The saints of old with shadowy hands
      Are pulling at your ropes.
Behind ye holy martyrs
      Uplift the palm and crown,
Before ye unborn ages send
      Their benedictions down.
Take heart from John de Matha ! —
      God's errands never fail » (³⁶).

The same ideally symbolic concept of the American flag served to inspire John Dryden, a Catholic poet — he was converted from Anglicism to the Church of Rome in 1686 — who wrote these two beautiful lines :

« A constellation is but one,
Though it is a train of stars ».

From that came the concept of the Star-Spangled Banner — a constellation of stars symbolizing unity and harmony.

To follow a little farther the fortunes of Old Glory, it should be recorded that 16 days after the Continental Congress officially adopted it (³⁷), on August 2, 1777, it flew for the first time at Fort Schuyler (Fort Stanwix), in the neighborhood of the future township of Rome, N. Y. Somewhat later the Catholic Dominic Lynch

baptized the settlement with the august name of the
« Sacred City of the Pontiffs ».

Two outstanding early American Catholics were Roger B. Taney, Chief Justice of the Supreme Court in a
vital period of its history ([38]), and Christopher Colles
(1738-1821), who designed one of the first machines in
this classic land of invention : he was among the first to
propose preserving water by means of a reservoir. The
present Croton aqueduct that furnishes New York City
derives from this project. As early as 1784 at the request
of the New York State Legislature, he undertook the feat
of joining Lake Erie with the Hudson River by a canal.
The audacious scheme conceived by this Catholic, who
was previously an engineer in the Continental Army, was
adopted by Governor Clinton and became a reality 15
years later ([39]).

Achievements, Catholic achievements in both spiritual and material spheres — an entire volume of its
own would be needed merely to list them. But to what
purpose ? Do these brilliant pioneering feats — at least
as they concern external things — represent the most
significant aspect of Catholic glory on the new Continent,
the most substantially vital aspect ?

Quite evidently, no.

Remember that a Catholic, Thomas Enright of Pittsburgh, was among the first three American soldiers to
fall in the first World War, on November 3, 1917; that
Joseph Lavelle, another Catholic, was the first American
sailor to die in the same war; and that Lt. W. D. Meyer-
ing of Chicago, also Catholic, received the first Distinguished Service Cross — that is eloquent enough, but
it is not all.

We add that the first American officer to die in that
war, Lt. W. T. Fitzsimmons, was an alumnus of the
Catholic St. Mary's College in Kansas and that the last

officer to die, only five minutes before the Armistice of 1918, was a Catholic chaplain, Father William F. Davitt of Springfield, Mass. But even this, while significant enough to make America's Catholics proud, does not constitute by itself what St. Francis, in the steps of the Apostle, would have deemed « perfect gladness » and the final glory ([40]).

One might take a step forward, in the ascending scale of values, and recall the Jesuit coadjutor, Brother Giles Mazier, who first forged the copper of Lake Superior (around 1675) and chiseled a pyx with local silver. This is perhaps still in the sphere of material activity, although the act was in the service of the supernatural.

The ineffable achievement of Catholic America was that of having introduced the civilizing and redeeming message of the Saviour in most of its States and to have first celebrated in them the bloodless Sacrifice of the Mystic Lamb of God that « Takes away the sins of the world ». In how many States? The figure is lost in history. Yet one may set down, among others, States such as Maine, Vermont, North and South Carolina, Alabama, Georgia, Florida, Mississippi, Texas, Louisiana, Indiana, Ohio, Michigan, Illinois, Wisconsin, Iowa, Minnesota, Missouri, New Mexico, Oregon, California and Arizona — more than half, among the 48, that are entirely Catholic. But is the story then complete?

An esteemed American historian, the convert Carlton J. H. Hayes, one time United States Ambassador to Madrid, revealed much when he wrote that when one spoke of American Catholicism « the truth imposes that America is the daughter of the Catholic Church ». It is well to repeat it : America is more truly the daughter of the Catholic Church than of Europe itself. However, you look at the history of her culture, America has always been Christian; Europe not. In other words, the Church has given America more than it has given Europe. Hence if the Church is European — in the worthy opinion of Belloc, it is for stronger reasons American. Protestantism did not exist when Christopher Columbus set foot on American soil; and although the majority of the European immigrants who stabilized the English colonies in the 17th century were Protestants, they were separated by so brief an interval from their Catholic ancestors and Catholic traditions that the best of what they brought with them was, willy-nilly, Catholic... Wherever one looks in the United States, at whatever of its institutions or ideals that are usually considered an aspect of true Americanism, you find that no matter who has created or formulated them their embryo, their antecedent must be sought in Catholic theory and practice. That is what I mean when I say that America is the daughter of the Catholic Church ([41]).

THE MISSIONARY EPIC

The Catholic religion, as practised in what is today the geographic area of the United States, was brought into existence through three separate phases of ecclesiastic activity.

The first was essentially a missionary phase, aiming to convert and civilize the natives. The second aimed chiefly at safeguarding the souls of the first colonists who subscribed to the Catholic faith, no matter from what part of Europe they came. The final phase was the most intense and successful. Carried out in the post-Revolutionary period, it was organized by the ecclesiastic hierarchy constituted in North America on November 6, 1789, because the Declaration of Indepedence ushered in a new era in the spiritual and religious life of the nation, as well as in its political life.

II — With the second landing of Columbus in « little Spain » on November 27th, 1493, began the movement of evangelizing the New Continent. At the time, it is calculated that there were several million Indians living in the Western Hemisphere, probably a million of them in the territory now known as the United States. Today's Indian population is estimated at fewer than 300,000, of which 200,000 inhabit the United States and Canada.

The Indians varied widely in their customs, folklore and language; it is estimated that their languages derived from more than fifty different glottological groups. Nevertheless, the tribes were generally ruled by a *sachem* or chief, assisted by counsellors. For the most part, they lived in wigwams. In the Southwestern area, New Mexico and Arizona, they carved rude dwellings or *pueblos* out of steep cliffs as a means of self-protection. Non-nomadic tribes cultivated grain, potatoes and tobacco. Buffalo, deer, reindeer and sometimes fish constituted their diet.

The Belgian missionary Father Louis Hennepin still remains probably the foremost analyst of Indian psychology. After a six-year scientific missionary expedition in America, Father Hennepin wrote his master work *La Description de la Louisiane*, first tourist book on the Northwest of the United States. In the final chapter entitled « Indian Indifference », the author tells us :

« These Indians have such remarkable indifference towards everything that nothing similar exists under the face of heaven. They listen willingly to everything told them and accept everything done for them. If we say : " My brother, pray God with me ", they pray and repeat word for word all the prayers taught them; "Kneel", and they kneel; "Lift your hat", and they do so; "Be silent", and they are silent; "Do not smoke", and they stop smoking. If you give them pictures, a crucifix or a crown, they use them as ornaments as if they were gems or porcelain. When I said to them : "Tomorrow will be a day of prayer", they replied : *"Niaova"* (all right). If I said to them : "Don't get drunk any more", they would answer : "Very well, I agree". But when they were given liquor by the French or the Dutch

— and the Dutch never hesitated to exchange liquor for furs — they would get drunk just as they had before. When I asked them if they believed, they invariably replied in the affirmative, yet almost all the Indian women baptized by our missionaries and married to Frenchmen in the Church, abandon and change their husbands often, because they are not subject to our Christian laws ».

Father Hennepin's judgments, written in the 17th century, were confirmed in the 19th century by a saintly Italian named Father Felice de Andreis. This missionary, who strove zealously to convert the natives, gave his views in a letter written to Father Sicardi : « Let us go out among the fifty different nations of Indians who recognize only one God, which they call in their language *Chissemenetu,* that is Master of Life, to whom they address a few prayers and the first puff of their pipes. To please their God, they sometimes practise horrible cruelties on themselves, this constituting the sum total of their religion. They live like the wild beasts they hunt, hunting being their sole occupation and only source of food. They go about half naked and trade with the whites, exchanging furs or game for liquor, red paint for their faces and silver rings for their noses or ears. The spirit of liberty and independence, common to all Americans, reaches its highest development in the savages, who consider themselves the only truly free men and far above all other men. It is really frightful to see, and one doubts that their reason is properly developed. They have in general considerable respect for priests, whom they call *mekkaie* or *uroiatte,* which means black skirt. If their veneration of priests is somewhat extreme, at the same time they show great indifference towards the Christian religion, which they consider designed only for us and not for them, as they have their own naturalistic religion, or rather superstitions. Among them there are some

Catholics and despite the efforts of the Protestant missionaries to convert them to their beliefs, they have always
repulsed them, declaring that true *mekkaie* have neither
wives nor children, as the Protestant ministers usually
have, but live wholly for God and for the good of their
souls ».

This pronouncement by a simple, devout Italian missionary has been illustrated on a more scientific level
by recent ethnologists. We are no longer mystified by
that aspect of Indian prayer, until now almost completely
misunderstood, which constitutes an apologetic proof of
the existence of God.

« A ceremony with an accompaniment of prayer is a
custom among certain Indian tribes of North America
which has erroneously been called a " sun dance ". This
is because only in its more recent forms, somewhat degen-
erated, this ritual has acquired a certain relation with
sun worship. Among the ancient tribes which still practise the genuine ritual, this " sun dance " is roughly considered an equivalent of the sacred performances of our
Middle Ages, that is as a mystery of the creation of the
world. It is, in fact, a representation, often dramatic,
of the creative hand of the Supreme Being, interpreted
through the myths that relate to it. This « mystery » is
no mere commemoration, but has a purely devotional basis,
because through the accompanying prayers it seeks to
call down the blessings of the first creative energy on the
bystanders, on their families and on the whole tribe.
Thus, for example, the prayer of supplication : " My
Father, we sit here on earth in humility, with a poor
heart, and ask your tender mercy." For mercy they
certainly mean material things, like food and health; but
they also ask for moral grace, such as fraternal charity
when they pray : " My Father, make us love each other
more." Or else their prayers are wholly spiritual, as

when they cry : " My Father, make our thoughts reach unto heaven, where there is saintliness." Then there is a prayer that says : " The Father, the Man up above, promised his benedictions and his grace. Still we invoke him above to keep the participants at this feast on the righteous path ". The feast closes with the plea : " My Father, come, come and stay with us." This rite is executed by many North American tribes either as an independent function or as a prelude to more elaborate ceremonies » (¹).

This illuminating description by Dr. Michel Schulien, scientific director of the Lateran Ethnological Missionary Museum, was confirmed by another report on the cultural ceremonies carried out by the Algonquins and particularly those of the Lenape tribe, which populated parts of New Jersey, Delaware and Pennsylvania.

The Lenapes «are certainly a people who have retained the most ancient cultural forms. When first discovered, they did not even know the art of making pottery, stockbreeding or agriculture. They lived by hunting bears and buffalo and harvesting wild rice that grows on the lake shores. Apart from the family, they have no social organization whatever ».

They celebrated their festival in the autumn, when the leaves fell. The festival lasted twelve days in memory of the twelve heavens, in the highest of which lives the Supreme Being. It opened with a « mystery of the creation ». Their absorption in prayer grew from day to day. All the rituals were interwoven with speeches of supplication, thanks and praise.

Sentiments of gratitude, of elevation to God and joy in Him shine through the following excerpts : « I do not feel capable of asking a blessing from the Great Spirit. It is truly remarkable that He should feel sympathy for us, He our Father, our Creator... »; « It is a joy to the soul to see how all things born are given to us, how our Father, the Great Spirit, has provided everything so well »; « I am grateful to you, O Great Spirit, that we have been able to live until now... If one thinks of his children, how happy he is to see them enjoy good health ! We rejoice because we realize how much we are blessed by the goodness of our Father, the Great Spirit ».

In their prayers of supplication, they asked for good crops, good hunting, cessation of storms, safety from floods and earthquakes and, perhaps with even greater fervor, brotherly charity and peaceful thoughts; in general, the grace of the « straight, white path », the « path of the Great Spirit », which is indeed a morally pure life on earth, spent under the eyes of the Supreme Being. From the « straight, white path » they hoped to proceed into the great beyond on the path that leads to the twelfth heaven, seat of the Great Spirit, so that they might live near Him. And they added : « O Great Spirit, give us everything we have asked of you, you who are you, our creator. Think of your children ».

This Lenape ceremony is one of notable loftiness, full of noble symbolism and a rich source of moral and religious energy. With the Lenapes, we have faith in a Supreme Being, a morale symbolized by the « white path » of the Great Spirit and a cult based on ceremonies, offerings and prayers — a concept of the world in which the intellect, will and sentiment find their natural order and repose in worshipping God and in preparing for a better life. A scholar who has profoundly studied these people, an American professor, points out that this is a « genuine, original religious concept ».

Some tribes, however, such as the Timucuas in Florida, the Natchez in Mississippi and others in certain remote areas of California, practised human sacrifice of both children and adults, following the rites with a cannabalistic feast. The Cherokee tribe believed that the flaming spirits of power and victory lived in the land of the Sun — the East — while the black spirits of death lived in the twilight land of the West.

Primitive forms of faith, therefore, were not wanting among these Indians. The founder of Quaker Pennsylvania, William Penn, who visited them in their wigwams, participated in their feasts and banquets and reasoned with them on spiritual matters, wrote : « These poor savage people believe in God and in the soul but without a knowledge of metaphysics ». Has any primitive people indeed ever existed that did not believe in the Divine ?

III — More than anyone else, Christopher Columbus aspired towards the spiritual renascence of the Indians. The historian Herrera wrote of him that, « zealous of God's honor », he « yearned to convert the Indians and to have the faith of Jesus Christ spread and embraced everywhere ».

At the solemn hour of her death, Isabella of Castille (1451-1504) revealed her sublime saintliness when, thinking of the Indians who had become recent subjects of the royal crown, she dictated these final dispositions in their favor : « ... Item : with regard to the Islands and Terra Firma beyond the seas granted us by the Holy Apostolic See, these lands discovered and those that remain to be discovered, it has been our intention... to gather together, induce and convert the people of those lands to our holy Catholic faith; moreover, to send to the said Islands and Terra Firma, prelates, men of religion, priests and other learned and God-fearing persons to instruct the citizens and inhabitants in the Catholic faith and teach them to clothe themselves properly and put due diligence into such tasks as outlined more fully in the letter of the said concession; which I charge and give mandate to the Princess, my daughter, and the Prince, her husband, that they do and execute in this manner and that this be their principal goal, in the attainment of which they put much solicitude and do not permit the Indians... to suffer any injustice to their persons or their property; that they give orders that the Indians be treated well and with justice and should they suffer any damages, such be repaired...»

This deeply human missionary clause contained in Isabella's testament was written into the *Recopilacion* of the Indies, and provided the basis of the « Laws of the Indies », of which the Bishop-historian Piedrahita wrote : « It would seem that not men but angels dictated it » ([2]).

A symbol of this sovereign missionary ideal cherished by the Catholic King and Queen towards the New World will be found in the Missal, printed on the finest parchment, richly gilded and decorated, glittering with gold and precious jewels, now exhibited in the Royal Library of Spain. This Missal was dedicated to their nephew, Emperor Charles IV, and contains this inscription : « Ferdinand and Isabella, most devoted sovereigns, embellish this book with the first gains (a shipment of gold) from the Indies ».

Charles V's missionary propensities are well known, particularly after the first publication in 1941 of a document describing the tasks assigned by the Emperor to those he sent to Florida : « And we command that the first thing the captains and friars and others on the spot will do the moment they step on the soil will be to declare, through interpreters who understand the Indians and the inhabitants of that land, that we have sent our men to teach them decent customs and to suppress their vice of eating human flesh, to instruct them in our holy faith, to preach to them so that they may be saved, and to draw

78

them to our subjection so that they may be treated much better than they are being treated now, enjoying the favors and privileges of our other Christian subjects... ».

Catholic Spain at that time generously upheld the nation's missionary pact with the Pope. In 1506, the Regent Cardinal Cisneros decreed, with typical Franciscan missionary wisdom, that no ship set sail for the Indies without missionaries. Years later, Charles V, impressed by Lopez da Gomora's stupendous declaration — « Spain did not discover America; God discovered it so that He might convert it to his holy law » — renewed this edict to the letter.

But before long, a tragic schism was to divide these men of God and their sublime ideal from the explorers, captains of fortune, traffickers and colonists, unfortunately many of the latter deported criminals, all intoxicated with the prospect of finding themselves unexpectedly in possession of a vast world of immeasurable resources.

There followed — and one is obliged to mention it — the hour of the pitiless denunciations made by the proud, upright Spanish Dominicans, the hated « Inquisitors », led by Arbuez and Torquemada, who rose up like blazing archangels of divine justice in defense of the Indians. Isabella in her tomb must have been placated, if not appeased.

The Dominican Antonio Montesinos, who landed in New Spain in 1510 with the first party of Dominicans dispatched to the American Continent, launched the initial campaign in defense of the oppressed Indians. One year after his arrival, he opened his public attack with true Dominican zeal. Father Montesinos considered abuse of the natives more than a sin that cried out for God's vengeance; it was, in his opinion, a shame and a disgrace for Spain ([3]). He was subsequently repatriated to answer charges of treason, but his vigorous self-defense brought about some measures of relief for the Indians.

Soon after, he was followed by another great Dominican, Bartholomew Las Casas, first Bishop of Chiapas (⁴), whom Pope Benedict XV hailed in his Encyclical *Maximum Illud* as a «glory and luminary», praising the «work he undertook to protect the wretched Indians from the infamous tyranny of men and rend them from implacable enslavement to the devil ».

Another Dominican, Da Villa, testified : « Such was the horror aroused in the Indians against the very name of Christianity, thanks to Spanish cruelty, that missionaries arriving in the New World were instructed to explain to the natives : " We are not Christians like the soldiers. We are *patres christianorum* ". We share with them a common faith but in life we have nothing in common with them ». Giuliano Garces, first Bishop of Tlaxkala, was another Dominican who denounced the greed, avarice and immorality of the *conquistadores*.

A fifth great Dominican was Francisco de Vitoria, whose name is immortal in the history of international law. Professor at the University of Salamanca from 1526 to 1539, he was often consulted by Charles V for his views on theology and law, which de Vitoria held indivisible. He was the first to propound the scientific aspects of the problem posed to the world by the Indian natives.

This occurred early in the Spanish exploratory campaign when the *conquistadores,* inebriated by their successes, sought to justify armed conquest of the new land as a duty in the name of civilization and faith. For the anti-Moslem crusades they substituted another against the idol worshippers of the New World. Scholarly Father de Vitoria supported in scientific terms the protests raised by so many Dominicans, from Father Montesinos to Father Las Casas. He contested any false rights of usurpation assumed by Christian peoples in the Western hemisphere, declaring that native peoples ought to enjoy the same rights that regulate relations between the European States — rights which he maintained were sacred and a common patrimony of the New and Old Worlds.

Thus, for the first time in the history of law, de Vitoria argued for the inherent sovereignty of every politically organized social group, a sovereignty not assumed from without but rather a natural privilege, and he arrived at a logical conclusion : the equality and independence of all groups capable of governing themselves and therefore eligible to enjoy every first-class privilege laid down by international law. If America conceded unqualified political liberty to the Philippines on July 4th, 1946, it did so by applying directly the principles set forth by this Dominican professor who did not hesitate to stand apart from current moral thought.

To answer these open denunciations, the merciless colonizers tried to justify themselves by fabricating theories of racial heresy, intended to cast doubt on the Indians as descendants of Adam's loins or to demonstrate that they had no power of reasoning like the white men.

The prolonged controversy between the *conquistadores* on one side and the missionaries and scientists on the other, could only be resolved authoritatively by the infallible Teaching of the Church; thus, the various pontifical directives issued in timely, detailed terms by Pope Paul III during his reign (1534-1549). We recall particularly three Bulls, the first of which, *Veritas Ipsa* (1537), was a sanction of de Vitoria's ideas. In this document, the Pope recognized first of all that the Indians were true men; subsequently he declared that « they and all other peoples still to be discovered, even those outside the Catholic faith, were not to be deprived of their liberty or

81

the enjoyment of their property, nor were they to be reduced to slavery ».

In his second Bull, *Unigenitus* (1537), Paul III reaffirmed the equality of whites and Indians in all matters of human rights, and forbade any damage to the Indians in respect to their persons and goods, threatening grave punishments to any transgressors. With his third Bull, *Altitudo Divini Consilii,* Paul decreed that the baptized native was to have no choice among the women with whom he cohabited, but must marry the one he took first, unless it were impossible to establish such priority for certain. In such a case, the Indian who lived successively with various women must marry the one with whom he was cohabiting at the time of his conversion and renounce all the others. In this way he raised the status of Indian brides and instituted among the savages the practice of monogamy.

The question has often been debated as to whether it was the interests of the greedy *conquistadores* or the religious movement that dominated the era of exploration and conquest of the American Continent. In his drama, *The New World of Columbus,* Lopez de Vega requires idolatry, one of his principal characters, to rail against the Spaniards in the New World and their religion :

> « *Providence, do not permit them*
> *To bear such injustice against me,*
> *Because it is avidity that rules them,*
> *And spurs them on to such deeds.*
> *Under the guise of religion*
> *They seek only gold and silver,*
> *And the delights of undiscovered treasures* ».

There is undoubtedly truth in these words, but only as they apply to adventurers who exploited the New World to enrich themselves through quick, illicit gains. But the same cannot be said of the missionaries. Where the *conquistadores* worked for man, the *padres* worked for God. Taken together, in this vast field of experiment in civilization stretching from Florida to California, we can conclude that the good outweighed evil. Notwithstanding the intemperance of some of her *conquistadores,* the Spanish Catholic civilization may be compared with the agave, picturesque plant of Central America, destined by nature to blossom forth in magnificent flower only once and then die, as if from excessive effort. It is appropriately said of Spain that her ultimate decline developed from Columbus' discoveries rather than the exodus of the Jews and Moors of the Inquisition. « Spain exhausted herself in the stupendous effort of colonizing and civilizing the New World » (⁵).

For the work they did towards evangelizing the American Continent, the French and Spanish were equally considered « crusaders for souls » by Protestant historians themselves. America is chiefly indebted to them and their fervor for her rapid, intensive exploration. « The chief impulse... came from the zeal of spiritual conquest that carried the French missionaries from the Atlantic Ocean to the Hudson Bay and the Mississippi, the Spanish missionaries to the southeast corner of the Continent » (⁶).

At any rate, the accusations brought against the Catholic *conquistadores* are certainly not new, and only the adventurers themselves can be held responsible for their deeds. An 18th-century Spanish proverb describes them appropriately : « Under the guise of religion, they go in search of silver and gold ». Lopez de Vega, on the other hand, interpreted the lofty aspirations of those not seeking adventure and gain in these words :

« *Al Rey infinitas tierras,*
Y a Dios infinitas almas ».

Thus he expressed their two-fold purpose in the sublimest terms of Christian idealism. *The Constant Prince* of Calderon likewise synthesizes the noble aim of Iberia's finest colonizers :

« *We have come to increase faith in God;*
His will shall be the honor
And His the glory ».

IV — Now begins in earnest the epic story of the missionaries among the American natives, a story that has written many golden pages in the annals of the apostolate, in the martyrology of the Franciscans and Jesuits, in the history of every branch of science. These « divine, impatient » missionaries belong almost entirely to two different religious Orders, the Franciscan and Jesuit. They covered the territory which, after a series of military, political and diplomatic maneuvers as well as financial purchases, was to become the present United States.

In the north, the French took Quebec as the center of their operations. From here Franciscans and Jesuits carried forth their missions in every direction, spreading out through southern Canada and into the very heart of the Continent. In this, the missionaries conformed to the Foundation Bull issued in 1674 by the Archbishopric of Quebec, which covered all the French possessions in North America, including Terranova, Acadia and the whole of « New France », from the Atlantic down the Mississippi Valley to Louisiana. Thus, an apostolic field considerably vaster than the whole of Europe lay open to the mystic fervor of these spiritual conquerors.

Meanwhile, another hardy missionary expedition, sponsored by Spain, initiated its evangelical work in the Antilles and indeed, seventy years after Columbus' discovery, peaceful legions of heroic missionaries, likewise predominantly Franciscan and Jesuit, had already arrived in Chile from Mexico and were heading from the Pacific eastward towards the Atlantic, establishing missionary settlements among the Indians in the areas that today comprise Florida, Arizona and later California.

Gradually, however, the Jesuits took first place in this missionary work until they became heroes without rival in that immense world to be converted.

From Canada they crossed the Great Lakes and penetrated from Sault Ste. Marie, Michigan, to New Orleans and the Gulf of Mexico. The Mississippi River traced, with imposing majesty, the way by which the heralds of Truth taught the Gospel. This trail led them to St. Louis, focal point from which they set out to establish missionary stations among the Yazoo, Natchez, Osage and Sioux Indians, and secured a foothold in New Orleans where, however, the Capuchins had already preceded them.

The situation was reversed in Mexico and later in Lower California. Here the admirable Jesuit missionaries consecrated to the conversion of the red-skins first founded the St. Francis Xavier missionary stations and gave to the world a wealth of invaluable services that yielded benefits not only to the missionary cause but to science as well. When these valorous pioneers were expelled by decree from Spanish territory, their missions were transferred by another royal edict to the Franciscans of the missionary college at San Fernando, Mexico.

Under the leadership of Father Juniper Serra, the Franciscans remained to make California the jewel of all

North American missions, and laid the foundation of a new spiritual empire on the shores of the Pacific.

V — Some will observe that the Dominican Order does not figure at all in this noble array of pioneers and missionaries among the American Indians. How is it, they will ask, that they do not occupy a place no less worthy than that of the Franciscans?

History answers this question by reminding us that during the era of evangelization in the two Americas, Providence reserved another sector for the Order of St. Dominic, that of South America. Let it suffice to cite the names of such States as San Domingo or metropolitan cities like Rosario to perceive how deeply the Dominicans penetrated into that area of the Western Hemisphere.

Arriving first in the New Word in 1510, the Dominicans enjoyed the enviable privilege of having given the first bishops to Manila, to the Antilles and, with the courageous Las Casas, to Chiapas, the Mexican city which still today prefers to call itself the « royal city of Las Casas ».

Abused at the hands of the *conquistadores,* the Indians never found a more loyal friend than the heroic Las Casas. He was held in no less esteem by the South American Continent, of which Las Casas recorded the vicissitudes of its remote origins in his *History of the Indians.* Thanks to his influential intervention, the Code of New Laws for the Indies was promulgated in 1542. In addition, he merits the honor of being the first priest ordained in the New World and the first to demand civil and religious liberty for all.

The Dominicans penetrated first into Chile, to which they contributed their first martyrs. Five Dominicans accompanied Pizaro into Peru, heart of the Inca empire, whose first Catholic Bishop was the Dominican Vincent Valverde. In this territory, the Order flourished like a flower on a smiling spring morning. The dates of their activities give eloquent testimony : in 1530, the Dominicans established their province of San Domingo; in 1532, St. James of Mexico ([7]); in 1539, St. John the Baptist in Peru; in 1551, St. Vincent of Chiapa and San Antonio in New Granada; in 1590, St. Catherine of Quito and 1592, St. Lawrence of Chile.

Indeed, America found shining stars of saintliness in many sons of the Dominican Order. Among them was Saint Louis Bertrand (1526-1581), missionary among the Indians of Panama and New Granada, where he baptized some ten thousand persons; but after seven years, broken-hearted he left this land, apparently because he could no longer endure the cruelties committed around him. He opposed them to their bitter end, but he was not given grace to eliminate them ([8]).

Then there was the angelic Santa Rosa, patroness of Lima, first « rose of saintliness » offered Christ by the New Continent, not to mention Martin de Porres, « the Negro saint » of the Third Order of St. Dominic in the province of St. John the Baptist, Peru ([9]). In Ecuador, the « lily of Quito », blessed Anna Paredes, absorbed not a little of the spirituality of the Dominican apostles.

First cousin of Santa Rosa of Lima, she was beatified by Pope Pius IX on December 16, 1850.

A North American priest, the Reverend Pise, sang of the saint of Lima in his *Lyra Catholica* :

> « *First flow'ret of the desert wild,*
> *Whose leaves the sweets of grace exhale,*
> *We greet thee, Lima's sainted child,*
> *Rose of America, all hail !*».

To complete this panoramic view of Dominican achievements among the natives of South America, we need only mention the names of the glorious universities founded by this order : San Domingo (1538); Santa Fé in Bogotà (1612); Manila, in the Philippine Islands (1645); Quito (1681); and Havana (1721).

Although final proof is still lacking, it was most probably a Dominican who, garbed in his white robe, celebrated the first Mass in the United States in the year 1521, during Ponce de Leon's second expedition along the western coast of Florida, where Charlotte Harbor now stands. At any rate, if he cannot claim this primacy, then the honor must certainly go to his colleague, the Dominican Antonio Montesinos, who celebrated Mass in June, 1526, near the site of the future Jamestown, boast of English colonization, during the Ayllon expedition. Incidentally, Father Montesinos, who inspired Las Casas to his great deeds, also passes for the first abolitionist in America.

VI — An important question is the difference between the Catholics and Protestants in their relation with the Indians.

The contrast could not have been more striking. As we have seen, in its program of converting the Indians, the Church strove mightily to transform the Indians, both through the inward grace of salvation and the external one of civilization. In addition to being evangelizer in the basic sense of the word, the priest was their teacher, father, protector, doctor and comforting angel. We will see what practical results were achieved within human limits.

In this respect, Bolton wrote : « In one sense, the treatment of Indians in the Latin countries differed essentially from that of the Anglo-Saxons. The Latins considered the Indians worthy of being civilized and their souls worthy of salvation. That, to a great extent, was due to the influence of the Church » ([10]). The benefits reaped from sowing the seeds of Christianity and civilization were tangible enough : « Education had an incalculable historic import » because to the receptive Indian mentality, it opened up new horizons and awakened a « sublime » desire for liberty among the younger generations ([11]).

Apart from certain notable exceptions, such results were not apparent in the Protestant missionary campaign. It was once wittily observed that the first thing the Puritans did when they touched the soil of the New Continent was to fall on their knees and then to fall on the natives.

That this approaches the truth is revealed in the very non-Catholic missionary psychology. Convincing enough are the first testimonies left us by the vanguard of the Calvinist missionaries who arrived from Holland in what is now the State of New York. The Calvinist pioneer, Rev. Megapolensis, who even learned the language of the Mohawks so that he could preach to them, once described what he considered the finest fruit of his Calvinist catechizing : an Indian able to recite prayers in Dutch and the catechism by heart. « And even he », the missionary confided in desperation, « has begun to drink brandy, has cast aside the Bible and transformed himself into a pure beast ».

His colleague, Rev. Jonas Michaelis, writing from New Amsterdam in 1628 to a friend in Holland, had this to say about the Indians : « I find the Indians in this Land completely savage and barbaric, alien to every decency and civility, as stupid as garden fence posts and given to every vice and bestiality : diabolical people who

89

serve no other than the demon. They possess so much witchcraft, divination, magic and perverse tricks that they cannot be held in check even with chains or padlocks. Moreover, they are thieves and traitors. As for their cruelties, they are worse than inhuman, worse than barbarians and Africans. It is difficult to perceive how such a people can be led to a true awareness of God... The best course of action might be to abandon parents to their own devices and begin with the children. But it would be difficult to put such discrimination into practice » ([12]).

This opinion expressed by Rev. Michaelis was widely echoed and some years later, we found even the Dutch East India Company asserting that it was « morally impossible to convert adults to the Christian faith » ([13]).

James Truslow Adams sums up the situation in New England by stating that the whites traded with the Indians, fought them, occasionally preached to them and then, as far as possible, exterminated them ([14]).

It is now customary for Protestant historiography to belittle Spanish colonization, but other unprejudiced historians are obliged to add that such blameworthy conduct towards the Indians was even worse in the case of the English and Dutch colonizers. « An honest comparison between the methods of the rival nations », wrote a recent historian, « demonstrates conclusively that the conversion, civilization and educational development of the natives were the principal aims of the French and Spanish, while the other nations seemed to have no other goal than extermination ». Another historian confirmed this statement : « From the English point of view, the Indian was, or at least was considered an encumbrance to civilization and their purpose to remove him for their own convenience was dictated by a policy wholly in conflict with their loudly trumpeted principles of patience and tolerance ».

Radically different was the motivating force behind the Catholic missions which followed not only a wholesome policy of colonization but also a profound inner conviction. Canada's primitive legislation recognized the neophyte among the savages as a free citizen of France; and Champlain, Governor of Canada, coined the maxim : « The salvation of a single soul is worth more than the conquest of an empire ». Recalling these facts, Bancroft gave his solemn judgment : « It was neither commercial initiative nor the ambition of kings that brought French power into the heart of our Continent, but rather religion».

There were, however, admirable examples of self-dedication to the cause of Indian redemption in New England. Among the noblest of these Protestants were : John Eliot (1604-1690), hailed as the Puritan « apostle of the Indians »; Roger Williams, who lived among the Indians of Narragansett Bay; David Brainerd, who spent the end of his all-too-short life (1718-1747) preaching to the Indians of New Jersey and drew high praise from that powerful cleric, Jonathan Edwards, his biographer.

However, none of these three traveled more than a few miles from the civilized centers of the protecting coast; moreover, they were regularly paid for their work. Eliot, for example, was financed by the Governor of Massachusetts and, from 1649 onwards, by the Society for Preaching the Gospel in New England, founded by none other than the English Parliament to compete with a similar Catholic organization. Nevertheless their efforts produced little in the way of enduring benefits, and Eliot was to see the rewards of all his labor swept away by war and discredit.

When Everett says of Eliot that « the history of the Christian Church contains no example of greater, more decisive, indefatigable or efficient work », or when Matthew Lelievre hails him as « the first missionary of modern times » (^{15}), surely they had only the Protestant world in mind. Within this limit, such praises may be sincere. It was not without good reason that Richard Baxter, Cromwell's Puritan chaplain, said of Eliot : « There is no man in the world that I honor above him ».

These tributes notwithstanding, an objective historical judgment must make certain reservations as to the methods Eliot adopted and the results he obtained. Was it not this same Eliot who taught the Indians to smash the Catholic crucifix? He has been praised to heaven for having translated the Bible into Indian for the Indians. However, it has never been pointed out that he took this Bible from the mother Church; furthermore that it was inopportune and fruitless, to say the least, to put the sacred Book into the hands of a people whose intelligence was wholly inadequate to grasp and assimilate it into a life concordant with its teachings (^{16}).

Nevertheless, he was both an avantguardist and a brilliant exception — an exception that makes all the more admirable that other apostolate which proved so great an achievement and brought honor to Catholic Spain and France. Indeed, Eliot flourished like a solitary rose in the arid Puritan desert.

VII — Long before the English founded their first great colony in 1606, the soil of America had already been reddened by the blood of 22 martyrs of the Roman Church : eleven Franciscans, eight Jesuits and three Dominicans in Virginia, Florida, New Mexico and Colorado. Two centuries later, when the Declaration of Independence was proclaimed in Philadelphia, already 85 Catholic heroes had died for the blood-stained « Declaration of the Catholic Faith ».

First honors in the evangelization of the American

aborigines go to the Franciscans, whom the Indians called the « barefooted » to distinguish them from the Jesuits, the « Black Robes ». According to O'Gorman, an account of the twofold missionary campaign of the Franciscans and Jesuits is equivalent to « telling the story of the French mission in the United States ».

On Hispaniola and Cuba, the very spots where Columbus landed on his first two voyages to America, the Minims established their first small monasteries and affiliated schools for the Indians. From these simple beginnings developed the first Minims' province in the New World, Santa Croce (1505).

Leaving aside the question as to whether Father Juan Perez took part in Columbus' first voyage, we are nevertheless certain of the names of the two very first missionaries, two humble lay brothers, who embarked at Cadiz on September 25, 1493, as members of the great explorer's second expedition. According to the account given us by their contemporary colleague, Nicholas Glassberger, a Franciscan chronicler of Bavaria, resident in the monastery of Nuremberg : « In 1493, having heard of the glorious adventure Columbus had undertaken and, fired with zeal for the salvation of the Indians, two humble, courageous Belgians, Brother Jean de la Deule and Brother Jean Cosin, asked and obtained... permission to depart for this new missionary territory. After five years spent in edifying the Indians of the Antilles and preaching the holiness of the humble life, they returned to their homeland, bringing with them two native youths. One of them died shortly afterwards and was buried with brotherly love in the shadow of their monastery ».

These two forerunners of the Franciscan mission in America, full of indomitable zeal, stressed to Father Olivier Maillard, their vicar general, the urgent need of sending priests, a request granted them by the King after the project was discussed. Towards Easter of 1500, the Breton Franciscan Father Jean Baudin, was assigned to the New World together with a number of colleagues. These were followed on September 25th of the same year by another Franciscan expedition, of which Brother Jean de la Deule was a member, arriving at the port of San Domingo. This chronicler tells us that within the space of a few years, these heralds of the Franciscan apostolate baptized some three thousands natives ([17]). In 1501 Hispanola initiated negotiations with Rome for the establishment of its own hierarchy.

Upon royal request, on November 15, 1504, Pope Julius II appointed to the bishopric of San Domingo the Franciscan Garcia de Padilla, who would have had the honor of being bishop of the New World's first diocese except that for various reasons, he was prevented from reaching his See. The first apostolic vicar, therefore, is believed to have been Father Juan Perez, supporter and champion of Columbus ([18]).

Thereafter followed a series of Franciscan primacies. First bishop of Mexico was Juan de Zumarraga (1468-1548), who achieved a number of « firsts », including the title « protector of the Indians ». He was responsible for reformed legislation which, together with the « new laws », saved Mexico from a bloody civil war; a school for young Indian girls; the famous Tlaltelolco College at Santa Cruz; and the introduction of the printing press into the New World ([19]).

Meanwhile, in North America there is evidence of an episcopal jurisdiction in Florida as early as 1527, when the Franciscan Juan Perez, of Valencia, was appointed Bishop of Florida by Charles V, but died in 1528 while he was en route to Mexico. « Although he was never consecrated, he had full episcopal jurisdiction and therefore can be regarded as the first prelate within the present territory of the United States » ([20]).

Subsequently, the Minims struck out in all directions and with such devotion that by 1511, three of them had been martyred in the Antilles and by 1535, they had already achieved fame for having converted no fewer than 1,200,000 Indians within the area known as New Spain.

Even before Jamestown and Quebec were founded, the New Continent had its first school at St. Augustine, Florida, established by the Minims ([21]). Another Franciscan, the venerable Antonio Margil, founder of the missionary college at Zacatecas, which was to furnish a number of missionaries to Texas and California, was honored in 1836 by Pope Gregory XVI, who ranked him among the foremost saints of the two Americas.

As with the first bishopric in the New World, the Franciscan Order can also claim the first halo of martyrdom in the United States, Canada and Mexico. In 1542 and 1544, Father Juan de Padilla, « protomartyr in the United States », and his humble lay brother, Brother John of the Cross, made the first supreme sacrifice. The Catholic historian Lawrence F. Flick observed that these « protomartyrs shed their blood for the faith just about the time that Europe was being thrown into confusion through the rise of Protestantism ». In fact, in 1520, Luther was excommunicated; in 1522, Zwinglio was suspended peremptorily (*suspensus a divinis*) by his bishop; in 1533, Henry VIII married Anne Boleyn; in 1536, Calvin established himself at Geneva; and in 1542, the Scottish John Knox renounced his faith. Thus, the present territory of the United States was consecrated to God by these Franciscans even before Protestantism was fully organized ([22]).

The great, pious French explorer Samuel Champlain (1570-1635) known as the « father of New France »,

95

asked directly for Franciscan help. Commenting on the second volume of his *Voyages,* he addressed the Regent Maria de' Medici : « I have always desired to make the Lily flourish in New France together with the Roman-Catholic-Apostolic religion ».

To this militarist-statesman goes the credit for having conceived and achieved an alliance with the Huron tribe. Scattered about in 25 villages, the Hurons, counting a population of some 30,000 souls, honored the alliance firmly and faithfully, asking in return France's cooperation in their war against the Iroquois tribes of northern New York. Those who paid for this alliance were chiefly the missionaries, who suffered every sort of atrocious reprisal.

VIII — The first French Franciscan expedition (1615) consisted of a party of five missionaries, including their guardian Jean Dalbeau (1586-1652), founder of the first monastery at Quebec, St. Mary of the Angels.

Among this small group was Father Joseph Le Caron (1586-1632) of Paris, formerly chaplain to the Duke of Orleans. Four signal honors are due him : he was first missionary to the Huron Indians; he was first to discover Lake Huron; he compiled the first dictionary in the Huron language; and lastly, he stoutly championed the rights of the Indians put under French political jurisdiction. In an eloquent eulogy to this « Franciscan without ambition », Bancroft recounts how Father Le Caron ventured into the land of the Mohawks, passed northward into the hunting grounds of the Wyandotts and, bound by his religious vows, traveled on foot or by canoe begging from the Indians until finally he arrived within sight of Lake Huron. Certainly Father Le Caron appears to have had extraordinary moral fibre as explorer, fighter and man ([23]).

The other two members of the party were Father Nicholas Viel and Brother Gabriel Sagard, the latter a great, if humble, lay brother. From 1622 to 1625, these two devout men lived among the Hurons in a bark-lined cabin, adopting the primitive customs of the natives in order to guide them better towards civilization and the Gospel. In the Spring of 1625, three Huron Indians perfidiously threw Father Nicholas into the lake together with his companion Ahuntsic, a Huron neophyte. On the site of the tragedy, now known as Sault-au-Recollect, a commemorative statue was erected on May 30, 1903, depicting the martyr with the Gospel in his left hand and the Cross in his right, over his heart ([24]).

When Father Sagard took the missionary Cross, Anne of Austria, consort of Louis XIII, presented him with a portable altar and sacred vestments for his priestly offices. He was highly resourceful in his humble work. When sacramental wine was not to be found in that rigid climate, he resorted to the juice of small, unripe grapes, *vitis Canadensis*. Soon he became the favorite of the Indians who, in 1624, gave him permission to go to Quebec but only on his solemn promise that he would return. He did return, and this time took voluminous notes on the missionary work carried out in that area.

Back in his home country, he presented his report to the Duke of Montmorency, Viceroy of New France, in which he bore out his colleague Father Le Caron by unmasking the trading agents, whose nefarious influences impeded the work of the missionaries. More than that, he convinced his superiors of the need for a mission from some more powerful Order than the humble group of Franciscans as the only means of correcting a situation which he maintained was growing more intolerable every day.

To this end, Brother Gabriel suggested the Company of Jesus. After considerable discussion by the authorities of the Holy See, this proposal was put into effect in 1625 by Cardinal Richelieu. Thus, in the very same year, the Jesuits took their place side by side with the Franciscans in the apostolate of New France.

In this matter, Brother Gabriel revealed himself as a strategist and diplomat no less skilful than Richelieu; through a strong intuition, he knew the proper moment to act. The remarkable sons of the Company of Jesus had already preached and died in Japan, had taught astronomy in the court of Pekin, had evangelized and won the Brahmins, brought the Cross into Abyssinia, preached in Brazil, shed their blood in Florida, set up a Christian republic in Paraguay, and were now about to offer the tribes of North America the same magnificent gestures they had performed in so many other parts of the world.

This indefatigable lay brother then prepared his historical and geographical notes for publication, and his volume *History of Canada,* including an account of the journeys made by the Minims to convert the unbelievers, appeared in Paris in 1636.

In the meantime, other Recollects were arriving in the New World, among them Father Joseph de la Roche Dallion, sent to work among the Hurons. In 1626, he accompanied the Jesuit Father Jean Brebeuf on a special mission to Three Rivers. The following year, Father Brebeuf, who was to die a martyr in 1649, discovered the first oil at Niagara. This we know from a letter he wrote to a friend in Paris on July 18, 1627. According to Shea, he had identified oil in a spring near the present village of Cuba, in Allegheny County, New York ([25]).

The first Catholic priest to set foot in what is now known as the « Empire State », as well as the first to evangelize among New York State's Indians, Father Brebeuf wrote this edifying passage on his first contact with the neutral aborigines (October 18, 1626) : « I asked their permission to live in their land so that I could teach them the Law of our God and the way to go to Paradise. They welcomed my offer and gave me to understand that they would be pleased to have me return to them » ([26]).

He spent considerable time with the Hurons as missionary and interpreter, even traveling with them in their canoes when they went to meet French traders of skins and furs. He carried out this mission until the English Protestants in 1629 required him to repatriate, precisely because of his accomplishments.

Now we come to another distinguished group of Recollects. First among them was Father Superior Gabriel de la Ribourde (1610-1680), future martyr stationed at Fort Frontenac (1673). On the La Salle expedition to the West, he officiated at Fort Niagara and blessed the Griffin, first ship to plow Lake Erie. Another was Father Zenobe Membré, chaplain at Fort Niagara in 1679, who took part in the La Salle expedition to Fort Crèvecoeur, near Peoria, Ill.; acted as peace mediator between the Iroquois and the Illinois; and traveled with La Salle down to the mouth of the Mississippi, later writing an account of this voyage, which his cousin and colleague, Father Christian Le Clercq, published in his *Etablissement de la foi* ([27]).

Father Le Clercq, a Recollect of Flemish origin, deserves special mention. For 12 years he worked as missionary among the Micmac tribe and, after learning their language, he developed a system for writing it — an ideographic system, it appears, based on hieroglyphics — by which he was able to teach the natives to read their own language. He received posthumous recognition for his merits in 1880 when an historian of America's Indians attested that the system of characters he introduced, used by the Micmacs for over two centuries, « added not a little glory to the Franciscans » ([28]).

In addition, American historiography of the colonial period found in Le Clercq's works a prime source of information; indeed, when he returned to France, he dictated two voluminous works on missionary history and geographical exploration among the Indians. His first volume entitled *Premier établissement de la foi dans la Nouvelle France* (Paris, 1691), narrates the discoveries of La Salle as described by a Minim, Anastase Douay, who took part in the tragic expedition into Texas. This book has acquired such value that it was sold for $2,100 at a New York auction sale in 1935. The other volume is entitled *Nouvelle Relation de la Gaspasie* (Paris, 1691).

We will discuss Father Louis Hennepin more fully later on. Of his wide popularity, it is sufficient to point out that more than 60 editions or resumés of his works have been published in six European languages. Another Recollect worthy of mention is Father Melitone Watteau, chaplain of Fort Niagara, to whom La Salle, staunch friend of the Recollects, presented a tract of land on May 27, 1679, to build a residential convent and cemetery. With this gift, the Church of the Franciscan Order came into possession of its first property in the State of New York. When the Griffin was launched on its rather less than brilliant adventure, Father Watteau remained at Niagara and thus was the first ecclesiast charged with carrying out holy ministrations among the whites of New York.

Champlain, La Salle, Frontenac and La Mothe-Cadillac had a singular preference for the Recollects. Champlain in fact always chose these brave, pious religious as chaplains of his forts and of his various expeditions, drawing particularly on these of Flemish origin.

The glory of Franciscan history in North America lies in the fact that the sons of St. Francis of Assisi toiled from Louisiana to Texas, from Alabama to California, from Utah to Nebraska, from Florida to New Mexico, to introduce these vital sections of the United States to the world, consecrate them for their splendid future and integrate them into Christian civilization.

JESUITS ON THE RED PATH OF GLORY
TWO LILIES AMONG THE NEGROES

CHAPTER IV

With the arrival of the Jesuit Fathers in Canada, the missionary campaign took on a fresh decisive impulse. Summoned by the Recollects and officially sent by the Viceroy, these holy men of the Company of Jesus initiated their apostolic duties in 1625. Other expeditions were to follow in the two successive centuries until the number of Jesuit missionaries reached a total of 329, of whom 32 died in martyrdom or else as victims of their own charity. Seven of them never crossed the Atlantic, having been born of French parents living in Canada, where they joined the Company.

The plan drawn up by the pious Champlain aimed at Christianizing the Hurons, cordial allies of the French from the beginning of the French penetration into their territory, and to civilize and appease their neighbors, the Iroquois Federation, consisting of the Five Nations: the Mohawks, the Oneidas, Cayugas, Onondagas and Senecas. Conversion of the Hurons was considered essential because they, like the Iroquois, were not nomadic tribes, but permanent dwellers in their territories, and this augured well for the work of civilizing them and thus erecting a buffer state against the English and Dutch.

The Jesuits followed the Recollects in this difficult task, difficult above all because of the insurmountable obstacles pitted against them by the Iroquois Federation, which occupied both banks of the Mohawk River in New York State. These Five Nations counted over two thousand proud, invincible warriors, whose power increased to a terrifying degree in 1640 when they succeeded in obtaining gunpowder from the Dutch merchants of New Amsterdam.

It appears that the Iroquois' incurable hatred of the French arose from a thoughtless action on the part of Champlain himself when, after discovering the lake that now bears his name, he subjected some Mohawk Indians to futile cruelties. The tribes' hatred passed from generation to generation, subsequently becoming more bitter because of political complications. Eventually, the Iroquois declared war on the Hurons, whom they considered servile to the French.

The missionaries took part in the quarrel between these two factions of unappeasable, pagan savages in the hope of effecting a peaceful solution. These apostles of conciliation toiled with a perseverance nothing could sway, not even the imminent prospect of martyrdom. A two-fold ideal, religious and patriotic, inspired them, since they were well aware that more than the peaceful Hurons, the Iroquois held the politico-military key in their hand, and therefore only that nation that could claim their friendship would succeed in establishing a balance of power.

In this first decade among the Hurons, the Jesuit mission counted 18 religious — the « white medicine men » or the « Black Robes », as the Indians dubbed them. In the course of 24 years, from 1626 to 1650, another seven colleagues joined the group, of which a high percentage ended in martyrdom. Continually hindered in their efforts by mandates and emissaries sent by the intractable Iroquois, these Jesuits worked tirelessly in an apostolate that brought them few personal rewards but won many natives to the faith. Some of their Indian neophytes gave their lives in sacrifice to their convictions, among them Stephen Te Ganonakoa, murdered by the Cayugas at Onondaga on December 25, 1690; the virgin Frances Gonannhatenha and Margaret Garangowas, killed by the Mohawks and the English on March 10, 1692; and Stephen Hooniventsionta-Wett.

When the missionaries themselves did not meet a violent death, they wore out their lives through a thousand hardships, through privation, imprisonment and shipwreck. It was from excerpts taken from their writings that the historian Shea was able to compile his fascinating volume on their bloodless martyrdom, entitled *Perils of the Ocean and the Forest*. Another historian, Bishop Kip of California, maintained that they were the first « fearless pioneers of civilization and of the Christian faith » along the shores of the Great Lakes, of whom America will « perennially keep a memory » (¹).

II — Following is the Golden Album of men who suffered or died in the territory of the present New York State at the hands of its inhabitants or neighbors :

a) *Canonized martyrs*
1642 Brother René Goupil, born at Angers, 1607
1646 Father Isaac Jogues, Arles, 1607
1646 Brother Jean La Lande, Dieppe, (?)
1648 Father Antoine Daniele, Dieppe, 1601
1649 Father Charles Garnier, Paris, 1606
» Father Jean Brebeuf, Condé, 1593
» Father Gabriel Lallemant, Paris, 1610 (²)
» Father Natale Chabanel, south of France (?)

b) *Confessors of the faith*

> 1644 Father Giuseppe Bressani, b. Rome, 1612,
> d. Florence, 1672; subjected to horrible tor-
> tures by the Iroquois (³)
> 1652 Father Buteaux, perished in an ambuscade
> 1653 Father Joseph A. Poncet, b. Paris, 1610 d.
> Martinique, 1675; tortured by the Iroquois,
> but saved in time by a rescue party.

In his *Important Notice to Those Whom it Will Please
God to Summon to the New World,* St. Jean de Brebeuf
used in his text the word of our Lord to St. Paul : *Osten-
dam illi quanta hic oporteat pro nomine Jesu pati,* and
described with graphic reality all the sufferings awaiting
the new missionary to the barbarians, a continuous series
of atrocious tortures. « Our lives hang by a thread... any
disgruntled native can burn down your cabin with you inside, or split your head open... The food would be insipid if
the liquid given our Lord to drink on the Cross did not
render it tastier than the most delicious dishes... You
are in the presence of death every moment ».

« But that is exactly what we want ! » came the reply
from Europe.

« Very well then, whoever you are, come, come !
Have no fear of hardships; there will be plenty of them
for you and your sole consolation will be to find your-
selves crucified with the Son of God ».

Thus he concluded : « Jesus Christ is the true greatness of the missionary. You must seek only Him and His
Cross when you come to these people. With Jesus you
will find roses among the thorns, the sweet with the
bitter, everything in nothing ».

The man who wrote these words for others practised
them for himself. These directives encouraged him in his
consecration to the Missions, sustained him in his arduous

apostolate and guided him to a heroic end. Father Brebeuf was truly worthy of his Norman antecedents, who
had fought at Hastings under William the Conqueror,
as Goyau reminds us. He was courageous beyond all description in his missionary life and even more so in death.

A vivid account of his martyrdom has been left us
by Christophe Regnaut, Jesuit Lay Brother and companion
of Fathers Brebeuf and Lallement in the Huron Mission
of St. Ignatius, scene of the macabre event.

On the morning of March 16, 1649, the two fathers
had left home for the neighboring village of St. Ignatius,
less than a quarter of an hour away. It was nearly time for
religious instruction and catechism. Before they were
aware of what was happening, the two priests were over-
powered by Iroquois Indians, over a thousand of whom
appeared without warning, intent on burning the Huron
village. Stripped naked, the two victims were bound to
a tree trunk and Father Brebeuf's martyrdom began at
once in the presence of Father Lallemant.

First his hands were cut off and then red-hot hatch-
ets placed under his armpits and on his shoulders.
Because he challenged his torturers, his mouth was
smashed by a stone and a burning firebrand thrust down
his throat. Then the Indians tore off his living skin and,
by way of ironic blasphemy baptized him three times
with boiling water. Lastly, they tore out his heart, which
an Indian chief proceeded to devour.

But for all their cruelty, they were conquered by
his indomitable resistance. Thus, they fought to drink
his blood so that they might imbibe his superhuman
courage.

Father Brebeuf's Catholic brothers everywhere exalted him. The Ursulines of Quebec hailed him as the
personification of grandeur and courage. The Protestant
Parkman, who studied this hero in every detail, described

him as the « Ajax of the missions », and continued : « Nature lavished on him all the passion of a powerful organism and religion bowed him to the glory of God». It is not to be wondered at that Father Brebeuf's head has been kept in the Hôtel Dieu in Quebec as a relic. A silver bust of the martyr, set on an ebony base, supports the venerated head, brought to the city by the Hurons themselves. In the same place, another reliquary holds the two thigh-bones of his companion martyr, Father Lallemant.

Father Lallemant wrote down the motives that drew him to missionary work, and concluded : « Courage, my soul. Let us perish in a saintly manner, to give this pleasure to the holy heart of Jesus ! ». He sealed his vow with this offering : « My Lord and Saviour Jesus, I vow never to fail on my part the grace of martyrdom if, through Your infinite pity, You will give me this grace one day... And I offer You, O my loving Christ, my blood, my body and my life, not that I might die for You but because You were worthy to die for me. Therefore I will take from Your hands the cup of suffering and I will invoke Your name : Jesus, Jesus, Jesus ! ».

The heroic death of Father Brebeuf occurred towards three o'clock in the afternoon. Three hours later began Father Lallemant's torture, which lasted until nine the next morning. When the Iroquois withdrew, the martyrs' bodies were carried to burial in St. Mary's, headquarters of the Huron mission.

How can one say enough on behalf of Father Jogues ?

Born in Orléans in 1607, the same year as Ruyter, future Dutch admiral who burned the English ships, and Jean Petitot, miniaturist, and dying in the same year as the scientist-genius Leibnitz first saw the light of day, Isaac Jogues yields to none of the three for moral fibre, strength of character, sensitivity or cultural achievement.

As the historian Bancroft observed, he and Raymbault spread the Gospel thousands of miles in the interior five years before John Eliot preached to the Indians only six miles from Boston Bay. With Garnier he worked among the Petun tribe and, with Raymbault, ventured as far as St. Mary's Lake. Near Georgian Bay he founded St. Mary's Fort, called by Parkman « the savage outpost of the world », a center from which missionaries struck out in all directions. He was the first white man to see the shores of Lake Superior and gave, even if indirectly, considerable impulse to commercial trade of the first order.

Father Jogues proposed conversion of the Indians in the Lake Superior area, as well as of the Sioux tribe, who dwelt at the source of the Mississippi. But his exploits were cut short when he was captured on August 3, 1642, near Three Rivers while he was journeying to Quebec. After cruel tortures, he was led to the Indian village of Ossernenon on the Mohawk, known today as Auriesville, 40 miles north of Albany.

A companion in this, his first captivity, was Brother René Goupil, Jesuit Lay Brother, whom Father Jogues received in the Company with the same spirit of fraternal solidarity with which he was later to write his biography. The end of this angelic youth was no less flashing than the hatchet that unexpectedly cut him down. This occurred soon after an aged, superstitious savage, with whom Goupil and Father Jogues lived in captivity, saw Goupil make the sign of the Cross over one of his young grandchildren. « Go, kill that French dog », said the Indian to a kinsman. « The Dutch have told us that the sign he just made is useless. I fear something worse; I fear it may bring us misfortune ». Consequently, one evening when Father Jogues and Brother René were strolling in the forest reciting the rosary, they were suddenly aware of being followed by two Indians. All at once, one of the savages drew forth a tomahawk and brought it down on Goupil's head with such force that the young missionary fell face forward on the ground, pronouncing the holy name of Christ.

Father Jogues thereupon fell on his knees and awaited his turn, but the assassins commanded him to rise and go to the village, which he did after absolving his colleague. « It was September 29th (1642), the feast of St. Michael », Father Jogues wrote in his *Notice,* with the vision of René Goupil's martyrdom still before his eyes, « when this angel of innocence, this martyr of Jesus Christ, gave his life to Him who had given him His own ».

Father Jogues remained in captivity another 13 months, suffering beyond all human limits. In a stupendous account which communicates to us something of the fascination of Father Jogues' powerful personality, Bancroft described the period of his imprisonment and tells us that while Father Jogues expected the same fate as befell Goupil, his life was spared this time and he was given greater liberty. Sitting atop a sunny hill, he recalled the Passion of Christ and eased his own suffering by reflecting that after all, alone in that vast region, he could worship the true God of the earth and sky. Wandering through the majestic forest of the Mohawk Valley, he carved the name of Jesus on tree barks and took possession of the land in the name of God, often lifting his voice in solitary song. Thus, « France brought her flag and faith to the confines of Albany ».

He was about to be burned alive when the Calvinists of Fort Orange, now Albany, persuaded him to save himself, and take refuge in a ship about to weigh anchor. Thus he managed to arrive safely in New Amsterdam. Here Johann Megapolensis, Dutch Calvinist minister, welcomed him in his house, situated where the Cunard

Line docks now stand, and restored him to health while negotiations were carried on between the Dutch and the Iroquois for ransom. In the same way, to the credit of the Dutch Calvinists, Father Bressani was saved the following year (⁴), and Father Joseph A. Poncet nine years later, after the latter had been captured by the Iroquois at Three Rivers.

According to the annals of the Catholic apostolate in New York, Fathers Jogues, Bressani and Le Moyne did their utmost to bring Megapolensis back to the Catholic faith, which he had previously renounced. (Megapolensis was an assumed name; his real name was Van Grootstede). Judging by a letter this Calvinist wrote in 1658 to Father Simon Le Moyne, in which he strained every effort to point out the errors of the Catholic Church, one is obliged to conclude that he persevered in his heresy, notwithstanding his admiration for the heroes of the faith he condemned.

Nevertheless, the gesture of this « good Samaritan » and other Dutchmen towards Father Jogues and other confessors of the faith was imbued with a rare moral beauty. In the few weeks Father Jogues spent as guest of Governor General Kieft while awaiting a ship to take him back to his native land, he was accorded all the honors due a hero of the Christian faith. It is little wonder that another Calvinist minister in New Amsterdam, observing how horribly Father Jogues had been mutilated for Christ, fell on his knees to ask his blessing and then, in the same burst of admiration, escorted him to his school and presented him to his pupils, declaring : « Today you have the privilege of beholding a saint ».

In the autumn of 1643, his ship finally set sail for France, and he arrived on Christmas day of that year. The regent Queen Mother of Louis XIV welcomed him in court with great honors, calling his adventures « a true novel », while Pope Urban VII graciously conceded him the rare privilege of celebrating holy Mass, although his fingers were either mutilated or burned. « It would be unjust », the Pope observed, « if a martyr of Christ were not to drink the blood of Christ ».

Such honors lavished upon him by Catholic Europe began to disturb him and he yearned to make the perilous return journey to his Hurons. Departing in 1646 on his last dangerous peace mission, he sensed his ultimate fate as a martyr, a presentiment borne out on October 18, 1646, when he was felled in an ambuscade near Lake George. Struck by a mortal blow from a tomahawk at the threshold of his cabin, he was decapitated by a second blow delivered, no doubt, on behalf of a bestial Iroquois superstition, by which the assassin sought to placate his idols and thus bring to an end an epidemic which had broken out among the Mohawks, whom he was visiting for the third time on a mission of aid and peace. His head was stuck on a pole as a trophy and his body thrown into the turbulent waters of the Mohawk River, which carried it to the Hudson.

Referring to Father Jogues' sacrifice, Bishop Kip wrote in admiration : « Thus died one of that glorious troop of men who showed the greatest devotion to the cause of Christianity, the like of which had not been seen since the time of the Apostles : men whose lives and sufferings tell a tale more touching and pathetic than any other in the history of our country and whose names will always be held in grateful memory ».

Catholics, Protestants and Indians demanded alike that he be paid due honors. After he was glorified by the Church in July, 1939, the State of New York erected, at a cost of $75,000, a statue to St. Isaac Jogues on the shores of Lake George, which he had discovered and named « Lake of the Holy Sacrament ». Thus it was called by the French and English colonists until 1775, when the English General, Sir William Johnson, renamed it in honor of King George III of England. In 1867, Parkman suggested calling it « Lake Jogues » ([5]).

Of another Jesuit confessor of the faith, Roman-born Father Francesco Bressani, Bancroft has painted a portrait worthy of Goya. Taken prisoner while he was en route to the Hurons, beaten, handcuffed, mutilated, whipped by the entire population of a village, burned and tortured, he was eye-witness to the tragic fate of a colleague, who was boiled alive and eaten. In spite of all these horrors, some mysterious power protected him and he was ultimately rescued by the Dutch.

The college opened by the Jesuits in Quebec was noteworthy as a cultural center and, more important, as a point of departure for the missionaries during its existence from 1635 to 1768. What Poller termed « the most heroic period of missionaries in the annals of America » found in the college its propelling power. From here missions went out to the Indians along the banks of the St. Lawrence, the Saguenay and northward to Hudson Bay; to the Iroquois, the neutral nations, the Petunis, Hurons, Ottawas and, continuing their advance, to the Miamis of Illinois and other tribes east of the Mississippi, descending gradually to the Gulf of Mexico.

Thanks to the zeal of Father Andrew White, apostle of Maryland, and his associates, the initial effort was made to evangelize the Indians of the interior. These religious carried out the first Jesuit missions among the Indians who lived along Chesapeake Bay and the Potomac River, including the Anacostas and Piscataways, who seemed best disposed to receive the message of the Gospel. Father White was first to evangelize in what is now the District of Columbia. In 1639, this pious priest established

115

a mission in the center of the Piscataway country, 15 miles south of Washington. In a solemn ceremony he baptized their *tayac,* or « emperor » Kittamaquund and his daughter Mary, given the baptismal name of Mary Kittamaquund Brent, a child of eight or nine who never again attended the English Protestant school at St. Mary after this event.

From then on, the Jesuits, occasionally assisted by English Franciscans, became the established missionaries of « Mary's State ». Between 1700 and 1805 some 90 Jesuits worked in this mission, among them 60 English, 16 Americans, the others German, Irish, Welsh, Belgian and French.

In the western zone as far as the Pacific, the missions among the Indians were led by Jesuits who set out from the extensive province of Mexico, which included California at that time. This province of the Company of Jesus counted in its most flourishing period, slightly fewer than 600 men evangelizing among 122,000 Indians. The historian E. Herbert Bolton noted that the « Black Robes » of New France counted their conversions in the hundreds or, if you like, in the thousands. Those of New Spain, who certainly worked in a more fertile vineyard, counted their baptisms in the hundreds of thousands, one might even say in the millions » ([6]).

III — To their unselfish dedication and heroism, the Jesuits added a passion for scientific research and methodology. Among them were vastly learned explorers as well as the writers and historians who produced the *Reports* and *Edifying Letters,* so highly esteemed in European literature of that time. In the 16th and 17th centuries, the Jesuit disciples were all scientists and explorers ([7]). From the Order's Canadian headquarters,

116

Father Dolbeau set out to explore all the mountainous districts north of the St. Lawrence River; Father Alloues in 1665 pushed westward to Lake Superior, establishing two missions there; Fathers Dablon and Marquette set out to re-plant the Cross at Sault Ste. Marie; and other Jesuits joined St. Lusson and La Salle on their exploratory mission to retrace the steps of Father Le Caron, discoverer of Lake Huron. Two years later, Father d'Albanel plunged into the inextricable forests of Canada to arrive eventually at Hudson Bay. Meanwhile, in 1673, Fathers Marquette and Joliet departed from a missionary settlement in the present State of Michigan to discover the Mississippi.

The story of the discovery of the Mississippi — *Missi Sipi* means « great river » in the Algonquin tongue — is more romantic than any novel, and the protagonists of this historical epic were in turn Spaniards, Frenchmen and Italians, all Catholics. In November, 1672, Governor Frontenac wrote to Prime Minister Colbert of France that he considered it opportune and « to the public interests » to send an explorer — Joliet, as it turned out — to « discover the South Sea and the Great River which, they say, empties into the Gulf of California ». Even the Mississippi's geographical identity was unknown.

How many explorers boasted of having discovered the Great River? ([8]).

We know with reasonable certainty that Hernando De Soto's expedition reached the Mississippi on June 18, 1541, and that his party was the first group of Europeans ever to travel on its waters. Some maintain that De Soto first saw it on the spot where Memphis now stands, while others avow that the momentous discovery occurred in Tunica County, in the present State of Mississippi. That such a river existed was already known to the white men, in fact it had actually been traced on the earliest

Spanish maps, bearing the name « River of the Holy Spirit ». In the strictest sense, therefore, it cannot be said that Marquette and Joliet discovered it (⁹).

In 1519, Alonso de Pineda identified the mouth of the river and in 1528, Cabez de Vaca is said to have crossed it. In the 17th century came the missionary explorers. From that time on, exploration of the Great River became a passion, an almost mystical expression of a Christian victory won by the clerical protagonists of the expeditions of 1673, 1678-9, 1720, 1726 and later until 1823. None of them dreamed that along its 2,500-mile route one day would rise such cities as Minneapolis, St. Paul, St. Louis and New Orleans, nor could they foresee that the Mississippi Valley would, in the distant future, form the spiritual heart of the nation, out of which were to be carved five powerful States, inhabited by more than one-fifth of the total population of the United States — an industrial area richer and more prosperous than any of those conquered by Alexander the Great or Julius Caesar.

Nor could they tell that along its majestic route, within two centuries the Mississippi would give the Church three of its most important dioceses, all dedicated to French Catholics : St. Louis, in memory of the Crusader king; Dubuque, in memory of a French-Canadian adventurer; and St. Paul, named after the patron saint of Minnesota's first church, built in 1841 by Father Lucien Galtier.

The importance of the Marquette-Joliet contribution lies in their discovery of the fact that the interior of the American Continent belongs to the Mississippi, which divides it into two parts, tracing a notched line from Canada to the Gulf of Mexico. Thus, they established the true identity of the mysterious Great River.

Singing the praises of the Virgin Mary, Father

Marquette, accompanied by Joliet, prepared to explore the territory after having skirted Lake Michigan to the Wisconsin River. Arriving by canoe at a point near the Wisconsin, the explorers found themselves abandoned by their two Indian guides, and Marquette, referring to that critical moment, recorded : « The guides turned back, leaving us alone in an unknown world — alone, but in the hands of Providence ».

Traveling in a fragile canoe, obliged to negotiate treacherous rapids, they finally arrived at the lordly river and began to descend it, a voyage that was eventually to fix the geographical map of North America. During the expedition, Father Marquette recorded the exact lines of America's topography and could therefore correct the prevailing belief that the river emptied into the Vermilion Sea (the Pacific) rather than into the Gulf of Mexico. Of the ecstatic moment when he realized his dream, Father Marquette wrote : « Full of assurance, we entered the Mississippi on June 17th (1673), so full of joy that I cannot describe it ».

His exploration indeed proved a revelation. At approximately the half-way point, the travelers saw the Missouri flowing into the Mississippi; farther south the confluence of the Ohio and even farther south, the confluence of the Arkansas. At length, convinced that the river flowed into the Gulf of Mexico and not into the Pacific, Marquette and Joliet turned back towards Michigan to avoid any disagreeable encounters with the Spaniards. These two courageous men therefore explored the imperial river for a length of some 2,550 miles, traveling 120 days by canoe and one-fifth of the way in total solitude.

What was the motive that spurred these two hardy souls to undertake their glorious adventure? Father Marquette explained it succinctly in his *Journal* : « To

do and suffer everything for such a glorious initiative ».
He says no more than that, but from a psychological
study of the man and his religious ardor, we can easily
surmise the rest.

Worn out by the superhuman effort required to
carry out his mission, Father Marquette died a few months
later at the age of 38 in a rustic cabin on the shores
of one of the lakes in the area where he had dedicated
himself to the service of God.

It is difficut to determine how many points on the
American map are named after this French Jesuit. At
least the following have been named in his honor : a
lake, a river, a bay, four cities (in Kansas, Michigan,
Iowa and Wisconsin), two counties and innumerable towns
and villages, a railroad, a national forest and a *département*
of northern France. In addition, he has been represented in marble and bronze, in high and low relief, in
mosaics and in irridescent stained glass.

Five years after the Marquette-Joliet undertaking,
another expedition set out to investigate the Mississippi
under the leadership of La Salle. Among those participating were Enrico Tonti, a Neapolitan, and a trio of Franciscan Recollects, Father Louis Hennepin, Father Gabriel de la Ribourde and Father Zenobi Membré, historian of the La Salle expedition, all three former members
of the Franciscan monastery at Quebec.

The La Salle party planned to push southward to
the mouth of the river in order to establish *de facto*
French rights to the whole interior of the Continent. But
unruly Sioux Indians frustrated their hopes almost at
the outset by capturing members of the expedition, and
it was only through the intervention of Greyolson, Sei-
gneur du Lhut, that they were released. Although the
group never got beyond Minnesota, nevertheless Father
Hennepin left a notable record of the ill-fated journey,

giving in his volume *Description de la Louisiane* (Paris, 1683) the second description ever written of Niagara Falls.

From a town founded in Illinois by the expedition and named after Father Hennepin, the illustrious Minim set forth on his last fortunate exploratory mission, undertaken by order of La Salle. The hardships of this mission and Indian tattle gave rise to the rumor that Father Hennepin and his two colleagues had all perished in their hazardous adventure. In fact, when Father Jeunet returned to Quebec, where a Requiem Mass had been sung to the three Recollects, he was astonished to see two of them, whom he greeted with the *Lazzari redivivi* salute.

The Mass, however, well served one of their number, Father Gabriel de la Ribourde, who failed to return with his companions. Formerly chaplain of Fort Frontenac, this noble Burgundian was driven by his passion for missionary work and science to follow the fortunes of the La Salle-Hennepin expedition despite his advanced age of 72 years. He was intoxicated by the wonders he had seen — the overwhelming panorama of Niagara Falls, the thick forests bordering on the Great Lakes, and now the promise of a voyage down the fabulous Mississippi. The virgin land that unfolded before European eyes in the highly civilized century of Louis XIV held a new, irresistible fascination for these adventurers from beyond the sea. Hennepin described the New World as a «delight » and « the terrestrial paradise of America ».

On September 9, 1681, while Father Membré worked with the enterprising Neapolitan, Enrico Tonti, to repair their canoe after the severe test to which it had been put during their difficult journey, Father de la Ribourde was reciting his breviary in a shady wood not far from the banks of the Illinois River. By evening, his companions had completely lost trace of him. A party of Kickapoo Indians, « nomads » in name and fact, recognizing him as a Frenchman, murdered him, stripped him of his garments, his breviary and the journal he kept as a record of his voyage — these objects were subsequently tracked down and recovered by a Jesuit colleague —and threw the body in a ravine. America had one more martyr that day ([10]).

It appears that Father Hennepin died in a Roman Franciscan monastery just when he had promised himself to return to his favorite mission. His love for missionary work was never exceeded by scientific curiosity. In his volume *New Voyage,* he wrote : « It is grand and glorious to win a battle and subdue rebellious spirits. But it is without doubt infinitely more glorious to win them to Jesus Christ, illuminating them in their profound ignorance and blindness ».

Still the fascination of the Great River continued to attract intrepid missionaries. Another French Jesuit, Father Pierre François Charlevoix (1682-1761) sought to reach the Pacific aboard his ship, the Duke of Orleans, by way of the Great Lakes west of the Mississippi. When the attempt failed, he descended the river to its mouth and, as misfortune would have it, his vessel, en route to San Domingo, was shipwrecked off the Bahamas. Barely saving his life, he reached the coast of Florida and returned to the Mississippi, traveling northward as far as New Orleans. By order of the French Government, in 1720 he undertook a journey of inspection throughout the French possessions in America and subsequenly turned his observations to good account as basis for a scholarly volume entitled *History and General Description of New France* (Paris, 1744), which was translated into English by Shea.

Still another Jesuit scientific conquest was achieved in another part of the Continent by the brilliant, devout

Father Eusebio Chini (1645-1711), a priest of Italian origin, having been a native of Segno, Valle di Non, near Trento. His notable contribution was that of having established and confirmed through unquestionable proof the contours of Lower California. Considerable confusion prevailed on this subject in the cartography of the 16th and 17th centuries. While some celebrated mapmakers of that era designated Lower California as a peninsula, nevertheless the noted Franciscan Sebastian Munster in 1540 and Mercator in 1541 demonstrated their ignorance of this territory's peninsular identity in their maps.

The learned geographers could do little but copy each other. But the missionaries enjoyed the privilege of moving about and executing their research on the spot, preceding the traders and, in innumerable instances, the professional geographers themselves. Thus, Father Chini, dynamic herald of the Cross, was able to carry out a long series of explorations beween 1687 and 1707, and his discoveries became the basis of the first true map of California, now in the Archives of Mexico and published in *Historic Mexican Documents* (third series, Vol. IV, pp. 817-819). His diary, including the famous description of his travels overland to California between 1689 and 1691, and his *Cosmographic Manifesto on California which is not an Island but a Peninsula* resolved once and for all the ancient controversy on the supposed insularity of California.

For three centuries after Columbus' discovery, declared the Protestant historian Bolton, the history of North America was the history of the Catholic missions; the Catholic missionaries, he added, brought the torch of civilization and set up the Cross of Christ in the solitary expanses of what is now the United States, Mexico and Canada. Practically three-fourths of the cities in these countries have risen from beginnings established by the missionaries.

We continue to glean such praises from Protestant historians who surely cannot be suspected of partiality. The Calvinist Prescott recognized that the « French and Spanish sought above all the salvation of souls »; moreover, he maintained that their footsteps are as imperishable as America itself. Like the Rocky Mountain peaks dominating normal altitudes, so did the Jesuits in North America « tower aloft» in the early stages of the nation's romantic history. The Methodist Bishop and historian Hurst declared that « the annals of martyrdom contain no more glorious tales than those of the Jesuits at work among the Indians ».

There are other testimonies of this nature too numerous to mention, but probably the most eloquent of them are those volunteered by the Indians themselves. Addressing Methodist and Baptist missionaries who sought to convert them, the Indians retorted : « Go and learn. Do as the " Black Robes " did and then we will believe what you tell us ».

Indian eulogies of the Jesuit missionaries often took on a solemn, primitive beauty. Father Vivier once heard from the lips of an Indian chief this happy estimate of a " Black Robe " : « We have never sought to do him good in any way », he said to his tribe. « He has lived far from us for a long time beyond the sun and yet he thinks of our village. He wants to do us good and when our sons die, he does what he can to send them to the Great Spirit. The " Black Robe " must be very good...».

IV — Jesuitical missionary literature, including the priceless *Relations* ([11]) and the *Edifying Letters,* came into existence for the purpose of educating and inspiring European readers. The *Relations* began when St. Francis Xavier instructed Joam Beira to write St. Ignatius in Rome and Father Roderiquez in Lisbon « such news as, once known in Europe, would induce those who heard to offer glory to God ». These letters, subsequently called *Relations,* acquired great authority, particularly those dispatched from New France. Indeed, Parkman considered them an important source of American history, declaring that « they hold a high position as authentic, trustworthy documents ».

Father Biard inaugurated the first *Relations from New France* in 1616, and a series of them was written in 1626 by Father Charles Lallemant, first Jesuit Superior in Canada and uncle of the martyr St. Gabriel Lallemant. In one of these letters, written to his brother Jerome, later Superior of the Huron mission, Father Charles spoke with enthusiasm of the exhilarating work that was being done towards evangelizing New France.

Forty-one volumes constitute the series of letters written from 1632 to 1672, of which 32 volumes are called *Relations* and two volumes (1645-55 and 1658-59) are called *Letters from New France.* With their periodic publication, these works won widespread credit and gradually became a monumental collection of missionary literature intended to arouse among the faithful an interest in the spiritual conquests of the Jesuits.

Other authors of these works included : Father Paul Le Jeune, who published eight series of letters between 1632 and 1639; Father Bartholomew Vimont, author of nine, between 1640 and 1648; Father Paul Raguernau, five (1648-1653); Father François Mercier, five (1654-58;Father Jerome Lallemant, 13 (1659-1671). As Rochemonteux observed, the *Relations* « reveal a single aspect, the finest and most consoling to know, that of Christian progress, its toils, its heroic struggles, its fecund energy and audacious enterprises ». But how much more information is caught in these lively pages, to be discovered by ethnologists, geographers, historians, diplomats, naturalists and students of folklore !

In 1673, after 57 years of publication, the *Relations* were barred to the public by decree of the Congregation of Propaganda, which banned publication of them without its own permission, a permission which the French Government in those years of power did not wish to grant ([12]).

A group of these *Relations* covering the years 1634-1673, was put on auction in New York in 1935, fetching a price of $11,000, a sum which shows the rare value and importance these works have today for the reconstruction of the missionaries' activities and the beginnings of American history. Indeed, the Protestant historian, Reverend Barnes, defines the *Relations* as « the most complete account and report that has ever been published in the English language » ([13]).

Chateaubriand, from the time of his rupture with the Church and even more so during the crisis that brought him back to it, drew considerable inspiration from these documents, and his intimate friend Joubert often found him absorbed in missionary literature. Their influence on him is clearly discernible in his novel *Atala,* in which the character Father Aubry describes his quiet, albeit dynamic life as a missionary among the Indians from Kentucky to Florida. Wrote Chateaubriand : « I felt the superiority of this stable, active life over the errant, lazy existence of the savage ».

The passages which this same author dedicated to the missions in his volume *Génie* demonstrates the full measure of his enthusiasm for the *Relations*. At one point he exalts them in these words : « Civilization has trodden everywhere in the steps of the Gospel, contrary to the religions of Mohammed, Brahma and Confucius, which have impeded the progress of society and forced men to grow old in their infancy ».

Elsewhere Chateaubriand wrote : « Here again is one of the great new ideas that can only belong to the Christian religion. Not even the ancient philosophers ever left... the delights of Athens to civilize the savage, teach the ignorant, cure the ailing, dress the poor or sow harmony and peace among enemy nations. But this is what the devout Christians have done and continue to do today. Oceans, tempests, polar ice, tropical heat, nothing stops them ».

From these same *Relations,* the Italian historian Muratori took a good deal of excellent material for his masterpiece, *The Happiness of Christianity.* Even the anti-religious philosophers drew from them various ideas for their theories, which they have tried to pass off as scientific. No less did Voltaire take from the same source the theme of his *L'Ingénu* as well as his ideas for the travels of *Candide* in Eldorado. Again, Rousseau found in the same pages the inspiration for his fantastic « good savage »; he believed that in his stories, under the obvious idyllic and panoramic qualities of his writing, he had hit on a solution to the enormous and crucial problem of the « state of nature », using this as a pedestal for his unrealistic theories of « primitivism ».

The author of *Paul and Virginia* likewise took his ideas from *Relations,* especially in the character of the sage who educates and counsels — a « kind of philosopher », says Chateaubriand, « who certainly could not substitute for the priest, apostle, missionary and civilizer of races ».

Ronsard and Montaigne, taking recourse to preconceived notions, opposed the missions which, in their opinion, disturbed « happy innocence ». These moralists ignored the original sin and concluded that in those vast expanses of the New World, uninitiated into the vices of civilization, reigned a « saturnalian golden age ».

Supporting such unrealistic and pagan philosophy, La Fontaine advised all « to remain in your own country and learn from nature », while Boileau scandalized the economists by wondering « *à quoi bon ravir l'or au sein du Nouveau Monde* ». However, the far-seeing missionaries dedicated themselves to the work of moulding a new spiritual and civil life for the primitives living in the grip of evil, and in their *Relations* narrated a story which the admiring world, judging realistically and independently, called « the mystic epopee of faith ».

When the glorious Company of Jesus was ousted, its multiple activities were taken over by the Lazzarists, Priests of the Foreign Mission, Franciscans and Dominicans, who did their utmost to maintain the standard of efficiency set by the Jesuits and even to improve where they could. Nevertheless, the eventual reistantement of the Jesuits was universally saluted with joy, and their missionaries, whose colleagues had already given so much sweat and blood, returned to New York, to Maryland, Kentucky, Missouri, Pennsylvania and Louisiana. And first to greet the « Black Robes » were their grateful friends, the Indians.

For indeed, they did not seek, as did Coronado, the seven fabled cities of Cibola with their massive walls of gold, nor did they ever dream of seas studded with pearls. They saw America only in the light of its idealistic transfiguration. And to elevate the aborigines and pioneers to such lofty altitudes, the Jesuits chose as fields for their holy work the most strategic points. In their sleepless, feverish search, the missionaries imitated Thompson's « Greyhound of heaven ».

128

V — Were the results of so much effort on the part of the Missionaries worth while? And what were the results they obtained?

Two historians, both judging the matter from a superficial, one-sided viewpoint arrived at negative conclusions.

According to the Methodist Hurst, the collapse of the Spanish empire brought down with it the whole structure of the missionary campaign. It fell and vanished, he declared, like a story that has been told. Another historian, O'Gorman, is unable to « find anything that remains of their work. Names of saints in the melodious Spanish language appear on the map wherever the Spanish religious, passed, sweated and died. In New Mexico and Arizona a few thousand Christian Indians still survive, descendants of those whom the religious converted and civilized. And that is all ».

Both these attitudes are open to discussion. Neither of the writers has chosen to acknowledge, for example, the indestructible scientific achievements of the missionaries. Then there is the tendency to ignore the Cross, to minimize Spanish missionary activity in the New World and lump the *conquistadores* together with the *padres*. An unforgiveable error has been committed in granting all credit to the colonial accomplishment achieved by New France and New England.

Examining the question in the light of reality, one is obliged to point out that the cultivated Spaniards proved their worth everywhere as builders of cathedrals, monasteries, hospitals, universities, government buildings and fortresses to defend them all. They did not create temporary works but established cities on a stable foundation in both the material and spiritual sense. Their purpose was always the same : to conquer whole regions in the name of the Catholic Church. The Philippine

Islands and Spanish America offer shining proof of achievements others never dreamed of.

It was the missionaries, furthermore, and not the merchants, statesmen or educators, who introduced European culture into the New World. James Truslow Adams, in *The Epic of America,* notes with astonishment that the Spanish were able to achieve so much in such a short space of time. The author, descendant himself of the Pilgrim Fathers, concludes his objective report with the statement that the birth of American civilization was more a missionary merit than a gift brought by the Puritans. « The American dream owes more to the wilderness than to the Puritans », he wrote.

The English, and particularly the Puritan preachers, baffled their converts with excessive doctrinage and with futile attempts to find corresponding Indian terminology with which to expound the ideas expressed in such words as « adoption », « election » and « justification ». It has been fully established that the French Catholic missionaries claimed an intellectual superiority over the English Protestant missionaries in the later periods. The coherence of Catholic tenets and ceremonial splendor naturally produced a more effective impression on Indian mentality than did the teachings of the many garrulous sects into which the English colonists were divided. The religious fervor of the French and their excellent parochial organization, even in areas sparsely populated, were well noted by the Indians who, by consequence, accused the English colonists of impiety.

In 1701, when the English ordered the withdrawal of the Jesuits, the Abenaki tribe retorted : « You are too late to start teaching us your prayers, after we have known you so many years. The French were more far-seeing than you, and as soon as they knew us, they taught us to pray to God. Now we pray better than you do » ([14]).

Another observation must be made : in those sections of America colonized under the protection and guidance of the Catholic missions, the Indians are better off than elsewhere and have learned to be useful or, at worst, not to be burdens. Thus, the missionary settlements, true experimental laboratories of collective colonization, reaped excellent results. Everyone will agree that the secularization of these missionary colonies brought about a regression in many ways. As a result, the government of the United States has granted special Reservations to Indian tribes so that they might resume their own way of life, practising their own religions and traditions, after having been decimated by warfare with enemy tribes and white men, by sickness and epidemics, by addiction to liquor given them by Europeans, and other ruinous factors.

The so-called « Five Nations » — Cherokee, Chickasaw, Choctaw, Creek and Seminole — today live on their own Reservation in the State of Oklahoma, enjoying special privileges for having assimilated the American way of life more than any other tribes. Thus, America has reverted to the ancient missionary idea of Indian colonies. But without spiritual light and the fraternal bonds of Christianity, the native cannot find true stability or civilize himself; he cannot, in other words, remake his soul and achieve an inner equanimity.

In 1870, after the ravages of the wars with the Indians, President Grant attempted to solve the Indian problem by Christianizing the tribes. His « Indian Peace Policy » proposed to pass administration of the Indian colonies from the military to civil authorities and missionaries. He presented this plan to Congress with the express purpose of giving « the Agencies over to such religious denominations as had heretofore established Missionaries among the Indians » ([15]). The plan was both

just and practical. Unfortunately, it was not executed
with due impartiality and through wholly arbitrary procedure, some 80,000 Catholic Indians passed under the
supervision of Protestant missionaries.

To correct this damage, in 1874 the Bureau of Catholic Indian Missions was founded in Washington, an
organization which has effectively carried out the work
of the Catholic Church ever since. It is worth noting that
the Act of 1870 was abolished in 1884. This Bureau
was financed by a special fund until 1887; now it
is supported half by an annuity left by Catherine Drexel,
half by an annual Lenten collection on behalf of
the Indian and Negro missions. Observing the laudable
work this agency was carrying out, in 1904 President
Theodore Roosevelt granted contracts totalling $100,000
a year, taken from the Indian Funds, with the Bureau
as beneficiary, particularly for the building of schools.
In 1908 the Supreme Court ratified this gracious and
just concession. The Bureau, moreover, secured special
concessions for the Indians, for example, the right of
Indian parents to choose schools for their children. In 1906,
it obtained retroactively sums of money due students
of the missionary schools, until then in dispute. In addition, in winning exemption of Catholic students from
government schools under Protestant influence, the Bureau saw to it that these students were provided with
religious services and Catholic instruction.

In May, 1904, with the cooperation of the Bureau
of Catholic Indian Missions, the Marquette League was
founded in New York with the purpose of promoting
missionary work. Towards that end, it collaborates with
ecclesiastical authorities in preserving the Catholic faith
among American Indians and bringing new converts into
the arms of the Church. Taking the apostle Father Marquette as its model and inspiration, the League has until

now spent several million dollars in its generous and sacred aim of bettering the spiritual, moral and material welfare of America's aborigines, subsidizing and financing schools, establishing new missionary stations, providing chapels for the poorest tribes, and other such works. It subsidizes catechisms, donates money and clothing, and provides remote settlements and the Indian Reservations with offerings for Masses, gifts of chalices and sacred vestments.

Another similar organization, the Society for the Preservation of the Faith among Indian Children, was formed in 1901 with headquarters in Washington.

An approximate idea of the missionary work being done was given by the U.S. Indian Bureau in 1923, with the following statistics : 650 missionaries among the Indians, of which 40 were Protestants in charge of 40,072 faithful Protestants, and 240 Catholics in charge of 52,316 natives of the Roman Catholic faith ([16]).

If the Indians as a race survive today even in small numbers, it is owing to the charitable, human, Christian spirit of Catholic aid proffered them through the Catholic Missionaries since the 16th century. History tells us, for example, that in Australia, where there were no missionaries to look after the natives and defend their rights, as Father Montesinos and Father Las Casas and many others did in America, these races have completely disappeared. The Philippines, on the other hand, show a striking contrast. Here where the Spanish Catholic missions were at work from the very beginning, we can see what Catholicization has meant for these islands : one of the examples given to the world of savage peoples who, through the missionaries' teaching of the Gospel, have succeeded in elevating themselves to the point where they are now sufficiently mature to rule themselves.

And again : if the Indian race is becoming extinct

133

in the United States, at least a goodly number of them have passed on to eternity radiant with the light of benediction and sustained in their expectation of certain immortality.

Was the ardor of the missionaries, therefore, ineffective ?

America does not think so because she knows that she owes her greatness to them, that on missionary fervor rests the cornerstone of her authentic aristocracy : faith, unity and Christian civilization, essentially classic because it is a Latin civilization, essentially Catholic in the universal sense. The Cross, symbol of integral civilization, gleams today from Washington to Buenos Aires from New York to Sao Paulo, from San Francisco to Chicago, thanks to those far-seeing pioneers who clung so tenaciously to their goal.

As for France, if that nation could look across the seas with confidence, however short-lived, and conceive a glorious empire in her « New France », she owed such hopes not to her philosophers but to those humble Recollects summoned to Quebec by Champlain and to the « Black Robe » Jesuits of Paris and Arles, who fully merited the title « statesmen of the Kingdom of God » bestowed on them.

Voltaire, protegé of Madame de Pompadour and Chatelet, living sumptuously in the royal palace in Berlin as Chamberlain to the Lutheran king-philosopher, reflected for a moment on the missionaries struggling and dying in the far-off New Continent for the glory of Christ and France, and asked his compatriots : « Why do they persist so obstinately for a few acres of snow? ». Even in his *Candide,* referring to the skirmishes between the English and French, he spoke of « two nations at war for a few acres of Canadian snow ». His « few acres » were in point of fact roughly twelve million square miles of land that could have developed into a Christian empire, the gem of the French colonial possessions, had it not been for the indifference of the politicians and anti-clerical philosophers like himself.

Perhaps based on Voltaire's cynicism — and Voltaire even once declared himself happy to witness the decline of his nation's prestige — in the famous phrase originated in the French Parliament : « Anti-clericalism is not an item for export ». In a biting retort to Volterrian anti-clericalists, Chateaubriand declared : « We do not pretend to have the gift of prophecy, but you can be sure — and time will tell — that the scientists sent abroad equipped by the Academy with instruments and plans will never accomplish what a humble religious will do with nothing but his rosary and his prayer-book... ».

An impartial Protestant historian, conjecturing on the destiny of North America if the Catholic missions had won indisputable supremacy, recognizes in Quebec, from which radiated the civilizing force of a great part of the United States, « an example of what France could have accomplished for the entire Continent » ([17]). This deduction was not meant by the author to be in the least negative or derogatory.

England, on the other hand, sought to implement her designs of supremacy in North America through immigration and political maneuvers. The Seven Years' War, from 1756 to 1763, brought disastrous results to France and ended all the brilliant possibilities in the New World, where French missionaries and scientists had already laid such solid foundations for a Latin Catholic civilization. By the war's end in 1763, England emerged master of Spanish Florida and all French possessions on the Continent. In the same year, England banned all French missionaries from the very soil which they, together with the Spanish missionaries, had prepared with so much sweat and blood.

This was England's supreme show of her instinctively imperialistic and inflexible power, a demonstration of a dominion that rules out every fair and tolerant conciliation. The outcome could not, however, be other than negative for England herself; American independence, now rapidly maturing, was to come into existence as a fortunate result. For England, this meant the loss of a continent.

Only the young Republic, then, was to benefit from the Catholic missionaries sent to the aborigines : and America found in them her best patriots and the most vigorous supporters of her independence movement. In the 18th century they assured the collaboration of all free spirits — French, Canadian, Irish, Spanish, Italian, Polish, etc. — who, when the hour sounded, spontaneously rallied to the rising Federation with the vision of self-government before their eyes.

Moreover, it was the Catholic missionaries who enlisted the aid of the Indians and won them over to the faith of freedom. If Father Peter Gibault, the « patriot priest of the West » — the west signifying the area extending from Ohio to Minnesota — had not united the Catholic Indians with the young Republic in the war of liberation, the political map of North America might well be different from what it is today ([18]).

The missions among the Indians paid off a debt to these aborigines, America's original masters, not only in the name of evangelization, but also in charity and Christian justice.

VI — This magnanimous gesture bore a bountiful crop of mystic, supernatural fruit, for many Indian tribes received the two-fold blessing of Christianity and Catholic civilization. Today the following tribes in North America are either wholly or partly Catholic : Abenaki, Black Feet, Coeur d'Alène, Chippewa, Crow, Gros Ventre, Huron, California Diggers, Flatheads, Mohawk, Osage, Ottawa, Pottawatomie, Iroquois, Passamaquoddy, Pueblo, Sioux and Yakima, to mention only the the best known. The Iroquois, responsible for the sacrifice of so many Jesuit lives, now count over 4,000 souls dedicated to the Catholic cause despite their vastly diminished numbers. Where they once appeared indomitable, they have become deeply faithful. In 1831, their Catholic leaders sent a gift to Pope Gregory XVI of moccasins and a hand made belt, accompanied by this message : « You are our Father, never will we recognize another. If our descendants forget you and fall into error, show them this belt and they will return immediately to your fold ».

An even more gracious gift to the Pope and to America, however, is the Iroquois tribe itself. Such a gift was made possible through a chosen creature of God, a member of the Iroquois tribe, Catherine Tekakwitha, the « Mohawk lily ». She was born in Auriesville New York in 1655. At her baptism, received at the age of 20, a heavenly joy inundated her soul. To free herself from the inhuman cruelties of a pagan uncle she fled from home to reach St. Francis Xavier's mission Caughnawaga (Canada). On her arrival there, it seemed to her that « she had reached Paradise ». The predestined girl died in 1680, having become a living model of those Iroquois, who according to the chronicles of the first Missionaries, emulated the fervor of the early Christians. " Who will teach me what is most pleasing to God, that I may do it ? " (Words of Kateri). To the philologists as well as to those Indians who knew her, no name could have been more appropriate : Tekakwitha means « she who puts things in order ». In fact, comments a biographer : « She put the order of Divine Law into the lives of many pagans ».

There are some who, reflecting on the venerable Catherine Tekakwitha, turn to the theory of heavenly revenge against modern racial prejudices. Certainly in this redskin saint one finds the grace and beauty of holiness wedded with the splendor of justice. The ten Jesuit missions in the State of New York need not proclaim their good cause, says one historian, in order to demonstrate their worth; it is enough to mention Catherine Tekakwitha. « What have all the skyscrapers of our sleepless cities ever produced that can be compared with her ? » ([19]).

Father Chauchetière, Catherine's biographer and friend, said of her : « The Holy Ghost worked through her and directed her in everything, so that she pleased God and men; the latter to such an extent that the most wicked admired her, and the good found in her a model to imitate ». When she died, her tomb at once became the goal of a legion of pilgrims, many of whom were men of influence and high ecclesiastical authority. Through Catherine Tekakwitha and her true story of sainthood, the Indians were introduced to the Faith and strong bonds established with the Church of the " Black Robes ". More than one hundred tribes have addressed the Holy Father by letter, bearing him expressions of love and fidelity. Such a letter was received by the Pope some 20 years ago; « Holy Father », it read, « although we Indians are poor and unhappy, our Creator had pity on us and guided us to the Catholic faith. And still pitying us, He gave us « Kateri Tekakwitha ».

This noble disciple of the Jesuit missions uttered two memorable phrases that measure the extent of her divine illumination. To a fanatic redskin who sought to tear her from her faith — perhaps he had surprised her in an attitude of prayer — and was about to smash her skull with a hatchet, she said : « You can take away my life but not my Faith ». On the brink of death, after having received the Blessed Sacrament, she spoke her last words : « Jesus, I love you ».

As far back as 1744, Father Francis Xavier Charlevoix wrote that the young girl was universally known as the Protectress of Canada.

A few years ago, Father Henry Béchard, S.J., Vice Postulator of the Cause of Beatification of the Servant of God, had the idea of raising a monument to Kateri in the Iroquois mission. His wish became a reality on August 8th 1955. Today the bronze statue erected to honor Kateri's memory in the Caughnawaga mission reminds the passers-by that the ground once sodden with the blood of the first holy missionaries has produced a magnificent Christian fruit : « the Lily of the Mohawks ».

After the blessing of the monument, Msgr. John Panico, Apostolic Delegate to Canada, evoked the Servant of God's heroic virtues. He recorded the first miracle which occurred 15 minutes after her death : her face slightly disfigured by small-pox, became exceedingly beautiful. « We have therefore gathered here to honor her », said His Excellency.

The blessing of the statue dedicated to her memory in St. Francis Xavier's mission, her mission, has no other meaning. But this honor would be very incomplete on our part, should we not have the earnest desire of imitating her spiritual life, particularly her love of Our Lord in the Most Holy Eucharist and of Our Blessed Lady.

This monument represents Ven. Kateri bearing a Cross and a Rosary. If we love Our Blessed Lord Who immolates Himself on the Altar, if we love the Blessed

Mother and pray to Her as the Church wishes us to pray to Her, we too, may hope to end our lives in an outpouring of love of God and our neighbor, pronouncing, as Kateri did, the sweet Names of Jesus and Mary.

Msgr. Panico then made some appropriate reflections on the example of Kateri's heroic virtues, and concluded with words which deeply impressed those present and were echoed by the press of the Country : « As Apostolic Delegate to Canada it is my earnest wish to see Venerable Kateri raised to the honor of the Altars. I know it to be the wish of His Holiness, Whose interest in the Cause can be ascertained by the fact He has diminished from 4 to 2 the number of miracles required for her beatification. Pope Pius XI told Msgr. Forbes, former parish Priest of this region, that Canadians must contribute their share of prayer to Kateri's Cause of Beatification. The Holy Father gloriously reigning is of this same opinion. May I be permitted to add in this Marian Year that the Queen of Heaven leans towards us expecting our prayers and sacrifices. She will present our petition to Her Divine Son to obtain for us the two miracles which will transform the name of Ven. Kateri to that of Blessed Kateri ». May this solemn wish find its fulfillment in the words of the Sovereign Head of Catholicism.

The Apostolic Delegate's words were followed by a marvellous address of the Minister of Post, Alcide Coté, representing the Federal Government of Ottawa. Pointing to the pagan atmosphere of Kateri's times, he insisted on the pernicious influence of modern paganism : « this impressive ceremony of the unveiling of the monument to Kateri Tekakwitha », he said, « beside being a beautiful reality, evokes a great lesson. Kateri's entire life was a heroic fight, the victorious issue of which was to break away from ancient paganism. That is why her figure appears today on the background of Canadian life as a lighthouse putting Christians in our Country on guard against the dangers of modern neopaganism under all its forms, especially under those of atheist communism which aggressively penetrates all over the world.

Confronted by this contemporary paganism the life of Kateri presents itself as an inspiration, and as an eloquent lesson, for all Christians in this Country ».

VII — The Holy Father, Pius X, besides nourishing a great affection for the Indians and colored people, struck out the false principles of racism, declaring that « those who enter the Church, whatever be their origin or their speech, must know that they have equal rights as children in the House of the Lord, where the law of Christ and peace of Christ prevail » ([20]).

According to these divine laws of charity and solidarity which are dictated by our common origin and by the equality of rational nature in all men, no matter to what people they belong, Mother Catherine Drexel became the Apostle of the Indians and Colored People in the United States of America.

Her father, Francis Anthony Drexel, a banker by profession, was born at Philadelphia, U.S.A., on June 20, 1824. He was well known everywhere not only for his wealth and financial genius but also for his righteousness. Mother Drexel was the second child of Francis Anthony Drexel by his first wife, Hannah J. Langstroth. The first child, Elizabeth, and his only child by the second marriage to Emma Bouvier, Louise, both died before Catherine, leaving the Drexel fortune principally to Caterine, whose house was the goal of a procession of poor people three times a week. She had « holes » in her hands. Her father pretended not to see. It was estimated that before leaving to embrace religious life she had given $100,000 in charity.

As a young girl Catherine took a great interest in reestablishing and supporting schools on Indian reservations. She took up a survey of the plight of the Indians and learned that almost 250,000 of them were practically abandoned and over 9,000,000 Negroes were forgotten.

In 1899, with the help of Rt. Rev. James O'Connor, Bishop of Omaha, and Most Rev. P. J. Ryan, Archbishop of Philadelphia, she formed a new congregation of religious women devoted exclusively to missionary work among these two races. The greater portion of the income which she derived from her father's estate was used in maintaining and furthering these missionary projects.

The first members of her new community made a two year's novitiate with the Sisters of Mercy and then opened their motherhouse in the old Drexel homestead, Torresdale, near Philadelphia.

As time went on, Catherine founded houses, schools and hospitals for the Indians and poor Negroes. Today the Congregation of Sisters of the Blessed Sacrament numbers : 591 professed sisters, 30 novices and 8 postullants. It has 48 postulant convents, 12 secondary schools, and the direction of St. Francis Xavier University in New Orleans, the only one in the world for the exclusive service of the colored students. From her own deposits and helped by her sisters' charity, during their lifetimes, she daily spent hundreds of dollars while she herself traveled from one house to another as the poorest of women, never permitting herself anything but the day coach, in order to save that money for the benefit of her Negroes. And yet think of this — the Drexel estate at the death of her father, February 15, 1885, was estimated at about $15,000,000. Her sisters having preceded her in death, Catherine inherited their share. At the death of her sister Louise, in 1945, she came into possession of an account worth $1000 a day.

Even during the last years of her religious life, her sisters were obliged to have recourse to every kind of stratagem in order to make her give up a pair of worn out shoes. They went to her cell when they knew her to be fast asleep, and pulling her old shoes, which looked more like old slippers than anything else — from under her bed, they exchanged them for a new pair. That was the only way of persuading her.

Mother Drexel was vigilant and active for her institution until a few moments before her death. None could have guessed that she was 94. Even after death her face bore traces of beauty and aristocracy. A few days before someone having reminded her of the millions she had pulled out of her pocket and distributed to the poor, she answered : « the salvation of souls is worth more than all riches ».

Through these wonderful souls of North America the efforts of the Catholic Missions among the people of that Continent were crowned with blessings and exalted in sacrifice and holiness : the epic, lyrical aspect of the divine poem which God perpetually composes for his Church.

GEORGE WASHINGTON AND CATHOLICISM

CHAPTER V

The most recent biographers of George Washington (1732-1799), Father of his Country and a « modern Cincinnatus », recount certain charming legends about him (it is hard to say whether in jest or in earnest) that have thrown an aura of almost unreal ideality around this fascinating aristocrat.

Frederick the Great's praise of his military prowess (¹); Washington's visit to Betsy Ross, the « Quaker rebel » of Philadelphia who embroidered the five-pointed stars on the first American flag; and his confident prayer spoken as he knelt in the snow of Valley Forge in the cruel winter of 1777, a prayer overheard by the good Quaker Potts from a nearby grove dripping with icicles — all this might be relegated to the delightful but insubstantial realm of fantasy.

If it is less difficult to vouch for the authenticity of the famous prayer of Valley Forge, that is not so much because Potts overheard it and then reported it in truly Quaker terms — « I saw a man in prayer; George Washington is certain to beat the English ! » — but rather because most of the records of Washington's life confirm the legend. Indeed Washington constantly surprises and bemuses us with the richness of the language with which he addressed his God, a language far removed from the Masonic stereotypes of 18th century deism, as for example his « All-Powerful Dispenser of Providence », « Benign Father of the Human Family », « Supreme Head of the Nations », « Great Giver of Every Public and Private Good » ([2]).

Washington was a devoutly religious man, and modestly reserved — a fact that cannot be denied. As such, he was subject to a shameful cabal of opposition, quite to be expected in the age of the Encyclopedia. He was essentially a man of action; yet at the same time he possessed a mystical temperament. For example, from his eleventh year onward he initiated the custom of praying aloud before sitting down to eat, which he would do whether or not there were guests or ladies present to observe him.

Among his signed manuscripts there has come to light a little book called *Daily Sacrifice,* in which the young George, by then 20 years old, composed morning and evening prayers for every day of the week. Those for the first three days, Monday to Wednesday, are complete. The morning prayer for Thursday ends at the bottom of the last page, and no one knows whether the remaining prayers have been lost or were never finished.

It is well known that Washington maintained a pew in church for himself and his family; that he attended Sunday services assiduously; that in the Army he frowned on cursing, oaths and foul language ([3]); that he read the prayers of the service to his troops; and that throughout his life he never once denied his boyhood assertion that for him « it would be impossible to argue logically without the awareness of a Supreme Being ». In organizing the militia, he founded the institution of the Chaplains, « whose absence reflects dishonor on the Army ».

Early every morning Washington retired to his

library to read a page of the Holy Bible and pray. He always held the Bible in the greatest veneration. When his adopted son and daughter were respectively eight and six years old he wrote expressly to London to order a richly bound Bible for them. In his letter he specified that their names be written in gold letters within the cover. This Bible may be seen today in the Library of Congress.

The tourist who visits the Chapel built in Washington's memory at Valley Forge in Pennsylvania may see an inscription in copper recalling that on June 1, 1774 he observed a day of fasting, prayer and humility. The inscription, put up by the House of Commons of his home State of Virginia, is confirmed by the entry in his own diary : « June 7 : Went to church and fasted all day ». His respect for Sunday as a day of worship, physical and spiritual repose, was a lifetime habit. When he lived at Mt. Vernon, he used to go by carriage, over rough roads, at Pohick, seven miles away, or to Alexandria, some ten miles away.

In announcing the Declaration of Independence, Washington said : « The peace and safety of (the) country depends, under God, solely on the success of our arms ». In his classic speech at Gettysburg, Lincoln appropriated this same, almost mystical expression of Washington's : « under God ».

During the period of the War for Independence, one Wittman — an American Tory — was captured as a British spy and, having confessed, was condemned to death. The evening before the execution, an old man named Peter Miller presented himself at Valley Forge and asked the General to pardon Wittman.

« But why », Washington asked him, « do you ask mercy for one whom you yourself have called your archenemy ? »

« I ask it because Jesus would do as much for me »,
the man replied.

Thereupon Washington signed Wittman's pardon
and, putting the document in the man's hand, he said :
« I thank you for this example of Christian charity ».

At the signing of the Declaration of Independence,
Washington asked God publicly to keep the United States
under His holy Benediction. Previously, in 1775, shortly
after assuming the perilous burden of Commander-in-
Chief of the patriots, he wrote the Massachusetts legislature thus : « I earnestly implore the Divine Being,
in whose hands are all human events, to make you and
your constituents as distinguished in private and public
happiness, as you have been by ministerial oppression and
private and public distress ».

Washington's antecedents, the Cavaliers of Old
England, came to the Colonies after the setting of Cromwell's star, partly for reasons of conscience, partly in
search of religious freedom and in adherence to something surviving from the mediaeval Catholic Church that
lingered in Anglicism, like the aroma in an antique phial
of perfume. And indeed everywhere in Washington's
public utterances his deeply ingrained piety is evident.

In his opening address, in the Philadelphia State
House, to the Congress that set out to draw up the lines
of the Constitution, Washington said : « Let us create
a model that the wise and honest can aspire to. The
task is in the hand of God ». And the call did not go
unheeded. The Congress, described by Jefferson as « an
assemblage of demi-gods composed of the ablest men in
all America », produced in the Constitution (to quote the
English statesman Gladstone) « the most marvelous work
of any time to issue from the mind and vision of man ».

In his First Inaugural Address, Washington offered
his « fervent supplications to that Almighty Being who

rules over the Universe, who presides in the Councils of Nations and whose providential aids can supply every human defect, that His benediction may consecrate to the liberties and happiness of the people of the United States a government instituted by themselves ». Later in the same speech he said : « No people can be bound to acknowledge and adore the Invisible Hand which conducts the affairs of men more than the people of the United States ».

And in his last discourse, called the Farewell Address the great man proved the sublimity of his philosophy when he warned his countrymen : « Of all the dispositions and habits that lead to political prosperity, religion and morality are indispensable supports ».

The poet Longfellow echoed the Farewell Address when he wrote these lines :

> « Thou, too, sail on, O Ship of State !
> Sail on, O Union, strong and great !
> Humanity with all its fears,
> With all the hopes of future years,
> Is hanging breathless on thy fate !
> We know what Master laid thy keel,
> What Workmen wrought thy ribs of steel... »

Washington's friend and biographer, Supreme Court Justice Marshall, wrote this eloquent testimony : « Without verbal ostentation of religion, he was a sincere believer in the Christian faith and a genuinely devout person ». Something similar, in more recent times, was said by Henry Cabot Lodge : « He did not make a parade of his own religion because in this as in everything else, he was simple and sincere to perfection. He did not experience the torture of doubts nor did he ask questions, but he always believed in a sovereign Providence, in a merciful God before Whom he knelt and addressed his own prayers, in dark hours as well as triumphant ones, with a faith as profound as it was innocent ».

II — American Catholicism, too, has nothing but praise for George Washington.

When Washington and the Church first encountered one another, the Church was only a fragile plant, a delicate mountain-flower. In 1776, at the time of the Declaration of Independence, there existed in the growing Republic only about 35,000 Catholics and 30 priests east of the Mississippi. The majority of the population — British in origin, outwardly correct but firm in its splendid isolationism and its anti-Roman supremacy — might well have won absolute Protestant control in a New World that had suffered so many bloody sacrifices and yet was so widely illumined by the light of Catholic thought.

« To such a deporable situation », declared Pope Pius XII in his Encyclical of November 1, 1939, *Sertum Laetitiae*, « a remedy was proposed by the famous George Washington, a man of firm character and penetrating mind. He formed a solid friendship with Msgr. John Carroll, Archbishop of Baltimore. Thus the Father of his Country and the first Prelate of its Church, bound by ties of good will, as a lasting example to posterity and as a lesson for times to come, almost with a handshake indicated that respect for the Christian faith must be the sacred and solemn rule of life for the American people ».

III — Was George Washington born on the 11th or 22nd of February? The more than 200-year-old family Bible, preserved under glass at Mt. Vernon, contains this notation on its first page : « George Washington, son of Augustus and Mary, his wife, was born the 11th day of February, 1732, about ten o'clock in the morning, and was baptized the 5th of April ».

Since his birthday is celebrated every year on the 22nd, there might arise some doubt about it, except that a later notation in the Bible explains the difficulty in saying that the date celebrated on the 22nd came about because, in 1752 — 20 years after Washington's birth, while the Colonies were still under English rule — the English Parliament finally decided to conform with the rest of the world and to correct the error of the Julian Calendar by adopting the reformed Calendar of Pope Gregory XIII, which eliminated 11 days of September, 1582.

IV — Washington's family was notable for the reverence with which it held the Bible, a fact significant, perhaps, because it indicates survivals of the old love for the Vulgate which in England, as elsewhere characterized the deep-seated piety during the Catholic restoration.

The coat of arms of Washington's maternal ancestors — the devout Ball family to which Washington's mother Mary, the « Rose of Epping Forest », belonged — consisted of the Latin words : *Coelumque tueri* (Look heavenwards), lineally derived from the text, *Cumque intuerentur in coelum* of the Acts (I :10), a reference to the Apostles on Mt. Olivet looking toward Paradise as the Saviour leaves them to ascend to His glory. This is no irrelevant detail, because it shows again the pre-Protestant tradition of piety which, often enough in the Anglican world, was inherited from the older family branches.

153

Also, Colonel Joseph Ball, maternal grandfather of George Washington, acted in a purely Catholic spirit when, as a member of the Virginia General Assembly, he did everything possible to pass a law providing that « a certain number of young men from good Virginia families be initiated into theological studies at the expense of the Municipality ».

Another example of family piety is the little poem in praise of Christmas Day that Washington wrote at the age of 13.

V — Washington had his first real and immediate contact with Catholics — and also with the author of a scholastic text — as a boy of scarcely 14, when he was learning to « write, read and cipher » at the school of the Anglican Church at Fredericksburg, Virginia. His instructor was a Mr. Hobby, who also acted as sexton in the rectory. For long hours at a time this Colonial pedagogue had his pupil copy and re-copy in a fine handwriting certain *Rules of Civility*.

The little book survives today. *Rules of Civility* was a primer for young schoolboys that outlined 110 rules of scholastic conduct. At that time it must have been fairly well-known to the Catholic youth of Maryland, who, in preparation for the priesthood, were sent to the preparatory schools maintained by the Company of Jesus in French Flanders (St. Omer) and Belgium (Douai).

The ethical and educational importance of this little work in the forming of Washington's character is worth discussing, if only to render justice to the good Jesuits who proved, indirectly, to be his tutors.

To Moncure D. Conway, in 1891, is due the credit of having first traced the origin of the maxims, which date back to a little treatise called *Bienséance de la Conversa-*

tion entre les Hommes, prepared in 1595 by the « pensionnaires » of the French Jesuit college of La Flèche and sent by them to their brothers at Pont-à-Musson. One of the latter, a Father Perrin, translated the maxims into Latin, adding his own chapter on table manners. This Latin edition appeared in Pont-à-Musson in 1617, in Paris in 1638 and in Rouen in 1651, and there were also versions in Spanish, German and Czech. The French edition had already been brought out in Paris by 1640.

After these first discoveries, Conway happily came across an English version of the same maxims in the British Museum, first published in London in 1640 by Francis Hawkins. He was also a Jesuit, a Londoner born in 1628, who took his vows in 1662 and lived till 1681, having served as priest and instructor in the schools of the Company.

Between 1640 and 1672 there were at least eleven editions of this English version translated by Hawkins. A copy of it came into the possession of Washington's boyhood teacher, Mr. Hobby. It was this book that he had his distinguished pupil transcribe, for the improvement both of his character and his handwriting. Thus there came into existence the precious manuscript of the small boy, which is the prize of the Washington papers acquired by Congress from his descendants in 1834 and 1849 and which remained in the State Department till 1903, when they were transferred to the Library of Congress ([4]).

All his biographers consider the little book, copied so carefully by Master George, as psychologically and historically a « vital key to the understanding of his character ». The rules that it sets forth imply self-control, modesty and a proper consideration of others, the ethics of the Gospel and the renascent spirit of Jesus, as represented in the Saviour's words : « I am among

you as one who serves (Luke XXII : 27) ». Here are
the last three of the booklet's revealing maxims :

108. « When thou speakest of God and His attributes, do so seriously and in terms of reverence ».

109. « Let thy recreations be manful, not sinful ».

110. «Strive to keep alight in thy breast that spark
of celestial fire called conscience ».

Washington the man embodied all these principles,
and the Jesuit pedagogue was in the long run well paid
for his labor. The maxims cut deep, as into bronze, into
his character and forged it.

One of his biographers, Roscoe Thayer, remarks
on the subject : « The religious precepts taught him in
his youth remained steadfastly with him throughout his
life. He believed in the moral virtues, and for him to
believe them meant to practice them ». The strength of
Washington's character had an influence upon everyone
around him and indeed was a psychological factor of
major importance in the forming of America. J. Truslow
Adams has pointed out that the darker the times became,
the more Washington's contemporaries clung to his indomitable courage, as to the last edge of dry land amid
the rising tide.

Another biographer, Owen Wister, has written that
the strong, forthright and passionate nature of the boy
received an impress from the maxims that was decisive
in preparing him for the adventure of life and momentous
for the country itself. And that was because the Jesuit
teacher's pregnant phrases were an idea-force and an
idea-light in the mind of the future Father of the Republic,
who held always that « every person who comports himself
as a good citizen, responsible only before God for his
religious opinions, must be allowed to worship God according to his own conscience ».

VI — On this golden rule of divine liberty to worship, contemporary Catholics and Washington were in full accord. And Washington's life is full of instances that show how he put this rule into effect.

In June, 1775 Washington was commissioned by Congress as General and Commander-in-Chief of the patriots, and he assumed active command of the Army in Cambridge, outside of Boston, the following month.

Boston, the city of the Puritans, with its unyielding anti-Catholicism, at that time enjoyed an annual « Pope and Devil » parade on November 5, which celebrated a disgraceful series of religious struggles in England a century before, such as the so-called « Oates Plot » of 1678 which, in an explosion of anti-Catholic frenzy, cost the lives of many Catholics and several priests, wrongfully accused of subversion. It is indeed a curiosity of Puritan folklore that Guy Fawkes' Day should have been transformed and parodied in New England in the irreverent Pope's Day.

However that may be, this ignoble ceremony — the procession conjuring up memories of the « Gunpowder Plot », unrolling amid mocking and obscenely vulgar parodies — provoked violent riots every year between anti-Catholics and Catholics. How indeed could the Catholics — many of them with the impetuous sensibilities of the sons of Erin — listen cold-bloodedly, for example, to the *Song for the Pope's Day?* One of its verses is in the following vein :

« Don't you hear my little bell go chink, chink?

Please to give a little money to buy my Pope a drink » (⁵).

On November 5, 1775, General Washington issued an ordinance which, after saying that the « observance of the ridiculous and childish custom of burning the Pope's effigy » would no longer be allowed, added that

157

« one can do no less than express surprise that there are in this Army officers and soldiers so destitute of common sense as to insult the religious sensibilities of those Canadians whom we seek to win as friends and allies ». The measure implied in this ordinance has rightly been called « the first note for religious freedom to reverberate in the growing Republic ». And no such irreverent parodies were ever held again ([6]).

A little more than a month before, on September 17, 1775, Washington gave Benedict Arnold, the officer in charge of a military expedition to Catholic Quebec, explicit instructions on the respects for others' religious beliefs. They are these : « As the contempt of the religion of a country by ridiculing any of its ceremonies or affronting its ministers or votaries has ever been deeply resented, you are to be particularly careful to restrain every officer and soldier from such imprudence and folly, and to punish every instance of it. On the other hand, as far as lays in your power, you are to protect and support the free exercise of the religion of the country and the undisturbed enjoyment of the rights of conscience in religious matters, with your utmost influence and authority ». (Cf. Ford, *Washington's Writings,* III, pp. 123-4). In this document to Arnold, Washington described the Catholicism of the Canadians as the religion of « our brothers » — an expression indicating his deep conviction on the subject.

Washington, in a letter of October 3, 1785 to George Mason, revealed another facet of his tolerant spirit when he wrote that no one's feelings were more opposed than his own to any sort of constriction whatsoever in the matter of religious principles ([7]). His serene impartiality is all the more evident because of the striking contrast between him and the political men of his period. There had been years of red-hot passions against the Church, and now the politics of the day seemed made expressly to rekindle them. At the time of England's proclamation of religious liberty to Catholics in neighboring Canada (the Quebec Act of 1774), there was so violent a popular reaction in America that some students of the period even call it « a principal cause of the American Revolution itself » ([8]).

Protestant bigotry, instead of being pleased with the Quebec law which it should have been, if only for reasons of political utilitarianism, discerned in it something of a threat. Protestants persisted in viewing this act of justice belatedly rendered to Catholics as an evil no less great than the political and economic injustices of which they themselves were victims. It was indeed an inversion of the true sense of justice, and it led, soon enough, to the loss of Canada's military support. America paid dearly for this anti-Catholic bigotry.

John Trumbull, Washington's aide, in his poem, *McFingal,* attacked England along with Catholicism, saying in effect she had « entered into business with the Roman church to acquire infallibility and had thrown open the door to the Papacy to befriend the scarlet prostitute » ([9]). About that time, the Continental Congress of 1774-75, at one of its first sittings, not foreseeing a possible future alliance with a Catholic nation such as France, launched an attack typical of Protestant sectarianism, declaring that « Catholicism had deluged England in blood and diffused impiety, bigotry, crime and rebellion in every part of the world ». This attack was addressed at once to England and Canada, which had at that time allied herself with England. Nor was King George of England spared, when a Massachusetts paper of the time altered his title sarcastically to « Defender of the Faith and the Pope ».

Echoes of the Protestant reaction to the Quebec Act are heard in the war song, *America to Arms* :

« Awake, awake, America, put cheerful courage on !
If tyrant oppress you, arise and say " Be gone ",
For let no Papist bear the sway, nor tyrants ever reign. »

And even Washington's friends were implacably anti-Catholic, such as John Adams, with his catch-phrase : « Catholic Christianity, cabalistic Christianity » ([10]).

As bit by bit American politics moved towards an alliance with Catholic France, there were further outbursts of anti-Catholicism, on the part of Americans who would have espoused the English cause in the war that was already under way. The *Rivington Gazette* of June 30, 1779, in a poem called *The Vicar of Bray,* urged America to break off the alliance with France, « land of Papists, peruked marquises, valets and priests » ([11]).

Such was the air that Washington breathed, but he retained an ivory-tower serenity. The Great Patriot's reverent attitude towards the Church provoked repercussions all around him, but little by little it influenced the entire Continental Congress. One of the first to be impressed was Msgr. Carroll, who at the end of the Revolution wrote to a friend in Rome : « In these United States, our religious system has undergone a revolution which if possible may be considered even more extraordinary than the political one » ([12]).

VII — On May 27, 1787, four years after the conclusion of the war, while delegates from the 12 States to the Constitutional Convention were assembled in Philadelphia to draw up the Constitution, Washington made this laconic entry in his diary : « Went to the Roman church in Philadelphia for High Mass ». The church he referred to was old St. Mary's, the original sanctuary of the city's Catholics.

This gesture, made with so much equanimity, could

hardly fail to rebuff the sour, anti-Catholic spirits, for Washington, if he wanted, could have silenced them by observing that a patriot breathes more freely in a Catholic church than in an Anglican cathedral, where the unvarying liturgical formulas invoked « the victory of the King over his enemies ». How, in Washington's case, could he be expected to give it the approving « Amen » of his consent ?

Some inconvenience happened in this respect a few years before, in New York City, at a time when the English forces were pressing the American rebels by land and sea. The rector of the famous Anglican church dedicated to the Holy Trinity, " Trinity Church ", was then the Rev. Charles Inglis. Immediately after the arrival of the revolutionary forces in the city, in April, 1776, the Rev. Inglis received a message that General Washington would be attending church and would be happy if the usual prayers of the liturgy, blessing the King and the Royal House and condemning his enemies, were omitted. To Washington, leader of the cause of liberty, these prayers could not but appear excessive. The Rev. Inglis replied that the clergy, with himself at its head, refused « to depart from their duty ». From that, one infers that the usual prayers were stubbornly recited on that occasion, and it was thanks only to Washington's superior mind and innate reverence for holy matters that the episode passed without incident. For the historical record, it should be added that this Anglican loyalist — perhaps as a reward for his rigid British intransigence — was promoted to the position of first Anglican bishop of Nova Scotia, the first colonial see instituted by the Church of England ([13]). In Philadelphia, at any rate, at the solemn Masses of the Roman Catholics, incidents and semi-provocations of this sort were never in danger of taking place.

161

Here might be mentioned the acquaintances, relationships and friendships that Washington had with various Catholics of Virginia and Maryland. Among these were Thomas Sim Lee, the governor of Maryland; Ignatius Digges, his neighbor and friend, and various members of the Carroll family ([14]). Other Catholic families Washington knew were the Bent and Young families and, particularly, that of William Digges of Warburton. The relations of the future President and the Digges family were exceptionally cordial, as the Diaries prove with their many references (prior to 1775) to fox-hunting parties with Mr. Digges, reciprocations of dinner invitations and visits of their wives ([15]).

Stephen Moylan of Philadelphia was likewise highly esteemed by Washington, who made him his aide-de-camp in 1776 and assigned him the organization of the First Pennsylvania Regiment of the Dragoons, which was the predecessor of the American Cavalry Corps. Moylan was the younger brother of the Bishop of Cork, Msgr. Francis Moylan.

In September, 1791, the College of Georgetown opened its doors to its first students, a month before the land marked out for the projected capital of Washington was put on sale. Among its first scholars were Austin and Bushrod Washington, young relatives of the President. Their connection with the school indicates a peaceful and friendly relation between the institute and Washington. The faculty was once received at Mt. Vernon and, shortly afterwards, Washington personally repaid the visit and was received by Professor Matthews, representing the college.

Other intimates of Washington were the McCarthy family of Virginia, of solid Catholic stock. Ann McCarthy of Westmoreland County was actually a cousin of Mary

Ball, Washington's mother (¹⁶). But further researches on this subject would take us too far.

VIII — A happy exchange of official messages between Washington and the Catholic Church occurred between 1789 and 1790, on the occasion of the great statesman's nomination as first President of the Confederation created by the new Constitution (April 30, 1789).

Both Catholics and Quakers — that is, the two religious groups persecuted up to that time — took part in the voting. A noteworthy letter of congratulation — a superb document of lofty patriotism — in the name of the clergy and Catholic laity was sent the President by Msgr. Carroll, then the leading Catholic dignitary of North America. In addition to his signature, the message was signed by four Catholic laymen who were among the most prominent men in the national life — Charles Carroll of Carrollton, Daniel Carroll of Maryland, Dominic Lynch of New York and Thomas Fitzsimmons of Philadelphia (¹⁷).

In the Archdiocesan Archives at Baltimore is preserved the original copy of the President's cordial answer, dated March 12, 1790, in which he thanks them for their good wishes, assures them of the nation's gratitude for Catholic participation both in the Revolution and the establishment of the government, and voices the wish that all members of the Catholic Church in America, « animated wholly by the pure spirit of Christianity », may enjoy every temporal and spiritual happiness.

This noble presidential document is considered remarkable for the imprint it bears of a great spirit of tolerance and sympathy. And it has in large part inspired the diplomacy of later American statesmen in regard to the Church.

IX — During Washington's two terms in the Presidency (1789-1797), two rulings were inserted into the Constitution that reflected Washington's fair-minded attitude toward religion — the Sixth Article and the First Amendment.

On September 17, 1787, the article guaranteeing religious freedom was drawn up — it was ratified June 21, 1788. Its text as finally approved reads as follows : « No religious test shall ever be required as a qualification to any office or public trust under the United States » (Art. VI, Paragraph 3).

Here it may be recalled for the record that before the ratification of the Sixth Article, the Hon. Charles Pinckney of South Carolina had proposed two others, both rejected. The first, very similar to that finally adopted, said that the religious persuasion of a person should never be asked in qualifying him for public office; the second, that the United States legislature should not make laws in regard to religion or in any way concerning or limiting the freedom of the press.

The fundamental disposition of the Article, which protected the civil rights of all citizens, threw out every trace of the British anti-Catholic legislation that had affected the life of the Colonies in so sinister a fashion and that had stemmed from the Act of 1689, which forbade any Catholic to take public office in England.

But the Catholics, along with other American religious groups, particularly the Presbyterians led by the Rev. Dr. Allison and the Baptists of Virginia, suspected that, in spite of everything, the Sixth Article might not offer in actual practice a clear-cut, explicit guarantee of civil and religious freedom.

In fact, after independence was attained, it was not long before the government tended to give precedence to

Protestantism. The newspapers of the time prove it. They were full of anonymous communications and sometimes articles that were explicitly anti-Catholic. To one such article, appearing in the *Columbian Magazine* of Philadelphia almost on the eve of the Constitutional Convention, Msgr. Carroll wrote an answer which the journal's editor — with little journalistic propriety — did not see fit to publish until after the Convention was adjourned and even then in expurgated form.

Two years later, on the eve of the First Congress, which was preparing to adopt a Bill of Rights to be incorporated into the Constitution, another deliberately derogatory article appeared in the *United States Gazette* of New York, with this transparent and eloquent title : *The Importance of the Protestant Religion Politically Considered*. Here one read that it was Protestantism that « had laid the foundations of this new great empire » — the eternal commonplace of a one-sided story — and it asked special privileges for Protestants, exemptions based on favoritism and in fact (though this was said in a roundabout manner) a subsidy of the Protestant clergy.

Msgr. Carroll reacted this time with a forceful article defending religious freedom which appeared on June 10, 1789 in the same magazine. In it, among other things, the Apostolic Prefect (who five months later was elected First Bishop of the See of Baltimore) said : « I am anxious to stand guard against the impression to which such insinuations lead, not so much to defend the professing of individual faith as much as to maintain forever intact in our new empire the great principles of religious liberty... If intolerance or myopic prejudice have still now prevented the cure of these ills, every friend of peace and justice is obliged not to aggravate them further ».

Clearly, there was a need, to prevent any resurgence of intolerance, for the Federal Government to state ex-

165

plicitly that it had no juridical authority whatsoever on matters of religion. To meet it, an unequivocal law — the First Amendment — was passed.

Story, in his ample study, *On the Constitution,* has underlined the urgent need for such a pronouncement, particularly in a spiritual world such as America was in 1789 — « so that Catholics and Protestants, Calvinists, Jews and infidels would be able to sit together at the common table of the National Assizes, without anyone enquiring about the faith or religious customs of any individual ».

The First Amendment was proposed by Nicholas Gilman of New Hampshire, after a reactionary from Massachusetts, Major Lusk, had called the Sixth Article too liberal, saying he « shuddered at the thought that Papists and pagans might be able to take office». Reactions such as these only made the passage of the Amendment seem more necessary. Among Catholics, Msgr. Carroll, his cousin Charles Carroll of Carrollton in the Senate and his brother Daniel in the House of Representatives all worked to have the Amendment passed and exerted an influence that Catholic historians — among them Shea — have till now rather minimized.

When the House of Representatives in deliberative assembly on August 15, 1789 opened debate on the proposed Amendment, Daniel Carroll took a leading part in the discussion and asked Madison, the Speaker of the House, to support the Amendment without reservation. Madison listened with favor, and the Amendment was passed, with 31 votes to 20. Its opening lines read : « Congress shall make no laws touching religion or infringing the rights of conscience ».

As such, then, the Amendment, together with others like it, went to the Senate, which, being convoked behind closed doors, allowed no official observer into its sessions in those days. We know that the chairman of the Committee on the Judiciary, who was also that of the Senate Committee on Conference, was Senator Charles Carroll of Carrollton. Whether or not he spoke on this occasion, we do not know. Perhaps the fact that the Amendment was adopted is proof enough that he supported it. This is its final text, as officially approved by the Senate : « Congress shall make no law respecting an establishment of religion or prohibiting the free exercise thereof ». The Amendment became the law of the land when it was ratified in 1791 ([18]).

Charles Carroll, at the age of 80, speaking at the golden anniversary of the Declaration of Independence (August 2, 1826), thus characterized its first, shining purpose : « I take the occasion to recommend to the present generation and to that to come the principles of that important document as the last earthly heritage their ancestors could leave them, and I pray that the civil and religious liberties they obtained for my country may be bequeathed to the most remote posterity and be extended throughout the entire human family » ([19]).

In addition to the Carrolls, Gilman and the other Catholic statesmen mentioned here, there is the splendid figure of Madison, who in 1784, while the Virginia House of Delegates was considering a project to subsidize « ministers of Christian religion », remarked that « religion, whatever may be one's duty toward the Creator, is not within the cognizance of civil government » ([20]). Nor must the great statesman Jefferson, to whom redounds the credit for the actual wording of the First Amendment, be forgotten ([21]).

But above all there looms the noble figure of the Father of his Country. At the end of his great career Washington wrote of his satisfaction that « in this land of equal liberty » each person could worship God according to the inspiration of his own conscience, adding that it was « our proud boast » that individual religious beliefs deprive no one of the law's protection or of the right to seek and occupy the highest offices of the United States ([22]). If everyone had pondered these authoritative words, certain recent acts of intolerance and discrimination toward individuals because of their religion would never have occurred.

Today all religious legislation in America is substantially based on the Sixth Article and the First Amendment, which together constitute the Magna Carta of religious freedom. Crystal-clear as a theory of Euclid, they are the instruments that assure religious liberty for all. They proclaim the inherent power and force of the ideal of freedom of worship; in comparison, the religious legislative ideal that seemed right to the Puritans tumbles like a house of cards ([23]).

X — On December 14, 1799, George Washington passed away. It was insistently rumored at the time that the priest Francis Neale was summoned from Piscataway, on the other side of the Potomac, and that he spent four hours with Washington before he died. The Negroes repeated this rumor, and so did the Maryland Jesuits. But at best the basis of the report is sparse and unverified.

Washington was buried at Mt. Vernon on the 18th, and five days later Congress assembled in Philadelphia, voted to set the date of the following February 22 as a day of official mourning.

In a circular distributed to the clergy on December 29, 1799, Msgr. Carroll told of the arrangements made for the participation of Catholics in this celebration. The Catholics grateful in their hearts to Washington, were second to none in the rites that paid him tribute.

Msgr. Carroll, on February 22, 1800, in St. Peter's Church in Baltimore, delivered a solemn eulogy and discourse in memory of the great statesman. Soon afterwards it was published (Baltimore, 1800; republished in New York, Kennedy, 1932) and those who heard it, as well as those who read it, considered it one of the best of all the pronouncements on that sad occasion.

Great feeling is present in it, and at moments one grasps the classic sense and heroic tone fitting to the period. Here is a single thought from it : « While he (Washington) was alive, we believed we were in a more solemn world, because we breathed the same air, lived on the same earth and enjoyed the same Constitution and laws as did the sublime, great-hearted Washington. He was invested with a glory that radiated splendor all around him. For the salvation of his country he often challenged death, which appeared to him in its most terrible aspects. He confronted it with constancy and calm; and in his last breath — we can believe him to have known the sovereign passion of his soul — he prayed Heaven to bless his country and he consigned it to the perennial protection of that Providence which he worshipped in all reverence. May his prayer be granted ».

The words that close this majestic obituary constitute a patriotic prayer by the first of America's Catholics : « May these United States flourish in religion pure and stainless, in morality, in peace, in union, in liberty and in the joyous use of their excellent Constitution, as long as respect, honor and veneration surround the name of Washington, as long as there survives a memory of his sublime human actions ».

In the fall of 1815 — Archbishop Carroll died on December 3 of that year — he was unwillingly obliged, because of failing health, to decline the honor offered him, both as bishop and intimate friend of the President, to pronounce the benediction at the laying of the corner-stone of the first monument to be erected to Washington in the capital. Another was to rise later at Baltimore, in the elegant crossroads at Charles and Monument Streets — a graceful Doric column of marble, 180 feet high, with a statue of the hero at its summit.

In any case, in gratitude for the honor accorded him, the prelate chose another occasion to commemorate « that illustrious personage to whom the monument was erected, whose memory, without the aid of marble, would remain indestructible in the hearts of his fellow country-men » ([24]).

XI — Indeed, all the best known men of the time, including Catholics, in official as well as non-official circles, revered Washington's memory.

When the United States capital erected its marble monument to him in Monument Park (it was begun in 1848 and finished in 1884), Pope Pius, in 1854, wished to be represented by a commemorative plaque — a marble slab from the classic Roman temple of Concordia, on which was inscribed : « From Rome to America ». Rome was at that time the capital of the Pontifical States. One does not forget the spiteful act of the Know-Nothings, who on a night in March, 1854, tore it out, smashed it and threw it into the Potomac — an act which did not succeed in blotting out the feeling of admiration the Pope had for Washington, which was shared throughout the Catholic world ([25]).

To understand this unhappy incident better, it should be recalled that the capital, between 1854 and 1856, was governed by an administration that expressed the fanaticism of the Know-Nothing party. Some of the bolder of its partisans, to carry out this indirect affront to authority, even fired on the Monument's guard.

Lafayette, Washington's great friend, in presenting him the main key of the Bastille, wrote that it represented the tribute of « the son of my adopted father, of the aide-de-camp of my general and of the missionary of freedom to the patriarch of freedom ».

Solemn, even vibrant with emotion, is the eulogy of Châteaubriand : « Something silent surrounded his actions; he acted slowly; one would say he felt himself invested with the liberty of the future and feared to compromise it. It was not his own destiny that this hero of a new stripe regarded but that of his country. Washington was the representative of the needs, ideas, lights and opinions of his age : instead of going against the motion of its spirit he assented to it. He wanted what had to be wanted : the same thing to which he was pre-destined, and from it came the coherence and continuity of his life — his own glory and the patrimony of civ-ilization ».

It is worth noting what Lamartine, then French minister of foreign affairs, said on March 28, 1848, to a delegation representing the National Italian Associa-tion. Giuseppe Mazzini, its president and spokesman, had mentioned Machiavelli. In reply, Lamartine hastened to substitute the name of Washington for that of the Florentine secretary. « Among the glorious names that you have cited », he said, « there is one that I reproach you for, because of the significance usually attached to it : Machiavelli. Substitute rather the pure name of Washington. Here is a name that deserves to be pro-claimed, for it incarnates the ideal of modern liberty. The world has no longer need of a politician and a conquer-or, but of a man who is disinterested and devoted to the people. A European Washington : that is the century's need; the people, peace, liberty : those are its exigencies ».

The Italians — especially poets and artists — were

inspired by the greatness of the Liberator. Vittorio Alfieri sent Washington an inscribed copy of his *Brutus,* which may be seen today at Mt. Vernon, and Washington inspired Alfieri's *Five Odes to Free America,* a copy of which was sent the President in 1790 by Count Paolo Andreani of Milan ([26]). The great Catholic French sculptor Houdon ([27]), whose exquisite statue of Washington (1788) may be admired in the State Capitol at Richmond, was followed by a Roman sculptor, Giuseppe Ceracchi (1750-1802), designer of the busts of Cardinals Albani and Rinaldi, as well as that of Pius VI and other personalities of his day. To Ceracchi fell the honor of creating the first marble bust of Washington, in 1795. It is today in New York's Metropolitan Museum.

A similar honor was accorded Antonio Canova, another sculptor of Popes. This was when the State of North Carolina voted for the erection of a monument to Washington in the capital at Raleigh. Canova set about his task after meditating on the *History of the War of Independence of the United States,* by the Piedmontese Carlo Botta, the first complete story of America and the Revolution to appear in Italy ([28]). Canova used the earlier model of Ceracchi and then, following his own classical instinct, showed the hero with an Alfieri-like head, wearing the costume of a Roman general — an allusion to his strong, war-like Roman temperament — in the act of signing the famous letter when he renounced his Army command to retire.

After Bonaparte was proclaimed First Consul in France, he ordered a ten-day mourning period for the whole nation upon Washington's death and announced the sad news to his armies in this Order of the Day: « Soldiers, Washington is dead. This great man fought against tyranny and assured the independence of his country. His memory will remain always dear to the

French people, no less than to all free men of the Two Worlds ! ». Some days later, while celebrating the first European commemoration of the American Independence, Napoleon had the thousand flags at Les Invalides, republican war trophies, lowered in tribute before the bust of the hero. On his part, Mazzini called Washington « the pure light of freedom ».

Today, when one looks at the precious model of Canova's statue at Possagno ([29]), honoring this elect son of Virginia who was « worthy of a crown », one thinks of the inscription at Mt. Vernon that records his sovereign gifts :

> « Hero, Patriot, Christian,
> When all was won, you renounced all,
> To seek, in the bosom of family and nature,
> Retirement and immortality
> In the aspirations of religion » ([30]).

CATHOLICS IN AMERICA DURING THE
EPIC STRUGGLE FOR INDEPENDENCE

CHAPTER VI

The great French thinker, statesmen and financier Turgot (1727-81) wrote almost prophetically on the eve of the American Revolution : « The Colonies are like fruit that has not been plucked because it is not yet ripe. As soon as America is in a position to govern herself, she will do what Carthage once did ».

The American Revolution — epic of patriotism aware of its own moral strength and foreseeing its manifest destinies — was the heroic prelude to the independence of the United States. Beginning on July 4, 1776, with the Declaration of Independence, after already a year's warfare with England, the glorious revolutionary struggle was to last seven more years before being finally crowned with peace.

If for America it was the measure of her people's maturity, the Revolution was for Catholicism the touch-stone of its relation to the cause of independence, of its potential ability to survive and of its vital capacity to expand, conquering its opponents in a fierce struggle that brought as its coveted prize the blessings of the most ample religious and civil freedom.

The influx of immigrants from old Europe to the new Continent played no little part in the crisis of the country's growth. Were these immigrants dependents of the Old World powers, or were they a part of a new national organism destined to create its own history? Such was the dilemma confronting the most liberal and advanced spirits of the day. Almost without intending to, England took a stand that made the need for its solution seem more urgent than ever before. The Stamp Act of October, 1765, provoked the first but already firm voices of protest. The State of Massachusetts invited the 13 original States to a special congress to articulate America's displeasure. Nine of them answered. The die was cast, and from that time forward England's authority was questioned, and colonial grievances were aired against laws affecting the English « born within the territory of the mother country ».

England, as usual, did not understand and persisted in pursuing her dangerous course. Discontent mounted against her. The tax imposed on tea, in 1774, was the coup de grace, with the result that an entire cargo of the precious merchandise was thrown into the sea and the clippers that brought it were burned. There followed, in Philadelphia, the opening of the first Colonial Congress, which from the first revealed its true revolutionary nature, for it refused to acknowledge the English Parliament, broke off all business relations with the mother country and organized the Committees of Public Health.

America was not yet formally constituted as an independent nation, but she was striving to become one, and she pledged her arms in defense of her sacred right to the destiny marked out by Providence and history as a republic conforming to reason and God's laws.

The immortal patriots who assumed the responsibility and plotted the strategy of the Revolution — Washington, Jefferson, Patrick Henry — had from the first a precise picture of the situation as it was developing : on the one hand, the men who sincerely wanted independence; on the other, the loyalists clinging to a dated past, among them a class of Colonial employees who drew their salaries from rich planters and businessmen and were satisfied with the mediocrity of their lives. These, if they fought for England, did so with weariness.

And yet not all of those who espoused the rebel cause were firm of character. What could be more painful, for instance, than the ambiguous correspondence of the dedicated anti-Catholic, Benedict Arnold, whose plot against the patriots was foiled by the Polish general Kosciusko? And how disillusioning was the petition, the so-called « Olive Branch », sent by some 46 members of the Second Continental Congress meeting in Philadelphia between May 10, 1775 and September 12, 1776? (¹). Or the irresolution of the « Sons of Liberty », who at the outbreak of the Revolution raised a flag on which was written : « No Popery ! » This motto was further enlarged in the sermon of an Anglican minister who then sided with the rebels to : « No King, No Pope », as an act of spite against King George, who had signed the famous Quebec Act conceding to Catholic « subjects of His Majesty and professing the religion of the Roman Church the right to practise the free exercise of their own religion » (²).

II — The hour of the American Revolution was not simply that of Protestantism; it was, one must say, the hour *par excellence* of Catholicism, the hour to test its potentiality and political maturity, its loyalty to the cause of freedom and its capacity for expansion in the imminent future.

One premise must be noted here. At the outbreak of hostilities, there were in the 13 rebel Colonies, out of three million inhabitants, only 25,000 Catholics all told, with 20 or 30 priests as their spiritual guides.

Today original sources and unedited documents are gradually coming to light to reveal the early roll of honor of Catholics who supported the cause of independence — a goodly figure considering their sparse numbers at the time. Specialists of the period emphasize the loyalty of Catholics to America, and the historian Griffin, for instance, has not succeeded in citing a single instance of a Catholic of the upper classes who showed hostility to the Revolution and « loyalty » to Great Britain ([3]).

The anti-Catholic movement provoked by the Quebec Act was artificially fomented by a new party called the Loyalists. These men were drawn up in serried ranks against the Revolution. It is estimated that 20,000 residents of the country — predominantly of English descent and Protestants — took up arms to scotch the movement for independence. The rich literature of this purely anti-American phenomenon, rightfully called « the other face of the American Revolution », is very clear on the subject and should be borne in mind whenever the loyalty of Catholics toward America is irresponsibly questioned ([4]).

The Church followed the course of the epical struggle with the keenest interest. In Rome, Msgr. Lazzari wrote a diary that kept abreast of the day-by-day development of the Revolution, and indeed Catholics everywhere showed their whole-hearted sympathy with the cause.

Here is a summary of contributions by ethnic groups of Catholics.

III — The early-day patriots who were readiest to sympathize and later to cooperate with the American rebellion, whether on American soil or on their own emerald isle, were the sons of Ireland ([5]). Anglican England, offended by their attitude, did not fail later to taunt Ireland on the subject when the question of Home Rule arose ([6]). In that crucial period America took her place in the front rank to support Ireland's own demands for independence.

Of the 56 signers of the Declaration of Independence, at least 13 were of Irish origin, of which one, Charles Carroll of Carrollton, representing Maryland, was a Catholic ([7]). If the majority of them were registered as Protestants, that may be explained by the fact that they were Orangemen, hailing from Ulster, which Cromwell had forcibly Protestantized, using the most refined blandishments and the shrewdest politics. Nevertheless, the single fact that they sided with the Colonies may represent a silent but formidable disavowal and open revenge against their hereditary oppressor.

These Irish patriots were primarily soldiers in arms, and there were many of them. Statistics show the American army included over 1,500 officers of Irish ancestry, with names like Reed, Carey, Moylan, McHenry, Fitzgerald, Sullivan, O'Brian and Butler. The roll calls of the Veterans Office in Washington list 695 Kellys, 494 Murphys, 227 Connors or O'Connors, 331 McCarthys, 322 Ryans, 286 Reillys, 243 Connollys, 221 Burkes, 230 O'Briens, 178 O'Neils, 184 Fitzgeralds, 155 Donnellys. They formed whole regiments which became famous for their bravery, such as the line infantry of Maryland and that of Pennsylvania, which gave Washington his best soldiers ([8]).

In referring to these great soldiers, so many of whom were Catholics, Robinson has written that « in the Revolution there was no field of battle where Irish blood was not generously shed for American independence ».

Irish Catholics of all 13 Colonies gave their own contributions — and they were of every sort, not only military — to the cause of freedom. Timothy Murphy, called the « most romantic hero » of the period; the brave Dillon; James Lynch of Syracuse, for many years custodian of Congress; John Fitzgerald, whom Washington appointed his personal secretary and aide-de-camp when he took over the Army at Cambridge; Dominick Lynch, who advanced the money to buy the property on which was to rise New York's first Catholic church, St. Peter's — these are names to be noted.

Particularly in the States of Maryland and Pennsylvania the Irish Catholics figure in the honor roll of the architects of American liberty. Maryland, a State that prided itself on its Catholic origins, put itself in the front rank with three sons of distant Irish derivation — the famous brothers Daniel and John Carroll and their illustrious second cousin, Charles Carroll of Carrollton, all educated in the Jesuit school of St. Omer in French Flanders.

These three Carrolls maintained the traditions inherited from their ancient, almost royal house. In the 12th century *Book of Leinster,* preserved in Trinity College at Dublin, there is a Gaelic poem in which the bard apostrophizes the famous sword of a victorious ancestor : « Hail, Sword of Carroll... ». The old nobility of the family was transmitted to the three and was transformed into greatness in religious and political matters.

Daniel Carroll (1733-1829), the elder of the two brothers, a man of liberal feelings and European culture, occupied the highest political posts, as representative of his native Maryland in the House of Representatives, as a member of the Colonial Congress (1780-84) and the new Congress (1789-91) and also as State delegate to the Constitutional Convention in Philadelphia (May to September, 1787), which drew up the Constitution. Carroll was one of its signers, an honor shared with another Catholic, Thomas Fitzsimons, representative of Pennsylvania. For the part they took in the Philadelphia convention, King George put a price on their heads and ordered their property confiscated.

More than a mute, passive spectator at this famous convention, Daniel Carroll took an active part in its work. Together with Judge James Wilson of Pennsylvania, he fought intelligently the movement to have the President elected by Congress and supported election by the people.

And in truth, if the Constitution as formulated in 1787 opened with the words : « We, the people », it ended with Carroll's word's : « Or to the people ». Here one sees the influence of Aquinas and Bellarmino, for Carroll, in making his report to the Committee of Eleven on August 13, 1789, on behalf of Maryland, proposed the adoption of his own Amendment (Article X), which was unanimously accepted and which read : « The powers not delegated to the United States by the Constitution, nor prohibited by it to the States, are reserved to the States respectively, or to the people » ([9]). Carroll called the Constitution « the best form of government the world has ever known ».

Returning to Baltimore, Carroll doubled his efforts to defeat the subtle sophisms of Samuel Chase, then his anti-Federalist opponent, and to have the Constitution ratified by Maryland. When it was decided to found a worthy national capital, Carroll was one of the three committeemen picked by Congress to carry out the project. In fact, it was Carroll himself who selected the actual site of the White House (he was one of the principal landowners of that aristocratic area). On April 15, 1791, with his colleague, David Stuart, Carroll laid the cornerstone of the District of Columbia ([10]).

The Protestant writer, J. Moss Ives, in his book, *The Ark and the Dove,* describes this humble brother of Archbishop Carroll as a « man undervalued in the constitutional history of America ». A little-known detail of his career is worth mentioning here : when there was some uncertainty as to whether Washington would accept a second presidential term, notable persons such as General MacHenry and Alexander Hamilton stated they considered Carroll the logical successor to the Father of his Country. Majestic as a long-lived tree, Carroll died lacking only four years of completing a century.

The story of his famous younger brother, Msgr. John Carroll (1735-1817), the first leader of American Catholicism, will be dealt with in the following chapter ([11]). A sole mention of his contribution to American independence shall be made here. In the early days of the Revolution (1776), the « Jesuit Patriot », as J. J. Walsh rightfully called him, took part in the celebrated official trip to Quebec, along with three delegates elected by Congress ([12]) — Benjamin Franklin and two Catholics from Maryland, Daniel Chase and Charles Carroll of Carrollton. The commission was charged with drawing Canada into the American orbit. In appointing him with the others, Congress described Msgr. Carroll as « a cultivated and capable gentleman ». As Catholic, priest and Jesuit, he was well qualified for this mission to persuade Canada to join the American cause.

The mission resulted in failure. Whose fault was it ? Primarily, it was the fanatic anti-Catholic spirit of the American colonies, and not, as has been so often repeated, the stiff opposition of the Bishop of Canada, Msgr. Briand, or of the great majority of Canadian Catholics, in whom the Americans' political attitude inspired nothing but distrust and pessimism. Among other things, Father Farmer, the pastor of St. Mary's in Philadelphia, was unwillingly obliged, on April 22, 1773, to urge his ecclesiastical superior, Msgr. Briand, not to come to Philadelphia for Holy Confirmation. He was fearful of possible riots and did not want to put his church in danger of losing what little liberty it had won at the cost of so many sacrifices and over so long a period of time. « It is unbelievable », Father Farmer wrote his colleague at Mascouche in Canada, « how much hatred, in every part of America, surrounds the very name of Bishop, among anti-Catholics and even among members of the so-called Anglican Church ! » ([13]).

Bishop Briand did not, indeed, forget this experience, which was a clear symptom of a situation hardly favorable to church freedom. Likewise, he remembered the bitterness with which Congress, in June, 1774 (the same Congress that sent this mission), had received the wise Quebec Act that declared Canada's Catholic Church spiritually free.

The Quebec Act was in large part a masterpiece of ecclesiastical diplomacy by Msgr. Briand, whom history has not unjustly termed « the second Founder of the Canadian Church ». By that law, Canadian Catholics were admitted to positions of public trust and granted their religious freedom. The same prelate was responsible for the modifications in the Test Oath that made it acceptable also to the Holy See and also the law of Habeas Corpus, which conceded to Catholics the rights and privileges of English subjects.

Thus it was natural for Msgr. Briand to adopt an attitude of implacable opposition to the neighboring anti-Catholic nation that was taking up arms. He went to the point of refusing the Sacraments to any Canadian who espoused the American cause and Christian burial to any who died for it.

So far the Bishop went, but no farther. Canada's loyalty to England was rooted in a three-fold logic. First, there was the logic of statistics, for Canada then numbered

185

in its population 150,000 Catholics, on whose rights the American colonies wanted to trample. Second, there was the inevitable logic of the French Alliance and the instructions given by France to M. de Bouvouloir, official French observer in America, to accept the *fait accompli* of Canada's passing to the British after the French evacuation of 1776. And, in the third place, there was the logic that sprang from the Quebec Act, based on the motto of « As ye sow, so shall ye reap », which, however belatedly, helped swing Canadian opinion to the English side.

Moreover, this orientation in favor of England was the only possible reaction for Canada to the offensive message ill-advisedly sent to the English people by Congress the day after the passage of the Quebec Act : « We think that the Legislature of Great Britain is not authorized by the Constitution to recognize a religion that overflows with bloody and impious dogmas. And we cannot but express our surprise that an English Parliament could consent to the domination in that country (Canada) of a religion that has inundated your island with blood and has diffused impiety, bigotry, persecutions, sins and rebellion in every part of the world ». The antagonism provoked by this missive appeared irremediable.

If the mission of 1776 was a failure, was it the fault of Franklin and the two Carrolls ? Not at all. According to the testimony of two English generals, it was thanks to the labors of that mission that the great mass of Canadian Catholics remained neutral during the American Revolution. The substantial consequence of Canadian neutrality was of itself a great positive step.

One must not disregard however, the Canadians who did fight for American independence — the special regiment called « Congress' Own », which was composed almost entirely of Canadian Catholic troops, and the

« priest-patriots », then contemptuously called « Americanists » but today honored in American history — Father Gibault; Father Flouquet, a Jesuit of Montreal and an associate of Colonel Hazal, who was peremptorily suspended (*suspensus a divinis*) in June, 1776; the Abbe Louis Lothinière, formerly of the Order of Malta and chaplain of the « rebel » Canadians ([14]); and Father de la Valinière, « the authentic rebel », whose espousal of the American cause resulted in his deportation to France in October, 1779 ([15]).

A truly great man of the era was Charles Carroll (1737-1832), who was called « of Carrollton », after his estate of 10,000 acres, to distinguish him from others of the same name ([16]). Born in Annapolis, he was sent at the age of eight by his father to French Flanders to study in the famous Jesuit College of St. Omer. Here he remained six years, after which he studied at Rheims for an additional year under the same instructors. For two more years, he attended the famous College of Louis le Grand in Paris, passing from there to the study of civil and common law in Bourges and London ([17]). In 1765, equipped with the best education and European cultural background the times afforded, he returned to his family home in Maryland, with no thought but to render the maximum service to his country and his church.

Family tradition made strong demands on him. His grandfather, an Irishman also named Charles Carroll, had graduated from Douai and later attained such distinction in the English Parliament that Lord Baltimore, then in England, brought him to Maryland to fill the post of Attorney General of the province. It was thus that this branch of the Carrolls was transplanted across the ocean. In the new land, the grandfather breathed Maryland's air of religious freedom with such enthusiasm that he changed the ancient and Catholic family motto, *In fide fortes et in bello* (Strong in faith and war), to another one : *Liberty in all things.*

The grandson named after him was not unworthy of his ancestor. Scarcely had the outline of the coming struggle for independence manifested itself on the political horizon than Carroll took his stand, first by writing articles for the *Baltimore Gazette,* under the pseudonym of « First Citizen », later with direct participation.

Carroll sent his articles from his home in Annapolis (the « Athens of America » of the day), and once an antagonist who signed himself « Antillon » wanted to learn who this « First Citizen » was. Carroll replied : « Who is " First Citizen ? ". A man who lives in a land of prosperity, who is a good friend of liberty and a sworn enemy of illegal prerogative ».

A politician's career was at that time barred to a Catholic even in a State that prided itself on its exceptional liberal traditions as Maryland did. Discriminated against, Catholics could not vote and, if they owned property, their taxes were doubled.

In 1763 Carroll's adversary — none other than the Hon. Daniel Dulany, the State Secretary dubbed « the Pitt of Maryland » — discourteously described him as a « Papist » and « a man disqualified by law for a political post ». Nevertheless, the agitation against the English Stamp Act offered Carroll the chance to prove himself a vigorous champion of public rights in the Colony of Maryland. And his extraordinary intellectual power quickly overcame every political discrimination.

He soon headed his own State Legislature, and in 1774 took part in the first historic Continental Congress, which sounded the reveille of American independence throughout the world. Reluctant to cross the Rubicon, Maryland had instructed its delegates « to disavow in the most solemn manner any project furthering the independence of the Colonies ». But Carroll evaded these orders and held firm to his principles.

Having thus placed himself in the ranks of the patriots, he began to receive appointments, the first of which was the assignment by Congress to the Quebec mission of 1776. On July 4, 1776, Carroll had the solemn responsibility of voting his State's approval of separation from Britain; and on the 2nd of August, together with 55 colleagues, he affixed his signature on the official parchment announcing the Declaration of Independence. He was the only Catholic to whom this honor befell.

He signed it Charles Carroll, adding to that the words « of Carrollton », not for ostentation but to spare others of the same name from being compromised by an act which, besides being a pledge of honor, put his own life in danger. For the Declaration of Independence closed with an open rebellion that involved the responsibility of its signers : « These united Colonies are, and of Right ought to be, Free and Independent States... all political connection between them and... Great Britain is and ought to be totally dissolved... For the support of this Declaration, with a firm reliance on the protection of Divine Providence, we mutually pledge to each other our Lives our Fortunes and our Sacred Honor ».

That the signer's standing was in jeopardy, is borne out by the experience of John Adams, the future President so hated by the Tories : « I was shunned like someone infected with leprosy; I walked alone in the streets of Philadelphia, bent under the weight of responsibility and unpopularity ».

Carroll's full signature prompted a good-humored jest on the part of one member of the Congress, who observed that « there were so many Carrolls that Charles could feel safe from any eventual reprisals ». After writing his name so unmistakably, Carroll is said to have added : « Now King George will know with which Carroll he is dealing ! »

He served on the Board of War, which brought him into close contact with Washington, who often sought his advice. He was besides a member of the historic Senate of the period and played a large part in drawing up the Alliance with France. He was also a member of the Maryland Senate and of the committee that wrote its constitution. In 1804, at the age of 67, he retired to private life to pass his remaining 28 years in the peace of his country estate, surrounded by children and grandchildren and esteemed by the country as a national patriarch. He was the wealthiest man of the nation.

At 75, in 1812, Carroll wrote thus to his daughter, Mrs. Caton : « In the years still left for me to remain with you, my daughter, pray to God's mercy that they may be spent in preparing me for the life eternal, whether it be eternally happy or unhappy » ([18]).

As one by one the signers of the Declaration passed away, America's affection for him seemed to increase. Adams and Jefferson went to their deaths in 1826. In a memorial ceremony on August 2 of that year in Faneuil Hall in Boston, Daniel Webster paid tribute to Carroll as the sole survivor of the signers, likening him to a venerable oak that rises alone in the middle of the plain. Two years later, as a testimonial of national esteem, Congress awarded the *Pater Patriae* the high honor of the Privilege of Free Post. On July 4, 1828, Carroll, at 91, officiated at the ground-breaking ceremony of the Baltimore and Ohio Railroad, first great railroad of the Western Hemisphere. It was his last public act. In October of the following year, after the last session of the first Provincial Council of Baltimore, a group of eminent prelates, among them Msgr. James Whitfield and the Bishops of Cincinnati and Boston, went to the old man's residence to tender him the respect and gratitude of the entire Catholic world of North America.

Three years later — on November 14, 1832 — laden with years and honor, Charles Carroll of Carrollton passed peacefully away. In the Senate it was said of him : « For many years he was the last precious relic of the group of July 4, 1776. The triumph of the tomb over this living monument to the birth of our nation, whom a grateful people held in such affection, calls for a national mourning ».

Catholics cherish his words, spoken shortly before his death : « I have come almost to the threshold of 96 years; I have always enjoyed the best of health! I have been blessed with great riches, prosperity, public esteem and more of the good things than the world usually concedes; but in looking back, the one thing that gives me the greatest satisfaction is that I practised the duties of my religion ».

Besides the great Carrolls, Catholic Maryland contributed to the national cause a pleiad of minor stars — Captain John Smith of the Maryland Regiment, who saw much service in the Revolution; Captains Neale, Semmes, Brent, Brooks, Kilty, Boarman and Mattingly. Accurate researches show that Maryland alone, with its uninterrupted traditions of Catholicism, gave 8,000 soldiers of Irish origin to the American cause ([19]).

Philadelphia might well be called the city of Irish patriotism instead of the « Quaker City ». St. Joseph's Chapel and St. Mary's Church, no less than the two famous buildings on Chestnut Street, Independence Hall (where the Declaration of Independence was signed) and Carpenter's Hall, all witnessed scenes that demonstrated the mystic passion for liberty of Catholics who had been persecuted and denied their rights for so long. The Biblical inscription on the famous Liberty Bell, now preserved in Independence Hall, well expresses the love of country for which so many sons of Erin laid down their lives : « Proclaim liberty throughout the land unto all the inhabitants » ([20]).

There were in Philadelphia a large percentage of anti-militaristic Quakers, whose religion forbade them to take up arms or pay war taxes. On the other hand, the Irish of Pennsylvania joined the State's famous infantry battalion in such numbers that General Lee called it «the Irish Infantry ». The battalion was composed largely of Catholics who in a measure were showing their gratitute to the city of Philadelphia for the religious tolerance it accorded them.

Irish patriotism is reflected, too, in the personalities of the Jesuit fathers of Philadelphia — Father Harding, friend of Franklin, and Father Farmer, who when asked by the English General Howe to act as chaplain for a regiment of Orangemen in the enemy camp, refused the handsome sum of money that accompanied the offer by saying that « all the gold of England » would not keep him from his « rightful office ».

The businessmen of Philadelphia's Catholic community all allied themselves to the American cause. One was Colonel Stephen Moylan (1734-1811), born in Ireland and a resident of the City of Brotherly Love, who at the outbreak of the war betook himself to Boston to enroll. Washington, recognizing his business acumen, made him Field Adjutant, and later he was appointed by Congress as Commissary General of the Continental Army. A dynamic man, Moylan organized on his own initiative a squadron of light cavalry called « Moylan's Dragoons », the first of its kind in Pennsylvania, and fought with it throughout the war, attaining the rank of Brigadier General. Moylan was also first president of the famous Irish patriotic society of Philadelphia, the

Friendly Sons of St. Patrick, founded in 1771 on March 17, the feast-day of Ireland's patron saint ([21]). He has happily been called « a gentleman of fortune ».

Three Philadelphians — Thomas Fitzsimons, his kinsman George Meade and Robert Morris — were among the men most responsible for the financing of the war. Fitzsimons (1741-1811) was born in Ireland and migrated to Philadelphia when barely 17. As provincial deputy to the constitutional conference in Carpenter's Hall, he was the first Catholic to occupy a public office in Philadelphia. His ships sailed the seven seas, and his commercial foresight won him the name of « father of the protective tariff system ». At the outbreak of the war, Fitzsimons organized a company of regular militia that took part in the Trenton campaign. He was a member of the historic Constitutional Convention of 1787 and a signer of the famous document. He also represented Pennsylvania in the first three Congresses of the united nation and was among the founders of Georgetown College ([22]).

Philadelphia knew other illustrious Catholics. Among them was Mathew Carey, who, from 1785 to 1824, was America's greatest editor. Besides being editor of four editions of the Douai version of the Bible and 49 of the King James version, he was known as the « pamphleteer of the Republic » ([23]). Let us recall, too, Thomas Lloyd, called « the father of American stenography », because he was court secretary for the Pennsylvania and Federal Congresses and founded the *Congressional Record*. Lloyd studied at St. Omer under the Jesuits, with Leonard Neale, who induced him to quit his native Ireland for America. When Washington took the oath of office on the balcony of Old Federal Hall on Wall Street in New York and delivered the historic Inaugural Address, Lloyd was beside him to take it down in shorthand and later transmitted it to the world ([24]).

193

Two other Irish Catholics of note were the humble, heroic boatman Patrick Colvin and the splendid John Barry, « father of the United States Navy ». Although from different social spheres, they both helped shape the fortunes of America in her golden hour.

A resident of Trenton, New Jersey, on the Delaware River, Colvin earned his living as a ferry-boatman. A good Catholic, he traveled every Sunday to Philadelphia, 32 miles away, for Mass, and his name figures in the register of St. Mary's. On Christmas Eve of 1776, when the cause of the young republic seemed hopelessly lost, Washington, with a handful of badly clothed, shivering soldiers and one cannon, conceived the master stroke of crossing the Delaware River at night to attack the English camped at Trenton the following morning. Two men came to the aid of his scheme — the two boatmen operating the ferries in either direction across the Delaware between Trenton and the State of Pennsylvania. Both Irish, one was a Presbyterian named McConkey, who operated Taylorsville ferry; the other was Patrick Colvin, who ran the one from Morrisville. The attack in the morning took the English by surprise, according to Washington's precisely pre-established plans, and Colvin shuttled back and forth across the river, carrying reinforcements until the enemy was dispersed (²⁵).

John Barry (1745-1803) was born in Wexford, Ireland. He was about 15 when he came to America and established permanent residence in Philadelphia. His vocation throughout his life was the sea. On October 13, 1775, the Continental Congress, then in session in Philadelphia, authorized the purchase of two armed vessels to initiate a much-needed Continental Navy. Barry was among the first to enlist and was officially assigned command of the Lexington, first of the two ships (December

7, 1775). It was this « No. 1 commission » that earned him the name of « Father of the American Navy ».

It has been said that as long as John Barry lived, « Britannia did not rule the waves ». On April 11 of the following year, Barry entered Philadelphia harbor with his first war booty. « Thus », writes the historian of *Origins of the American Flag,* « the Lexington was the first ship to have borne the Continental flag to victory on the ocean ». The Lexington's victory prompted John Adams to remark, on April 12, 1776 : « We begin to make some little figure here in the Navy way » ([26]).

His feats of arms were all brilliant : capture of the Harlem, the Mars, the Minerva; crippling of the Atlanta and the frigate Sibyl; transportation to and from France of high diplomats, including Lafayette in 1781. In 1794 he reorganized the cadres of the Navy. It is said that the English general, Sir William Howe, commander in chief of the English forces in America, offered Barry 20,000 guineas ($100,000) and command of the best English frigate if he would leave the rebel side, just as Howe had already tried with Father Farmer. Barry answered : « Not all the money the British government could control, nor the command of all the fleets it could bring upon the seas would tempt me to desert my country » ([27]).

Barry married twice, and both times to Protestants, who quickly — in the manner of Henrietta Blondel — became converts to Catholicism.

An episode that shows how he personally campaigned for the cause of liberty took place in the cold winter of 1780, when hunger and mutiny threatened to dissolve the revolutionary forces. Barry roamed through the crowded streets of Philadelphia, recruiting soldiers and soliciting subscriptions. The most generous — more than a half million dollars — was donated by the Friendly Sons of

St. Patrick, and Thomas Fitzsimons, the noted Catholic businessman of the city, himself subscribed $25,000.

Today Barry lies in the old cemetery of St. Mary's in Philadelphia, beside his two wives. The inscription over his tomb describes the orthodoxy of his faith : « In full belief in the doctrines of the Gospel, he abandoned himself to the arms of his Redeemer ».

There are many monuments to Barry — a marble statue and memorial fountain, erected in 1876 in Fairmount Park, Philadelphia; his portrait, a copy of an original by Gilbert Stuart, that occupies a place of honor in Independence Hall; a bronze statue put up in Independence Square in 1907; and John J. Boyle's statue of him in Washington, which was dedicated by President Wilson in 1914 [28].

A Catholic heroine of Irish origin was Molly Pitcher (1751-1800), spirited wife of an artilleryman, John Corbin. She seems to have been a native of Carlisle, Pa., although there is some doubt about her maiden name and some claim she is merely a vague figure of legend. One hears of her feats of arms, at the side of her husband — perhaps as a nurse or a vivandiere — in the siege of Fort Washington and the battle of Monmouth Court House, New Jersey. It was at Fort Washington that, seeing her husband killed before her eyes, she forthwith took his place by his cannon and fired it tirelessly throughout the day, which ended in victory. General Greene is said to have presented her to General Washington, who made her a sergeant with the pay and pension of a noncommissioned officer. On the battlefield of Monmouth and in her native Carlisle, two monuments today recall this indomitable Catholic heroine [29].

We have cited here only a few of the Irish personalities involved in the Revolution. It would be impossible to mention the thousands from the rank and file. Recent researches tell us that at the period Americans of Anglo-Saxon origin — that is, 60 per cent of the entire colonial population — constituted only 25 per cent of Washington's troops. Thirty-eight per cent, on the other hand, were Irish soldiers — Protestants and Catholics — as revealed in the muster rolls, which list more than 12,000 officers and men with characteristically Irish names.

The loyalty and valor of the Irish-Americans are legendary. Judge Jeremiah S. Black once said, in a vivid phrase : « I have seen black swans and I have heard white ravens croak. But I have never yet heard mention of an Irishman who was disloyal to America ». And J. Parke Custis, Washington's adopted son, paid a tribute to the famed regiment of Pennsylvania infantry that is worth recalling. It was in connection with the incident that saved West Point, « the key to the Hudson », when threatened through the treachery of Benedict Arnold. So difficult were the circumstances that Washington, deeply perplexed, confided to Lafayette : « Whom can we trust now ? » With the intuition of a military genius, Lafayette answered : « The Pennsylvania Regiment ». And it was an inspiration. The hand-picked militia, entirely composed of Irishmen, after a forced four-hour march by night, succeeded in holding the imperilled fortress. Of this feat Custis remarked : « The good services of the sons of Erin deserve high honors in the story of independence. May the shamrock of St. Patrick be interlaced with the laurels of the Revolution ! »

And Horace Walpole, in a letter from London in 1776, barely concealed his disgruntled surprise at the solidarity of the Irish in the Revolution. « All Ireland », he wrote, « is America-mad ».

IV — The Italians also did much for the American cause, although little or nothing is said of them, because of their small numbers. (There were in Washington's time hardly more than 2,000 in America, scattered far and wide, and certainly not in positions of first rank).

Their contribution is overlooked, for when one speaks of Catholic participation in the Revolution, one invariably thinks of four main classifications — (1) the colonials of Anglo-Saxon or Celtic stock; (2) the Catholic Indians of Maine and elsewhere; (3) the Canadian volunteers; and (4) the French and Spanish allies.

Italy was in a crisis at the time, being divided into some ten small states or kingdoms. At most, Italians had no reason other than sheer idealism to intervene with arms in the American insurrection, whereas the others — Lafayette and the French generals, the Indians and Spanish and Baron Steuben, who reorganized the Federal troops at Valley Forge — were surely motivated by anti-English sentiments and hopes of gain by their military cooperation, however little they might have acknowledged it.

But the Italians had no such motives. With instinctive sympathy, they loved America for her fresh and youthful spirit. And on her part, America appreciated the passion of Catholic Italy for the modern Atlantis. Not insignificant is the fact that the first American diplomat sent to Europe, after Franklin, was Ralph Izard, commissioner to the Grand Duchy of Tuscany, and that the first treaty of friendship and trade offered by the United States to a European country, after France, was that with the Venetian Republic which was signed by Adams, Franklin and Jefferson.

The most precious contribution of Italy to rebellious America lay in her own great ideal of political independence, her affirmation of human liberty and of rights that may not be suppressed, and her own stand against the tyranny of the state. The Declaration of Independence, which recognizes that all men are created equal, that government depends on popular consent and that a free assembly has its unalienable rights, represents the fruit of centuries of painfully garnered Christian experience in striving for individual dignity and freedom. Likewise, the American Constitution is Christian and not agnostic, being founded on the sovereignty of moral law and the right to worship God.

Behind these two documents one discerns the impulse of Catholic genius of all times, from the Apostles up to the English Magna Carta of 1215, which was urged upon King John by Archbishop Langton of Canterbury, the spirit behind English constitutional liberty. They represent, too, the ideal of political liberty expressed by St. Thomas Aquinas and, in the post-Renaissance period, by two profound thinkers, Suarez and Bellarmino.

The memorable pledge of King John in Article 39 of the Magna Carta — « No freeman shall be arrested, or detained in prison, or deprived of his freehold, or outlawed, or banished, or in any way molested; and we (the King) will not go forth against him, nor send against him, unless by the lawful judgment of his peers and by the law of the land » — was formally incorporated in the principle of « due process of law », which is the basis of the American government ([30]).

The influence of St. Thomas Aquinas on the American Constitution is obvious. Certain phrases of his *Summa,* as well as some concepts in his *De Regimine Principum,* are rich with the germs of individual and constitutional liberty. William Hard, author of *The Spirit of the Constitution,* has clearly stated that the original speculations « in the theological halls of Europe » laid the groundwork for that document ([31]). Green, in his classic *History of the English People* (I, 251), declares, alluding principally to St. Thomas Aquinas, that « politically the teaching of these scholars was (in England) of immense value, because it was based on religion and gave an intellectual form to the constitutional theory of the relations between king and people which slowly emerged from the struggle with the Crown ».

After the Renaissance, the Jesuit Suarez harked back to Thomism in his political thought, as well as in his theology and philosophy. Edmund Burke, diligent student of Suarez' writings, turned his ideas to good account for the Whigs — the liberal English of the 18th century — and through them they penetrated to the American Founding Fathers, as an almost pure source of American governmental philosophy.

Most potent of all influences, immediate or remote, on American statesmanship, however, was that of Roberto Cardinal Bellarmino ([32]). In contesting the doctrine of the divine right of kings, Bellarmino asserted that « the people always transfer their own powers to those who govern them but in such a way as to retain potential authority in their own hands ».

Two sovereign principles are implicit, but also operative, in a democratic regime : (1) the principle that « all men are equal, not in wisdom and in grace, but in essence and in the nature of humanity », and (2) that « political rights come from God and are necessarily inherent in man's nature ». These two thoughts from Bellarmino's political system are the basis of the ideal of liberty incorporated into the Declaration of Independence — an ideal tended like a flower in the fecund soil of Catholic Italy. That these ideas were not Bellarmino's alone but those of the official Church is demonstrated by two Briefs of Pope Paul V, in 1606 and 1607.

There is a certain Protestant tendency to minimize

the importance of this Catholic influence and to claim that these ideas are discoverable far back in history ([33]). According to some, one can find in Moses' Ten Commandments traces of the essential idea later distilled in the Constitution ([34]); and according to others, in the Acts of the Apostles. They add that Jefferson, framer of the Declaration of Independence, was inspired if not by Locke at least by Harrington, author of *Oceana,* and by the Calvinistic philosophy of which he was a disciple.

The truth is that those who belittle the Catholic paternity of political thought embodied in the Constitution, unmask themselves by their stubborn championing of a worn-out theory that Catholicism, perpetually aligning itself with oppressive power, is still impregnated with the old pagan leaven.

The following three principles quoted from Bellarmino's *De Clericis* and *De Laicis* and compared with excerpts from the Declaration of Independence will show how the 17th century thinker and the framers of the document conceived liberty in identical terms :

Bellarmino said : « In a free state all men are born free ». The Declaration of Independence says : « All men are created equal ».

Bellarmino said : « Being naturally free, the people themselves hold immediately and directly the political power, with the result that it cannot be transferred to others ». The Declaration says : « They (all men) are endowed by their Creator with certain unalienable rights... and that to secure these rights Governments are instituted among Men, deriving their just powers from the consent of the governed ».

Bellarmino said : « For a legitimate reason the people can change the government ». The Declaration says : « Whenever any Form of Government becomes destructive of these ends (life, liberty and the pursuit of happiness), it is the Right of the People to alter or abolish it, or to institute new Government ».

In view of these parallels, as someone has observed, how can the Declaration of Independence be other than « an accurate transcription of Catholic thought? ». Or better still, a « Catholic document? ». The people, the people, insisted Bellarmino, and, with no less force, the Constitution of America, more than 170 years later, opens its preamble with the words : « We, the people of the United States ».

Bellarmino made the ancient thesis of « indirect power » famous throughout Europe ([35]), and as early as 1610 the learned Cardinal was bitterly denounced by William Barclay, the Scotch Catholic jurist and professor of law at Angers, in his work, *On the Power of the Pope.* His son, John Barclay, who published it posthumously, became a disciple of Bellarmino. Opposed to the doctrine of the absolute power of a king, at a time when these theories were fomenting political persecutions of the Church in Venice and England, Bellarmino answered it with his famous treatise, *On the Power of the Roman Pontiff in Temporal Matters.* This work refuted William Barclay with the counterthesis of authority seen as the attribute of a people assembled to form a state with the God-given right to elect its own representative.

In 1680 Sir Robert Filmer, defending the divine monarchical right in his *Patriarca, or the Natural Power of the Kings,* rejected Bellarmino's principle of popular sovereignty, but at the same time he included in his work a synthesis of Bellarmino's doctrine, drawn from *De Potestate Pontificis* (l. I. c. VI, p. 257). As a result, Bellarmino's thought was passed on easily to America in this volume, which was far simpler for the laity to read than the Cardinal's own ponderous tomes. Of the two, Bellarmino, with his convictions and equality and human rights, intrigued the American patriots far more than Filmer did, with his pro-royal negativism ([36]). In 1698 Algernon Sidney refuted Filmer and declared he owed a debt of gratitude to Bellarmino. Even Locke, writing against Filmer, expatiated on his summary of Bellarmino. When Jefferson was a student at William and Mary College, he could hardly have been unaware of Filmer, Sidney and Locke.

In fact, in Jefferson's vast library ([37]), there was a copy of Bellarmino's *De Laicis,* along with Filmer's *Patriarca,* and on this evidence Catholic and non-Catholic writers have unanimously agreed that Jefferson wrote the Declaration of Independence under the great Cardinal's influence and owed a special debt to the principles he outlined in *Treatise on the Law.*

A student of the subject asks : « Were Madison and Jefferson aware of their indebtedness to Bellarmino, or did they use Filmer's presentation of his doctrine without knowing the original? Did the Americans realize they were risking life, fortune and their sacred honor to support a theory of government proclaimed by a Catholic priest? We cannot answer such questions, but Catholics would be well pleased to know that the basic ideas, from which the greatest of modern revolutions was born, issue from the writings of a Prince of the Church » ([38]).

Chesterton suggests : « The Church is always in advance of the world. St. Thomas was an internationalist before all our internationalists. Joan of Arc was a nationalist before there were nations. Bellarmino described democracy before people, in any part of the world, dared to be democratic ».

To leave idealism for reality, we turn now to the Italian Catholics who collaborated actively — with their arms and minds and money — with the cause of American liberty.

This is largely a story yet to be written; for the most part, it has come down to us by oral tradition. The « Little Italys » of America retell these legends with pride. Such a one is the episode of a soldier at the Battle of Monmouth, who is identified only as « Francesco, the Italian » and was one of the heroes of the day. This humble foreign soldier at the cost of his own life, so legend says, saved Washington from being killed by the bayonets of the English cavalry that had already slain his horse. There is also the case of the 20-year-old Richard Tagliaferro, who fell in the Battle of Guildford Court House in Virginia and whose name is inscribed on a monument to the heroes of the engagement under the motto : *Palmam qui meruit ferat* ([39]).

In the first rank among Italian names is that of the patriot Paul Revere (1735-1818). His Italian origin has been variously traced to Liguria, Piedmont (the most likely opinion, in view of the family name) and even Trieste. Most probably he was born while his immigrant parents were traveling to America, and his birth registered at the first port of call — Boston. He showed the mark of his native Italian talent in his exercise of the family profession of silversmith and coppersmith. The engraved metal plates of the frigate Constitution are a sample of his work, as well as other pieces notable for their craftsmanship and style.

He was passionately devoted, from the beginning, to the rebel cause. Revere participated in all Boston's insurrectional movements of 1774, such as the refusal to take oath, the Portsmouth mission that led to the capture of Fort William and Mary (one of the first manifestations of rebel military force) and the Boston Tea Party. The following year he performed the epic act of his romantic, adventurous life. Near his dwelling there was an ancient church (called Old North Church), from whose bell-tower, tradition says, Revere and other conspirators sounded warnings of enemy ships arriving in port, as well as the deployment of enemy land forces.

At any rate, on the night of April 18-19, 1775, Revere discovered that a sizable number of troops were disembarking from ships recently arrived in the harbor and were preparing to march on to Lexington, some 40 miles distant, to seize by surprise the most important deposit of arms in the Confederacy. Without losing an instant, Revere leaped on his horse and galloped through the night towards Lexington to warn the other patriots, the Middlesex farmers and the Minute Men to stand ready with arms. At every house, at every hamlet along the route, he shouted : « Arise ! To arms ! The English are coming ! ». A man warned is a man half saved, and the English expedition, thanks to Revere, marched to their famous defeat.

The splendid story — illustrating, one might say, the typically impulsive Italian character — lives on in Longfellow's vivid poem of 1860, which for all its romantic gusto is indeed a page of history ([40]). There is not a child in America unfamiliar with this episode, and there are few schoolrooms that do not display the traditional picture of the horseman riding through the night, alerting his compatriots to defend themselves. Samuel Adams had Paul Revere in mind when he exclaimed that day : « What a glorious morning for America is this ! »

Philip Mazzei was another Italian patriot of the revolutionary era. Born at Poggio Caiano, near Florence, on Christmas Day, 1730, he was brought up in the cultural climate of Tuscany and received his degree in medicine at the Hospital of Santa Maria Nuova. But his was an enormously versatile talent : by turns, during his life, he was merchant, farmer, naturalist, soldier, man of let-

ters, journalist and diplomat. He left the Florence of
Grand Duke Leopoldo after being wrongfully accused
of possessing and writing books frowned on by the Church.
In Naples, however, he effectively vindicated himself
of these charges, which were annulled; and indeed he
always remained attached to the Church of his ancestors,
even when he resided in staunchly Protestant Virginia.

About 1771, after 16 years as a merchant in London,
he became acquainted with a group of Virginians who,
recognizing him as a man of fertile initiative, proposed
that he introduce to their State two Tuscan specialties
— viticulture and viniculture, as well as the culture of
olives and silkworms. Mazzei was enthusiastic over the
idea. He left for Tuscany, where with six skilled agri-
culturists he acquired tools and seeds. After many vicissitudes (his associates were at the last minute panic-
stricken by the approaching adventure), he sailed with
them from Leghorn for the New World. He settled in
Albemarle County, not far from Jefferson's famed residence, Monticello.

This proximity to the great statesman, who admired
everything Italian and as a planter's son was passionately
devoted to the soil, turned out to be infinitely valuable
to him. Jefferson had made a special trip to Italy to study
the cultivation of rice in Lombardy, with the intent of
introducing it to America, as he had already done for
broccoli and peppers. He was hence delighted to hand
over to his enthusiastic neighbor Mazzei 2,000 acres of
land near Monticello, to which the Tuscan added 700
more of his own, for experiments in agriculture.

The Revolution interrupted this placid Georgic idyll
on the estate that Jefferson called « The Hill », and one
day Mazzei and his group of Tuscan viticulturists laid
down their rakes to take up guns in the Albemarle Militia. When word came that the English had disembarked

at nearby Hampton, Mazzei enlisted as a simple soldier in a regiment organized at Williamsburg.

Mazzei worked with Jefferson and Patrick Henry in their campaign for religious freedom in Virginia; he lectured in various churches and circulated leaflets on the subject. Known to almost all the founders of the Republic, Mazzei was given a special assignment as an agent for Virginia. Among other things, he was sent to Tuscany to solicit military funds from Grand Duke Leopoldo. On this mission, as John Adams declared, Mazzei showed a zeal and an attachment to the honor and interests of America extraordinary in a foreigner. From Florence he went to Paris, during the period when Jefferson was American ambassador to France, succeeding Franklin. Mazzei spent his time there writing a massive volume, at Jefferson's suggestion, called *Historical-Political Researches on the United States of America,* which came out in France in four volumes in 1788. Carlo Botta drew upon Mazzei's work for his own celebrated history.

Mazzei was eligible for a consular position, but prejudice against him, as a foreign-born Catholic, stood in the way. When he returned to America, he found all his work in agricultural experiment had gone to ruin in his absence, because a Hessian baron — prisoner of the Battle of Saratoga — had rented « The Hill » and had let horses loose on the property, destroying six years' toil in one week. Home-sickness for Europe, and especially his beloved Tuscany, came over him and he decided to return to spend the last years of his life there. Before leaving, he wrote President Madison (who spoke and wrote fluent Italian) : « I am leaving, but my heart remains here. I do not know what will happen to me after I lose sight of Sandy Hook, but I know well that wherever I am and in whatever conditions, I will never relax my efforts on behalf of the well-being of my adopted country ».

He rendered a last service to America when he selected two Tuscan sculptors, at the request of the architect Latrobe, and sent them to America to complete the adornment of the new Capitol in Washington. On his death in Pisa on March 19, 1816, his old friend, former President Jefferson, said : « I learn this news with much sorrow. During forty years of friendship I grew to learn his worth, and our friendship was maintained after separation uninterrupted by a constant exchange of letters. The esteem which he enjoyed in this country was due to his zealous cooperation from the very first hour with the cause of independence » ([41]).

Another humble but great Catholic who figured in the history of American independence was Francesco Vigo (1747-1836). A recent biographer calls him a « forgotten framer of the American Republic » ([42]), and John T. Paris devotes much space to him in his *Romance of Forgotten Americans* ([43]). Yet the great American historian Bancroft knew of him and, unlike others who have called him either a Sardinian or a Spaniard, identified him correctly as « an Italian from Piedmont » ([44]). In his native parish at Mondovi, his baptismal registration may be seen today in the church records.

When he was very young, he went to work in Spain. There he made the acquaintance of the Spanish governor De Leyba, who when transferred to America brought Vigo with him, with the understanding he would deal in pelts and furs with the Indians. Vigo established himself first in New Orleans and then in St. Louis, from where he trafficked with all the Indian trading posts, from Kaskaskia and Cahokia on the Mississippi and Vincennes on the Wabash, as far north as Michinakinaw. These were areas controlled by the English, who maintained, in the midst of a Creole-French population, garrisons that kept the Indians within the English orbit.

At this period a bold and adventurous young man was gaining prominence in the frontier world — George Clark (1752-1818), a native of Jefferson's and Mazzei's Albemarle County in Virginia. At the age of 26, Clark represented Kentucky in the Virginia legislature, and in this capacity, as well as that of major in the militia, he conceived a plan which, if it were to succeed, would conquer the entire West for democracy.

On the eve of the Revolution, Clark, convinced that the Kentucky borders were in danger if the British chose to expand from Detroit over the vast neighboring territory inhabited by the Indians, proposed to Virginia's governor, Patrick Henry, the capture of all the Indian trading posts and the seizure of Detroit itself. It was an audacious proposal of incalculable importance to the immediate development of the nation.

To aid him in his venture Clark enlisted the services of Vigo, the immigrant merchant from Mondovi, and the patriotic missionary, Abbé Gibault, who worked with the Indians and colonial French in the vast territory.

Vigo's role in this risky, yet romantic enterprise was threefold: (1) he furnished Clark, when he was preparing for his historic expedition of 1778-79, all the particulars of Fort Sackville, outpost of the English general, Hamilton; (2) he gave him an absolute guarantee of the loyalty of the citizens of Vincennes; and (3) he advanced all the funds needed for the armament and equipment of the troops required for the campaign, since the French refused to deal in Virginia dollars — the only currency at Clark's disposal — and the Indians demanded either piastres or furs.

In strict accordance with Clark's plan, Vigo traveled disguised as a Cuban merchant from Kaskaskia to Vincennes, a distance of 240 miles through marshes and deserts infested with hostile Indians, to acquire all the military information on the British stronghold of Fort Sackville that was indispensable to Clark's project. On his way back, to report on his explorations, he was arrested by General Hamilton's sentinels, while awaiting a propitious moment to cross the Wabash. With surprising presence of mind, pretending all the while to be a Cuban merchant, he swallowed the compromising notes he had on him and let himself be imprisoned in Fort Sackville, where, in the very heart of the fortress, he finished gathering the most secret information needed to capture it.

The brave Father Gibault, the other participant in the scheme, then warned the English of the danger that the entire Catholic population of Vincennes would revolt against the Protestant soldiers. Vigo was released, promising on his honor to « return to St. Louis without doing anything en route that might be contrary to the English ». He kept his word and galloped at full speed to St. Louis, but then, with equal haste, hurried to Clark's headquarters at Kaskaskia, where he gave him his full report.

When it came to a practical situation, Vigo was also an able man. On December 4, 1778, Vigo gave Clark a bank check of local money equivalent to $6,716.40. With this, Clark acquired 170 « long knives » and other arms, gunpowder and military uniforms. At a pre-arranged moment, his troops marched on Vincennes, and on February 25, 1779, Fort Sackville was captured. The garrison was taken by surprise, for General Hamilton supposed that the invading forces were a major unit. Actually, Clark had only 130 men with him, who had had to endure untold sacrifices on the 240-mile march over muddy, inundated terrain.

Father Gibault and Vigo used all their considerable

influence to win over the French Catholic inhabitants to the patriots' cause, as well as the Indians of the area, who joyfully took the oath of allegiance to the growing Republic. The exceptional importance of the conquest by the Clark-Vigo-Gibault triumvirate was revealed in full in the Treaty of Paris of 1783, which legally gave to the United States government all the territory between the Mississippi and the Alleghenies ([45]).

As for Vigo, Clark's irreplaceable ally, he was never reimbursed in full for the financial advance that represented all his savings from so many years of hard work ([46]). The small payments that dribbled in were not enough to take care of him in his old age. In 1834, Prince Maximilian of Wied, passing through Vincennes, found Colonel Vigo, who was then 90, living in the most squalid misery. « The Americans », he wrote, « hurried to promote Vigo but now leave him to die of hunger ». With good reason, J. T. Paris, in his *Romance of Forgotten Americans,* called Vigo « the Robert Morris of the Northwest Territory », in the sense that the great financier of the Revolution himself died in relative poverty in Philadelphia.

Fifty years later, Congress voted to pay to Vigo's heirs, descendants in the third generation of Vigo's widow, about $50,000 for the loan made by Vigo. Fifty dollars went to the Court House in Vigo County, Indiana, to buy it a bell, according to a wish expressed by the colonel in his will, and $20 were given to the heirs of the undertaker Andrew Gardner, who supplied the coffin on credit for the colonel's remains.

The Italians who served the cause of American liberty represent the highest contribution that could be made — that of intelligence, heart and personal sacrifice ([47]). In turn, America has been grateful to Italy.

V — It is perhaps little known that Catholic Spain in 1779 declared war on England and made a direct contribution to the United States with a loan of money. This gesture was decidedly useful in creating a favorable attitude among Americans toward all the Spanish residents of their territories or in adjoining ones for indeed the Spanish were everywhere at the time — on all the borders, in Canada, in the Spanish colonies around the Gulf of Mexico and in the French ones of the Illinois area.

Of first importance were the Spanish of New Orleans and Florida, who contributed to the victory of the Republic under Count Bernardo de Galvez (1755-1786), the Spanish administrator, governor of Louisiana and viceroy of Mexico, who is remembered in the name of the Texan city, Galveston (Galvez-ton) ([48]).

The contribution of Catholic Poland, which at that time (1772) had just been dismembered and divided up between Russia, Austria and Prussia, is even more significant. Two personalities stand out in high relief.

One is the great Thaddeus Kosciusko (1746-1817), brilliant descendant of a royal Lithuanian house, who as a youth crossed the ocean to espouse the cause of democracy. Jefferson described him as « the purest lover of human liberty » and President Harrison dubbed him « the Martyr ». In his capacity as engineering officer, he was entrusted by Washington in 1776 with the construction of fortifications at West Point, which prevented the English from taking Albany and gave Major General Clinton and the « Irish Volunteers » a chance to hold them at bay.

With his defensive works on the Delaware River, he aided Washington in the brilliant strategic movement at Trenton. His fortifications at Ticonderoga assured the successful American retreat from Canada and gave the rebels a solid foothold in the Battle of Saratoga. According to Trevelyan, it was this success on the heights of Behmis and at Saratoga, « the Thermopylae of America », that assured the aid of France. The cadets of West Point call Kosciusko « the father of American artillery » ([49]).

The other Pole is Count Casimir Pulaski (1748-79). After he and his father led an insurrection of Polish Catholics rebelling against the harsh yoke of servitude, he was exiled to America and joined the Continental Army in 1777. Distinguishing himself at Brandywine, he was promoted to brigadier general and the following year, with the consent of Congress, organized the Pulaski Legion, an autonomous cavalry and light infantry unit. At its head he entered Charleston in 1779 and took part in the liberation of the city. Various members of the Legion were Polish noblemen who had followed Pulaski to America. He met his death during the assault on Savannah on October 11, 1779, at the age of 31, repeating the holy names : « Jesus, Mary and Joseph » ([50]).

VI — The French are mentioned last, only because their contribution was more valuable than any other. It was the last burst of the military splendor of the royal house of France. What typifies this generous outpouring of French sympathy and aid to the American cause was its very spontaneity, something like the response of one heart to another and the magnetic attraction between one ideal of democracy that had already matured and the French ideal about to be born. Lafayette expressed this tacit sentiment in a revealing sentence in his memoirs : « At the very first news of the American struggle, my heart was already pledged to it ». The two countries were bound by impalpable spiritual threads. Yet were the

French interventionists aware that the movement for
liberty across the ocean was substantially different from
the movement in France that was to lead to regicide,
sanscullotism, terrorism, persecution of the Church and
the guillotine ?([51]).

The attraction of the French for American democracy was perhaps a reflowering of the old love for a still
mysterious land that for two centuries had inspired French
idealists, missionaries, students, explorers, adventurers
— the whole dynasty of Champlain, Cartier, De Monts,
Marquette, Joliet, La Salle, Hennepin, Bienville — and
left its imprint in the names of hundreds of cities, from
New Orleans and New Rochelle to St. Louis.

From the first Continental Congress, the patriot rebels were fully aware that without French aid their
struggle for freedom could hardly succeed. According to
Truslow Adams, Washington's strength of character was
one of the two factors that saved the Revolution from
becoming an abortive rebellion. The other was the alignment of the European powers against the English. The
Philadelphia assembly made a grave mistake in reject-
ing the Canadian delegates — cousins of France — for
the sole reason that Canada was a Catholic country. The
mistake, fortunately, was not repeated in the case of
France.

With admirable foresight, the 70-year-old Benjamin
Franklin was dispatched to France as envoy to the court
of Versailles, where he arrived December 31, 1776. Washington wrote him, at a crucial moment of the Revolution : « If France does not send her army, the cause must
perish, for our troops are beginning to mutiny, funds can
no longer be collected to pay them, they are without food
and their feet, half out of their shoes, are cut and bleed-
ing ». On February 6, 1778, in the Treaty of Alliance,
King Louis XVI made Catholic France the ally of the

United States — the only one until 1782 — and recognized its national independence. And thanks to French financial, diplomatic and — more importantly — naval and military aid, the American Revolution took a resolute turn.

At the stipulation of the French alliance, the United States was loaned $6,353,000 by the French government, then represented by Beaumarchais. France did this not without risk or sacrifice on her own part. Some historians have forthrightly described the loan, with the resultant impoverishment and discontent of the French people, as one of the immediate causes of their revolution of 1789. In addition to this loan, France witnessed a stupendous act of generosity, for when the Royal Treasury found it was unable to supply other funds to implement the clauses of the Treaty of Alliance, bishops and clergy, already heavily taxed, voted in 1879 to collect an additional sum of six million dollars to send overseas in aid of the American struggle [52].

French diplomatic assistance was also highly profitable and took many forms. Every possibility of material and moral cooperation, indeed the whole weight of France, helped throw the balance of the war in America's favor. With the appointment of her first plenipotentiary ministers to the United States, France gave her formal recognition of the worth of the American cause and confirmed her decision on the international diplomatic plane. In the story of American diplomacy it will always be noted that the first diplomatic corps of the young nation was Catholic, for the first two powers to recognize it, ahead of all others, were France and Spain.

The first of these Catholic ambassadors was Conrad A. Gerard [53]. His successor was the great Marquis Chevalier de la Luzerne [54], whose good deeds during the Revolution justify J. J. Walsh's eulogy : « The Catholic

Church in America probably owes more to De la Luzerne than to any other individual, with the possible exception of Bishop Carroll, its first great prelate, and Charles Carroll of Carrollton ».

In a military way, the Alliance meant the contribution of French arms to the United States wherever opportunity presented itself for the French fleet to engage in battle with the English, in all the waters of the world — even the Indian Ocean. All told, the French aid involved approximately 30,000 men, in land and sea forces, along with 90 military heads under the command of General Washington.

The English, first thrown into confusion and finally overcome, heaped anti-clerical contumely on the rebels. To quote McCarthy : « The loyalist newpapers published nonsense of every type, announcing that the King of France equipped a fleet with the sole purpose of turning the Americans into Catholics, like his own subjects. Each one of his ships was said to be laden with holy water and barrels of consecrated oil. A thousand crates crammed with relics, rosaries and crucifixes, with an enormous supply of hair-shirts, cowls and whips, were part of the cargo. One ship contained thousands of consecrated hosts and missals and bales of indulgences. Naturally, to assure the conversion of the heretics, the good King did not forget the tools of the trade, such as racks, hooks, chains and branding-irons. To instruct the citizens of the New World in the use of such instruments, an army of priests, secular and religious was organized. . . A contract was drawn up for the erection of a Bastille in New York, so that America might benefit from the blessings of the King of France and the Pontiff ».

While idlers occupied themselves in fabricating such fantasies, France sent with her picked troops the flower of her chaplains and the elect of her officers, generals and admirals.

How many chaplains of the French Army and Navy were there? More than a hundred, and of these 20 were Capuchins. Specifically, the chaplains of the French forces serving in the United States numbered 109 — 11 regular Army chaplains; 38 with D'Estaing's squadron; 32 with De Grasse; 12 with De Guichen; 16 with De Ternay. Several of them, after independence was achieved, lived on in the United States and became distinguished in one field or another ([55]).

Of the more prominent leaders from France, all born Catholics, here are a few names. One is that of Comte Claude de Saint-Simon (1760-1823), future founder and exponent of humanitarian socialism, who began his adventurous career in the French Army that went to America, serving with distinction in the campaign against Cornwallis. Another is Augustin Mottin de la Balme (1736-1780), who offered his services to America two years before Lafayette. As inspector general of the American Cavalry, De la Balme fell victim to an ambush of the Little Turtle Indians on November 5, 1780, at his camp near Fort Wayne, while he was proceeding with a platoon of voluntaries to the attack of the English garrison at Detroit. The episode of his end is related in the war story, *Massacre of De la Balme* ([56]).

Then there was the Marquis de Lafayette (1754-1834), the 20-year-old idealist whose head swimming with liberal fancies but who in reality — by his own confession — was solely anxious to gain the glory that he called « his brevet of immortality ». Washington, his friend, assigned him the command of a division, with which he participated in the battle of Yorktown. By one of those mysterious threads of sympathy that often bind men and nations, Lafayette has become the Frenchman who more than any other captivated the heart of America. « Prince Charming », « Idol of the nation », « Cavalier of Liberty » are a few of the phrases by which he is known. His American adventure has also been called his « brilliant folly », and indeed it has the quality of an ancient *chanson de geste*.

In 1831, Mazzini declared that « it was only singular circumstances and Washington's friendship that procured for Lafayette a fame beyond his merits ». But Mazzini's judgment did not affect by one iota the American's high esteem for him. One recalls General Pershing's famous words upon his arrival in Paris in 1917, spoken at Lafayette's tomb : « Lafayette, we are here ! » ([57]).

But Lafayette was not the real French hero of the Revolution; there were two true heroes — Rochambeau on land and De Grasse on the sea.

Count and Marshal of France, Rochambeau (1725-1807) was sent by Louis XVI to the aid of the Colonies with the rank of Lieutenant General, at the head of an expeditionary force of 6,000 soldiers. The paltry number of these troops at first led him to consider declining the mission, but his zeal for the American cause induced him to accept it. Rochambeau had been brought up by the Jesuits in their College at Blois and almost became a Jesuit himself; after he completed his novitiate, his brother's death made him suddenly heir to the family estate, which deterred him from taking final vows. With his contingent, Rochambeau arrived at Newport, Rhode Island, in July, 1780, and at once joined forces with Washington's army on the Hudson. From that moment till the capture of Yorktown, he collaborated with the Liberator in his dual capacity of general and French diplomat. On his embarkation for France, Congress officially gave him the nation's thanks ([58]).

The Comte de Grasse (1723-1788) was a born sailor. When barely 11, he enlisted in the famous navy of the

Knights of Malta and fought for the defense of Catholicism and civilization against the Turks and Moors. After he enrolled in the French Navy, his courage on the seas made him famous : at 31 he was a lieutenant, at 39 a captain. In 1781 he fought against the English at Tobago, in the Leeward Islands of the West Indies. Arriving at Haiti the same year, he was met by a French frigate with special dispatches from Washington and Rochambeau. Jointly they asked him to take part in a combined sea-and-land action against the English forces, evidently intending De Grasse to deliver the decisive blow.

He at once drew up his own strategic plan, which the same frigate delivered to Washington and Rochambeau, who by August 15 had a perfect understanding of it. Then began the epic period of seven weeks which brought the war to its effective conclusion ([59]).

De Grasse took 3,500 of Saint-Simon's soldiers aboard his convoy of 28 ships, and on August 30 he anchored in Chesapeake Bay, where another French admiral, Comte de Barras, had been waiting for him for three days, with four other frigates and 19 French transports. In a dispatch Washington congratulated De Grasse on « the happy arrival of such a formidable fleet of His Most Christian Majesty in Chesapeake Bay ». His satisfaction was well justified, for indeed this was the most powerful naval force — 51 ships — that had been seen since the time of the Spanish Armada.

The English admiral, Lord Graves, despite a tentative attack on De Barras' forces off Chesapeake Bay, found he was unable to put up a fight against this potent alignment of two fleets, with 20,000 French sailors, and tacked about for New York. That was why he could not lend Lord Cornwallis, trapped at Yorktown with 7,000 men, the aid from the sea he had promised him. The story of the English naval retreat has been called « the mari-

time Waterloo ». And the paralysis thus enforced on the
English fleet then inspired the strategy of the allied
armies of Washington, Rochambeau and Lafayette, to
which was added Saint-Simon's army, which De Grasse
had transported freshly equipped for war ([60]).

VII — While the traitor Benedict Arnold was devas-
tating Virginia, Lafayette held Cornwallis in siege, to
give the converging land and sea forces time to approach
under the commands of De Grasse, Washington and
Rochambeau. Lord Cornwallis and his 7,000 men, who
were barricaded in two forts, then came under the con-
centrated fire of Hamilton and the French Count Guil-
laume Deuxponts. Finding himself cut off from any
possible avenue of retreat, Cornwallis had no recourse but
to surrender on October 19, 1781, a final act that signalized the virtual close of the War of Independence ([61]).

In that culminating moment of victory at Yorktown,
borne by De Grasse's and Rochambeau's 32,000 men and
Washington's 6,000, the chivalry of the Catholic nobility
was revealed. For when an English officer offered the
sword of the conquered general to Rochambeau, he refused
it, ordering him to deliver it to the American commander-
in-chief. The Catholic wished to defer all honors to Washington and his federal troops.

Colonel Tilghman — an Irishman from Maryland
— was dispatched by night to Philadelphia with Washington's message announcing to Congress the English surrender. The first and only thought the Assembly had on
receiving it was to repair immediately to the nearest
church to give thanks to God for « having crowned the
Allied flags of the United States and France » with so
stunning a victory ([62]). Six days later, on October 26,
1781, Congress issued a proclamation recommending to

the various States that they set aside the 13th of the following December to thanksgiving for the victory and prayers for an honorable and lasting peace.

For the Catholics who played so heroic a part in the American success, the sense of gratitude to the Lord of Victories was expressed by the French ambassador to Philadelphia, the Chevalier de la Luzerne, brother of the Bishop of Langres, who had mortgaged his private fortune to aid the revolutionaries. This excellent diplomat had a religious service held in the Jesuits' church of St. Mary's on November 4, with a solemn Mass, sermon and *Te Deum,* to which he invited the Continental Congress, the Supreme Executive Council and the Philadelphia Assembly (⁶³). Father Seraphin Bandol — a Franciscan who served as chaplain to the French Legation — delivered a sermon on the occasion that James Thatcher in his *Military Journal* described as « not only animated and elegant in its French but also warm in its feeling of devoutness and gratitude to our Divine Benefactor ».

France was no less grateful for the victory of her troops at Yorktown. The news, which took a month to get there, was brought aboard the swift ship La Surveillante, which De Grasse had summarily dispatched. Upon hearing it, King Louis had but one thought — to thank the God of Victory and ordered a *Te Deum* sung in the churches of every diocese in France « for the success borne » — so read the royal proclamation — « over the English by His Most Christian Majesty's armies together with those of General Washington » (⁶⁴).

Washington never forgot his gratitude to France for her essential services in concluding the war — nor indeed his gratitude to Catholicism in general. In his noted letter of 1790 to Msgr. John Carroll and three leaders of the Catholic laity, he wrote : « I hope that our citizens will never forget the part you have played in the accomplishment of their revolution and the establishment of our government, or the important aid they have received from a nation professing the Roman Catholic faith » ([65]).

On April 19, 1783 — exactly eight years to the day from the opening of hostilities at Lexington — Washington ordered the definite cessation of the war. Immediately afterwards, Franklin, together with a commission in which Jefferson and three others participated, was designated to negotiate the peace treaty with Lord Selborn, the English prime minister. The preliminary negotiations resulted in the ceding to America of the whole territory east of the Mississippi that had been secured by Clark, Vigo and Gibault. On September 3, 1783 the Treaty of Paris was solemnly signed, and America began her history as a free and independent nation ([66]).

JOHN CARROLL AND THE CATHOLIC HIERARCHY IN THE UNITED STATES

CHAPTER VII

In North America, the Catholic Church, until the time its autonomous hierarchy was created, was directly dependent on the Propaganda of the Faith in Rome, or on corresponding hierarchies already constituted in Quebec, for the French missions of Illinois, and in Mexico, for the other missions, prevalently Spanish, scattered through Florida, Texas, New Mexico and California ([1]).

The original 13 American colonies, from the start of the colonization of Maryland, fell automatically under the ecclesiastical jurisdiction of the Vicar Apostolic of London. On September 6, 1688, Innocent XI nominated Dr. John Leyburn Vicar Apostolic of all England. The Colonies were naturally part of his jurisdiction and of that of his successors — Bishops Gifford (1703-34), Petre (1734-58), Challoner (1758-81) and Talbot (1781-84).

More precisely, Msgr. Richard Challoner was the last to exercise supervision over Catholicism in America, for after the United States won independence, his successor, Msgr. Talbot, deliberately withdrew his authority from the distant Continent. Just prior to the Revolution, the Vicar Apostolic of London directed the affairs of the Colonies through Father Lewis, Superior of the Jesuits of America.

Catholic life at that time revolved around Maryland, which ecclesiastically represented all the States during the Revolution. The Report sent the Holy See by the Rev. John Carroll showed there were 15,800 Catholics in Maryland, of which about 9,000 were colonists, 3,000 children and another 3,000 Negro slaves. In addition, there were 7,000 Catholics in Pennsylvania, 1,500 in New York and 200 in Virginia. To administer to this population of souls dispersed over an enormous area, there were 19 missionary priests for Maryland and another five for Pennsylvania.

II — The notable personality among these 19 Maryland priests was Father John Carroll (1735-1815), an American of Irish origin, who grew up under the protecting shadow of the Company of Jesus, which administered spiritually to all American Catholics. An Italian writer living in America, G. Prezzolini, happily describes him as « the most important figure of American Catholicism; in a sense, the founder of it, with the characteristics that it has today, not as a foreign sect but as one of the national religions ».

Young Carroll was educated by Jesuit priests first in his native Maryland, at Bohemia Manor, and then, from 1747, in the most renowned Jesuit colleges in France and Belgium, particularly at St. Omer, preferred European college for English-speaking Catholics. In 1753 Carroll made his profession at St. Omer; in 1761 he was ordained at Liège by Bishop Pierre Jacquett and until the regrettable suppression of July 12, 1773, taught philosophy and theology in the colleges of his order at St. Omer and Liège ([2]).

In 1773 an incident befell him that illustrates a phase of his spiritual development. While visiting the

Sanctuary of Loreto in Italy, with his pupil, son of Lord Houghton, he had an experience which, as he wrote shortly afterwards to his brother Daniel, he would never forget. At that moment there came to him a sudden awareness that « the greatest blessing that he could receive from God would be that of instantaneous death ». Recovering himself, he added : « Yet if that is denied me, His holy and lovable intentions can be fulfilled entirely through me ». Newman, in a quite different state of mind, had a similar presentiment of high destiny awaiting him at Leonforte in Sicily.

Father Carroll was in Rome only a few months before the suppression of the Company of Jesus. The same year Lord Arundel of Wardour Castle offered him, to no avail, an ecclesiastical residence in England. Almost as though on a sacred impulse, he returned to America about the middle of 1774, after 27 years abroad, on one of the last ships that left England before the Revolution. He returned with a fine program of service clearly outlined in his mind. His biographer Walsh wrote : « He burned with the yearning to return to his native land, to serve it ».

Father Carroll found in his homeland about 20 of his former Jesuit associates tending the souls of some 23,000 Catholics. He settled in the maternal home at Rock Creek in Maryland, north of the present District of Columbia, where he carried out his own missionary apostolate, ministering to the welfare of souls in Maryland and Virginia. Because of the Legislature's intolerant ruling that forbade Maryland's Catholics to maintain a church open to the public, Father Carroll had a tiny chapel built on his mother's estate for semi-private use. Here, on Sundays, when distant missions did not prevent it, he quietly assembled the Catholics of the neighborhood and celebrated Mass for them.

In 1774 he established at Forest Glenn, Md., the Rock Creek Mission, known today as the Church of St. John and called « the Bethlehem of the Faith of Eastern America ». It was from here that Father Carroll was summoned to join the Congressional mission headed by Franklin that sought to secure Canada's neutrality in the War of Independence. In 1784 he was still pastor of this church when the Pope promoted him to Prefect Apostolic of the United States. Today the first Mass bell and liturgical books used by Carroll are preserved here, together with the marble plate that stood above the little pine-wood altar. The altar itself, however, is preserved in the crypt of the National Sanctuary of the Immaculate in Washington (³).

III — At the close of the Revolution, Catholic America felt more than ever the need for an autonomous hierarchical government, separate from that of England, the better to guarantee the development of the Church in the new nation.

Since no mention was made of liberty for the Catholic cult during the preliminaries of the peace treaty between England and America in Paris, Msgr. Pamphily Doria, the Papal Nuncio to France, was requested to speak of it to King Louis XVI. In his name the Comte de Vergennes, Foreign Minister of France, approached the American delegates on the matter, but it seemed to them it would be superfluous to insert in a treaty a constitutional principle that would look as though the war had been fought only for religious independence from London (⁴).

A thorny problem then arose. The idea of continuing dependence on the Vicar Apostolic in London having been discarded, it was asked whether ecclesiastical jurisdiction should be given to the Bishop of Quebec (such was Bishop Challoner's first thought) or to France, which for more than a century had done so much to Catholicize Canada. Or, on the other hand, should America be given its own hierarchy?

Vergennes had given instructions from the start to De la Luzerne, French envoy to the new republic, to « let things follow their natural course and, as for the French, never to weary in trying to find an honorable, just and disinterested solution in regard to the Americans ». Although some Frenchmen, such as certain missionaries in Canada, showed a leaning for a church of French, or at least French-Canadian character, Vergennes not only insisted that American Catholics be free to choose the nationality of the Superior assigned them but also stressed the necessity of selecting a citizen of the young nation as Vicar Apostolic « with the authority of a bishop ». If the suggestion of a French bishop came up in the various negotiations, it sprang from the Francophile Franklin. De la Luzerne first and later Marbois, being on the spot, were in a position to assess American public opinion and were not slow in realizing that Americans preferred an American bishop. Marbois in 1784 praised Father Carroll in a letter to Paris : « I do not know him personally. Yet I know he enjoys a fine reputation, and I believe it would be desirable if His Holiness elevated him to the episcopal seat as head of the Church of Pennsylvania and Maryland » (5).

A student of the complex problem, E. S. Kite, gives this resumé of the delicate situation : « The idea of putting a French bishop at the head of the Church in America never made much progress because it was never accepted by the French government in any form and remained a purely abortive idea of Franklin and certain Italian prelates » (6).

Certainly the historian Shea exaggerated when, unaware of recently uncovered documents, he mentioned a French attempt to « enslave » the infant Church in America. Baisnée and others stressed the generous and disinterested action of France, which « cooperated with the Holy See and the American representative to answer the needs of the Church in a land that she had aided and whose independent status she had recognized » ([7]). And the first to admit he was wrong was Franklin himself, once he was better informed on the subject.

This is indirectly but conclusively proved by the mention made by the Nuncio, Msgr. Pamphily Doria, to De la Luzerne when he assured him that if John Carroll were chosen as Vicar Apostolic in Maryland, it « would give pleasure to Congress and especially to Mr. Franklin, who had recommended him personally » ([8]).

IV — In the development of diplomatic negotiations for the practical creation of the Catholic hierarchy, the Curia proceeded with its usual wisdom and sought first to strenghten the structure of American Catholicism before appointing a bishop.

After relations with the Vicar Apostolic in London were broken off by war, the Maryland clergy assembled at least three times to make necessary decisions in the matter. These meetings took place at Whitemarsh, in a modest building that an Irishman had left incomplete and given to the Jesuit missionary Father John Ashton for use as a Mass house.

Here six deputies of the clergy assembled for the first time on June 27, 1783 in a meeting convoked by Father John Lewis, then Vicar General for Bishop Talbot of London, to discuss means of paving the way for the superintendence of the Church in the new republic.

During the second meeting, on November 6 of the same year, a committee was chosen to draw up a petition asking the Pontiff for the nomination of Father Lewis as Superior of the Church of America, with certain privileges of a bishop but without necessarily his title. The authors revealed in this petition an all too modest version of the future reserved for their young country. It is not surprising that when the rest of the clergy were told of the petition's form and content, it was held that the tone was not respectful enough. In consequence a second commission was chosen, headed by Father Carroll, to draft another petition, in which it was asked *ex novo* that the clergy be allowed to elect its own Superior. The Holy See investigated, and on June 6, 1784, Father Carroll was elected Superior of the Missions of the 13 States of America, with the authorization to administer Confirmation.

Again at Whitemarsh, on October 11, 1784, the Constitution of the Catholic Church of America was formulated by the new Superior and several other priests.

On February 27 of the following year, Father Carroll accepted the office of Prefect Apostolic, the official document for which had arrived in November the preceding November 26.

In another meeting in March, 1788, the American clergy — in a respectful petition signed by Msgr. Carroll and Fathers Robert Molyneaux and John Ashton — indicated to the Holy See that a Bishop, with full authority and jurisdiction, was more urgently needed in America than a Prefect Apostolic. The Vatican's reply was that the United States clergy would be permitted, as an exception (*pro prima hac vice tantum*), to choose its own candidate as bishop as well as the city where the episcopal see would be established.

In 1789 the 24 priests of Maryland and Pennsylvania met at Whitemarsh in solemn conclave, and this time, without a dissenting vote, Msgr. Carroll was nominated as their Pastor and Bishop. Their procedure was sent to Rome, and on November 6, 1789, Pius VI's Bull, *Ad Futuram,* named Msgr. Carroll first Bishop of the United States, with his see at Baltimore. Hence he is today honored with the fine title of « Father of the American Catholic Hierarchy ». His consecration took place in Lulworth Castle in Dorset, England, on August 15, 1790, presided over by the Benedictine Charles Walmesley, titular Bishop of Ramatha and Vicar Apostolic of the Western District, assisted by two Jesuits, Father Charles Plowden and Father James Porter (⁹).

The Rev. Father Plowden, at the impressive ceremony, delivered an address in which he sounded a mystic-patriotic note. In it, as Shea has pointed out, he underlined the significant fact that the dismemberment of Great Britain, in giving life to the new empire of the Western world, illuminated the action of divine Providence because « its first and precious fruit was the extension of the Reign of Christ and the diffusion of the Catholic religion which, till then hindered by restrictive laws, was now released from its bonds and left at liberty to exert the full energy of divine truth ».

The episcopal seal adopted by Msgr. Carroll shows, to fine effect, the bishop's hat, crossed keys of St. Peter and in the center the star-crowned Virgin carrying the Divine Son. Inside the inscription reads : « 1790 : *Joannes Epis. Baltimorensis* ». Around the seal in the wide margin another inscription of Biblical derivation is an invocation of humility and faith : « *Ne. derelinquas. nos. Deus. noster.* ». Bishop Carroll's first act, shortly after he took over his See in December, 1790, was to order that the Litanies of Loreto in honor of the Virgin be regularly recited in the churches under his jurisdiction before the celebration of the Mass.

Historians have pointed out that in the same year,

1789, that Carroll was named first Bishop, Washington was elected first President of the United States. The first initiated the hierarchy of the Catholic Church that meant the dawn of a new era for the Catholic religious life of the country; the second initiated the organization of the government of the state. Thus « in their formal organization, both Catholic Church and America proceeded along parallel lines » ([10]).

The passage of time has only emphasized the importance of this birth of a hierarchy. The Popes themselves have had many occasions to recall it. On the first centenary, the great Leo XIII paid tribute to it in his Letter, *Longinqua Oceani,* and in 1939 — at a distance of a century and a half — the no less great Pius XII declared in his Encyclical, *Sertum Laetitiae* : «In desiring to render more radiant a garland of holy joy, we cross in thought the boundless vastness of the sea and we are with you in spirit, together with all your faithful, in celebrating the happy completion of a century and a half since the constitution of the ecclesiastical hierarchy of the United States ».

From the day of Msgr. Carroll's consecration, the rise of Catholicism in the United States has continued uninterruptedly, in spite of difficulties, and has kept pace with the nation's material prosperity. Between the constituted hierarchy and the corresponding rhythm of this material advance there seems to be a correlation almost like that of cause and effect. To many indeed this seems providential.

V — The personality of the newly elected Bishop has always seemed in the religious sphere akin to that of his cousin Charles Carroll of Carrollton in the political sphere — a personality of absolute preeminence.

The Papal Bull nominating Carroll as Bishop contained an injunction for the opening of a college and seminary. Nothing was closer to the Bishop's heart. After conferring with Msgr. Dugnani, Papal Nuncio to Paris, he entered into negotiations with Father Emery, ninth Superior General of St. Sulpice in Paris, as a result of which Father Emery and his Sulpicians decided to found a seminary in Baltimore at their own expense. The project came closer to realization upon the arrival in America, aboard the ship St. Pierre, of Father Nagot, director of the Bourges seminary, and Tessier, former professor of the Viviers seminary, together with five seminarians in theological studies — the first nucleus of professors and students.

Indeed we find the Sulpicians at the base of the American hierarchy. Msgr. Flaget and Msgr. David became the first and second Bishops of Louisville and Msgr. Chabrat, Bishop Coadjutor; Msgr. Dubourg, in Louisiana and Florida; Msgr. Maréchal and Msgr. Eccleston, respectively third and fifth Archbishops of Baltimore; Msgr. Dubois, first actual Bishop of New York; Msgr. Bruté, first Bishop of Vincennes; and Msgr. Verot, first Bishop of St. Augustine [11].

In July, 1791, they acquired the so-called « Inn of the First Mile », with four adjacent acres of land, and on the 18th of that month the Seminary of St. Mary — first seminary in the United States. On May 25, 1793, the new Bishop ordained his first priest, the French-born Stephen T. Badin (1768-1853), and on March 24, 1800, his first priest of American birth, William Matthew [12]. On his death, Archbishop Carroll left a hundred priests in his diocese alone.

In the beginning the Church in America was extremely poor its only source of income being voluntary contributions of the faithful, subsidies that came irregularly from the Propaganda in Rome and money acquired from some fund-raising expeditions to South America.

Shortly after his return to America, Msgr. Carroll, in his first address to the people and the clergy, hailed the forthcoming institution as a seminary « in which to rear ministers for the Sanctuary and to serve religion in such a way that we shall no longer be dependent on foreign and uncertain coadjutors ». This ideal was never lost sight of : in the first hundred years of its existence, one Cardinal, 30 Bishops and 1,400 priests passed through the halls of the seminary.

As with all works destined for future greatness, the first years after the institution of the hierarchy, were not without difficulty. There were moments of uncertainty as to the advisability of having such brilliant instructors from France. Msgr. Carroll repeatedly praised the Sulpicians and wrote to their Superior General in Paris : « As I have told you on other occasions, I have nowhere found men worthier than your priests for character, talent and virtue, or better adapted to instruct our priests. One of the gravest misfortunes that could befall this diocese would be to have to lose these gentlemen of the seminary ».

Gosselin, in his life of Emery, the Sulpician superior, relates that in 1804, when Pope Pius VII was in Paris to take part in the coronation of Napoleon, Emery spoke to him of recalling his Sulpicians from America — there were more than 12 of them — to bring new life to the seminaries of France, which would mean the closing of the Baltimore institute. The Pope's reply was : « My son, let them be. Let the seminary continue, for in its time it will bear rich fruit. To recall your directors, to put them into other seminaries would be equivalent to robbing Peter to pay Paul ». The high-minded Emery understood, obeyed and in time did observe the marvelous fruits which, as we have seen, were not long in coming ([13]).

Indeed, the Sulpicians educated the flower of the

American priesthood. The first rector of Catholic University, Msgr. Keane, was brought up by them, as was the great Cardinal Gibbons. One of their illustrious rectors, Alphonse Magnien (1878-1902), instituted the College of St. Augustine, near Catholic University in Washington, in order to carry on the Sulpicians' work ([14]).

In 1791 Msgr. Carroll founded the famous College of Georgetown, « the oldest Catholic cultural institution in the United States, which in 1805 passed to the Jesuits, who had been restored by the Bull, *Catholicae Fidei*, of 1801 ([15]). On March 1, 1815, the college, under the administration of Father John Grassi, was authorized by Congress to confer diplomas. In time it prospered so well that it achieved the status of a university, and today, as Catholic University of Washington, it counts an academic body of 400 instructors and about 3,000 students.

Georgetown was a long cherished dream of this noble Bishop who had himself been educated in the Jesuit colleges of France and Belgium. On March 12, 1807, the Jesuit, Leonard Neale, Bishop Coadjutor of Baltimore and then President of Georgetown, ordained the first four priests of the reborn Company of Jesus. And in recognition of Carroll's efforts on behalf of Georgetown, the Company named John Carroll University in Cleveland, Ohio, after him.

What St. Mary's Seminary is for the clergy, Catholic University is for young Catholics destined for civilian careers. Two other institutions, both in Msgr. Carroll's state of Maryland, must be mentioned — the College and Seminary of St. Joseph, founded in 1809, and the « Little Seminary » at Ellicott City, dedicated to St. Charles and in great part erected through the generosity of Charles Carroll of Carrollton, which serves as a preparatory school for the larger seminary ([16]).

VI — Only 15 months after his consecration as Bishop, Msgr. Carroll convoked (on November 17, 1791) the first diocesan Synod of Baltimore — the diocese at that time being practically equivalent to a national one — to which 22 priests of five nationalities came.

This *pusillus grex* was the first grain of seed for the future huge Catholic Church of America. This Synod elaborated the elements of ecclesiastical life and regulated the question of voluntary maintenance of the clergy by means of contributions from the faithful.

Evident everywhere was a growing fervor, the urgency of new projects, the spring-like budding-forth of a thousand initiatives. The parochial congregations, spread over wide areas, had like aims : some formed in New York, Boston and Charleston. There were a dozen missionary stations, founded by the Jesuits, in Maryland, four in Pennsylvania, three at Vincennes (thanks to the apostolate of Father Gibault), one in Delaware.

From this fragmentary panorama, the lynx-eyed Church, anticipating the times ahead with bold strategy, selected the four points most appropriate for the extension of the Catholic hierarchy in America. On April 8, 1808, Pius VII fixed it along these lines : the see of Baltimore was hierarchically constituted the Metropolitan See and as a consequence Bishop Carroll was elevated to the rank of Archbishop; and four Suffragan Sees were created at Boston, New York, Philadelphia and Louisville. The Bishops destined for these Sees were Msgr. Cheverus (Boston), Msgr. Dubois (New York), Msgr. Egan (Philadelphia) and Msgr. Flaget (Louisville) ([17]). (Note the French element in this roll of honor).

Then came the need for erecting his own Cathedral. Having acquired the land at the cost of $20,000 and approved the designs by Latrobe, architect of the Capitol at Washington, Msgr. Carroll blessed the first stone on July 7, 1806. In 1810, the energetic Archbishop convoked the Congress of the Hierarchy, and on August 18, 1811, His Grace received the honor of the sacred Pallium. On December 3, 1815, weighted with years, honors and glory, the Archbishop died in Baltimore. His mortal remains were temporarily placed in the chapel of his beloved Seminary of St. Mary, where they remained till 1824, when the crypt for his monumental tomb, under the high altar of the Cathedral, received them.

Here the spiritual leader of America's Catholicism lies in the majesty of death, but « his spirit marches on » in the Bishops who in uninterrupted succession continue the exercise of his power as magistrate, minister and governor.

History's judgment of the work and pastoral success of this outstanding personality has been unanimously positive and favorable. His first biographer, Brent, has emphasized the noble patriotism which, no less than religious zeal, animated him : « He was a patriot, and he loved his native country, and Americans must never forget that his acts and his blessings, as man and as Christian prelate, were directed to their nation's interest and independence ». Spalding praises his administrative gifts : « This saintly man pursued a glorious career; he was endowed with wisdom and prudence which all held worthy of love and high esteem. « Shea, another biographer, evaluates the firmness of his statesmanship : « With his life of wide experience, in the midst of civil and religious vicissitudes, in the tempests of which his faith in the Church's mission never wavered, a notable period ended in the history of the Church of the United States ».

Finally, Bishop O'Gorman, the historian of American Catholicism, affirms : « He appeared on the scene when the sky was darkest for the Church; he left it when the light shone upon it more fully and more warmly because of his positive actions » ([18]).

VII — The venerated patriarch brings us to the mention of the Assizes, or Provincial Councils — later Plenary Councils — in which the hierarchy found its own voice. All these Councils assembled in Baltimore and were not unlike the German Catholic gatherings in Fulda, at the tomb of St. Boniface.

The first seven Provincial Councils — at least in substance they could not be considered Plenary — took place between 1829 and 1849. Eventually, as the number of dioceses and ecclesiastical provinces grew, the first Plenary Council was called in 1852, with the authorization of the Holy See. Present were six Archbishops, 32 Suffragan Bishops, two Bishops of other jurisdiction (of Monterey and Toronto), a mitred Abbot and eight Superiors of religious orders. In a half century the Church had made gigantic strides forward.

The second Plenary Council, presided over by Archbishop Spalding of Baltimore, took place October 7-21, 1866, and its final solemn session was honored by the President of the United States himself, Andrew Johnson. The third ([19]), which incorporated the present-day canon law of the American Church, based on the Canonical Codex, met between November 9 and December 7, 1884. Its President and Delegate Apostolic was Archbishop Gibbons of Baltimore. Its decrees were subscribed to by 14 Archbishops, 61 Bishops or their representatives, six mitred Abbots. These three councils have been likened to the great Councils of the Church of Africa.

In 1869-70 the American hierarchy participated for the first time at the Ecumenical Council at the Vatican.

VIII — One of the later developments in the American hierarchy occurred on March 15, 1875, when Pius IX created the first American cardinal in the venerated person of John McCloskey, then Archbishop of New York.

Since then, the roman purple has been conferred on ten other American Church dignitaries. Eight of these were American-born; the other two, of Irish origin (J. M. Farley and J. J. Glennon) acquired American citizenship. This is the honor roll of names: James Gibbons of Baltimore (1886), J. M. Farley of New York (1911), William H. O'Connell of Boston (1911), D. J. Dougherty of Philadelphia (1921), G. William Mundelein of Chicago (1924), P. J. Hayes of New York (1924), John Glennon of St. Louis, Edward Mooney of Detroit, Samuel Stritch of Chicago and Francis Spellman of New York. The last four were elevated to the purple by Pius XII in the Secret Consistory of February 8, 1946, after the second World War [20].

On January 8, 1893, Pope Leo XIII founded in Washington the Apostolic Delegation, then dependent upon the sacred Congregation of Propaganda [21]. The first dignitary elected by the Pope as representative of the Holy See to the Delegation — which was strictly ecclesiastical and not diplomatic — was Francesco Cardinal Satolli (1893-96). In some parts of the Protestant world this nomination was received with distaste. Catholicism was parodied as « Satollicism », and others called him « an American Viceroy sent to Washington by the Vatican ». But the mission had its precedents in former times, although informal or semi-official, in such emissaries sent to America as Bishop Plessis of Quebec (1763-1822); Comte de Fourbin-Janson (1785-1844), Bishop of Nancy and Toul; Cardinal Bedini (1806-64) and Canon Salzbacher — all proving the basic need for it [22].

Indeed, the idea of sending Cardinal Bedini to establish a permanent Nunciature in Washington had been aired some four decades before, as is proved by the Brief of July 12, 1854, now in the archives of the Propaganda in Rome. But the increasing incidents aggravated at that time by the secret order of Know-Nothings proved it was then impractical.

In 1908, in view of developments, Pius X in his Constitution, *Sapienti Consilio* of June 29, removed the American dioceses from the authority of the Congregation of Propaganda and placed them under the common law of the Church, subject to the normal Congregations and Offices of the Holy See. In other words, the American Church entered its vigorous majority and ceased to be a « land of missions ».

IX — Three institutions are dependent upon the American Episcopacy — Catholic University in Washington, the Mission to the Indians and Negroes of the United States and the North American College in Rome. Besides these, under the high direction of a committee of American Bishops, there is an American seminary at the Catholic University at Louvain, founded in 1875 by Bishop Spalding of Louisville with the approval of the Cardinal of Malines and under the patronage of the Bishops of Belgium.

One of the cradles in which the finest flower of American priesthood has been educated is the North American College, in the very shadow of the Basilica of the First Apostle, solemnly consecrated on December 8, 1859, by Msgr. Bedini. The first 13 students at the time had as their rector the Benedictine P. B. Smith. Its full title is : « American College of the Roman Church of the United States at Rome ». It was a project close to the heart of Pope Pius IX, together with two American Archbishops, Hughes of New York and Kenrick of Baltimore, who hoped to preserve and extend the Roman traditions and strengthen the bonds between the See of Peter and the American Church.

Already in 1854, when a large group of American Bishops were in Rome for the proclamation of the Dogma of the Immaculate Conception, Pius IX had been told of the Americans' keen desire to have in Rome a seminary like those of other nations. The Provincial Councils studied the practical execution of the project, which resulted in a collaboration of Pius IX and the Committee of American Bishops. Accordingly, in 1857, the Pope acquired in Via dell'Umiltà, in Rome, the former monastery of the Sisters of the Visitation, then occupied by soldiers of the French garrison stationed in Rome. The cost was $52,000, and the building was put at the perpetual disposal of the American Church, with a proviso that the latter assume the obligation of repairing it and financing it.

Indications of the good feelings of the Popes toward the College are not lacking. For instance, when John P. Stockton was American minister to the Papal States (1858-61), Pius IX once visited the College and it is said the occasion marked the first time the Pope had dined in public in 50 years. On that day the Pope told the American minister he was happy to meet him « in America ». On October 25, 1844, Leo XIII, in his Letter, *Ubi Primum,* awarded it the name of « Pontifical College ».

Immediately afterward, the College underwent its trial by fire, from the disputes lasting over a decade with the Italian government, which between 1866 and 1867 tried to confiscate a mass of Italian and foreign ecclesiastical property. Weary of vain warfare with the forces of

Masonic anticlericalism, Cardinal McCloskey and Archbishop Corrigan had recourse in 1884 directly to the President of the United States, Chester A. Arthur, denouncing the ruling that appropriated what was virtually American property.

The Secretary of State was thereupon instructed to tell the American minister in Rome to inform the Italian government that the confiscation would injure interests that were almost entirely American. The upshot of the matter was that the College was saved and freed from any further threat of confiscation. Shortly afterwards, its rector, Msgr. William O'Connoll, acquired for $20,000 the Villa Santa Caterina at Castel Gandolfo as a summer residence for the seminarians. In 1903, another rector, Msgr. Kennedy, enlarged the neighboring property of the College, at the cost of $50,000 more.

Statistically, in its first 70 years of existence, 2,100 priests emerged from the College, to be dispersed among all the States of the Union and in the great majority of its dioceses. In the Audience of June 5, 1934, on the occasion of the 75th anniversary of the institution, which Pius XI accorded its alumni and students, there were at this gathering so many high churchmen — two Cardinals, four Archbishops and 25 Bishops — that the number seemed sufficient to give an idea of the value of a tree that produced such fruit.

In 1862, the convert Manning, speaking in Italian to the Academy of Quirites, said : « We are not strangers to Rome. We are here in the house of Our Father, in this place where the peoples forget their boundaries and their rivalries, to remember that their unity is the Kingdom of God ». This noble thought of indestructible Catholic unity is what presided and still presides over the North American College of the *Urbs Sacra*.

X — October 14, 1953 marked a glorious date in the history of the Pontifical North American College : the Sovereign Pontiff Pius XII blessed the new College building on the Janiculum Hill.

The colossal edifice, the crowning of so many years of expectation and of so many sacrifices made by the Bishops and the faithful of the United States, rises in the vast zone of the ex-villa Gabrielli very close to the Urban College of Propaganda Fide. The new building has accommodations for 311 *alumni* each with his own room.

Several hundred distinguished guests gathered in the large chapel to assist at the blessing and the inauguration ceremonies. Fifteen Cardinals were seated on the right side of the sanctuary facing the papal throne. Among them were three distinguished *alumni* of the College : their Eminences, Edward Cardinal Mooney, Archbishop of Detroit, Samuel Cardinal Strich, Archbishop of Chicago, and Francis Cardinal Spellman, Archbishop of New York. Also present were the Cuban Cardinal Arteaga y Betancourt, Archbishop of Havana, and their Eminences Giuseppe Cardinal Pizzardo, Cardinal Protector of the College, Clement Cardinal Micara, Cardinal Vicar of Rome, Eugenio Card. Tisserant, Benedetto Card. Aloisi Masella, Adeodato Giovanni Card. Piazza, Pietro Card. Fumasoni Biondi, Celso Card. Costantini, Valerio Card. Valeri, Francesco Card. Borgonini Duca, Nicola Card. Canali and Alfredo Card. Ottaviani of the Roman Curia. Equally impressive was the vast number of American Archbishops and Bishops present.

Next to the Bishops were the Superior Generals of the various Religious Orders and Congregations.

Among the many representatives of the Religious Congregations and Institutions for women were the Mother Generals and Assistants of those Congregations having houses in the United States with Motherhouses in Rome.

Special places were provided for them in the sisters' choir.

The American Ambassador to Italy, Mrs. Clare Boothe Luce, was given a place of honor on the right side of the chapel near the Diplomatic Corps accredited to the Holy See, representing more than 40 different nations.

Among those present also were the Pro-Secretaries of State of the Holy See, Msgr. Tardini and Montini, the Substitutes Msgr. Grasso and dell'Acqua, the Secretary for extraordinary ecclesiastical Affairs, Msgr. Samoré and other Prelates of the Secretariate of State.

Among the personalities Prince Carlo Pacelli, Count Enrico Pietro Galeazzi, Architect of the Sacred Apostolic Palaces and of the College, the Hon. Giulio Andreotti, representing the Italian republic. The Holy Father who left Castelgandolfo by car at 9:35 arrived at 10:15. His Holiness was met at the door of the College by the Rector, H. E. the Most Rev. Martin J. O'Connor and the members of the Pontifical Anticamera.

After a few words of greeting in the Reception-Room, the Holy Father, wearing the familiar white cassock and ermine trimmed mozzetta was accompanied to the Chapel by Bishop O'Connor. He was escorted by the Noble Guard and preceded by his private Chaplain, Msgr. Alberto Piermattei bearing the Processional Cross. As His Holiness entered, the Choir sang the « *Tu es Petrus* ». After a short prayer at the faldstool the Holy Father ascended his throne on the left side of the sanctuary and delivered his address.

Speaking in English about the new College, His Holiness gave unstinting praise to the Church in America, and fired the hearts of the Seminarians with glorious thoughts on the Priesthood of Christ.

«For several years», the Holy Father said of the College, « We have followed with keen interest the preparations and the construction of your new seminary. Our Venerable Brother, the Rector, devoted, courageous, vigilant of every detail, kept us informed of its progress, until with our own eyes we saw it, reflecting the morning sun, like a city seated on a mountain. Its completion lights a stronger flame of hope for the Church in the United States of America and in the world. We belong to the Church militant; and she is militant because on earth the powers of darkness are never restless to encompass her distruction. Not only in the far-off centuries of the early Church, but down through the ages and in this our day, the enemies of God and Christian civilization make bold to attack the Creator's supreme dominion and sacrosanct human rights. No rank of the clergy is spared; and the faithful — their number is legion — inspired by the valiant endurance of their shepherds and fathers in Christ, stand firm, ready to suffer and die, as the martyrs of old, for the one true Faith taught by Jesus Christ. Into that militia you seek to be admitted as leaders. Imprisonment and martyrdom, we know, do not loom on the horizon that spreads before your eyes. In an atmosphere of untrammeled freedom, where the word of God is not bound », the Church in your country has grown in numbers, in influence, in strength of leadership, in all that makes for the good of the Commonwealth. The College on the Via dell'Umiltà has seen your priests increase from twenty five hundred to forty five thousand and more proud and glorious tribute to the unselfish, clear-visioned Catholic family life that prevails among you; a mission country become a seminary of Apostles for foreign fields. But the Church militant is one body, with one Spirit... with the same Lord, the same faith, the same baptism... (Eph. 4, 4). And that Spirit calls for more than a dash of heroism in every priest who would be worthy of the name, whatever the external circumstances of time and place. The spirit of the martyrs breathes in every priestly soul, who in the daily round of pastoral duties and in his cheerful, unrelenting efforts to increase in wisdom and in grace, gives witness to the Prince of Shepherds, who endured the cross, despised the shame " when he gave himself up on our behalf, a sacrifice breathing out fragrance as He offered it to God " (Eph. 5, 2).

We raise a fervent prayer to Mary Immaculate, under whose patronage you have placed your country, to Mary gloriously assumed into heaven, whom you have wished to honour in your chapel here, that She would always show a mother's loving care of the clergy of America, and guide you, beloved seminarians, bearers of such high hopes, along the way that leads to that holiness which will bring Her to recognize in you a greater and greater resemblance to her own divine Son.

And thus, venerable Bothers of America, this seminary will be your pride and your delight. All the dioceses of your country will, we hope, receive of its apostolic power. For generations to come it will stand as a monument to your love of Rome and devotion to the See of Peter, and your successors, and their successors will take inspiration from your enlightened and admirable pastoral zeal to carry the Church in your loved country on to yet greater conquests of souls for God's eternal Kingdom ».

After his address, His Holiness vested with the familiar ceremonial Stole. He intoned the *Veni Creator* and then sang the versicle and oration to the Holy Spirit. The Holy Father, with the Papal masters of ceremonies, blessed the chapel with holy water, then went in procession and blessed the main corridors. He returned to the chapel and sang the prayers to Christ the King, the Eternal High Priest, then invoked the intercession of the Blessed Virgin Mary, the Queen of Apostles, and S. Thomas Aquinas, the Patron of Schools.

247

From this new powerhouse of faith, of study and of prayer many new and fresh energies of sacerdotal ministry will irradiate in the future in North America.

XI — Msgr. Carroll did not like the appointment of Bishops imposed by foreign powers, such as happened, for instance, with the selection of the first two dignitaries of New York — the Irish Dominicans, R. L. Concanen (April 8, 1808) and John Connolly (October 4, 1814). Carroll wrote : « We would rather die than renounce the authority of the Supreme Pontiff. Yet it is necessary that we destroy in our countrymen's spirit this unjust prejudice that our church leaders are hostile to the Constitution by placing us under the authority of foreign governments ».

Archbishop Ambrose Maréchal, on his part, saw another foreign priest named as first Bishop of Richmond — Patrick Kelly, president of an Irish college, who after only 18 months in America, left to take over a see in his native country.

Hence there was timely need for the Propaganda Decree of 1834, describing the procedure for the nomination of Bishops to vacant sees in the United States.

Every Bishop must hold in readiness — sealed and addressed to the Vicar General himself, to be opened after his death — a duplicate list with the names of three priests that he believes most fitted to succeed him. The Vicar General must in his turn submit one of these lists to the Archbishop of Baltimore and the other to the nearest Bishop, or to the senior of the nearest Bishops, to whom falls the task of communicating his own opinion to the Archbishop.

From Baltimore the Archbishop must transmit this list (in case he disapproves of it, he must draw up a second one with other names) to each one of the Bishops of the concerned ecclesiastical province, and these, then, must communicate their own opinions to the Congregation of the Propaganda. Such a preliminary procedure on the part of the Bishops is obviously only a recommendation and is not equivalent to an election, nomination or postulation. This wise system is in accord with the democratic spirit of the American Church, whose motto is : « Liberty of the Church of the United States under sole spiritual dependence of Rome ». The great founder of the American hierarchy, Msgr. Carroll, worked to attain this ideal, as did his successors, Msgrs. Maréchal and Whitfield.

Every year — on the part of the Provincial and General Councils and the Diocesan Synods presided over by them — the Archbishops hold an assembly, gathering in a given city, designated according to precedence, to discuss matters regarding Catholic University or religious, social and missionary problems, with relation to American life.

All this indicates the vigorous youth and dynamic capacity for apostolic expansion typical of the Church in America and is but a prelude to further expansions of the American hierarchy. The monuments left by the men of the hierarchy are books, churches, schools, cathedrals, seminaries and universities, missions for Indians and Negroes, hospitals and asylums for those ailing in body and spirit. And through them the nation has been enlarged and stabilized on unshakeable foundations, because their episcopal throne stands solidly on the « firm rock of the centuries » — Christ, the eternal founder of the Church and the « immortal Bishop and Pastor » of souls ([23]).

249

DIPLOMATIC RELATIONS BETWEEN THE HOLY SEE AND THE UNITED STATES OF AMERICA

CHAPTER VIII

The compact masses of Catholics who have recently immigrated into the United States from all parts of the world in ever-growing numbers, imbued with a deeply religious sensitivity are drawn as by magnetic attraction to the Holy See at St. Peter's as the Cathedral of their spiritual teachings and the unifying center of God's people.

Such is the sentiment that animates millions of North American Catholics. One must bear in mind the watchful solicitude which the Catholic Church in Rome extends to all nations of the globe with a ready, maternal tenderness. In 1909, a professor at the University of Wisconsin, Carl Russell Fish, after thorough research in the Vatican Archives into the regularization of the Roman Catholic system in the United States under « conditions of national independence », confessed his surprise at the Roman hierarchy's delicate understanding of the feelings, thoughts and psychology of his people from America's earliest times to her emergence as an autonomous nation.

Let us remember, in passing, the matter of Italo-Catholic-American relations which date back to the year 1757, when a ship from the Papal port of Civitavecchia, flying the Papal flag, dropped anchor in New York. Bound for San Domingo, she had been captured by two American pirate ships for the rich Papal booty aboard, and guided to the port of New York, from which she was never to return.

II — All eleven successive Popes from Pius VI (1775-1799) to the incumbent Pius XII, more or less maintained religious and commercial relations with the United States Government.

Earliest official relations date back to 1783 during the papacy of Pius VI, when the first negotiations, carried out in Paris, resulted in a cordial agreement between the Papal Ambassador Cardinal Doria Pamphily and Benjamin Franklin, United States Plenipotentiary to the French capital.

On June 6, 1784, the American Reverend John Carroll was named head of the Missions of the thirteen American States, having all the qualifications to execute such a task. On September 25th of the same year, Leonardo Cardinal Antonelli, Prefect of Propaganda dispatched a letter of thanks to the United States Congress for « sentiments of respect » expressed by that body towards His Holiness Pius VI. When Msgr. Carroll was appointed Bishop five years later, Congress declared that « America believes with her citizens, honors God and venerates Christian worship ». This declaration was the more significant since all questions involving Catholicism were held of purely Catholic concern; religious matters were deemed outside the jurisdiction of the national governing body.

The relations between the Holy See and the United States were brilliantly inaugurated. To Pope Pius VI goes the honor of having created the North American hierarchy during the time of his fierce European struggles against jurisdictionalists, Jansenists and Napoleonists. Msgr. Carroll figured as first Bishop (1789), with Leonard Neale (1779) as his successor and the city of Baltimore as principal See.

III — On December 15, 1784, diplomatic relations were strengthened when the Papal Ambassador to Paris announced to the American Commissioners that his Government had put two ports at the disposal of American ships : Civitavecchia on the Mediterranean and Ancona on the Adriatic. More than accepting this offer, the United States reciprocated by inviting the Papal States to open consulates in New York, Boston and New Orleans.

An American of Italian origin, John Baptist Sartori might well be considered the first titular consul. Although he was appointed to this post in 1797, he did not arrive in America until 1800, taking up residence in Trenton, New Jersey.

IV — Sartori, however, did not receive his Letters of Authority — documents which his heirs still possess — until December 16, 1828. In the meantime, we meet another who substituted for him some years before, as is shown in the Vatican Archives. This was the Cavalier Ferdinando Lucchesi dei Principi di Campo Franco, who had already acted as Consul General in Washington for the King of the Two Sicilies. The Secretary of Propaganda and Secretary of State, Giulio Maria Cardinal della Somaglia, agreed in 1825 to establish a Consulate in Washington and on March 10, 1826, Cardinal Lucchesi was named Consul General. Apart from his commercial duties, the new Consul General was charged with seeking to develop our « spiritual and temporal relations with America ».

Lucchesi's term of office, however, was of brief duration; as Consul General for the Two Sicilies, in 1827 he was transferred by the Bourbon King to Brazil. A year later, on December 16, 1828, he was succeeded in his Washington post by G. B. Sartori, until then Papal Consul, but now the Pope's first Consul General in the United States.

V — Pius VII was deeply concerned with the destiny of North America's Catholics. In 1808, he enlarged the small American hierarchy and established four dioceses in New York, Philadelphia, Boston and Louisville. In 1820, dioceses were added in Charleston and Richmond and in Cincinnati a year later.

Credit is due him, furthermore, for reinstating the the Company of Jesus in the Anglo-Saxon countries (1813), including the United States, and for appointing 15 Bishops to the nascent North American Sees. Men of admirable moral fibre, these builders of God's mystical kingdom, and their very names are equivalent to a eulogy: Flaget, Bishop of Louisville; Cheverus, Bishop of Boston; Dubourg, Catholic leader in Louisiana and Florida; Maréchal, third Bishop of Baltimore; David, founder of the Nazareth Sisters of Charity; England, Bishop of Charleston and the Lazzarist Bishop Rosati, also of Louisville.

However brief the pontificates of Leo XII and Pius VIII and despite the obstacles put in their way by powerful anti-clerical forces of their day, nevertheless these two Holy Fathers left favorable impressions even in America by their wise choice of Bishops, among them the great Jesuit Fenwick, successor to Cheverus in Bosston; Michael Portier, who brought Catholicism to Alabama and Arkansas; Dubois, founder of the glorious seminary at Emmitsburg and third Bishop of New York; and the Lazzarist De Neckers, Bishop of New Orleans.

VI — Pope Gregory XVI (1831-46) demonstrated no less spiritual solicitude for the United States; a fervid champion of the Catholic missions, he was in return highly esteemed by the Americans. On April, 1946, on the occasion of the centennial anniversary of his passing, Pope Pius XII issued a message in which he declared that Gregory XVI « with almost prophetic intuition, foresaw the providential development of the Church in England and America ». In reply to a letter written him by Felice Cicognani, United States Consul in Rome, Secretary of State Martin Van Buren praised the Pope's favorable sentiments towards the United States (¹).

In Puritan Boston, a fine vessel christened the Sovereign Pontiff was launched in 1831, with the Christ of Gregory XVI, by the famous sculptor Beecher, handsomely decorating the prow.

Following Cicognani, first Consul of American birth to represent the United States in Rome (1837-47), came George W. Greene, nephew and biographer of the Quaker Nathaniel Greene, of Revolutionary War fame. Another successor was the more recent Edwin C. Cushman, descendant of Robert Cushman (1580-1625), one of the Pilgrim founders of Plymouth, who engaged the Mayflower for the Pilgrims' first voyage to America. We mention Cushing for the startling reason that he enlisted in the Papal Guards in Rome (²).

VII — For the remainder of the classic period, Pope Pius IX supervised relations between the United States and the Holy See with charity, spirit and an aristocratic sense of diplomacy.

From the very beginning of his papacy, generous

America felt for this lovable Pope the same throb of sympathy that rendered him popular even among the liberals of Italy. The American Margaret Fuller, married to the Marquis Orsoli, confided to the great writer Alessandro Manzoni that in policies of unity and independence, she leaned much more towards Pius IX than to Carlo Alberto (³).

Another eloquent testimony of American sympathy for the « Pope of the Risorgimento » was a document written by Lester C. Edwards (1815-90), American Consul General in Genoa from 1841 to 1849, after his private audience with the Pope on March 8, 1848. Let us give the word to the speaker, a brilliant diplomat and writer, who recounted the memorable event thus :

« At seven o'clock that night I went to the Quirinale where a Monseigneur conducted me to the audience chamber of the Pope and then withdrew. Pius was seated in front of a table on one side of the vast room, which was tapestried in purple velvet, with an exquisitely frescoed ceiling framed in gold. He was dressed in everyday clothes and wore a white skull-cap on his head. As soon as I entered, he rose from his chair. Half-way from the door, I knelt on one knee for a moment until he made a sign for me to advance. I approached closer and knelt again. He immediately held out his hand, which I kissed as I would have kissed the hand of a beloved, venerated father. He then took both my hands and told me to rise, addressing me with such kind expressions as only a Pope can find for one who so little merits them.

« " Holy Father ", I said, " Your Holiness knows that I am a Protestant; and do believe me when I say that I would not have submitted to this ceremony had it not come from my heart ".

« " Yes, my son, I know that ", the Pope replied. " Speak to me as you would to a friend you love, because

I feel like a father to you. Just as you acknowledge in my poor person the representative of the religion of our common Saviour, so do I acknowledge in you a faith equally honest and ideal ".

« " Your Holiness has had means of determining the sentiments of my compatriots towards you ", said Edwards. " They venerate your name because your generous, charitable works have shown you to be a sincere Christian, a just man and a friend of liberty ".

« " Yes, it does seem as if the Americans truly love us ", answered the Pope. " You are a great and free nation, and I hope that some day you will be united in the same flock under the same Shepherd. Your country is full of light, truth and liberty, and the warmest desire in my heart is to see every obstacle removed from the way of a final, glorious reunion, so that with the combined efforts and prayers of the two continents, we may emancipate and convert the world " » (⁴).

VIII — Despite the influence of exiled Italian patriots, New York amply demonstrated its cordiality towards the new Pope Pius IX. On November 23, 1847, the papers of the metropolis published this notice : « We, the undersigned, cordially invite our fellow citizens without distinction of party or religions, to gather in a public demonstration of sympathy with which the American people view the illuminated policies and liberal measures of Pope Pius IX and the Italian people's effort to win national independence and constitutional liberty. Monday at nine o'clock at the Broadway Tabernacle ». Seven hundred signatures of the city's most eminent citizens followed.

Several newspapers accompanied this announcement with comments on Pius IX and the liberal political reforms

he had instituted, which appeared to them phenomenal reflections of American ideals in the clearest Catholic mirror.
On the same date, November 23, the *New York Herald*
published an editorial which was truly symptomatic of
the new times. A Pope, it said who « had already astonished all Europe » with his advanced thoughts and measures, could not continue without diplomatic representation of « the greatest of all the free Christian nations ».

When the meeting began, the Broadway Tabernacle,
biggest public meeting hall in New York at the time, was
filled to overflowing. The city had never witnessed a
more imposing event. With Mayor William A. Brady
presiding, the gathering was honored by the presence of
two ex-Presidents of the United States, three Secretaries
of State, numerous Senators, diplomats and State
Governors.

No end of praises were heaped on the Pope. Among
other declarations, it was stated that « the emancipation
of Italy would be the signal for the liberation of all Europe
from slavery ». American policy then showed itself
extremely sensitive to popular opinion; only eight days
later, on December 7,1847, President James K. Polk, in
a special paragraph in his annual message to Congress,
announced his intention of initiating satisfactory diplomatic and commercial relations with the Papal States,
where the United States had been represented for the
previous forty years only by Consular agents : « The
interesting political events which are now developing in
those States », said the President, « render such measures
highly opportune ».

From the Legislature of Louisiana came a proposal
for closer relations between the United States and the
Vatican. An action of this sort could not fail to meet strong
opposition; nevertheless, in spite of the objections raised
against the proposal calling for American diplomatic rep-

resentation in Rome — a move which, in fact, had been advocated ever since Jefferson's mission to Paris — the Democratic Party supported it and the measure was brought before Congress, where it won an overwhelming victory with 137 affirmative and 15 negative votes in the House and 36 affirmative against seven negative in the Senate.

IX — After ratification, on April 1, 1848, Jacob L. Martin, a North Carolinian, was named first Chargé d'Affaires to the Papal States. Martin remained at his post until August 26th of the same year ([5]).

Noteworthy is his report to Secretary of State James Buchanan of his first audience with Pope Pius IX, which he described as highly cordial. « The goodness of his character and the gentleness of his countenance are proverbial », he wrote. The Pope assured him of « his great pleasure in entering diplomatic relations with a country which he holds in such high esteem », and listened with satisfaction to Martin's account of the progress made by the Church in America, remarking that he held a favorable opinion of the character of its clergymen.

X — Martin's appointment was evidently only temporary while awaiting the first of the five Ministers who were to represent the United States at the Court of Pope Pius IX. He was in fact replaced by Major Lewis Cass, Jr., who took over on January 6, 1849 and remained until November 27, 1858. Since a Congressional Act in 1853 raised this diplomatic post in Rome to the rank of Minister, in view of his promotion Cass may be considered the first Minister of the United States to the Papal States.

When Cass arrived in Rome, the Pope had taken refuge several months previously with Ferdinand, King of the Two Sicilies, at Gaeta, with the European diplomats following him. The presence of the American in Rome served to guarantee some measure of order. No less than elsewhere in Italy, Rome was then in the throes of a revolution, and, a witness to the excesses committed by the insurgents, Cass at first took a somewhat pessimistic view of the Italian people, whose mutual dislike drove him to express harsh and not, it would seem, unmerited opinions of them.

Nevertheless, gifted with a sense of realism that was alert to future commercial advantages — « I see in Italy a good market for tobacco, a product of universal use » — he persisted in his work. Only member of the diplomatic corps to remain in Rome and therefore of inestimable value, among his various duties he acted as trustee for the Pope. Thanks to him, the American flag continued to command respect during those difficult times of Garibaldi-Mazzinian revolutionary ferocity and the Stars and Stripes waved undisturbed over the Barberini, Altieri, Massimo and Falconieri Palaces, over Villa Pinciana and elsewhere. « The just and humane impartiality of the American representative in Rome at the time », it has been written, « defended whoever was threatened, no matter from what source these threats came ». Word was trumpeted abroad that Cass' sympathies lay with Garibaldi and Mazzini; nevertheless when the French troops entered Rome, it was to him that many compromised Romans turned for protection, which he gave them. Since he was a Protestant, his task was naturally difficult and delicate, nevertheless he performed it brilliantly (⁶).

American public opinion during the Pope's unhappy banishment to Gaeta showed profound sympathy for this august exile, nor did the plight of this spiritual sovereign, obliged to flee from his headquarters in the wake of violence, damage his moral prestige in the least. On the contrary, it confirmed a prediction made on June 12, 1848, by the newly converted journalist James. A. MacMaster in a letter to Brownson : « If (Pius IX) were ever to be imprisoned, it would detract no one whit from his moral power, indeed it would add to it ». Samuel Eccleston, Catholic Primate of North America and fifth Archbishop of Baltimore, deliberately invited Pius IX to cross the Atlantic so that he might preside over the Seventh Provincial Council of Baltimore.

From New York, his colleague, Msgr. J. J. Hughes, broadcast a warning : the liberty of the Holy See, he admonished, was no less necessary to the health of religion than to civilization. The journalist MacMaster echoed him by declaring that the Pope's fate was « tightly bound to the fate of the world ». Even the most devout Protestants rallied to the Pontiff and sent him a generous contribution, brought aboard an American ship that put in at Gaeta, not only to deliver the gift but also to pay him respectful homage.

The Americans did even more. The newspapers of the time, expressing themselves with somewhat crude frankness, invited the Pope to America. In December, 1848, the *New York Sun* declared that, once liberated from temporal power, the Pope «could find refuge in our happy Republic ». The authoritative *New York Herald* wrote on February 4, 1849, that the Pontiff « would be secure in the United States and no one would turn him out of his own home if he wanted one here, contrary to what his Catholic followers have done ». On January 12, 1849, the *Boston Evening Transcript* commented : « Let him come. We will convert him into a good Republican ! » Someone observed amusingly that it was the priests in Rome who effectively converted those good Republicans into excellent Catholics.

Lewis Cass' successor was John P. Stockton, who

acted as Minister from June 18, 1858, to June 5, 1861. In one of his first dispatches from Rome, this Princeton graduate and future Senator made some acute, farseeing observations on the Vatican : « The importance which the mission holds in the eyes of the European Catholic powers, the present political situation of the Continent and the relations between Propaganda and the Catholic Church in America and throughout the world, make Rome one of the most important observation posts abroad. Here the great powers are represented by plenipotentiary ministers, men of first rank in the countries that have sent them. It is said that the diplomatic corps in Rome is the largest and most distinguished in Europe. Probably more American families live here than in any other capital in Europe. It was a great mistake to classify this mission only in the light of its commercial aspects; a proper consideration of European politics, the dignity of our country, the greatest welfare and satisfaction of thousands of our citizens require that this mission be placed on a different footing ».

The third Minister was Alexander W. Randall, of Wisconsin, who served from August 6, 1861, until August 11, 1862, to be followed by Richard Milford Blatchford, of New York, until October 6, 1863. Fifth Minister was Rufus King, who remained at the post until the New Year of 1868 (⁷). As we will soon see, when Congress cancelled all funds for the support of the Vatican Legation as of June 30, 1867, King stayed on in Rome at his own expense until the end of that year, after which the Legation was abolished. On September 20, 1870, the United States was represented in Rome by D. M. Armstrong, first American Consul to the newly united Kingdom of Italy.

King's four-year residence coincided with stormy episodes in the history of Rome as, for example, when

Garibaldi threatened the city. On that occasion the American Minister was advised that « the presence of an American warship at Civitavecchia would be highly desirable since, if the Pope felt obliged to abandon Rome, he could find refuge in the United States ».

In reply, King declared that his country was a « land of civil and religious freedom, a refuge for all who wished to escape from the disturbances of a political or any other nature in the Old World », adding that « any time he thought it necessary to go to the United States, His Holiness would undoubtedly find a warm reception there and would be left completely free to carry out, without hindrances of any kind, his great work as head of the Catholic Church ». The American Secretary of State William H. Seward confirmed this wise pronouncement ([8]).

These were the five Ministers who represented the United States at the Court of Pius IX from 1849 to 1868 during the administrations of Presidents Polk, Taylor, Fillmore, Pierce, Buchanan, Lincoln and Andrew Johnson. In the fulfillment of their mission, they were immediately responsible to Secretaries of State James Buchanan, John M. Clayton, Daniel Webster, Edward Everett, William L. Marchy, Lewis Cass, Jeremiah S. Black and William H. Seward.

XI — What were the causes that led to the suppression of the American Legation to the Holy See in 1867 ?

First of all, let us assume that this action was not motivated either by religious conflict with the Catholics or by any lesser admiration of Pope Pius IX. In a country run on a two-party political system, the majority of the people decided this question after having been inspired or brought under pressure by reaction and by frictions arising from the internal political situation. That is all.

As it will be shown later in this book, the Catholic minority in North America has been compelled at times to take up a stout defense to preserve its very existence against the hostile Protestant majority, incited by powerful and eloquent non-Catholic adversaries and by continuous waves of immigrants who were bringing to the New World an anti-democratic education fermenting with all the rancid molds of Protestant North European anticlericalism. Thus, in January, 1867, when the House of Representatives debated the budget and administrative funds to be allotted for the ensuing year, the radical leader Hon. Theodore Stevens seconded a proposal submitted by Congressman Williams to remove Rome from the list of legation headquarters ([9]). On February 28, 1867, the House passed the amendment, and the motion calling for an allocation of funds to support the United States Legation to the Holy See was defeated ([10]).

The Senate did not vote this issue but only ratified the House amendment. Therefore, the law did not technically abolish the Legation but merely provided for a « diplomatic parenthesis » in the interests of a temporary financial economy.

It might also be added here that suppression of the American Legation to the Holy See by no means signified a definite breaking off of relations as understood in the diplomatic sense. Whenever an occasion has arisen, as during the Philippine and Second World Wars, the American Government has made use of the good offices of the Catholic hierarchy, often through special emissaries to the Church. Such an emissary was His Excellency Myron Taylor, whose function was that of a personal representative to the Holy See for both Franklin D. Roosevelt and Harry Truman. This underscores the urgent need of permanent official American representation to the Papal Court.

XII — During the time of Pius IX, the United States profited not only from the services of career diplomats but also from those of eminent North American Catholic Bishops appointed by the Pope to various posts in Catholic Europe, particularly to the Holy See. During the Civil War, President Lincoln sent Archbishop J. J. Hughes of New York to Europe as his personal representative, to enlist European support on behalf of the North, then fighting to purify the country of black slavery. To counterbalance this eminent Cardinal's mission, Jefferson Davis, President of the Southern Confederate States, dispatched Msgr. P. M. Lynch, Bishop of Charleston, S. C., to plead the South's cause before Pius IX in Rome.

A message sent to the Bishop by Judas P. Benjamin, Secretary of the Confederate States, is worth quoting : « Recent correspondence between the President and His Holiness Pius IX reveals the Holy Father's character, his strong desire for the restoration of peace on this Continent and his willingness to do everything possible, as head of the Catholic Church, towards achieving the desired results. The spontaneous act of His Holiness in addressing an exhortation towards this end to the two highest Church dignitaries of the North and South has evoked a powerful reaction from the President and the people of the Confederacy for such a surprising expression of Christian charity and benevolence. The President, therefore, has deemed it proper that, to express his people's cordiality towards the Sovereign Pontiff, a Commissioner should be sent to the Vatican Court to initiate political relations. He (President Davis) knows no one whose execution of such a task would be received by the Holy Father with greater satisfaction than yourself ». Then follow the instruction to the mission ([1]).

The foregoing examples indicate only a few of the

various diplomatic and spiritual relations between the United States and the Holy See during Pope Mastai's long and difficult pontificate; however briefly we have recounted them, they are sufficient to demonstrate that cordial understanding and deep appreciation of integrity and amicable loyalty which characterized a moral collaboration between two different goals, both of them admirable for the paths they followed and for the ideals that inspired them.

XIII — Pius IX loved this chosen land and in a succession of praiseworthy acts during his reign, revealed his profound affection for her and his dream of bringing America closer to Christ.

Among the acts he carried out, we recall particularly his appointment of Archbishop McCloskey of New York to the cardinalate (March 15, 1875) and the nomination of 46 other Bishops in the United States, among whom were the Msgrs. M. Demers, the two Spaldings, Timon, C. B. Lamy, I. F. Baraga, Wadhams, Corrigan and Ireland. The new dioceses established by Pius IX in North America resemble a firmament of stars : practically half the present number. In 1847, he founded dioceses in Albany, Buffalo, Cleveland and Galveston; in 1850, in Monterey, Savannah, St. Paul, Wheeling, Santa Fe and Seattle; in 1853, Burlington, Covington, Erie, Natchitoches, Brooklyn, Newark and Alton; in 1855, the diocese of Portland, Me.; in 1857, Sault Ste. Marie; in 1868, Columbus, Sacramento, Green Bay, Harrisburg, La Crosse, Rochester, Scranton, St. Joseph and Wilmington; in 1870, Springfied and St. Augustine; in 1872, Peoria and in 1877, Leavenworth, Kansas.

Moreover, he created new Apostolic Vicariates which have since been elevated to the status of dioceses : Nebraska (1851); Northern Michigan (1853); North Carolina, Idaho and Colorado (1868); Arizona (1869); Brownsville, Texas, and Northern Minnesota (1874).

A sublime spectacle! This venerable old Pope introduced so many areas of the New Continent to civilization and anointed them with the sacred oil of indelible dignity through religion and a holy hierarchy. Pope Mastai demonstrated another act of love towards America when he founded the North American College in Rome at his own expense, to prepare the flower of the clergy of the country so dear to him.

« If kings abandon the Pope, the people will still remain faithful to him », said Msgr. Dwenger one day in 1874 when he presented a group of American pilgrims to the Pope. In reply, His Holiness congratulated him on that « unlimited liberty », understood in the American tradition as religious liberty, that permitted a Bishop to speak such words to the head of the Church.

In another revealing incident, Pope Pius IX permitted himself this very human confidence to an American priest, Father Delay : « America today is the only country where I am truly considered a Pope in the eyes of the Government. In the nations of Europe, I have reason to fear that my acts are checked or rejected by the governments. But I can send any pontifical document whatsoever to America with complete freedom and without fear that the Government might oppose its publication » ([12]).

XIV — With Leo XIII's accession to the Papacy, relations between the United States and the Holy See became even stronger and more cordial. Pope Pecci looked on America with the deepest admiration, which was evoked in him by the vigor of that nation's erupting youthfulness and dynamic power. With his «solicitude for all Churches», **Leo XIII** followed America step by step in all her ascending stages. In 1884, he confirmed the decrees passed by the Third Plenary Council in Baltimore; in 1886, he promoted Cardinal Gibbons to the purple; in 1889, he approved the Knights of Labor union organization; in 1892, he founded the Apostolic Delegation in Washington and composed that monumental Encyclical, pronounced at the Chicago World's Fair, exalting the Catholic genius of Christopher Columbus on the fourth centenary of the discovery of America. Leo XIII furthermore participated in the Fair by sending a personal representative bearing precious curios. On January 6, 1895, the Pope addressed his other Encyclical memorandum *Longiqua Oceani Spatia* to the North American Catholic hierarchy; in 1898, as another proof of his spiritual solicitude for the American Church, he addressed a letter to Cardinal Gibbons, *Restem Benevolentiae,* taking Americanism as his theme; and in 1902, he sent another notable letter to the American hierarchy, which had participated at his Pontifical Jubilee. America loved him, non-Catholics no less than Catholics.

We recall particularly Cardinal Gibbons' eulogy of this Holy Father : « Pope Leo XIII is perhaps the most popular man in Europe today, if not in the world. The secret of his popularity is that he has understood the times; he has realized that we are living in the nineteenth century; he understands the needs of the people and sympathizes with their legitimate aspirations, like a brother and defender of the law. He has found the key to the heart of the people ».

From a more political quarter, we remember the congratulations sent by President Grover Cleveland, son of a Presbyterian minister, to the Pontiff on the event of his Jubilee; together with his good wishes, the President sent a copy of the United States Constitution, which celebrated its one hundredth anniversary on September 7, 1887. For this kind, respectful homage, Pope Pecci wrote the Cardinal of Baltimore : « We wish that Your Eminence would express to the President all our admiration for the Constitution of the United States, not only because it permits active, intelligent citizens to achieve such a high level of prosperity, but also because under its protection, Catholics have enjoyed a liberty that has undoubtedly spurred their extraordinary religious development in the past and that will permit them we believe to further America's political institutions in the future ». President Cleveland was so pleased with the Pope's letter that he requested the original copy of it.

XV — During his diplomatic relations with the United States, Pope Leo XIII undertook negotiations to settle the question of monastic property in the Philippines, a question which arose in consequence of the Treaty of Paris in 1898 when Spain ceded these possessions to the United States. The problem concerned · disposal of 405,000 acres of land, property of the glorious Spanish missions which had been cultivating faith and civilization in those islands ever since the sixteenth century.

In June, 1901, Cardinal Rampolla requested Archbishop Ireland, of St. Paul, to advise him on what suitable measures should be adopted to resolve this problem between the United States and the Vatican. A personal friend of Theodore Roosevelt, who was just then moving into the White House, Ireland urged the new President to send an envoy to the Vatican to settle the matter with the Church. Thus, on November 3, 1901, Secretary of War Elihu Root and Secretary of State John Hay named William H. Taft, future President and then Civil Governor of the Philippines. On June 5, 1902, Mr. Taft was granted a special audience with Leo XIII, during which he reminded the Pontiff of America's disposition to settle the matter amicably. The Pope then wisely put the delicate question into the hands of the Congregation for Extraordinary Ecclesiastical Affairs, which sent its recommendations to Mr. Taft after two weeks.

On this basis, a preliminary agreement was easily arrived at, and Msgr. G. B. Guidi was nominated Apostolic Delegate to the Philippines. There on December 22, 1903, the sum of $7,230,000 passed from the Governor to the Delegate for purchase of the land, and the question was closed. Taft's work brought the utmost satisfaction to both parties, and his mission to the Vatican occupies a place in itself in American diplomatic history. Several days before Taft left Rome, Leo XIII charged Msgr. O'Gorman to bring President Roosevelt « a token of my personal satisfaction — a mosaic made by the Vatican Laboratory portraying our Gardens » ([13]).

XVI — Pope Pius X, no less energetic than his predecessors, nominated 69 Bishops to the United States Church, among them the future Cardinals P. J. Hayes, of New York, and G. W. Mundelein, of Chicago, « first Cardinal of the West », and Archbishops J. Schrembs, of Cleveland, E. J. Hanna, of San Francisco, M. J. Curley, of Baltimore and Washington, « champion of Catholic education », and T. J. Shanan, Rector of the Catholic University of America.

On March 12, 1912, the Holy Father received Major Q. Butt, Field Adjutant to President Taft, who brought him the President's thanks for the promotion of three American Cardinals — Falconic, Farley and O'Connell — which occurred on November 27, 1911. This Pope won the hearts of the American Catholics above all for the fascination of his saintliness. In 1945, fourteen American dioceses promoted a prayer crusade for his beatification and declared October 14 « Pius X Day » ([14]).

XVII — No less cordial were the relations between Benedict XV (1914-22) and President Woodrow Wilson (1913-21).

Mr. Wilson pondered long and thoughtfully on this Pontiff's « Peace Note », absorbing it in letter and spirit. Wilson's words in which he referred to this revered Document, ought to be sculptured in gold on a new monument, erected by a grateful world to this humane Pope. « Every heart that has not been hardened by the terrors of the World War », the President said, « should be deeply touched by His Holiness' moving appeal; every heart should feel the dignity and strength of the human, generous motives that prompted such an appeal and should fervently desire that the road to peace which he so persuasively indicated may be taken ».

When President Wilson went to Europe to participate in the peace negotiations, Benedict XV wrote him to urge that the final peace terms should « not be a provocation for the vanquished ». It is a pity that cold political calculations should have triumphed over humane Christian reason; had the combined efforts of the President and the Vatican succeeded, the world would have enjoyed perpetual peace and the Second World War would have been avoided.

XVIII — Relations between Pope Pius XI and the United States were likewise very good. They were not even disturbed by the hostilities and religious prejudices let loose anew during the presidential campaign of 1928 when a Catholic, Alfred E. Smith, popular Governor of New York State, ran as candidate for the supreme office. Opponents argued that as a Catholic, he was subservient to the Pope, a « foreign power », and therefore could not be loyal to America. Because of such false propaganda, part of his electoral votes naturally went to his opponent, Republican Herbert C. Hoover.

In his message to the Eucharistic Congress, which took place in Omaha in 1930, the Pope declared : « I love the American people for their marvellous spirit of generosity and devotion. My prayers for them rise every day to the Father of all of us so that He may bless them and maintain them in His love ».

With his accession to the presidency in 1933, Franklin Delano Roosevelt inaugurated an era of closer, stronger ties with the Holy See. An American sociologist has observed that the principles which inspired President Roosevelt from the very beginning had been defined nearly a century before — on December 12, 1847, to be exact — by Msgr. J. J. Hughes, Bishop of New York, in his famous sermon *Christianity, Single Source of Moral, Social and Political Regeneration.* Indeed, the North American Episcopacy lost no time in proclaiming its support of the smiling, newly-elected President after he had delivered his historic message of July 24, 1933.

Pope Pius XI's Encyclical on Charity, in which the Pontiff analyzed the spiritual malady that tortures the world of today, was inserted in the official Senate Journal by unanimous approval of the Senate ([15]). The radio broadcast of his historic Encyclical *Quadragesimo Anno,* running to 20,000 words, established a record as the longest dispatch ever transmitted from Italy to the American newspapers. The transmission lasted seven and one-half hours and it was the first Encyclical wholly broadcast by radio to North America. Catholic leaders expressed their satisfaction when some of the proposals outlined in the Encyclical on behalf of the working classes were incorporated in the President's National Recovery Act. The Church subsequently declared it the duty of every Catholic to collaborate in the economic reconstruction plan proposed by the President.

Pope Pius XI dedicated a good many efforts to America, among them the appointment of 126 Bishops and the creation of these new dioceses : Monterey-Fresno, Pittsburgh and Raleigh (1924); Amarillo (1926); Reno (1931); San Diego (1936); Camden and Patterson (1937); Saginaw (1938); and Gallup (1939). His works rewarded him with considerable admiration and affection, particularly demonstrated on the occasion of his passing, when the two chambers of Congress went into official mourning and both President Roosevelt and Secretary of State Cordell Hull cabled their condolences to the Holy See ([16]).

XIX — When Pope Pius XII succeeded him, the United States, for the first time in its history, sent a special embassy to the coronation. The delegation was headed by His Excellency Kennedy, American Ambassador to London.

Pope Pacelli claims the distinction of being the only Pope to have visited both North and South America before assuming the papal triple crown. On a private, month-long trip in October, 1936, Cardinal Eugenio Pacelli, then Secretary of State to Pope Pius XI. visited the United States and met President Roosevelt. In the Sanctuary of the Immaculate in Washington, one can still see today a doubly sacred object : the altar at which the future Pius XII celebrated Mass.

Cardinal Pacelli brought back unforgettable impressions of the American nation : « The memory of everything we admired with our eyes will forever remain indelible and delightful in our heart », he wrote in his Encyclical of November 1, 1939. This voyage might well be described as an abundant sowing of precious seeds, soon destined by Providence to bear rich rewards. Traveling by plane, he covered about 10,000 miles from the Atlantic to the Pacific, visiting 12 of the country's 16 ecclesiastical provinces. The « flying Cardinal » saw everything, from humble mission churches to imposing Cathedrals, from schools, hospitals and asylums to the great Catholic universities, four of which conferred honorary degrees on him.

Senator Alexander Wiley, a Protestant, on the occasion of the birthday of His Holiness Pius XII, speaking in the Senate of the U. S., said : « President, today March 2nd, is the 79th birthday of His Holiness Pope Pius XII. It is therefore my pleasure and privilege to send my most sincere personal wishes and, I feel sure, those of my Colleagues of the Senate and of the House of Representatives, to this Great Spiritual Head. It is my hope and prayer that the Sovereign Pontiff may yet live for many years in full health in the service of humanity and I am sure that all righteous men whatever may be their race or religious belief, will unite with me. The long and painful illness of Pius XII from which he has not completely recovered, has been a cause of anxiety not only for all the millions of faithful of the Catholic Church, but for all those who have appreciated his noble and fatiguing efforts to preserve peace, liberty and spiritual life in the world. The historic appeals addressed by Him to the heads of every nation thereby to avoid the holocaust of a war, have moved all humanity. His Holiness Pope Pius XII is a Man both great and humble, weak and powerful; He is the Supreme voice of the Catholic Church, but his is a voice which speaks of the universal conceptions which are understood and appreciated by men and women of all beliefs. The Sovereign Pontiff is heir to a rich tradition of many centuries, but he is also exquisitely sensitive to the special needs of modern days.

I, as former President of the Senatorial Committee for Foreign Affairs and now as a Republican member of the Senate, am proud to express these words of profound and sincere homage to Pius XII. The numerous Americans who have had the opportunity of seeing Him and knowing Him during His stay in the U. S. twenty years ago, remember Him with the deepest admiration. The German people amongst whom he worked for twelve years remember Him with affection, as do the people of many other lands.

Eugenius Mary Joseph John Pacelli, born on March 2nd 1876, ordained Priest in the Basilica of St. Mary Major, April 2nd 1899, prelate in 1904, and after having been sent on many foreign missions, was named Secretary of State of Pope Pius XI, February 7th, 1930. During these long years of preparation He distinguished himself by the competence and zeal with which he fulfilled the important missions entrusted to Him, wherefore He was lastly elected Successor of St. Peter, Vicar of Jesus Christ. His Pontificate in an era particularly difficult for humanity, the impetuosity of the pitiless Communist conspiracy with its persecution against millions and millions of faithful, has given His Pontificate a significance which has never before been witnessed in the long history of the Catholic Church and of humanity.

A great number of anecdotes of the life of Pius XII might be mentioned, but I wish to mention just one, regarding the Russian dictator, Joseph Stalin. As a matter of fact the Russian dictator enquired during an international conference : « how many divisions has the Pope got? ». When this was referred to Pius XII, He said :

« they can answer my son Joseph that he will find my divisions in the other life ».

It may be that this unusual sentence in answer to the pitiless enemy brings to light the humility, compassion, comprehension and the faith of this spiritual Head; it may be that this sums up the fight of Christ against anti-Christ; in any case it expresses the conduct of this Servant of God Who does not fear the 175 Russian divisions, nor the atomic or the H-bomb, nor the power of the Communist Party in Italy and the world. This behaviour tells us of the esteem and confidence which the whole world professes for the Sovereign Pontiff representing real principle and the sole power, and Who is the Father of all men, be these Communists, Catholics, or of any other belief or party.

Therefore, now, by means of my speech, may the good wishes and the congratulations of the whole world reach His Holiness Pius XII. May Divine Providence grant Him many and many more years for the good of humanity ».

On November 5, 1936, two days before returning to Rome, the future Pontiff was invited to lunch at Roosevelt's Hyde Park home. The President had just then been re-elected with a vast majority over the Republican candidate Alfred Landon. A biographer of Pius XII was once asked : « Will it not be from that very seed that good fruit will grow — personal representation of the President to the Holy See ? ».

American historians may well take note of the future Pope's moving comment on the America he saw : « The youthful energy of this people is so strong and resistant that it can keep its history free of the many tragic pages that have filled the annals of other peoples in the past and present. It would be an illusion, however, to believe that this nation could long be spared the same tensions and the same struggles that have broken out in other parts of the world. Therefore, it is the noble duty of all American Catholics, together with their fellow citizens, to observe conscientiously the precepts of truth, of justice and brotherly love so that they may spare their country any possible danger of discord and social catastrophe. Happy is the people that, understanding harmony between the governing and the governed, can march along the royal road of justice, even at the cost of sacrifice and renunciation. The terrible firebrands that have laid waste other countries will not appear on her horizons. *Opus justitiae pax* ».

As early as October, 1932, Franklin Delano Roosevelt, then Democratic candidate for the presidency, quoted in one of his campaign speeches a passage from Pius XII's Encyclical *Quadragesimo Anno,* which he hailed as one of the greatest documents of modern times, written by « one of the greatest conservative forces in the world »; moreover, he emphasized the « radical » tendencies of the Pope's directives which, he declared, he hoped would serve him as inspiration.

President Roosevelt felt no less admiration for Pius XII's actions in seeking to maintain peace and later, in doing everything possible to prevent the spread of World War II and heal its bloody wounds.

XX — On December 23, 1939, President Roosevelt dispatched a message to Pius XII with the information that he was sending a representative to the Holy See with the rank of Ambassador, His Excellency Myron C. Taylor ([17]).

In this message, the President expressed himself thus : « Men know that the civilization handed down to us by our forefathers was built by men and women animated by the deep conviction that we are all brothers

279

because we are the children of God. Men believe that enmities can be cured by His holy will; that in His mercy, the weak can find freedom and the strong can find grace in helping the weak. In the distress and terror of the present times, it may be that these voices, as long as they are heard, will show us the way towards reconstruction of the world. It is well that, at this Christmas season, the world may reflect on this point ».

The next day, the news that Roosevelt was sending his personal representative to the Holy See added a resplendent light of hope to the Papal Christmas Allocution. « It is an announcement », said the Pope, « that could not have been more welcome because it signifies on the part of the eminent Leader of that great and powerful nation a valid, promising contribution to our efforts towards securing a just and lasting peace and towards providing war victims with relief from their sufferings on a vaster and more efficient scale ».

In his reply of January 7, 1940, the Holy Father said : « A characteristic note in Your Excellency's message has particularly touched us : your spiritual contact with the thoughts and feelings, hopes and aspirations of the common people, on whom rests the weight of pain and sacrifice in greater measure than has ever before been known. Perhaps no one can appreciate more than ourselves the significance, the strength and the moving warmth of Your Excellency's actions ».

A month later, on February 27, 1940, the Pontiff received in solemn audience the President's special envoy, according him all the honors due an Ambassador. His Excellency, Ambassador Taylor — an Episcopalian of Quaker origin — presented His Holiness a letter in which President Roosevelt reiterated his belief that the common ideal of religion and humanity could serve towards the re-establishment of a more lasting peace based on liberty, security and integrity of all nations under the protection of God.

Roosevelt's diplomatic initiative brought the youngest Republic once more in close contact with the oldest and most majestic spiritual dynasty on earth — a dynasty dating back to Virgil's « blond Tiber » and long outliving that of the Caesars. This contact again revealed a mutual understanding that was to bear fertile fruit. In his book *Moment of Decision,* Sumner Welles, Under-Secretary of State for a good part of the war, outlined projects for world reorganization after the war and affirmed that Pius XII, endowed with « great qualities of statesmanship », was one of the constructive forces that would work for the regeneration of mankind.

During the Second World War, public audiences were given almost daily by the Pontiff to troops of all nationalities, and audiences were frequently granted to groups of North American soldiers who did not want to leave the city of the Caesars without having paid homage to the Father of the faithful. In most cases, those groups admitted to these private audiences were only partly Catholic. Moreover, the paternal Pontiff often addressed special speeches in excellent English, revealing his anxiety to bring all into closer contact with God and with the pure sources of life illuminated by supernatural grace.

Within the brief space of a few months, vast numbers of American GIs enjoyed the privilege of sharing the sublime vision of Christ's Vicar who, with admirable effect, brought messages to men of different intellectual capacities, many of them not even of his flock, and blessed them with profound love, invoking heaven's benediction on those near and dear to them.

On July 8, 1945, Pius XII reminded the Americans that « in the last year, thousands of persons, indeed tens of thousands, have visited the Vatican's majestic halls. We meet them every day and speak with men of every age, of every social rank, of many nationalities. Behind these men we can picture in our mind's eye millions of other people throughout the world... ».

But is all this enough?

Certain symptoms which crop up from time to time lead one to assume that an unappeasable Protestant hostility stands ready to strike at Catholicism. In June, 1946, a group of members of the Federal Council of the Church of Christ in America, mouthpiece of about 30,000,000 American Protestants, induced President Harry S. Truman, a Baptist, to abolish Myron Taylor's mission which, they maintained, was unauthorized and unconstitutional. The special envoy to the Vatican was therefore recalled just when the peace treaty with Italy was being signed. In this gesture, Cardinal Spellman recognized the work of anti-Catholic « unhooded Klanism ». « Some object that such representation (to the Holy See) is contrary to the American principle of separation of Church and State », the Cardinal observed, and then pointed out that it is not very different, after all, from that of a North American ambassador to the Court of St. James where, ever since Queen Elizabeth, « the monarch is head of the Church as well as of the State... ».

THE ANTI-CATHOLIC CRUSADE :
ITS ORIGIN AND ITS LEADERS

CHAPTER IX

As we have seen, the American Constitution clearly guaranteed the most ample spiritual freedom in two basic articles. So firm and incontrovertible are these points that they inspired the apt remark of an American Archbishop, Ireland, to an Italian : « The Church in America is as free as the imperial eagle of your Alps ». President Theodore Roosevelt said, no less felicitously : « In our happy country, religion and liberty are natural allies ». More than a century before, De Tocqueville wrote in his classic work, *Democracy in America* : « Religion in America is a distinct sphere in which the priest is sovereign ».

II — Two cases, beginning with the first decades of the country's establishment, prove that the American government, far from oppressing the Church, protected it when its rights were in danger of being violated.

To cut short any confusion that might arise in a country of 300 Christian denominations, His Excellency Msgr. Carroll won in 1798 a most important legal case — the so-called Fromm case — in which Judge Addison, president of the Court of Appeals for the fifth district in Pennsylvania, delivered this sentence : « The Bishop of Baltimore exercises the sole episcopal authority over the Catholic Church in the United States. Every Catholic congregation in the United States is subject to his jurisdiction, and without authority received from him no Catholic priest may exercise any pastoral function whatsoever in any congregation of the United States ».

Another law of Carroll's time, of equally great import to the priesthood, dates from June 8, 1813. It reads : « Auricular confession, as a part of ecclesiastical discipline, protects the Catholic priest from being obliged to testify in court on facts or confidences received through the sacrament ».

This is the typical case that brought it about. Father Anthony Kohlmann, an Alsatian Jesuit ([1]), was unjustly named in the suit of one James Keating, who charged that the priest knew the identity of a thief who had restored stolen goods to him, having advised the thief to do so in the confessional. The Court of General Sessions, before which Father Kohlmann was ordered to appear, was composed of De Witt Clinton, then mayor of New York, and three other judges. The lawyer defending Father Kohlmann was Dr. William Sampson (1764-1836), an Irish Protestant and son of a Presbyterian minister who had come to America in 1798. His defense was so warm in its conviction and so strict in its logic that Clinton (although a Mason) and the others absolved the priest, deciding wholly in his favor that he had a right to keep a professional secret. In its just decision the court affirmed it could « neither approve nor authorize the application of insult to a Catholic's faith or torture to his conscience ». The principle was incorporated into the laws of the State of New York in December, 1828, and later other States followed suit ([2]).

Almost as though this solemn precedent were not enough, a similar juridical case came up in October, 1855, in Richmond, Va., which likewise led to permanent legislation. The Vicar General of that diocese, Msgr. John Teeling, after having heard the confession of a dying woman whose husband was later suspected of murdering her, was called to testify before the court in regard to what he knew of the case. Refusing to break the seal of confession, he was brought to trial. Once more the sanctity of the priestly cause was guaranteed and safeguarded by the sentence of a fair-minded judge, John A. Meredith, in the so-called « Teeling Law ». It says : « To abuse the confession, which is known to constitute a basic dogma of the Catholic Church, would be equivalent to disregarding the Bill of Rights. In view of the said circumstances, I can without hesitation declare that a priest enjoys privilege of exemption not to reveal what has been confided to him in the confessional ».

III — Yet we must not lose sight of another important aspect of the religious situation in America. Federal legislation aside, the individual States themselves reserve the right to regulate religious questions and the reciprocal relations between Church and State within the limits of their respective jurisdictions. That is why religious discriminations — humiliating inheritance from the past — were so slow in being withdrawn from the constitutions of the various States.

In 1783, by order of Congress, a collection of the constitutions of the 13 original States was printed. The purpose of this compilation was evidently to hasten their process of revision and adapt them to the altered climate of liberty and tolerance. Inscribed in the volume are several verses that are the personification of Liberty and proclaim her double aim :

« To cherish, in religion, Truth alone,
   Yet leave the faith of citizens their own » (³).

But not until 1806 did the State of New York repeal the clauses disqualifying Catholics for public office. Massachusetts abrogated similar clauses in 1821 and as late as 1833 broke off its union with the Congregationalist Church, finally lightening the burden of Catholic residents who had been obliged to pay taxes to maintain it.

Virginia repealed in 1830 its anti-Catholic laws and North Carolina did likewise in 1836. New Jersey maintained its anti-Catholic constitution in full force until 1844. As for New Hampshire, more backward than any other State, it finally eliminated from its constitution the article denying Catholics State employment in 1877, 88 years after the First Amendment.

One must keep in mind this subtle distinction between Federal and State attitudes toward religion in America, because it is precisely to that and to the residue of surviving anti-clericalism that we owe certain unexpected anti-Catholic movements now to be studied here.

IV — The critical years for the Catholic Church in the United States were those between 1820 and 1860. After this period, whether because of the growing political as well as numerical strength of the Catholics or because of the maturing of the nation as a whole, the furious crusade against Catholics gradually subsided, except for occasional incidents of a transitory and more or less localized nature.

Yet in this 40-year period the anti-Catholic struggle had visible repercussions — not only religious ones but political and cultural ones. Historians have severely condemned it. K. S. Wilson dubbed it « the anti-Catholic madness »; Maury calls it « the war of the impious »; Condon, « the revival of religious intolerance ».

And what were its determining causes? Jealousy of Catholic strength, fear of the increasing Catholic emigration and the consequent spread of papal interference in America — in a word, « the shadow of the Pope », as Williams has characterized that baseless dread.

V — The essence of almost all these definitions, if analyzed, lies in the survival of the Protestant English spirit as the origin of this underground of anti-Catholicism.

On one hand, the Protestant controversialists seemed to fight Catholicism in order to Protestantize the country; on the other, the American middle class saw in the emigration of so many Catholics, particularly Irish and German, a threat to the security of their own employment.

Indeed this spirit goes back to the reign of Elizabeth I and in the New World was perpetuated by a powerful middle class Protestant tradition that produced successively four organized movements : the Native Americans (1820-1844), the Know-Nothings (1844-1857), the American Protective Association (1887-1900) and, from 1921 on, the notorious bands of white-robed, hooded men known as the Ku Klux Klan ([4]).

It was the English aristocrats, statesmen and educators from Anglo-Saxon universities sent to America in colonial times who transplanted the seeds of dissension between the elect and the reprobates — that is, between Protestants and « Papists ». The pious Governor Dobbs of North Carolina, in announcing a « solemn fast and humiliation », transmitted his proclamation to Secretary Pitts in London, along with a hymn against « the

Papal Beast » that he had composed to be sung on Thanksgiving Day, 1759. According to him, his anti-Papal hymn
of some 12 strophes had the advantage of being « in line
with the prophecies up to date ».

Another governor, Beecher of New Jersey, in celebrating the tenth anniversary of Princeton College (September 24, 1755), inveighed against those « two mon-
strous furies that are Papism and Slavery ». In the same
period, one of the Methodist ministers who followed
George Whitefield from London to the Colonies, carried
a sharpened hatchet on his shoulders to break up « the
idols of the Papal Church » in the Cromwellian manner.

The English bête noire was then Catholic Canada,
from which so many Jesuit missionaries and secular
priests emigrated to convert the Maine Indians and some
of the first white settlers of New England. As late as
the 1780's, when the French ambassador De la Luzerne
offered to found a chair of French history at New Haven
College (Yale), his offer was rejected because such a
project might tend to introduce Papism to the State.

VI — As though this sort of anti-Catholicism was
not enough, there was from the first the influence of
colonial educators with textbooks bearing names such as
Benjamin Harris' *The New England Primer* and *The
Protestant Tutor,* not to mention popular publications
like Nathanael Ward's much-read *The Simple Cobbler
of Aggawam* which were filled with hostility toward
Catholicism.

Although it is true that the *Primer's* anti-Catholic
animadversions appeared only in certain editions, they
included such scandalous jingles as the following, reprinted from the works of John Rogers, whom Mary Stuart
had burned alive for his effronteries :

« Abhor that arrant Whore of Rome
     And all her blasphemies;
     And drink not of her cursed Cup,
     Obey not her Decrees ».

Such were the educational texts intended for the sons of Puritan « Round Heads » ([5]).

VII — The four principal sects of Catholic opposition, which all sprang from the English reform movement, were the Presbyterians, Dutch Reformists, Baptists and Methodist Episcopalians. Each of these groups furnished one or more leaders to the agitation against the Church ([6]).

Prominent among the Boston Presbyterians was the Reverend Lyman Beecher (1775-1863), first of the preaching dynasty of that name and descendant of one of the founders of the Puritan colony at New Haven in Connecticut. Shea has felicitously characterized him as « of great influence but quite without scruples ». A sample of this was his incendiary sermon in Boston the Sunday preceding the predatory assault on the Ursuline Monastery at Charlestown. « He is at least partly to blame for that attack », Auld writes. Beecher's *Plea for the West* of 1835 was delivered expressly to stop the march of Catholic pioneers into the American interior.

A contemporary of Beecher was the Reverend William Craig Brownlee (1784-1860), a Scotchman by birth and pastor of the Dutch Reformed Church of New York. A virulent enemy of Catholics and Quakers, author of such works as *Letters on the Roman Catholic Controversy* (1834) and *Treatise on Popery* (1847), he was largely the spirit behind the anti-Catholic, anti-Irish party, the American Protective Association. His colleague, the Reverend L. R. Reese, strenuously supported him in an ignoble campaign in his newspaper, *The Protestant*.

In line with these was another Presbyterian, the Reverend Robert Breckinridge (1797-1841). If he lacked Beecher's intellectual stature, he carried as much social influence, being chaplain of the national House of Representatives (1826-31) and professor of theology at Princeton. An outspoken adversary of Catholicism, which he was unable to understand, he engaged in Philadelphia in 1833 in a controversial dispute with the Reverend Dr. John Hughes, future Archbishop of New York, who was then pastor of St. John's Church. The Presbyterian later published the exchange under the title, *Roman Catholic Controversy* (1836) and also published *Papism in the 19th Century in the United States* (Baltimore, 1841).

Among other Presbyterians who similarly indulged in anti-Catholic attack were Nicholas Murray and the Reverend Dr. Spring of New York's Brick Presbyterian Church. The latter is particularly noted for the debate of October 31, 1840, before the Common Council of New York, in which Bishop Hughes pleaded for the freedom and secularization of instruction against the Protestant Society of Public Schools. Pointing his finger at the prelate, the Presbyterian intoned as though from his pulpit : « This gentleman has tried to prove that the scholastic system in force leads to non-belief. Now, Sir, don't think it strange if I prefer non-belief to Catholicism. Even a mind so fine as Voltaire's came to the conclusion that in the alternative between non-belief and the dogmas of the Catholic Church, he would choose non-belief. Sir, in a similar circumstance, I would prefer tomorrow to ally myself with the non-believers ! ».

The Baptists emerged also onto the anti-Catholic

battlefield, and their principal champions were Richard
B. Fuller (1804-76) and Alexander Campbell (1788-1866).
Fuller, although born and brought up an Episcopalian,
was Baptist pastor at Beaufort in South Carolina and
entered into polemic battle with Msgr. England, the
eloquent Catholic bishop of Charleston. The theme was
« Vindications of the Catholic Church ». Campbell separated himself from the Baptists in 1827 and organized
his own group, the Disciples of Christ, also called the
Campbellites. He is noted for his verbal battle with Msgr.
J. B. Purcell of Cincinnati on a theme of his own proposal :
« Is the Roman Catholic religion in some or all of its
principles or doctrines the enemy of civil or religious
liberty ? ».

In this arena of polemics the Methodist Episcopalians on their part, were not missing. Among their most
popular champions was the Reverend William G. Brownlow (1805-77), the « Fighting Parson » of Tennessee.
Converted to Methodism at a revival meeting, he was one
of its notorious « circuit riders » and later one of its spiritual Don Quixotes, eternally in a struggle with « the Devil », if not with a Calvinist, a Baptist, a Presbyterian
theologian or some hated Catholic priest. More petty
politician than Christian preacher, he defended slavery in
many celebrated arguments, but the black shadow envelop-
ing America was in his opinion the peril of Catholicism.
To exorcise it, he wrote article upon article. Convinced
that Jackson and the Democrats were allied with the Pope,
he branded them in his first book. Afterwards, he joined
the Know-Nothing Party and in 1856 brought out a bulky
volume entitled : *Americanism Contrasted with Foreign-
ism, Romanism and Bogus Democracy*. His extraordinary
intolerance almost made him laughable ([7]).

Another anti-Catholic Methodist was the Reverend
Charles Elliott (1792-1869), whose Irish forebears had

as their insignia the orange rather than the clover. A publisher of Methodist newspapers and president of Wesleyan University in Iowa (1856-60 and 1864-67), Elliott was an abolitionist. Yet if he held slavery a « sin », he likewise did nothing to repudiate anti-Catholicism. In 1851 he published in New York two volumes called *Delineation of Romanism and Acknowledged Standards of the Church*. With him may be bracketed another Methodist who fought slavery on one hand and Catholics on the other, the Reverend Hiram Mattison (1811-1868). He harangued against the latter in his book, *Romanism : Its General Decline and Its Present Condition and Prospects in the United States*.

To these may be added a host of minor Protestant writers all dealing with the same theme and from the same point of view — N. L. Rice, Samuel Edgar, Rufus W. Clark, S. W. Barnum, etc., etc.

VIII — The methods used to attain the double purpose of making Protestantism the exclusive religion of America and of ridding the country of Catholicism may be summarized along these lines :

a) False accusations and rash judgments that cast doubts on the loyalty of Catholics and their ability to adapt themselves to the spirit of liberty, maintaining that they were awaiting orders from Rome to crush every republican movement in the nation.

b) Resolute tendency to exclude immigrants from employment and public offices. In order not to violate Article Six of the Constitution, which forbids any discrimination on the ground of religion, the position was shifted to a nationalistic basis, the claim being made that the right of employment should be granted only to those born in the United States.

c) Bitter campaign against women's convents, almost all of them dedicated to the instruction of the young and as such providing the most stubborn obstacle to the total Protestantizing of the country. To make them unpopular, they were discredited as « priests' prisons for women », and on occasion they were destroyed, as happened to the Ursuline Monastery at Charlestown near Boston — an event that is discussed later.

d) Attacks on persons, institutions and anything else connected with the Catholic Church; the list of churches that were burned down is a long one. On « Bloody Monday », August 5, 1855, the entire Irish residential section of Louisville was attacked and devastated, 20 houses were demolished and a hundred impoverished Catholics slaughtered.

All these attacks were preceded and accompanied by a wave of insults defining Catholicism as « Papist pseudo-religion », « Satanic religion », Romanist idolatry ». The phrase, « liberating the country from the jaws of the Beast », was often used, and the Democratic Party, the one preferred by Catholic voters, was vilified as « the party of rum, Romanism and rebellion ».

From places and institutions, the campaign of vilification was extended to the most venerated personages of the Church. It is enough to recall the « Outrage of Ellsworth » in Maine of October, 1855, when the highly esteemed Jesuit missionary, Father John Bapst (1815-75), was dragged out of his church by order of the Know-Nothings' town council, robbed of his watch and wallet, tarred and feathered and ridden through the town's streets on a rail.

But the gravest of all these insults was directed against Archbishop Gaetano Bedini, who while on his way to Brazil as Papal Nuncio in 1853, stopped in the United States « to pay his respects, in the name of the

Holy Father », to President Franklin Pierce. Some ten cities were witness to shocking scenes perpetrated, not without the support of the Know-Nothings, by a group of anti-clerical foreigners — mostly Italians — led by the apostate Alessandro Gavazzi of Bologna. Gavazzi, who harbored political grievances against the Archbishop, traveled through the country expressly to give vent to his hatred of him. He and his companions held a mock trial in the main square of Saratoga, N. Y., then strung up a dummy supposed to represent the Nuncio, with a sign attached to it that read : « Msgr. Bedini, assassin, condemned in effigy ». Later, in Philadelphia, the apostate was awarded, as a prize for a similar outrage, a ring with a fragment of the Liberty Bell. The disgusting parody was repeated in Cincinnati in December, 1853.

e) Polemic literature of propagandistic and actually scandalous intent, which sprouted like weeds. The New York journal, *The Protestant,* led the way in this respect, but the *Gospel Advocate,* the *North American Review,* the *Missionary of Mt. Zion,* the *Religions Telegraph of the South* and other Protestant organs were not far behind it. On August 14, 1834, a weekly named *Downfall of Babylon* appeared. It was printed first in Philadelphia and later in New York, and its editor, Samuel B. Smith, boasted he was a « former Popish priest ». Six days later the *American Protestant Vindicator* put in its appearance, a bi-weekly publication edited in New York by the Reverend W. C. Brownlow, already mentioned here. The same year saw the publication of the English translation of a pamphlet by a degenerate Jansenist dignitary, Scipione de' Ricci, with the title : *Secrets of Nunneries Disclosed.*

But the most scandalous work of the day was the notorious forerunner of a whole literature, consisting of some 50 novels, pamphlets and papers, for which it set the tone ([8]). It was Maria Monk's *Awful Disclosures of the Hôtel-Dieu Nunnery of Montreal,* published in New York in 1836. Apart from the untruths it told, it constituted the most influential work of the period preceding the Civil War, and it was launched by the Native American Party as an all-out attack on the Catholic Church.

The author, whoever it was — for if Maria Monk signed it, she certainly did not write it — was a puppet in the hands of one who used her cleverly to serve the cause of Protestant propaganda. Much of this propaganda was put out by the American Society to Promote the Principles of Protestant Reform, the so-called Protestant Society, which was founded in May, 1836, and lasted till 1869, when the publishing house most responsible for these works was forced to withdraw its entire stock under pressure of public indignation.

At any rate, the book bearing the name of Maria Monk made a fortune, sold 300,000 copies and was called « the *Uncle Tom's Cabin* of the Know-Nothing movement ». But the proof that the « awful disclosures » were a sheer fabrication was brought — we must fairly acknowledge it — by the Protestants themselves.

First among these was Colonel W. L. Stone Sr., editor of the *New York Commercial Advertiser.* Wanting to get the facts of the « disclosures » straight, he went to Montreal — scene of the supposed scandals — with the incriminating volume in his hand. There he was given full freedom to make an exhaustive on-the-spot study inside the Hôtel-Dieu nunnery. The results were so completely negative that Maria Monk was exposed as « an arrant imposter who had never been a nun nor had ever been inside the cloister of the Hôtel-Dieu ». As a result, Stone denounced the *Awful Disclosures* as « entirely and unequivocally, from top to bottom, untrue and the fantasy of a deranged mind, and a series of calumnies without parallel in the corruption of their invention ». This was the conclusion of the investigation : « I must solemnly declare that in this affair priests and nuns have been proven wholly innocent ».

Several decades later, in 1874, the autobiography of Maria Monks' daughter was published in New York, which with its account of her own conversion to Catholicism constitutes a splendid tribute to *Catholica fides*.

IX — Let us take a look at the four major anti-Catholic parties that emerged in the United States during the 19th century.

a) Native American Party.

Its name leads one to suppose it was a protective organization founded by the Indians, the aborigines of North America and as such the natural rulers of the country. But no; it was used to designate a political grouping of white immigrants who had come to America one or two generations before. It was a party of few ideals, whose program was mainly to exclude new-coming foreigners, particularly if they were Catholics, from remunerative jobs and public positions.

This « nativism » was an evolution of the preceding Federalist movement, formed in the main by Tory Protestants, who sought to establish Protestantism as a state religion and to promote legislation hostile to immigration, naturalization and equal rights for Catholics. That was the period when the New York Federalist John Jay succeeded in inserting into his State's constitution the law denying citizenship to every Catholic born outside the country unless he abjured his own faith and renounced every tie with the Roman Church.

This political organization was formally constituted

in New York City in 1835, but before that it was responsible for acts that have redounded little to its honor — particularly the total destruction by fire of the Mt. Benedict Monastery-Convent of the Ursulines at Charlestown.

The Congregationalists of nearby Boston nourished feelings that were especially antipathetic to this monastery for three reasons : (1) it maintained a school for young girls, many of them Catholic; (2) it was the first institution founded by nuns in New England; (3) it was envisioned and financed by one of their former Congregationalist pastors, the Reverend John Thayer, who was converted to Catholicism and who left upon his death the money to finance it. Besides, the superior at that time, Mother Ursula A. Moffat, was also a converted Protestant.

On January 19, 1832, one Rebecca Read left the community at St. Benedict and, being an easy prey of the anti-clericals, became a Protestant again, turning on her former benefactresses by writing a book called *Six Months in a Convent*. The adverse press was only too happy to print this book and its sequel. Although she denied it later, she prided herself on being « the humble instrument used by Providence to destroy the institution of Mt. Benedict ». In addition to the disloyal Rebecca, the music teacher at the convent, Mary St. John, perhaps influenced by the former, also left it. Monastic life was finding it difficult to establish itself in the hostile Anglo-Saxon world. Partisans of the Native Americans, incited by the Reverend Lyman Beecher from his Boston pulpit, used these instances as a pretext for the ignoble rioting against the institution.

The infernal plan got under way on the night of August 11, 1834. About 9 :30, the evil-doers tumultuously assembled in Charlestown in great numbers and at a given signal, shouting « Down with the convent ! », forced their way into the house of God, drove the defenseless sisters and their frightened charges into the garden and then set on fire faggots heaped around the venerated walls, throwing into the blaze the monastic Bible, valuable vases, the altar vestments and all the sacred furniture. The profaners then proceeded to the very tombs of the monastery garden, opened and desecrated them. Dawn was breaking when they put the crowning touch to their vile act by setting fire to the stables, the caretaker's house and the granary. The burning and destruction of the hedges around the convent amid diabolical cackling laughter was the final act of this malevolent mob.

Bishop Fenwick, coming post haste from Boston, had the anguished nuns removed to a place of refuge, from which they were later sent to the Ursuline monastery in Quebec. The following Sunday he used as the text for his sermon at Holy Cross the words of Our Lord : « Father, forgive them, for they know not what they do ». The sacrilege of Charlestown was described in a letter from Msgr. Fenwick to Msgr. Signay in Quebec as « an outrage without precedent in the annals of civilization », but his words show how little his confidence was shaken : « Notwithstanding the fact that they (the Nativists) have sought to wage a bitter war against us and that we must suffer as much in our own persons as in the property of our churches, we will triumph in the end : *Si Deus pro nobis, quis contra nos?* » ([9]).

A decade later, in 1844, during the presidency of Tyler, a similar outrage took place in Philadelphia. On the grounds that Msgr. Kenrick of that city had objected to the use of the Protestant instead of the Catholic Bible in public schools, the Nativists set fire to the beautiful Church of St. Augustine and attempted to do the same to the Churches of St. Michael and St. John. It was only the timely intervention of the troops that saved these last two from destruction, but the fire destroyed many Catholic homes in the district of Kensington and killed many of the inhabitants. On May 12, 1844 Msgr. Kenrick ordered the suspension of services in all Philadelphia churches because of inadequate security.

In New York City another incident of the sort almost took place but was luckily averted by Msgr. Hughes, who called on the mayor and told him he would be personally responsible for any act committed by the Nativist.

Between 1820 and 1860 the Nativist movement — which was anti-American as much as it was anti-Catholic — spread from north to south, from east to west. In 1860, in New York City and Brooklyn alone, there were some 60 propaganda centers of the Nativists. But notwithstanding its apparent vitality, nativism, founded as it was on reactionary motives, on arbitrary privileges incompatible with the principles of democracy, could not take root in the spiritual soil of America. Eventually it died out ([10]).

b) The Know-Nothing Party was formally organized in New York City in 1852 and was so called from the oath that required all members to answer inquiries as to the party's aims and existence with the invariable formula : « I don't know ».

It was to assume national importance, but at first it was simply a local organization composed of more or less secret groups or sub-groups related to the Nativist movement, from which it borrowed the « No Popery » slogan of unhappy memory.

At any rate, its regulations made no secret of its bias. The second article, adopted on June 12, 1854, said clearly : « A person to become a member of any subordinate council (of the order) must be Protestant, born of Protestant parents, educated under Protestant influence and not related by marriage to a Roman Catholic ». The third article said : « No member who has been a Roman Catholic may be elected to a post in the order ». And the oath administered upon admission to the order « in the presence of God and these witnesses », pledged the member among other things « neither to vote for nor support anyone for public employment unless he be an American citizen by birth and under no circumstances if he be a Roman Catholic ».

This rigid discrimination against Catholics has made the Know-Nothing movement contemptible : « It does not oppose German Protestants, English Protestants, Scotch Protestants or even Irish Protestants. It opposes only foreign Catholics. The party is essentially an anti-Catholic party, and it is particularly against the Irish, since the majority of these are Catholics ». If only for this reason, it has been said that the party « corrupted a wide section of the native American population. It was not the American people who wanted to declare war against the Church, but only a group of pseudo-religious fanatics and inconsequent demagogues who represented the American people as little as did the rioters they incited to massacres and acts of incendiarism. Their every gesture was an anti-American one, in contrast with all the principles of America's free institutions ».

And Protestantism, again allied with anti-Catholics, made another attempt to dominate the United States. Lay orators and ministers from their pulpits reopened the anti-Catholic campaign in the conviction that Bible and faith were better served by a war against the Mother Church. The lower classes thought that their economic well-being would be no less improved by opposing Catholic immigration and the appointment of Catholics to public positions.

In the first two years of its existence — which was

fated to flourish barely a decade — the Know-Nothing movement spread to 35 States or territories. At first it limited itself to supporting political candidates approved by its secret councils. But in 1854 the party took on an active role as arbiter in politics of the country. Its first successes were in the municipal elections of Philadelphia, Baltimore, San Francisco, New Orleans and New York, where it won 146,000 votes. The same year the party sent 40 representatives to Congress, among them Gardiner, governor of Massachusetts. The next year (1855) party members became governors of New Hampshire, Connecticut and Rhode Island and occupied some 75 seats in Congress, constituting one half of Massachusetts' delegation, two-thirds of Ohio's and the whole of Pennsylvania's. The Know-Nothings triumphed — however briefly — everywhere, from Maryland to Virginia, from Iowa to Wisconsin and Indiana, from Kentucky to California in the Far West.

And accordingly the Catholic Church in America suffered. One of the first objects of Know-Nothing animosity was the cottage at Providence, R. I., inhabited by the Sisters of Mercy, directed by the energetic Mother Xavier Warde. When in 1851 rioters attempted to attack it, Msgr. Bernard O'Reilly intervened with words that were clear and simple : « The sisters live in their own home; they never leave it for a single hour. As long as I live, I will protect them and, if need be, I will shed my blood in defending them ». Unaccustomed to such heroism, the rioters gradually dispersed.

The following year (1852) a group of Know-Nothings in New Orleans attacked the offices of the newspaper, *Le Propagateur Catholique,* that had been founded in 1844 by the Reverend Napoleon J. Perché, later Archbishop of the city, and also attempted an assault on the Ursulines' monastery.

303

The years 1853 and 1954 were marked by the historic manifestations in Saratoga and Cincinnati against the Pontifical delegate, Msgr. Bedini; by the « Outrage of Ellsworth » perpetrated against Father John Bapst; by the destruction of Pius IX's gift of a stone tablet for the Washington Monument; by the odious Inspection Laws against Catholic institutions in Massachusetts; and 1855 witnessed Louisville's « Bloody Monday » of evil memory and the infamous Church Property Bill of New York.

With these and other acts the Know-Nothings finally overreached themselves. The crimes of Louisville and the election in 1855 of the Democrat, Henry A. Wise, whose program explicitly opposed Know-Nothingism, to the Virginia governorship signalized the downfall of the party. In a speech on the eve of his election, Wise reminded his constituents that the nation was founded on religious tolerance and political liberty and bitterly attacked the Know-Nothings as illegal and unconstitutional.

Wise's overwhelming victory was that of a knight whose ideal is one of absolute equality. To the imposing crowd that acclaimed him at the Brown Hotel in Washington, he said : « I have confronted the Black Knight with his drawn visor; his shield and lance are now in fragments ». Know-Nothing partisans tried to intervene, but to no avail. Their fortunes, from this time onward, began to wane, and by the next year, when the Pennsylvania Democrat James Buchanan defeated the Know-Nothing candidate, Millard Fillmore, for the presidency, they were discredited as a political entity.

For his part, President Lincoln expressed his dislike of the Know-Nothings in a letter to Joshua Speed. If the Know-Nothings ever attain power, Lincoln wrote, they would reword the Constitution to read : All men are created equal except Negroes, foreigners and Catholics. If that ever happens, he commented, he would rather emigrate to some nation where love of liberty is not talked about so much — to Russia, for example, where despotism is enjoyed in a pure state, untainted by hypocrisy.

c) The American Protective Association (A. P. A.), which flourished between 1889 and 1897, was the third incarnation of this ever-reappearing anti-Catholic specter.

The new secret order traces its origin to March 13, 1887, at Clinton, Iowa, with the creation of its first council, organized by one Henry Bowers, a lawyer from Maryland. He was its perpetual national president, for he was reelected in 1898 and held the post till 1906, by which time his party was merely a shadow of its former self.

The A. P. A.'s regulations, echoing those of its predecessors, solemnly affirmed its anti-Catholic stand in saying that « the support of any ecclesiastical power of non-American character with equal or greater sovereignty than the government of the United States is irreconcilable with American citizenship ». Behind these premises, the party opposed the tenure of political office by anyone « subject to or in support of said ecclesiastical power ». Its ritual « oaths » excluding Catholics from public office became famous.

Its sole difference from the preceding movement consisted of its extending admission to the order to members born abroad, as long as they were not Catholics, and in the wide-spread use of a defamatory press, publishing false Papal Bulls and the like.

The A. P. A.'s first political victory took place in Omaha in 1891 and the next year in Kansas City, Mo. The latter victory emboldened its members to petition the governor of Missouri, William J. Stone, for the ostracism of all Catholic candidates from public office by means of black lists. Stone proudly answered that their association was neither democratic nor American and that he vigorously opposed it. Theodore Roosevelt also treated it with similar severity. The A. P. A. gradually spread from Iowa, Nebraska and Missouri to the neighboring States of Illinois and Ohio, forming the so-called « A. P. A. Belt ».

The A. P. A.'s anti-Catholic activity consisted mainly of various low actions. Between 1888 and 1892 its so-called Committee of the Hundred misused the press by flooding America with propaganda as contemptible as it was untrue. This campaign in a single year furtively issued 70 weekly publications solely intended to spread fear and diffidence among Catholics.

Another hostile act was its protest against the gift to Washington's « Hall of Fame » of a stupendous statue of Father Marquette, discoverer of the Mississippi, from the State of Wisconsin. The A. P. A. objected on the petty grounds that the Jesuit was a native of Laon. American good sense immediately overcame this obstacle when Congress voted Marquette a posthumous brevet of honorary citizenship.

The A. P. A. was also responsible for the campaign unleashed against Archbishop Satolli, appointed first Delegate Apostolic to the United States in 1893 by Leo XIII, and for the drive to cancel the federal government's subsidies to the Catholic Schools for Indians, on the grounds that the Redskins were hated foreigners who should be abandoned to their ancestral ignorance.

The electoral victory of Grover Cleveland marked the end of the A. P. A., and indeed a non-Catholic writer has observed that the movement served only « to reenforce Catholicism, since it succeeded in arousing sleeping sentinels and infusing new vigor and enthusiasm among the rank and file ».

d) The Ku Klux Klan was the final evolution of the three movements that preceded it. To avoid confusion, it should be pointed out that in the course of a half-century two entirely different secret organizations bore the name, derived from the Greek *kuklos,* circle, and the Celtic *clan,* club. The first order of the K. K. K. was organized at Pulaski, in central Tennessee, in the summer of 1865 by a group of young Confederate veterans, more or less for recreational purposes. The social disorders arising in the Reconstruction period and the attempts to « Africanize » the Southern States soon inspired its members to dedicate themselves to « regulating » the conduct of the Negroes. Thus the genuine K. K. K. at that time declared its intention to be an « institution of chivalry, humanity, service and patriotism ».

But the full story of this first Klanist organization, with its succession of orders like the Knights of the White Camellia, the Invisible Circle, etc., and its wicked campaign to terrorize the Southern Negroes with strange costumes and mysterious lingo, is beyond the purpose of this book ([11]).

The second secret order of the Knights of the Ku Klux Klan — which has more directly to do with the story of American Catholicism — was founded by the Reverend William Joseph Simmons, a Methodist skilled in organizing secret fraternities, on the night of November 26, 1915, when he led a group of 34 to a mountain-top near Atlanta, Ga. There, challenging « the first icy gusts of winter winds » and « under a flaming torch », they swore fidelity to the « Invisible Empire », whose leader was called the Grand Wizard. In organization and rituals, the new K. K. K. followed the old one of 1865 to the letter, including all the paraphernalia of white robes and hoods and all the fantastic nomenclature, along with an elaborate and mystifying initiation ceremony. The

307

feminine counterpart of the K. K. K., which however achieved little renown, assumed the name of Order of the Camellia.

As the K. K. K. was organized, each State constituted a Kingdom ruled by a Grand Dragon, each electoral district a Dominion headed by a Grand Titan, and each county was divided into Caverns under a Grand Cyclops. Each of these had its own orders of Furies, Hydras, Vultures and Phantoms.

Its program was a militant and intense affirmation of Protestantism. It meted out punishments to moral offenders (particularly in the case of Negroes and of judges who were too tolerant toward them); it demanded complete submission of the black race, defense against the « Roman Catholic menace » and economic boycott on the Jews. Among its slogans were phrases like « White supremacy », « Nordic supremacy » and « 100 per cent Americanism ». From the Nativists it borrowed the expression : « Americans must rule America ».

After the first World War, Simmons nominated Edward Young Clark, an ex-newspaperman and publicity expert, as « Imperial Kleagle ». Under him, 40 leaders called « Kleagles » were established in as many States. To these went four-tenths of the members' dues; a tenth went to Simmons (the « King Kleagle »), and the rest to the « Imperial Treasury ». By the end of 1921 the Klan numbered 100,000 followers and became notorious for a whole series of violent disorders performed by hooded mobs who whipped their victims and then tarred and feathered them, all in the cause of « anti-Catholic », « anti-Semitic », anti-foreigner » and « anti-Negro » ardor.

Internal dissensions transferred the sovereign powers from Simmons to a Texas dentist named Hiram Wesley Evans. The Klan continued to develop until in 1924 it numbered 2,500,000 members, especially in the Southern and Mid-Western States, and had become a decisive political factor. In Oregon it succeeded in having legislation passed suppressing parochial schools, and in 1924 it tried to exert its influence at the Democratic presidential convention to overthrow Alfred E. Smith, four times governor of New York and a militant Catholic. Smith was defeated as presidential candidate in 1928 by Herbert Hoover, garnering 14,620,000 votes to Hoover's 20,620,000. The three chief charges against Smith — the « Happy Warrior » — were invariably his Catholicism, his anti-prohibitionism and his affiliation with Tammany. But it was not the K. K. K. but rather the Protestant ministry that sought to discredit Smith on the grounds of his faith; he answered with the irrefutable argument that his spiritual loyalty to the Pope as a Catholic in no way affected his loyalty to the nation as a patriot.

In the State of Georgia, stronghold of the K. K. K., an organization called the Catholic Laymen's Association was formed in 1916 with the express purpose of countering the continuous attacks of the Church's enemies. Neutral on the political level, the association's task was that of clarification, of answering all inquiries, of publishing Catholic information and of challenging any false statements made by its adversaries. For example, when the Klansmen fabricated a false oath attributed by them to the Knights of Columbus, the association retorted by announcing with every publicity means at its disposal a prize of $25,000 to anyone who could prove the oath's authenticity. No one, it need hardly be added, turned up to collect it.

The result of the association's campaign surpassed all expectations, for out of 200 anti-Catholic newspapers and periodicals published in Georgia, only ten remained, the others disappearing like weeds burnt by the sun.

The bad faith of the anti-Catholic movement was thus unmasked completely, and although much Protestant ignorance on the subject of Catholicism persisted, a great many Protestants, given the truth of the situation, changed their attitude toward it.

The K. K. K.'s noisy campaign of terrorism gradually came to disgust all thinking Americans. The scandals — both financial and moral — attributed to them did the rest, and their attempt in 1928 to reorganize, under the new but no less fantastic name of Knights of the Green Forest, did nothing to improve their lot ([12]).

With the decline of the K. K. K., we can drop the curtain on all the anti-Catholic movements that sprang from the soil of America in the 19th and 20th centuries. Can it be that they represented anything more than a crisis of youth and a natural phase of adjustment in a country that was growing up? Certainly these successive currents, which resolved themselves into a single one, had neither their source in the federal power at Washington nor did they have its sanction. As a contaminating influence in politics, they made themselves felt only in individual States. Yet they represented a sad flowering of religious intolerance, as well as the egotism of men who sought to achieve through them easy notoriety, political power and personal advantage.

CATHOLIC DEFENSE: PROCLAMATION OF TRUTH AND PATRIOTIC LOYALTY

CHAPTER X

To combat the hostility generated against it, Catholicism has resorted to a two-fold defense : the classic defense, adopted by Christianity since the time of St. Peter (¹), based on logic and the *arma veritatis* of victorious Christian apology; and a fearless and pure patriotism, which has silenced those accusing American Catholics of being temporarily settled foreigners and sworn vassals to a foreign authority.

With these two weapons, both the priesthood and people have fought back, in the past and present century, and won the battle for their very existence against all adversaries.

II — In many cases, Catholics have not fought alone. Although their enemies have been predominantly Protestant, nevertheless other more reasonable Protestants have risen up everywhere in their defense.

During the Presidency of John Adams (1791-1801), turbulent political conditions in Europe swelled the influx of Catholic immigrants into the country, thus alarming the Federalist Party. The newcomers, however, unexpectedly found a valiant champion in James Madison, subsequently fourth President of the Confederation (1809-1817). On their behalf, he contended that there was nothing in the religion of the Catholic immigrants that could be held incompatible with the purest Republicanism (²).

Nevertheless, rising resentment against the Catholic minority at one point culminated in the passage of certain laws « against Foreigners and Seditionists ». One Sunday, at the portals of the Catholic Church of St. Mary in Philadelphia, a petition for the repeal of these laws was circulated among the faithful as they were leaving the church. Several Federalist agitators publicly denounced the sponsors of the petition, with the result that a riot broke out; thus, the agitators who sought to promote measures of intolerance appeared justified in defining the incident as « a riot by Foreigners and Seditionists ». But Thomas Jefferson, in a letter written on June 16, 1796, to General Lafayette, called it a deplorable affair and referred to the free and tolerant spirit of the Constitution.

Such exemplary interventions on behalf of the hard-pressed Catholics abound in American history, and there have been not a few instances of Protestant ministers who have not only defended but even exalted the victims of this persecution (³). Particularly notable is the Reverend H. M. Field who, during a trip to Rome in 1848, wrote a book entitled *The Good and Bad in the Roman Catholic Church,* in which he tried to conciliate Catholics with Protestants. « I write these pages », he declared, « in the hope of softening the sentiments of at least a few Protestants opposed to Catholics and their religion. We complain so much of Papal intransigeance, but is there not perhaps just as much on our part? ». A decade or two later, the Reverend F. C. Ewer flayed religious intolerance from the pulpit in his *Sermons on the Failure of Protestantism and Catholicism.*

More recently a monthly magazine entitled *Truth and Light,* edited by the Presbyterian Charles Windle, spoke out boldly against the anti-Catholic fanaticism of some Americans, in its program of combatting any propaganda founded on deceit and designed to intensify religious prejudice. For about 12 years, from 1920 to 1932 this small review conducted a commendable campaign which left its mark on many right-minded Protestants.

III — How have the members of the venerable North American hierarchy, the masters, defenders and pastors of the mystical flock entrusted to their care, reacted collectively and individually to the persecution of their Church?

In 1833, in a pastoral letter addressed to the clergy and laity, the Fathers of the Second Provincial Council of Baltimore noted « regretfully » a spirit which certain leaders of the press were flaunting « to the advantage of our non-Catholic brothers and which, in the past several years, has become more and more discourteous, even unjust towards us. Not only do they attack us and our institutions with unfair criticism and reiterate a thousand confused calumnies... but they have even denounced us as enemies of the Republic and openly proclaimed the fantastic necessity of obstructing our development and taking recourse to the most efficient methods of destroying our religion ». Because it was « not our principle to repay evil with evil or injury with injury », the Fathers exhorted their flock to answer their enemies with blessings.

In their separate areas, the Bishops have conformed to particular situations which have arisen, resorted to apologetic defense and argued the logic of those aspects of Catholic Truth which have been contested, falsified or ignored. From the ranks of the hierarchy and priesthood and, to a lesser extent, the laity, a legion of brilliant spokesman have risen up to defend the disputed faith (*).

In a letter written in 1826, Msgr. John England revealed that the Catholics of his generation were fighting « in detached squadrons ». This was necessary because in that period, the scarcity of workers, the vast expanse of the American Continent and its contrasting topographical characteristics, and, above all, the various situations which had gradually developed in each region, obliged the « detached squadrons » to carry on a sort of spiritual guerrilla warfare. Without modern telegraphy, telephone, radio, television or printing presses, there could be no defensive effort on a national or international scale. Each age uses the means it finds at its disposal.

Among the principal champions of the Catholic intellectual defense of the 19th Century, first in importance was Msgr. John England, Bishop of Charleston (1820-42). An Irishman from Cork, like all his compatriots since St. Patrick who seem born with a passion to defend Catholic Truth through polemic apology, he did not wait for his adversaries to attack; rather than fold his hands in prayer and commit to God His own defense and that of His church, he struck out with the two-edged sword of the new spirit.

Installed a little over a year in his small diocese, alert to the urgency of counteracting anti-Catholic literature, Msgr. England founded in Charleston (1822) a periodical entitled *United States Catholic Miscellany,* considered the first distinctly Catholic newspaper in the United States. With the appearance of the *Miscellany,* the press became a powerful weapon of apostolic defense : Msgr. England valiantly assailed the controversialists who aimed at the very heart of Catholicism in their efforts to Protestantize the nation. This he did by means of three series of letters : *The Calumnies of J. Blanco White*

Against the Catholic Religion (1826-28); *Letters to Dr. Bowen* (1828), in which he firmly opposed the Episcopalian Bishop of South Carolina; and in 1831, a polemical discussion on *The Republic in Danger*.

These three works of the vigilant Pastor confuted the grave, abusive charges repeatedly made against the Church : « Republicanism and Catholicism have no affinity or relationship whatsoever, nor can they ever be cordially united because of their basic differences ». In reply, Msgr. England bitterly observed : « Were it God's will that we should deal only with enemies who publish nothing but the truth ! But what a torment and affliction to find ourselves constantly obliged to deal with an Augean stable in which all the lies imported by European writers have accumulated ! ».

His immediate successor was the second Bishop of Boston, Msgr. B. J. Fenwick (1825-46), alumnus of the Jesuit school and therefore well versed in polemics. On September 5, 1829, he founded a dynamic publication called *The Jesuit* or *The Catholic Sentinel* ([5]). In his program article he stated : « The rapid increase and the respectability of Roman Catholics in Boston and throughout the United States loudly clamor for the publication of a newspaper in which the Truth of the Catholic Church, unchanged from the Apostolic era to our times, may be verily explained and accurately but firmly defended ».

After the press, came the pulpit. In 1830, the passionate oratory of the Presbyterian Rev. Lyman Beecher, father of Harriet, famous authoress of *Uncle Tom's Cabin,* inflamed New England public opinion with his violent diatribes against the Catholic Church. In that winter of 1830-31, Msgr. Fenwick felt duty-bound to strike back, and thus delivered a series of sermons to contradict him. Although snow blocked the streets leading to Boston's Holy Cross Cathedral, the building was packed with eager listeners, Protestants prevailing. In these sermons, the Bishop took as his theme the nature and characteristics of the Catholic Church and exposed the futility of the Protestant position. Adopting the very words of the more prominent so-called reformers, he turned the spotlight on their human, if not very recommendable characters. Conclusion : the Reverend Lyman Beecher ceased his attacks and withdrew from the battle.

With the same purpose of crushing the continuing attacks against the Catholic cause, Edward Fenwick, O. P., Archbishop of Cincinnati, on October 22, 1831, brought out the first issue of his journal, *The Catholic Telegraph,* which became at once the official organ of the diocese.

John Hughes (1837-64) stood like an invincible fortress against the anti-Catholic movement of that stormy period. In preparing his counter-attack — aimed chiefly at his most powerful foe, the Presbyterian minister Robert Breckinridge — the future Bishop and subsequently Archbishop of New York founded the *Catholic Herald* in Philadelphia in 1833. The power of the press as a weapon of counter-attack was soon clearly defined in the heated dispute between Philadelphia's champions of Catholicism and Protestantism, Father Hughes, pastor of St. John's Catholic Church, and Robert Breckinridge. According to an agreement between these two antagonists, the debate was limited to these main points : « Is the religion of Christ Protestantism ? » and « What is the infallible rule of the faith ? ».

The discussion, prolonged from January to October, was published in instalments in both *The Catholic Herald* and *The Presbyterian.* It was later put into volume form and reflected great credit upon Father Hughes for his ability and acumen. The results ? As in the case of the Reverend Lyman Beecher's debate with Msgr. Fenwick in Boston, Robert Breckenridge retired from the scene even before the controversy had reached its climax.

Moving from Philadelphia to New York, Msgr. Hughes, with his stout Irish heart, continued the battle against the enemies of his faith. Of memorable interest were his feuds with « Kirwan » and Senator Brooks. In 1847, one Nicholas Murray, hiding behind the pseudonym « Kirwan », addressed a volume of letters to Bishop Hughes. Despite the pressure of his various undertakings, the Bishop found time to answer the anonymous works with another entitled *The Importance of Being in Communion with the One Holy Catholic and Apostolic Church*. Meanwhile, the anonymous author revealed his identity and Msgr. Hughes returned to the fray with another series of letters published in 1847 under the title of *Kirwan Unmasked*. Later came the so-called « Brooksian controversy » provoked by Senator Brooks who had promoted in Congress a Church Property Bill empowering the State to confiscate any ecclesiastical property when a congregation was not recognized as a public corporation.

This same prelate waged other titanic campaigns to stem the invasion of the laity in ecclesiastical affairs, to prevent the Protestant Society of Public Schools from controlling public education and to assure Catholic freedom of education in their ever-increasing parochial schools — all in all, a complex of vigorous polemics undertaken to win a victory for the ecclesiastical, spiritual, scholastic and political liberty of Catholicism.

What Msgr. Hughes represented in the East, Msgr. J. B. Purcell, Bishop (1833-50) and later Archbishop (1850-83) of Cincinnati, represented in the West. Great were the praises accorded him for his week-long series of meetings beginning February 13, 1837, in defense of Catholicism. Two sessions were held daily in a Baptist church, now consecrated to the Catholic faith

319

and dedicated to St. Thomas. A native Irishman from County Cork, he was openly challenged to a marathon debate by the famous Alexander Campbell, founder of a cult of « Campbellites », who later was to announce — in the year 1866, just when he was called to appear before the Divine Judgment —the second coming of the Lord and the end of the world.

This self-styled prophet demanded a debate with the Bishop on these subjects : 1) The Catholic Church is worse than any other sect because it represents an apostasy of the Church of Christ and the Babylon of the Apocalypse; 2) The idea of apostolic succession is neither Biblical nor rational, 3) If the Church is infallible and unchangeable, then it is in conflict with the American spirit, which signifies progress. All these were ancient, worn-out slogans which Msgr. Purcell brilliantly destroyed like so many papier maché castles.

Msgr. J. Martin Henni, theologian who worked with Msgr. Purcell in the Fifth Provincial Council of Baltimore and subsequently first Bishop (1843-75) and first Archbishop (1875-81) of Milwaukee, defended Catholic Truth with his pen. Let it suffice to point to his volume *Facts Versus Assertions,* published in 1844.

In the same year of 1844, Msgr. Martin J. Spalding was named Vicar General of Louisville. To the anti-Catholic attacks loosed by the Protestant League, then newly organized in Louisville, he responded with a series of vibrant lectures, later published under the title of *Evidences of Catholicity.*

The Bishop of Philadelphia, Msgr. F. P. Kendrick, did not betray the Irish fighting spirit of a native Dubliner. His *Catholic Doctrine of Justification* dates back to 1841, while the first edition of his forthright *Vindication of the Catholic Church in a Series of Letters, or The Primacy of the Apostolic See Vindicated* appeared in 1845.

In 1845, Msgr. Michael O'Connor of Pittsburgh founded a journal, *The Catholic*, and opened St. Michael's Seminary. The apologetic press and the priesthood were the two greatest preoccupations of this saintly pastor who yearned to become a Jesuit. Later he devoted himself to direct polemics and on March 17, 1852, delivered a famous lecture on *The Influence of Catholicism on Civil Institutions in the United States*.

In Louisiana in 1844, Father N. J. Perché, future Archbishop of New Orleans (1870-83), founded and directed *The Catholic Propagator,* a militant publication which the local Know-Nothing group attempted to wreck in 1852. The battling Reverend Perché held his ground and distinguished himself in many controversies with his foes.

In 1855, the Know-Nothing movement swept Virginia like a cyclone. By good fortune, the Bishopric in Richmond was occupied by Msgr. John McGill (1850-72), who entered in lively debate with the editor of *The Richmond Whig* and defended the Church with exceptional vigor. Memorable was the Bishop's prediction in a letter to Robert Ridgway, editor of the *Whig*: « When Know-Nothingism will have become a name in history, the Church which you would like to destroy will still stand firm on the Eternal Rock on which it is founded, because it is upheld by the hand of God ».

Especially during the inactivity imposed by the Civil War on his itinerant pastoral duties, Msgr. McGill wrote a number of polemical works, including *The True Church Indicated to the Inquirer* and *Our Faith, Our Victory, or A Comprehensive View of the Principal Doctrines of the Christian Religion* ([6]).

The first Archbishop of St. Paul, Msgr. John Ireland (1888-1918), who strove valiantly to avert war between the United States and Spain, was a brilliant exponent of the high sense of patriotism of those Catholics whom the A. P. A. did its utmost to ostracize as « undesiderable foreigners ». In his campaign, he produced such powerful works as *Patriotism, its Duty and Value* (1894) and *The Church and Modern Society* (1903-4).

Innumerable other names remain to be added, among them Msgr. S. H. Rosenkranz, Auxiliary Bishop of Columbus, author of *The Divinity of Christ* (1866); the Dominican Msgr. J. Whelan, Bishop of Nashville, author of *Golden Chain* (1871), which demonstrated through historical analysis that « papal infallibility is not a novelty »; Msgr. James Gibbons, who promoted organization of the American Catholic League to fight the enemy's damaging propaganda, and wrote various celebrated works, among them *Faith of Our Fathers,* which has sold millions of copies in the United States alone since its first edition in 1877; Msgr. J. Horstmann, Bishop of Cleveland (1892-1908), author of *The Catholic Doctrine as Defined by the Council of Trent;* Msgr. Thomas O'Gorman, Bishop of Sioux Falls (1896-1921), who produced the renowned *History of the Roman Catholic Church in the United States* (1902) and *How Catholics Came to be Misunderstood;* Msgr. E. V. O'Hara, since 1939 Bishop of Kansas City, to whom we owe *At the Deathbed of Darwinism* (1905); and finally, the recently departed Bishop of Oklahoma, Msgr. F. C. Kelley, whose prolific pen produced such books as *The Last Battle of the Gods* (1907) and *The Forgotten God* (1932).

This enlightened apostolate *pro Christo et Ecclesia* carried out by the North American Catholic hierarchy has always insisted on open proclamation of Catholic action, has boldly confronted abuses aimed at it by Protestant sects and has not hesitated at times to solicit State aid commensurate with that granted to other confessional groups on one pretext or another. According to some observers, this latter action has not always been wise or tactful; nevertheless, in the opinion of the Catholic writer A. J. Riley, insistence upon Catholic schools, opposition to the Protestant Bible, diffusion of the Catholic press, creation of new dioceses, construction of imposing churches, observance of liturgical ceremonies in all their majestic beauty, the convocation of provincial and national councils — are essential to the vitality of Catholicism in America.

IV — In the wake of the higher elements of the North American Episcopate, the secular and regular clergy have supplied the 19th-Century Catholic Church with other groups of staunch defenders, many of them functioning as « separate squadrons » in the principal zones of the Confederation.

In the New York area, when opposition to the Church centered around the Protestant Association (circa 1832), which organized meetings and published the anti-Catholic journal *The Protestant*, a number of polemicists emerged from the ranks of the metropolitan Catholic clergy. One of the foremost of these was the Reverend John Power, rector of St. Peter's, who boldly entered the lists by engaging in debates with Dr. Bromley and other Protestant leaders of the anti-Church movement. Father Power and his faithful assistant, Dr. Felix Varsela, fought zealously in the columns of the Catholic periodical *The Truth Teller*. In this work they were ably abetted by the Reverends Thomas Lewins and Joseph A. Schneller, third pastor of St. Paul's in Brooklyn.

On his own account, Dr. Felix Varsela, erudite Cuban priest from Havana, missionary and later Vicar General of the diocese of New York, wrote the celebrated

Letters to Elpidio and directed the New York journal, *Catholic Expositor* (1842-44). His collaborator in this latter work was the Rev. Charles C. Pise, who answered the clamorous anti-Catholic novel *Father Clement*, a tapestry of calumnious insinuations, with his own successful novel *Father Rowland*. In 1843, he published another celebrated work, *Aletheya, or Letters on the Truth of Catholic Doctrine*, a series of 18 letters in which he demonstrated that Catholicism is wholly sincere in its support of republican institutions and loyal to God and America in equal measure.

The clergy of the Boston diocese contributed the Rev. Joseph Finotti (1817-72), a native of Ferrara, Italy, who directed *The Pilot* in Boston for many years. Pennsylvania furnished many apologist priests, among them Father Charles Maguire, who in 1825 wrote *The Defense of the Divinity of Jesus Christ and of the Mystery of the Divine Presence in Answer to an Anonymous Letter on Unitarian Principles*. In 1833, when the Presbyterian synod at Columbia, Pa., assailed the Catholic Church, the Reverend A. Gallitzin retorted with his *Six Letters of Advice*. He achieved widespread popularity with this and three other works, *Defense of Catholic Principles, Letters on the Holy Scriptures* and *An Appeal to the Protestant Public*.

Others worthy of mention are: Rev. James Keogh of the Philadelphia *Catholic Standard;* Reverend James Moriarity, author of *The Keys of the Kingdom, or The Infallible Promise;* the well-loved orator, Father Xavier Weninger, S. J., author of *Protestantism and Incredulity : An Appeal to Candid Americans;* and Rev. J. C. Perrodin, author of *Catholicism Versus Protestantism : Conversations of a Catholic Missionary with Americans*. These priests strove to affirm the truth, prove the legitimacy of the Catholic principle and apply it to their civic actions.

V — The Catholic laity, too, has added its intellectual collaboration to the hierarchy and priesthood towards the defense of the common faith, assailed from many sides.

To Rev. William E. Andrews, son of a convert, is attributed the first distinctly Catholic periodical to be published in New York; entitled *The Truth Teller,* its first edition appeared on April 2, 1835. Another priest, Thomas O'Connor, had founded a periodical in New York in 1810 but his weekly *Shamrock* or *Hibernian Chronicle* was only half Catholic, as it was equally dedicated to the defense of the Irish cause. O'Connor consecrated his pen « not only to the guardianship of Ireland and the honor of the United States, but also to defend Truth and the purity of... the Apostolic Church ».

Another priest, likewise son of a convert and vigorous champion of the Church against the persecution of the Know-Nothings, was Benjamin J. Webb, a Kentuckian. Editor of the *Catholic Advocate,* he published a series of letters in the *Courier-Journal* denouncing the violent excesses of those who dishonored Louisville on « Bloody Monday » in 1855.

Third champion priest of Catholic apology was the convert Orestes Augustus Brownson (1803-76) through his authoritative journal, *Brownson's Quarterly Review,* which he edited and directed from 1844 to 1875, except for an interval of seven years from 1865 to 1872. With competence and a vigorous personal style, he heroically fought Protestant, liberal, partisan and indifferent groups, always defending his faith without compromise. He assailed the Nativists (⁷) and the Know-Nothings as anti-Christian and anti-American. The Fathers of the Seventh Provincial Council of Baltimore (May, 1849) sent him a letter expressing their satisfaction with his achievements and Pope Pius IX awarded him a commendation in 1854.

Another convert was the priest James A. McMaster (1820-86), intrepid advocate of Catholicism who collaborated on the *New York Freeman's Journal* when it belonged to Bishop Hughes, but purchased it in 1848 and directed it until his death. His journalistic output, stamped with an unmistakeable personal style, anticipated that of Leon Bloy and the « savage man » of Papini-Giuliotti. Each of his articles blazed with a flashing protest. With unsheathed sword, he defended the rights of the Holy See and untrammeled freedom of education, favoring parochial schools against public schools, which horrified him.

Many other lay apologists and polemicists parade in close ranks from the early 19th Century to the present day. Among the modern ones of outstanding merit is J. J. Walsh, author of more than 40 works written alone or in collaboration and inspired by the contributions of Catholicism in the Middle Ages and the Papacy in terms of its contributions to the world in culture, good service, civilization, physical and moral well-being, etc.

We mention the titles of a few of Walsh's works which won him the well-merited commendation of the Order of St. Gregory the Great, a medal from the University of Nôtre Dame and the Order of Malta : *Popes and Science* (1908); *Catholic Ecclesiastics in Science* (1924); *These Splendid Priests* (1926); *These Splendid Nuns* (1927); and *American Jesuits* (1934).

After Dr. Walsh came such laymen as F. J. Kinsman, ex-Episcopalian Bishop of Delaware, author of *Salve Mater* (1920), *Trenton* (1921) *and Americanism and Ca-*

tholicism (1925); G. N. Shuster, author of *The Catholic Spirit in America* (1927), *The Catholic Church and Current Literature* (1929) and *Pius XI and American Public Opinion* (1939); and Michael Williams, director of the Catholic weekly, *The Commonweal* — in 1930 Igino Giordani hailed him as « perhaps the most original North American Catholic writer — to whose brilliance we owe such vivid apologetic works as *The American Catholics in the World War* (1921), *Catholicism and the Modern Mind* (1928), *The Shadow of the Pope* (1932) and *The Catholic Church in Action* (1935).

With these individual laymen should be mentioned the dynamic Knights of Columbus, who appointed a Commission of Religious Prejudice in 1916 to determine the basic motives of centuries-old antagonisms and eliminate as far as possible deeply-rooted misconceptions with dazzling torches of Catholic Truth.

Hierarchy, priesthood and laity — such is the compact triple phalanx that constitutes a single front of defense of the immortal principles of the Church. With its large Irish majority, this homogeneous group of defenders of the faith seems like a vast army of « pilgrims of that absolute » which is truth and justice.

VI — The second method of Catholic defense in North America was the purest, most sincere and adamantine patriotism, manifested in every circumstance and emergency confronted by the new Confederate States, which the Catholics so enthusiastically helped to create. Through their flaming spirit of total patriotic dedication, the Catholic profession became an « expression of the most intense fusion with the national spirit » ([8]).

Classic was the judgment of De Tocqueville, who spent two years in America from 1831 to 1833. Of the

Catholics he wrote : « They constitute the most republican and democratic class in America... They, especially the clergy, are a living example of the adage, " Render unto Caesar that which is Caesar's and unto God that which is God's ". In such a way, the Catholics in the United States are at once the most faithful believers and most zealous citizens » (⁹).

In the patriotic sense, De Tocqueville assigned a distinctive position to the North American Catholic clergy. In the span of a century and in the full light of its hierarchal reports, today we can accurately evaluate the patriotic picture of the Episcopate across the sea. Not at all the « political threat » that idle chatterers have warned against !

Beginning with Msgr. John Carroll, we do not find a single Bishop who does not distinguish himself by his patriotism. The very existence of a hierarchy distinctive for its particular American national character, independent of the Apostolic Bishopric in London, of the ecclesiastical jurisdiction of the neighboring French Bishopric in Quebec and of the trusteeship of the French Episcopacy, has eloquently proved the patriotic loyalty of the Catholic clergy in the new, expanding Republic.

VII — There is nothing more patriotically sublime than Msgr. Carroll's *Prayer for the Civil Authorities* which he composed in November 1791, for the First National Synod. For this particular prayer, which was read after the Gospel of the Mass, the Bishop came to « represent the heart of all the Councils legislating for citizenship, both civic and evangelical ».

After invoking heavenly benediction for the Pontiff and the local Bishop and priests, the liturgical prayer asked blessings for the United States President, George

Washington : « We pray Thee, Lord of Power, wisdom and justice, through whom authority is righteously administered, laws are passed and judgments decreed, to assist the President of the United States with Thy holy spirit of counsel and strength, so that his Administration may be guided in justice and that he might be eminently useful to Thy people over whom he presides... May the light of Thy divine wisdom guide the leaders in Congress and may there be light on every procedure and law adopted by our Government towards national happiness, growth of industry, sobriety and useful knowledge, and may there be for us a perpetual benediction of impartial liberty... ».

A golden halo of Christian patriotism illuminates this liturgical prayer which, ever since it was pronounced, has inspired the American Catholics.

VIII — Sometimes this fierce patriotic love manifested by the North American Bishops assumes proportions of a jealous passion. Even if some of them were born abroad, their affection for the United States fills their hearts with all the tenderness of a motherly kiss.

The Archbishop J. B. Purcell recalled with emotion that on August 7, 1823, when he was still a cleric at the Emmitsburg Seminary, he and Father Pise « unfurled the American flag to the winds on the highest tree of the Carnick Knob estuary ». The Reverend Pise never received a Bishopric ([10]), but was the only Catholic chaplain ever appointed to the United States Senate. The anti-Catholic Know-Nothing party objected clamorously when they saw the son of an Italian immigrant rise to such a position, but he defended himself in a passionate discourse delivered in the State Legislature at Annapolis on July 4, 1833.

To those who wished to see him removed from his post because he was « a subject of the Pope » and had « avowed his loyalty to that temporal leader », the Reverend Pise retorted hotly : « Must I confute this charge ? Must I declare before the Assembly that I know of no temporal bond between the Pope and myself ?... Like all other Americans, I am proud to be wholly dedicated to liberty... Our religion commands us to give honor to those who merit it and to render unto Caesar that which is Caesar's ».

Mention of this single Catholic Chaplain in the American Congress recalls to mind the very first chaplain in Congress Rev. Jacob Duche (1737-98) an Anglican minister, born in Philadephia of Huguenot parents. He who claimed the privilege of pronouncing the first prayer before the Continental Congress (on September 7, 1774) and of officiating for three months as chaplain, hastily abandoned the patriots' cause when the English took Philadelphia, and wrote an infamous letter to George Washington in which he tried to convince the General that his patriotic duty obliged him to desert the fight against Great Britain.

Of Msgr. Dubois, founder of the Marymount Seminary, it is worth mentioning his heartbroken declaration when, elected Bishop, he was charged with being « French » : « If I had not been an American for such a long time through sworn loyalty, custom, gratitude and affection which bind me to this land, then the 35 years I have spent in America as missionary and teacher ought certainly to give me the right to exclaim : " I, too, am an American ". ... But all of us are Catholics. In this common profession, are not all differences of birth and homeland pardoned us ? »

IX — At once deeply moving and fiery are the words addressed by Bishop J. J. Hughes of New York in a letter (May 17, 1844) to Mayor Harper of that city in reply to the ceaseless insults of the Know-Nothings : « I can still today recall my thoughts when I saw the American flag for the first time. At the time it never occurred to me that the day would come when that flag, emblem of liberty, would become divided, with the stars attributed to native-born citizens and the stripes to foreigners. Yet, not even recent events have undermined my confidence in that emblem of civil and religious liberty ».

The American Bishops of Hughes' patriotic moral fibre constitute no exception to the rule. In 1886, Bishop Ireland wrote in his *Memorial* : « Today it is easy to unloose a religious tempest in the United States. You need do no more than make it appear that the Church is the product of European nationalism ».

If individual personalities fought back with courage, no less courageous and patriotic were the « Acts » promulgated collectively by the hierarchy. Not without irony, the Fathers of the Fifth Provincial Council of Baltimore in 1843 issued this statement : « You see us, whose fathers shed blood like water to defend our common independence against a common oppressor; yet now we stand accused of forfeiting our civil and political liberty, putting it into the hands of a foreign prince, (the Pope) and of being unfaithful to our Republic ».

Nine years later (in May, 1852) the usual pastoral letter addressed by the Bishops present at the First Plenary Council of Baltimore to the clergy and people exhorted the faithful to continue service as good Americans, « not that there is reason to fear that your feelings could change from what they have always been but, rather that you may find in your religion more profound reasons to fulfill your civic duties ».

In 1884, in the official letter addressed to the Catholics of North America by the Fathers present at the Third Plenary Council in Baltimore, parents were urged to educate their children to take a greater interest « in the history of our country. We regard the crowning independence of our country, the winning of liberty and the adopting of its laws as the masterpiece of a special Providence because its architects, building even more wisely than they themselves ever realized, had the hand of God to guide them... If the heritage of freedom which they left us should ever be in danger, heaven forbid! our Catholic citizens will find themselves on their feet, out in front as one person, ready once more to give their lives, their fortunes and their sacred honor... ».

X — Bearing all this in mind, we can then demonstrate how North American Catholicism has always consistently coordinated its professed principles with the practical realization of its patriotic ideals.

The six successive wars fought in more than a century and a half by the North American Confederation can very well show whether the Catholic Church of the United States has emerged victorious in the supreme test to which it was put.

In addition to what has already been said, it suffices to mention that history is becoming more and more aware of the not inconsequential contribution made by the small Catholic population of the period of the American Revolution, while other ecclesiastical bodies, notably the Episcopalians, took an indifferent view of the cause.

When the war of 1812 broke out, the Bishop and clergy of the various dioceses encouraged the faithful to patriotic resistence. Bishop Cheverus, of Boston, worked hard with his priests to raise barricades and dig trenches. The historian Shea who examined the documents of the times, concludes the second volume of his *History of American Catholicism* thus : « In the war with England, they (the Catholics) have shown their patriotism on the field of battle and on the waves ». Among the notable Catholic leaders in that conflict was Commodore Thomas MacDonough (1783-1825) in command of the Constitution and known as the « Hero of Lake Champlain ».

The Mexican War (1846-48), provoked by offenses aimed against North Americans because of boundary disputes, proved advantageous for America, considering the half a million square miles which Mexico was obliged to give up, including all its territories north of the Rio Grande.

General Stephen Walts Kearney (1794-1848) who won this conflict, was a descendant of one of the first Irishmen of Cork to immigrate to William Penn's tolerant Philadelphia. From the same Kearney family of Philadelphia also came Commodore Lawrence Kearney and the audacious General « Phil » Kearney, hero of the Civil War.

Of great help to the conqueror of New Mexico were the Pima Indians, ancient pupils of the Jesuit Missions of Father Chini and his Franciscan successors who promptly offered him their aid.

The St. Patrick's Battalion, formed by Irish volunteers, also distinguished itself in the same campaign.

The enlistment rolls show 1,100 Catholic soldiers under arms in this war. On the whole, Catholic soldiers and officials, whether volunteers or draftees, rendered good service and covered themselves with glory in all phases of the Mexican War : from Palo Alto to Resaco de la Palma, from Monterey to Vera Cruz, from Cerro Gordo to Churubusco, from Molino del Rey and the assault of Chapultepec to the taking by storm of Mexico City.

Brigadier General of the enlisted men under General Zachary Taylor on the Rio Grande was James Shields, staunch Catholic who immigrated from Ireland in 1826.

Other Catholic officials participated in the Mexican War, later in the Civil War. Among them were Raphael Semmes of Maryland (1809-77),who won special distinction at Vera Cruz and Captain Giulio P. Garache (1820-1862) alumnus of Georgetown College of the Jesuit Fathers and decorated by Pius IX for services to the Church. Another alumnus of Georgetown College to play a major role in the Mexican War was William Wilson Corcoran (1798-1888), philanthropist who donated the splendid Corcoran Gallery to the nation's capital. He financed the entire campaign, advancing the entire cost to the government.

Because of the number of Catholics taking part in the conflict, Secretary of State James Buchanan asked the Church authorities for a few Chaplains; immediately they offered two Jesuit priests, Father Antonio Rey (1807-1847), Vice President of Georgetown College, and Father John McElroy of Frederick, Maryland, who were sent to join General Zachary Taylor in Texas. Father Rey distinguished himself in the heroic days of the siege of Monterey, which ended on September 24 with the capitulation of the Mexican General Pedro de Ampudis and his nine thousand men.

Remaining in Monterey, Father Rey preached to the Mexicans of the bordering ranches. Against the advice of his colleagues, he set out one day for Ceralvo, site of a Catholic community of mixed Americans and Mexicans. The particulars of that excursion are unknown, but a few days later his body was found pierced with lance blows.

The unity maintained by Catholics when the nation was split in two by the Civil War has always astounded students of America's religious problems. The Baptists maintained two separate conventions, in the North and South, while the Methodists, Presbyterians, etc., were similarly divided. The *U. S. Catholic Miscellany* foresaw this as early as 1856 : « The Catholics are the only body exempt from the fanaticism of the slavery question and the only group to uphold the Constitution by their creed ». The usual hostile elements attempted to attribute this phenomenon to the « foreign » nature of its unity, refusing to concede that Catholicism throughout the conflict was loyal to itself and to all America.

Thus Msgr. M. J. Spalding, in 1863, could write to Rome that the Civil War « revealed the difference between the true Catholic Church of all ages and nations and the local modern denominations taking sides in the storm, fire and blood. Truly our holy Church has shown itself to represent not the God of dissension but of peace and charity » ([11]).

When the conflict broke out, the Catholics rallied around the one true President of the nation. On April 15, President Lincoln called for 75,000 volunteers to defend the Union and on April 20, Archbishop J. B. Purcell told his flock in Cincinnati : « The President has spoken and we must obey the head of the nation... It is therefore our solemn duty as good and loyal citizens to march shoulder to shoulder with all our fellow citizens and to uphold the national honor ».

No less explicit was Archbishop Hughes of New York, despite the fact that many dioceses had suffered persecutions with monasteries, Catholic churches and homes destroyed, crosses smashed, priests and nuns insulted. However, with the assault on Fort Sumter, American Catholicism, with its generous heart, put aside every legitimate resentment. Archbishop Hughes proclaimed that « The Union must and will be preserved », and in a sermon supporting the army draft, declared : « This is not cruelty but mercy. This is humanity. You need not hate your enemies or become cruel in battle. You must be loyal and patriotic and do for your country what the country asks. Divine benedictions will reward those who fulfill their duties without hesitation and without violating any of the divine, human laws ».

In strict accord with the central government, the Catholics gave every possible contribution in their power towards a victorious solution of the conflict.

The military contribution offered by the American Catholics was truly notable, although its full extent still remains to be determined. We know, however, that from 145 to 175 thousand Irish Americans volunteered in the Union Army; and if we wished to appraise all the actions of these volunteers in the Civil War, we would have to rewrite the history of its more important battles : Antietam, Williamsburg, Bull Run, Gettysburg and Fredericksburg, in which the Irish soldiers fought in the front line of battle.

The excellent service of the Catholic superior officers speaks for itself. First of all, there was Kit Carson (1809-68), popular pioneer and hero of so many enterprises, among which he persuaded the Navajo Indians to join the Northern cause after they had agreed to unite with the rebels. For his brilliant exploits, in 1865 he was promoted to the rank of Brigadier-General ([12]).

Hero of both the Mexican and Civil Wars, James Shields was (1810-79) of Irish birth but American at heart. Appointed Brigadier General of the volunteers on August 19, 1861, he achieved heroic accomplishments

at Shenandoah Valley. In March, 1862, he succeeded
General Frederick W. Lander in command of a North
American division. Although seriously wounded, he
opened hostilities at Winchester and, on March 23, 1862,
decisively defeated Stonewall Jackson, who enjoyed the
legendary fame of being invincible. Because of injuries
he sustained, he was obliged to retire from service a year
later. The museum of the Catholic University of Nôtre
Dame preserves the sword of this hero, brought up in the
Catholic mission of Kaskaskia and destined to die in a
monastery in Iowa while visiting a relative there.

To George Meade (1815-72), Commander of the
Army of the Potomac, goes the credit of having won what
is considered the most important battle of the Civil War
or which, at least, marked its turning point. Lee, the
opposing general, advancing from the south through
Shenandoah Valley, planned to invade Pennsylvania so
that he could branch out from there and occupy General
Washington's strategic points, Philadephia, the national
capital, and New York. If their plan had succeeded,
Lincoln would have had to capitulate. General Meade
warded off this mortal blow engaging Lee in that epic
three-day battle (July 1-3, 1863) at Gettysburg, which
ushered in the military decline of the Confederacy ([13]).

When William Tecumseh Sherman (1820-91) was
nine years old, he was adopted by Thomas Ewing, a
Presbyterian later converted to the Catholic Church. The
young lad received a Catholic education in the Ewing
household and eventually married his protector's pious
daughter, Eleanor. Turning to a military career, in 1861
Sherman became Brigadier General and on July 21 of
that year, participated at the Battle of Bull Run. Later
he directed war operations in Kentucky. In 1863 he
obliged James Longstreet, Confederate Brigadier General,
to retreat from Knoxville.

A year later, commanding 100,000 men, he opened the campaign which destroyed the enemy in the Mississippi country and preceded the invasion of Georgia. With the fall of Atlanta in May, 1864, Sherman set out on his legendary « march to the sea ». On December 25, he wired Lincoln that he had made him a Christmas present of the city of Savannah. On May 24, 1865, he defeated General Johnston at Betonville, and accepted his opponent's surrender at Durham, N. C. For all these brilliant actions, Congress honored him and promoted him to General of the Army ([14]).

Thomas Francis Meagher, born in Ireland (1823-67) of Irish Catholic parents, completed his education in the Jesuit College at Clongowes Wood, Kildare. Because of his membership in the « Young Ireland » party, in 1848 he was condemned to death for treason, but was exiled instead to Tasmania. From there he entered the United States, where he was admitted to the bar. At the outbreak of the Civil War, Meagher threw himself body and soul into the adventure. In September, 1861, he defended the Union cause among the Irish in a historical speech delivered at the Music Hall of Boston. That speech remained doubly famous for its sublime exaltation of the American Flag and because it led to the organization of the 28th and 29th Regiments of Volunteers in Massachussetts.

Said the orator : « A national flag is the most sacred thing a nation can possess. It is the symbol of national authority. This morning as I looked out on Bunker Hill, what did I see ? I saw English troops evacuating the city of New York. I saw George Washington seated as first President of the United States. I saw the majestic forehead and the lean figure of Andrew Jackson. I saw the American sailor continue his solitary and heroic advance along the interminable currents of the Amazon River to open a new world — even in the New World — to industry and the conquest of the age. I saw the Bay of Smyrna, Austrian prey, redeemed by the Stars and Stripes. I saw the towers of Mexico and those majestic roads glistening in a greater glory than that which Cortez conferred on Spain. This and a host of other events passed like a vision above those stars while I remained in its shadow. Oh, that never, never again may that flag meet with another disaster ! Henceforth, the troops carrying it in action should have this motto to guide them : " Death if you will, victory if God will grant it to us, but no defeat and no retreat " ».

« Meagher of the sword », as he was dubbed, enlisted in the famous Irish Brigade in 1861, distinguishing himself in numerous deeds and writing pages of glory in the second Battle of Bull Run and at Antietam. At Fredericksburg, he commanded the Brigade in a furious attack on the enemy's position on the impregnable Mary's Heights, where the unit was so drastically reduced that Meagher, alarmed by the lack of men, resigned his post. Today General Meagher's sword is preserved next to that of James Shields' and the green flag of the Irish Brigade at the University of Notre Dame.

One of the three greatest generals of the conflict was Philip Henry Sheridan (1831-88), legendary hero of the American cavalry in the Civil War. Born in Ohio of Catholic parents he was graduated from West Point Military Academy and rose rapidly to the rank of Brigadier General. Aware of his military genius, General Grant put him in charge of the Army of the Potomac, with which Sheridan distinguished himself in a series of 18 brilliant victories that strengthened the North and disorganized the South. His soldiers called him « little Phil » with the same affection that the French soldiers had once addressed Napoleon as their « little Corporal ».

The powerful influence he held over his troops and the confidence he inspired in them were two of the attributes that brought him brilliant success.

Appointed Commander of the Potomac Cavalry in 1864, he acted as General Grant's right arm. His military exploits, now legendary, were similar to those of Napoleon and Garibaldi.

One of his outstanding operations occurred at Cold Harbor, Virginia, scene of one of the bloodiest battles in the entire war. It was here that General Grant, aiming at opening a breach to Richmond, capital of the Confederacy, met the enemy face to face. The battle that ensued resulted in a draw between the two armies. General Sheridan, summoned to lend support with his cavalry, drove the enemy from its strongly-entrenched position at Old Cold Harbor. General Meade then sent him this message : « Hold the fort as I am about to arrive ». Pinned down with his men, Sheridan obeyed, and despite powerful, incessant attacks from his opponent, General Fitzhugh Lee, he held out all through the night. The following day, reinforcements arrived — General Wright of the Sixth Army Corps of the Potomac and General W. F. Smith with the James Army. In August, 1864, Sheridan was made Commander of the Army of the Shenandoah and from this broad valley, he routed the Confederates within a short time.

In another brilliant strategic maneuver on September 19, 1864, after a 20-mile ride, Sheridan and 38,000 men defeated General Early, thus averting an invasion of the city of Washington. In this action, the Confederates lost 4,000 men out of 15,000 participating. Near Fisher's Hill, not far away, Sheridan won another victory a month later and on the 19th of October, began his famous ride at Cedar Creek, which was perhaps the most dramatic episode of the war and inspired Thomas Buchanan Read to write his famous poem, *Sheridan's Ride,* so dear to American patriotism.

At dawn of October 19, while General Sheridan was in Washington on military business, a powerful force of General Early's men took his troops by surprise; dislodged, they fled in disorder to Middletown. Arriving at Winchester and aware of what had happened, Sheridan rushed to the front 20 miles away, where his presence was enough to rally his men. Towards three o'clock in the afternoon, he organized a counterattack with such success that he not only retrieved the cannons taken from him by the enemy but captured 23 of their own. In General Grant's opinion, his exceptional action, in which victory emerged from what appeared sure defeat, « stamped Sheridan as what I have always thought of him, one of the ablest of generals ». Grant once told Prince Bismark that « never has a better general straddled a horse and led an army ».

In the winter of 1864-65, Sheridan won control of the Shenandoah Valley. At Missionary Ridge, his historical cavalry charges were a decisive factor in the ultimate victory and became a subject dear to poets. Another outstanding achievement was the epic Battle of Five Forks, a point considered by both Grant and Lee of the highest strategic importance, as here was the juncture of two railroads still open to Lee, who was defending them with five brigades. Grant entrusted Sheridan with the task of dislodging the enemy, which he did on April 1st, taking 6,000 prisoners. Two days later, Lee was obliged to evacuate Petersburg and Richmond and the Confederate Army began to disintegrate. In the next six days, with the final brilliant charges of his cavalry, Sheridan wrote the last crowning stanza of the Civil War. On April 9th, 1865, Lee surrendered at Appomattox Court House, and the Civil War passed into history.

Civil and military honors of every sort awaited Sheridan. Lincoln promoted him and Grant honored him, firing a salvo of 100 cannons. Poets extolled him as a hero and the people sang his praises in popular songs ([15]).

The United States Marine Corps also distinguished itself in the person of its leader, Commander James H. Ward (1806-61), Catholic convert and one of the founders of the United States Naval Academy. As Counsellor to the Navy, he was called to Washington to organize the flotilla of the Potomac, taking command on May 16th, 1861. He fell in battle, first naval official to give his life in the Civil War, at Matthias Point a month later while leading operations against Confederate batteries.

This glorious list of military Catholics participating in the Civil War is a truly historic phenomenon. To them goes not a small share of the victory which cemented the unity of America, which may well be characterized as a victory of the purest American Catholic patriotism.

Not to be overlooked is the spiritual contribution offered by the Catholics. A high percentage of religious men volunteering as chaplains were Catholic. Moreover, the nursing sisters performed a true miracle, considering that their organization dated back only about half a century.

Again, the Catholics played a key role in the diplomatic aspect of the Civil War. Where the Congregationalist Henry Ward Beecher made a lecture tour of Great Britain in 1863 to champion the Union cause before large audiences, American Catholicism was charged with executing more delicate diplomatic missions among the European powers ([16]). As we have previously mentioned, Abraham Lincoln sent his friend, Archbishop Hughes, to Europe as his personal representative. Carrying out this mission, at the French Court in Rome and other official European circles, he pleaded the Union's just cause in seeking to outlaw the crime of slavery and oppose secession of the Southern States. It was urgent that foreign public opinion be enlightened.

Perfidious Albion raised his hopes on the one hand but pursued an anti-union policy on the other, while rumors circulated of an Anglo-French alliance against the North, with the implied purpose of torpedoing American independence. Was it another instance of divide and rule? The « Trent Affair » of 1861, in which two Confederates accredited in France were discovered aboard the British ship Trent, supports this interpretation. But if such underhanded maneuvers in responsible French diplomatic circles were foiled, it was due in no small measure to the work of the Archbishop, who in consequence was honored by the American Government as « one of the greatest citizens of the Republic » (17).

Particularly difficult was the confidential mission to the Vatican carried on towards the end of the war by Msgr. Lynch, of Charleston, on behalf of the South. The gentle Pope Pius IX cherished little sympathy for Southern slavery and secession and found himself in an embarrassing position when Southern representatives sought to win him over to their side. In a letter to Jefferson Davis, as in previous letters to the Archbishops of New York and New Orleans, the Pontiff deplored the war and declared that he was praying for its conclusion, adding that he could never, as a Christian and head of the Catholic Church, lend any sanction or countenance to the system of African slavery. Yet, the Pope was reluctant to speak of the Civil War and once observed to an American : « As regards intervention in your affairs, I have no weapon left but this pen ». With every means at his disposal, he then solicited the North to accept the conditions proposed by the Confederacy, suggesting the same long-range policies later adopted by Grant.

In the brief war between the United States and Spain for the liberation of Cuba, Msgr. John Ireland, Archbishop of St. Paul, did his utmost on behalf of the peaceful God to avert it.

This ecclesiastic, close friend of President William McKinley and of various Cabinet members, went to Washington in April, 1898, at the request of the Holy See, since Pope Leo XIII, anxious to prevent an armed conflict and already in contact with Madrid, had fought to mediate after misgovernment of Cuba and the blowing up of the American battleship Maine in the port of Havana on February 15, 1898, saw the two nations drifting inevitably towards war.

The Archbishop's efforts at first seemed about to bear favorable results; in fact, he notified the Pope that the President wished for peace and would be willing to accept Papal mediation. Unfortunately, however, neither Leo XIII nor McKinley could overcome the policy of the capitalists or popular national enthusiasm for the war. Spanish diplomacy, notably evasive and dilatory, hastened the crisis, and on April 11, McKinley submitted the matter to Congress, which signified war.

Msgr. Ireland immediately repaired to Baltimore to confer with Cardinal Gibbons and the two prelates agreed that any further attempts to avert bloodshed would be futile. On April 22, Cuba was blockaded by sea and on April 24, Spain declared war, followed the next day by America. On the same day, Archbishop Ireland declared : « I have worked for peace, but if the national will is for war, then I pray, that victory alight on the banners of my country » ([18]).

America carried out a brilliant campaign. On May 1, the battle of the Bay of Manila signaled the destruction of the Spanish fleet. In the battle of San Juan Hill and subsequently in the capture of Manila and Santiago, the military and other assistance contributed by the Catholics proved to be of first order. With the fall of Santiago on August 12 came armistice. The following day, Msgr. Ireland, speaking on Catholic contributions to the war, could say with intense pride : « In this war, there has not been a battle on land or sea in which our Catholic soldiers and sailors have not risked their lives for the defense of America. Moreover, in most States statistics show that the percentage of their numbers has furnished more than the contingent asked for towards the defense of America » ([19]).

When World War I broke out, Cardinal Gibbons of Baltimore did much to muffle the mouths of the anti-Catholics, including the Protectors of America and the Ku Klux Klan : « On my word of honor », he declared, « I have known personally and well three Popes of the Catholic Church. I have been a priest for 32 years, Bishop for 15 and Cardinal for five. I have had the closest relationship not only with the Pope but with all Roman ecclesiastics. I know each priest in my diocese well and every Bishop in this nation. And yet in all my experience, never have I heard said, uttered or whispered anything about America and American institutions except words of affection. Never have I heard one syllable that could not be printed in capital letters and shown throughout the nation. Never have I heard of a plot or a scheme, but only words of admiration and love. Had there been any intrigue whatever I would surely have known about it. But of such things, I have absolutely not heard even the slightest whisper ».

Such were the patriotic sentiments that animated the American hierarchy when the United States declared war on April 6, 1917. Twelve days later, the nation's Archbishops, during their annual meeting at the Catholic

University in Washington, reaffirmed the loyalty pact drawn up 33 years before at the Third Plenary Council (1884) and then sent a collective letter to President Woodrow Wilson affirming their unbreakable solidarity with the national aims : « Firmly rooted in our Catholic tradition and history... in this hour of tension and trial, we affirm our most sacred and sincere loyalty and our patriotism towards our country, our Government and our flag... our people, now as ever, will rise up as one man to serve the nation. Our priests and our women... will once again win admiration and approval for their heroism and service ».

Nor were these vague promises. In a sermon pronounced during a military Mass at Fort Meade, Cardinal Gibbons declared : « Remember any wounds you might receive will be stars of honor. Go to war, go to victory, and God be with you ».

Williams has observed that the American Catholics were the first to volunteer for service [20]. Under the pressure of the crisis was formed the National Catholic War Council, through which American Catholicism achieved wonders in mobilizing and coordinating the 14 principal national Catholic Societies. Most important among these was the Knights of Columbus [21], which on April 14, 1917, affirmed « the devotion of the 400,000 members of the Order to the Republic and its laws », and assured its constant, unconditional support to the President and Congress... in the determination to protect the nation's honor and its ideals of humanity and right... ».

In response to the Order's appeal, the organization's war fund raised $14,000,000, and its war services were launched with the appointment of 1,134 secretaries and 209 chaplains and the erection of 260 buildings and community centers. The Order sent overseas 1,075 secretaries and 36 chaplains and opened 126 clubs. After the war, it opened 254 offices, gave out 498 scholarships to veterans and opened 48 schools for their civil reeducation.

Again, the Catholics showed themselves in this war to be admirable soldiers and officers. One of them, Major General McAndrew (1862-1922), personally directed the brilliant operations at Chateau Thierry, St. Mihiel and the Argonne Meuse.

Marvels of consecration, as usual, were the nuns, angels of mercy to all in need. The chaplains of the Army and Navy likewise revealed themselves as heroes. They considered their area of work a diocese apart — the Army and Navy diocese — constituted by soldiers and sailors of the Fatherland in arms which lifted the spirituality of their task.

Among a thousand or so such chaplains coming from 54 different orders and congregations ([22]) we mention only Francis L. Duffy, the popular « Father Duffy » (1871-1932) chaplain of the New York 69th Regiment of the Rainbow Division, a model of dynamic heroism venerated by the soldiers entrusted to his care ([23]). In his memory a statue has been erected in one of New York's most important squares.

Nor was there a lack of private patriotic initiative. Notable was the first Ambulance Unit accepted by America, contributed by Fordham University and operated by 150 of its students.

The rest is history which still remains to be written in all its details.

In the Second World War, again American Catholic chaplains won immortality in the fulfillment of their peaceful mission of administering spiritual aid to stricken troops. The number of those who gave their lives reaches 66 — 55 in the Army and 11 in the Marines — out of a total of 172 military chaplains of every denomination.

Thus, the Catholics account for 38% of the losses among American military chaplains.

These patriot priests who fell in action received some 57 decorations. No historian can but crown with a garland of laurel these patriot priests in the service of their fellow-men, who entrusted their souls to them under the rage of iron and fire.

Most pathetic of all were the nine chaplains who lost their lives in the sinking of two vessels converted by the crafty Japanese into prison ships — one destroyed in Subic Bay in December, 1944, and the other blown up two months later. We recall particularly among their number Father James O'Brien, of San Francisco, seen for the last time grasping a remnant of a floating raft, meanwhile giving absolution to those around him. While their prison ship went down, he sent the souls of the dying towards heaven.

One of the heroic chaplains of Bataan was the Rev. William Cummings, who coined the famous phrase « There are no atheists in fox-holes » during one of his sermons on Bataan. A missionary in Manila, he immediately enlisted as military chaplain when the war broke out. Under fire in the Bataan campaign, he coolly performed miracles. Once when the military hospital was bombarded by the Japanese, he saved the lives of many soldiers about to flee in disorder by jumping on a chair and reassuring them, thus averting panic and keeping them under cover. When his prison ship weighed anchor at Formosa in January, 1945, and headed for Japan, Father Cummings outdid himself in maintaining a high morale among his fellow prisoners. Twice daily he gathered them for talks with the cry, " Chaplain calling all the boys ". Each time he found new words of encouragement for his beloved flock, languishing and dying from hunger and thirst (five drops of water were allotted to each man

348

daily), dysentery and paralyzing cold, all the more brutal because the men were still wearing tropical uniforms. His electrifying words sustained many suffering spirits until one night when his comforting voice was heard no more : cold and hunger had taken their toll of this intrepid chaplain, whose fragile body had been nourished by little more than an indomitable spirit. For his bravery, he was posthumously awarded the Distinguished Service Cross.

War cancels all confessional differences and places the Catholic faith in a splendid light. Recently the 13th Tank Division, representing men of all denominations, donated gold chalices in homage to two Gold-Star chaplains who had served them. One chalice was presented to the Benedictine monastery of the Holy Cross in Canon City, Colo., in memory of the Reverend Lee C. Rechsteiner, who fell on the battlefield at Leyte, the other to the Monastery of the Redemptorists in Oakland, Calif., to commemorate the Reverend Father Clarence A. Vincent, who lost his life in Germany.

Other Chaplains returned home alive, yes, but scarred with wounds. So many of them won decorations for outstanding bravery that it would be difficult to remember them all or list them impartially. To mention a few, we begin with Father Donald Cleary, the « Flying Father ». Chaplain of Cornell University, in January, 1943, he began flying over England and the European Continent with his Ninth Air Force Division. A Marine chaplain, the Reverend Father Joseph Timothy O'Callahan, was awarded the highest decoration bestowed in the United States, the Congressional Medal of Honor, pinned on his uniform by President Truman in a ceremony at the White House. This was the noble priest's commendation for heroism demonstrated aboard the ill-fated Franklin in March, 1945. A Jesuit, he had taught logic, mathematics and philosophy at Georgetown and Boston. « He believes only in two things », his fellow officers said of him « in God and in the recruit ». Another officer described him thus : « O'Callahan was the bravest man I have ever met in my life. He rushed from one side of the burning ship to the other, and he was always to be found in the most dangerous spot. In the end, it was faith that saved one of America's greatest aircraft carriers, the faith of Father O'Callahan and the faith the men had in him ».

There were other courageous Catholic chaplains, such as the Dominican Father John Curran, survivor of the « death march » of Bataan who, during 41 months in the Fukuosa prison camp in southern Japan, administered the extreme unction to dying soldiers with holy oils smuggled to him by a Japanese sentinel married to a Christian and on whom General MacArthur personally conferred the Medal of Distinguished Service. Then there are the Reverend John Griffin, of the Archdiocese of Philadelphia, winner of the Bronze Star for courageous acts in maintaining continuous contact at tremendous personal risk between the front and the sentinels and telephone operators in the battered outposts; Major Edward J. Kellenberg, another Bronze Star hero, who flew 75,000 miles among the Pacific islands to visit military personnel and coordinate the work of the chaplains; the Rev. Albert C. Steffens, veteran of the campaigns in Sicily, Italy and Europe, who won three decorations, the Silver Star, War Cross and Soldiers' Medal; and the Reverend J. White, veteran of the First World War who became a priest in 1937 and later Dean of the juridical school of the Catholic University in Washington. Joining the Marines in 1945 with the rank of Captain, he was awarded the Bronze Star for courageous acts in the Central Mediterranean military expeditions while he was in charge of all the chaplains in that area. Already honored with a knighthood in the French Legion of Honor, in October 1945, President Truman promoted him to the rank of Commodore, the first priest in the history of the United States Marine Corps to receive such a distinction. Moreover, five Catholic laymen were among the 28 soldiers and officials decorated by the President with the Congressional Medal in October, 1945 while Catholic military men were similarly honored the following February.

Again in this war, the Catholics distinguished themselves in every zone of action. To mention one, General Joseph Lawton Collins directed the assault on Cherbourg and on the Siegfried Line after which he commanded the 25th Infantry at Guadalcanal and Munda.

The Catholic universities did not hesitate to contribute their share to the war effort. The glorious Georgetown University, for one, gave some 6,085 students, of whom 159 were decorated. Boston College gave 5,000 soldiers to the Army, of whom 136 perished, including Commodore John Shea, 517 were decorated and 34 cited in orders of the day. Some 12,000 alumni of Notre Dame served in the naval forces alone during the war.

Special mention must be made of the spiritual and moral rehabilitation services undertaken by the American hierarchy and Catholic population of the United States in generous response to the appeal made to them by the Holy Father on behalf of their war stricken co-religionists in the bitter conflict which shook all humanity to its very foundation. To humanize the furious conflict as far as possible and, once peace was declared, wipe out its sufferings and memories through merciful works — such was the most Christian aspect of the contribution realized by the American Catholics in the Second World War.

As the Allied troops advanced in the Orient, in East Africa and Europe, the Catholic war relief services, through a total of 22,000 volunteers, undertook the task of distributing its precious assistance in 44 countries and preserving civilization in the Old World.

In Italy, distribution of aid was entrusted to Msgr. John Boland, of Buffalo, N. Y., a venerable ecclesiastic with considerable experience in charitable and social work; Thomas F. Markham, pastor of Lowell, Mass.; Father Cesare M. Rinaldi, pastor of St. Anthony in Union City, N. J.; and Rt. Rev. Msgr. Andrea P. Landi, of Brooklyn. These men initiated their welfare work on Columbus Day, October 12, 1944.

Since 1945, these representatives have extended the charity work of the War Relief Services of the National Catholic Welfare Conference on a vast scale in Italy. Thanks to their efficient aid, the Pontifical Commission of Assistance could furnish considerable aid to the southern provinces, gravely stricken by the war. The work was completed with the donation of money which permitted the Pontifical Commission to distribute 112,000 free meals over the number previously fixed. In the winter of 1945-46, 20 communities in the province of Campania were added to the list of those already receiving relief.

In a year's time it was calculated that the total aid sent to the Holy Father by Catholic Americans in response to the appeal of the United States Episcopacy amounted to 3,223 tons, for a value of over eight billion lire. This represents 62% of all aid sent to Italy by the various American agencies. In October, 1945, some 50 American ambulances were sold to the War Relief Service for use in Italy. This organization, a private welfare agency under the direction of the National Catholic Conference for Social Assistance, used some of the ambulances to aid wounded soldiers and sick civilians throughout the peninsula, while others were sent to Germany and Austria with medicine and clothing which was distributed among ex-internees of the Nazi prison camps.

The American Catholic Assistance Center in Paris, directed by Father Hoban, distributed hundreds of tons of food and vitamins among the French population, particularly to needy infants.

When Germany capitulated in May 1945, another distinguished American priest was entrusted by Pope Pius XII with a very important mission, after having rendered brilliant services to the Vatican Information Agency and executing various papal aid projects during the war. Msgr. Walter S. Carroll, of the Pittsburgh diocese, at the behest of the Holy Father, made an inspection of the more infamous of the German concentration camps to estimate the needs of the newly liberated prisoners. The Allied authorities received him with a solicitude that well expressed their desire to collaborate with the Holy See in solving the complex problem of lending relief to the unendurable suffering of the Italians, Lithuanians, Estonians, Hungarians, Poles, Albanians and other nationalities deported to the camps, many of them seriously ill. In accordance with Msgr. Carroll's recommendations, the Vatican organized an aid mission under the direction of the dynamic Msgr. Carroll, dubbed the « wonder-working Monseigneur », which provided relief to enormous masses of internees, who were assisted impartially without any discrimination as to faith, race, nationality or political affiliation.

In executing this arduous work, Catholic America lent considerable help, not only through expert and selfless individuals such as Msgr. Carroll but also through the Catholic War Relief Services, which collaborated with the Pontifical mission. The task was carried out in the most strategic points, at Innsbruck (Mittenwald), Linz, Kassel, Munich, a zone which included 18 concentration camps, Ulm, Stuttgart and outlying districts such as the notorious Dachau, Mathdusen and Bebra, a center for masses of prisoners returning from Russia to Italy. From each of the principal stations swarmed groups of priests, doctors and sanitary assistants to work in the outlying camps. Within the radius of a few miles of Linz, the relief workers found some 200,000 refugees, while the number in the Munich and Ulm zones was even greater.

The problem confronting the Pontifical Mission was an enormously difficult one. In one camp north of Munich, for example, there were 8,000 Poles, among them 450 priests; in another an agglomeration of prisoners from the Balkan countries, a mosaic of human masses without a country.

From Dachau the Mission shipped out all the Albanians they found, many Italians and a group of Greeks in prison hospitals. The sick were transported in 17 American ambulances which Msgr. Carroll managed to obtain. He also obtained a hospital train to transport 300 ailing Italians to their homeland, supplying them with the necessary medicine and personnel. Moreover, he effected the repatriation of 2,000 Italians interned at Ulm, who had been unable to realize their dream of returning home because of bureaucratic obstacles.

These are only a few examples of the wonders achieved by the N.C.W.C. in 44 nations beginning in the autumn of 1943 when the first aid reached East Africa, the Middle East and India. Millions upon millions of war victims were given food, clothing and refuge by the 150 centers of Catholic assistance. Two millions in Germany alone, plus Belgium, Holland, England, Malta, Spain, Portugal, from Africa to Switzerland, from India to Egypt, Poles scattered everywhere, homeless Chinese, *ad infinitum*. There was a time when more than 6,000,000 war victims, differing in political and religious creeds as well as in the color of their skins, depended upon the N.C.W.C. for their very existence.

Through collections made in the American Catholic churches on the fourth Sunday of Lent in 1945, the American Episcopate offered the Holy Father another vast sum of money to continue and enlarge his gigantic « charity program ». To alleviate the bitter hardship suffered during the first post-war winter, that of 1945-46, the N.C.W.C. launched a campaign to raise food for the war victims, in which 100 American dioceses joyously participated to reach the goal of 20 million food parcels. When the campaign, in which 425,000 volunteers took part, was over, 15,000 parishes had surpassed their target by two and a half million food parcels. This contribution went far to combat famine in Europe and Asia.

The generosity of American Catholics was truly miraculous. From the autumn of 1943 to November, 1945, the American Catholic parishes collected 44,000 tons of food as well as clothing, for an approximate total of $35,000,000. In a cable sent in November, 1945, by the Pope to the Apostolic Delegate, Archbishop A. G. Cicognani, the Holy Father expressed his « cordial and paternal gratitude » to the generous American Catholics for « this ultimate proof of zeal and charity on the part of our dear sons in the United States and for their Christian effort to offer aid in such great measure to the innocent victims of war ».

XI — In conclusion, the patriotic loyalty of the Catholic Americans in itself constitutes the most concrete confutation of all the calumnies heaped upon them by their adversaries, from the early 19th Century Federalists to the Twentieth-century Ku Klux Klan. Despite all these spontaneous disinterested patriotic manifestations, in which the Roman Catholic Church in America has always shown itself in perfect accord with the American nation, still there are those in bad faith who seek to distort the facts and cry out in alarm that the Roman Church is seeking to « influence » the great Republic of the West.

But to those who question the crystal purity of its impartial loyal patriotism, the Catholic Church can well reply the apology of Oriental children to their playmates, the same apology used by the Divine Master to his adversaries :

> « We played the flute,
> But you did not dance;
> We sang lute songs
> But you did not weep ».

A STATISTICAL RECORD
OF THE DEVELOPMENT OF THE
CATHOLIC CHURCH IN THE U. S.

CHAPTER XI

An expert in ecclesiastical history, Reverend I. J. Laux, has said that « the advance of the Catholic Church in the United States by leaps and bounds, from 25,000 faithful at the time of the Revolution to 20,000,000 in 1931, is an outstanding phenomenon in Church history » ([1]). Certainly it deserves particular attention, as well as the various collateral problems it poses.

Statistically, the period preceding the Revolution offers scanty and inadequate data. Long before the arrival of the Pilgrims in 1620, Catholic missionaries had crossed the country in every direction, from Florida to California, from the mouth of the St. Lawrence to the Gulf of Mexico. These heralds of the Cross were the first explorers of the immense area, the first to have dealings with the Indians and open schools and missions among them. It is a pity that the statistics of their great work were not gathered. It has been said that in 1669 the faithful numbered 2,000; in 1708, 3,000; in 1755, 7,000; but these figures are hypothetical. The Vicar Apostolic of London, Richard Challoner, who had jurisdiction also over the Catholics of the Colonies, expressed his opinion in 1765 that Catholics in America were few indeed, outside of Maryland and Pennsylvania.

But in 1790 the United States government took its first census, in accordance with a federal decree that the nation's population was to be tabulated once every ten years ([2]). The date happily corresponds with the establishment at Baltimore of a center of religious authority for the new nation, under Bishop Carroll ([3]). In his letter accepting his appointment, Msgr. Carroll informed the Sacred Congregation of Propaganda that in the range of his own jurisdiction under the spiritual care of 34 priests, he roughly estimated there were 30,000 Catholics, of which 15,000 were in Maryland, 7,000 in Pennsylvania, 3,000 at Detroit and Vincennes, 2,500 in Illinois, 1,500 in New York and a few scattered through New England. He omitted those resident in territories then Spanish (New Mexico, Texas, Arizona, California), in Louisiana and along the Mississippi. These 30,000 faithful, of which 5,500 were of French origin, constituted one Catholic for every 131 of the entire white population of the 13 original States.

This modest initial figure served as the point of departure for the extraordinary advance of Catholicism in America — an advance so precipitous that it makes one think of a Rossini crescendo.

In the year 1800, when the total population of the country stood at 5,380,000 inhabitants, the number of Catholics had jumped to 100,000 — or one out of every 53. By 1808 Catholicism had spread so rapidly that Pius VII created four Suffragan dioceses — in New York, Philadelphia, Boston and Louisville. At that time the Church had 80 churches and 70 priests for a flock of 120,000 faithful, which in another two years mounted to 150,000, or one out of every 48 inhabitants.

When in 1815 the Rev. Charles Nerinck of Kentucky published his monograph, *A Look at the Present Condition of the Roman Catholic Church in*

North America, he estimated that of a population varying between 7 and 8,000,000, there were 300,000 Catholics. By 1820 the ratio was one Catholic to every 33 inhabitants, and by 1829, the year of the first Provincial Council of Baltimore, the Catholic population had swelled to an estimated 500,000, or one Catholic to 24. So swiftly did Catholicism grow that in 1839 Bishop England was able to report a figure of 1,200,000 faithful, with 545 priests and 539 churches and chapels. The following year, the federal census registered a total population of 17,000,000. On this basis one out of every 14 inhabitants was a Catholic (⁴).

Sixty years after the Treaty of Paris — in 1842 — the initial mere handful of Catholics had mounted to a figure of some 2,000,000, and the Church could boast of 33 dioceses, an Archbishop, 1,300 priests of nine religious congregations, 1,545 churches, a university at St. Louis, 20 seminaries, 17 colleges for men and 91 for women. The advance was so constant that the Fathers of the fifth Provincial Council at Baltimore in 1843 had reason to quote the Pauline paean : *Verbum Dei currit et dilatatur.* An eighth of the white population of the United States were members of the Church.

And the advance continued, achieving its own rhythm. On May 9, 1852, the first Plenary Council of Baltimore offered dramatic proof of the measure of Catholic growth in the United States. The first Provincial Council of 1829 had consisted of one Archbishop and nine Bishops; on this day, the solemn procession in the cathedral that opened the council included five Archbishops (Baltimore, New York, Cincinnati, St. Louis and New Orleans), 24 Suffragan Bishops, an Abbot of the Trappists, the Superiors of eight religious congregations, the officers of the Synod and the Bishops' theologians. The occasion reminded the historian O'Gorman of

361

the apostolic zeal of the early days of Christianity. At the end of the council, the hierarchy was enriched with another archbishopric and ten bishoprics ([5]).

The federal statistics for the year 1860 showed a population of 31,500,000, of which 4,500,000 were Catholics, the majority being Irish who had immigrated from 1841 onwards. The second Plenary Council of Baltimore in 1866 provoked this comment from a European observer : « Illegal for a half-century, rejected by the only colony it had founded, Catholicism now sees opening ahead of it an era of liberty. Its development is nothing less than a triumph — continuous, uninterrupted and growing daily » ([6]).

The 1870 statistics marked another step forward — 5,000,000 Catholics out of 38,500,000, with a ratio of seven and a half to one. The statistics for 1880 — for a nation that now included 38 States and nine territories — showed 500,000 more Catholics.

In 1889 the hierarchy of the United States celebrated its centenary; for the occasion, Pope Leo XIII, in his Letter to Cardinal Gibbons, drew attention to the fact that in contrast to the 40,000 Catholics of a century before the faithful now numbered 10,000,000 ([7]).

The 20th century was to see even greater advances. O'Gorman estimates that in 1904, out of 76,000,000 people in 45 States and five territories of the Union, there were 12,000,000 Catholics, or a sixth of the entire population.

In 1916, when the population reached the figure of 100,000,000, the census made this astounding revelation : « Catholics constitute two-thirds of the church members in all our cities with a population over 300,000; a half in all cities between 300,000 and 50,000; and almost a half (46%) in cities between 50,000 and 25,000. In two-thirds of the States, Catholics are more numerous than

members of any other denomination; and in 15 States —
the most developed and advanced — Catholics outnumber
all non-Catholics together » ([8]).

The eloquence of these statistics is irrefutable : out
of an average of about 42,000,000 members of all
churches, denominations and sects, 17,500,000 were Catholics — a third of the total. The fact was emphasized
in a speech by Cardinal W. H. O'Connell of Boston,
honoring Cardinal Gibbons at Catholic University; he
spoke of the « incredible development of the infant Church
of Maryland to the gigantic Church of America ».

New surprises were revealed in the official statistics
for 1930 : more than 20,000,000 faithful, four Cardinals,
16 Archbishops, 104 Bishops and 27,854 priests, of which
8,000 belonged to religious orders.

Fourteen years later, the *Official Roman Catholic
Directory of the United States* for 1944 published a figure
of 23,963,671 Catholics in the United States, including
Alaska and Hawaii. Moreover, it set at around 85,000
the number of conversions to Catholicism in the preceding year and noted that the ranks of the clergy now
comprised 25,299 diocesan priests and 12,450 priests
belonging to religious congregations — a total, therefore,
of 37,749 ministers of the sanctuary. It listed 14,791
parishes, plus 6,115 parochial missions, or a grand total
of 20,906 houses of God ([9]).

To this huge sum can be added 4,322 semi-public
chapels of educational and charitable institutions. Catholic educators, expressly dedicated to scholastic instruction, may be listed in this proportion : 4,647 priest-
teachers of every grade, from elementary school to
university; 3,223 priests in other educative branches;
76,908 sisters; and finally 7,633 lay scholars.

Further statistics are revealing : 368 orphanages and
refuges for the young; a total of 64,144 children benefit-

ing from Catholic assistance; 770 Catholic hospitals equipped with about 78,000 beds for 3,000,000 patients per year, all under the supervision of a veritable army of sisters.

We learn from the *Official Catholic Year Book* published in Washington (June, 1955) that the number of Catholics residing in the U.S.A., Alaska and Hawaiian Islands is 32,575,702. In the U.S.A. alone there are 32,403,332 faithful with an increase of more than 8,000,000 with reference to 1945.

The greatest increase in the number of Catholics has been in Brooklyn (53,570), Trenton (43,017), New York (41,784), Chicago (40,059), Saint Augustine (38,948), Philadelphia (32,000), Boston (30,155) and Newark 28,688).

The number of Archdioceses in the U. S. A. is twenty-six with a total Catholic population of 15,280,263 faithful, while the dioceses number 106, including the Vicariate of Alaska, with a population of 17,295,439 Catholics. Six of the Archdioceses have a Catholic population of over 1,000,000, namely those of Chicago, Boston, New York, Philadelphia, Newark and Detroit.

For the ninth consecutive year the number of converts has surpassed 100,000. In fact in 1954 there were 137,310 Baptisms of adults, showing an increase of 10,733 with reference to the year before. Adding together the number of converts of the last ten years one obtains the encouraging figure of 1,160,054.

From the *Year Book* we also learn that there are in the U.S.A. 208 members of the Ecclesiastical Hierarchy, a number never reached hitherto in the history of the Church in this country : these are divided as follows : 4 Cardinals, 34 Archbishops and 170 Bishops. In 1954 an increase of 1519 priests, 61 lay brothers and 4014 sisters was registered.

The number of students enrolled in the Catholic institutes has also increased and this has led consequently to an increase of teachers. The new teachers are partly lay (3668) and partly priests (4581). The total number of the Catholic scholastic institutes is 12,494 divided as follows : 78 diocesan seminaries, 385 seminaries of religious communities, 247 partly colleges and partly universities, 1557 secondary parochial and diocesan schools, 842 private secondary schools, 8843 elementary parochial schools and 542 private elementary schools. 15,901 seminarians are enrolled in the 78 diocesan seminaries, while 16,493 students attend the seminaries of the various religious communities.

There are therefore actually in the U. S. 32,394 candidates for the priesthood. During the course of last year there was a notable increase in the number of pupils attending the Catholic elementary schools : 302,340. The parochial schools alone are attended by 3,253,608 pupils, a number which assumes particular importance if one thinks of the many non-Catholic scholastic institutions existing in the United States.

Accurate statistics have finally revealed that a total number of 6,367,414 students attend Catholic schools and universities, showing an increase of about 8% with reference to last year.

We also learn that the 739 Catholic hospitals in America received 9,319,356 patients. These figures are significant. Comparing them with the number of Catholics residing in America (32,575,702) it is easy to understand that a great number of the patients are not Catholics.

To supply personnel for the Catholic health institutions, 53 new training-colleges have been opened, which together with those already existing are attended by

35,067 students. There are 299 institutions caring for 27,147 aged and invalid persons.

Well might it be said that « the little plant has become a great tree indeed », spreading its branches from the Atlantic to the Pacific.

II — The silent eloquence of all these statistics provokes certain reflections.

From a viewpoint of comparative geography, the Catholic Church of America surpasses today all the non-Catholic religious associations in the New England states, once the stronghold of the intransigent Pilgrim Fathers, as well as in the Middle Atlantic, the Central Northeast and the Pacific states. In addition, it outnumbers any other religious group in the States of Delaware, Maryland, Louisiana, Texas and California and the District of Columbia. It exercises its apostolate on three different ethnic groups — the white, the red and the black.

The amplitude of its sphere of action, seen in conjunction with its multitude of activities (hospitals, schools, institutions of every kind), adds every day to the importance of the Church in America as a positive influence for good in the entire world. Its practical functioning during the two World Wars provided additional evidence of this.

From, let us say, an apologetic point of view, the Catholic flowering in America put to the test the divine mission of the Church, whose prodigious vitality reflects something of the immortal youth of Christ Himself. Its growth in America, despite the four successive currents hostile to it (the Native Americans, the Know-Nothings, the American Protective Association and the Ku Klux Klan), and all the persecutions it endured, is even worthier of consideration in view of the fact that its successive waves of support — the immigrants — represented the poorest and most oppressed peoples of the earth.

From an organic point of view, the statistical vitality of the Church throws into relief the fact that Catholicism, exempt from the support of thrones, governments or political parties, has asked nothing but to be left in peace and to complete its own program, since it is in itself a symbol of liberty.

Finally, from the essential viewpoint of spirituality, these statistics tell us that Catholicism transcends them, for they only summarize its purely external elements and give numerical proof of its phenomenal reality. As everywhere, but perhaps even more in America because of its vastness, Catholicism is « spirit and life ». Its exterior aspect and the details of its statistics — necessary for comparative reference — are *sub specie aeternitatis* and are in themselves transient. But the Church's intimate essence and its intrinsic vitality are informed with the life of the spirit.

A revelation of this truth was made in 1939 by Pope Pius XII, echoing Leo XIII, in his Encyclical, *Sertum Laetitiae*. « In these 50 years », said the Holy Father, « the progress of the Church has not been retarded but has enjoyed the greatest expansion and the most robust growth. Luxuriant is the life that the grace of the Holy Spirit has brought to flower in the sanctuary of the heart; consoling are the multitudes of churches, where so many of the faithful draw near to receive the Bread of the Angels, the Nourishment of the strong... ».

BIBLIOGRAPHICAL NOTES

NOTE FOR CHAPTER I

(1) Cf. CARNEGIE, ANDREW: *The Empire of Business*, Garden City, New York, 1933; IDEM, *The Gospel of Wealth*, ibidem, 1933.

(2) American sociologists and educators have not tried to hide the evils that plague this youthful nation, conceived out of such overflowing energy. Cardinal Gibbons, for example, stigmatized divorce as « only slightly less deplorable than Mormonism and in a certain sense more dangerous, since Mormonism has the sanction of civil law ».

Cf. GIBBONS: *Our Christian Heritage*, 1889.

(3) We are well acquainted with the long battle of « Prohibition », by which the American Government sought to abolish the traffic and sale of alcoholic beverages.   In 1846 the State of Maine passed prohibitionist legislation, to be followed in 1852 by Massachusetts, Rhode Island and Vermont.   One by one other States joined them, leading up to the Congressional Act of December 1, 1917, which forbade the production of any liquors except beer and wine.   On January 16, 1920, the 18th Amendment, imposing national Prohibition, was enacted into law, having been ratified by both houses of Congress.   The measure, however, soon proved inapplicable or, at any rate, difficult and costly to enforce.

Furthermore, it provoked such nation-wide opposition that it was subsequently abolished by the 21st Amendment, passed by the Senate on February 16, 1933, and by the House four days later.

Free from Puritan excesses in this respect, excesses which the Puritan was wont to apply more to his neighbor than to himself, the Catholic Church was more indulgent in this question.   At one moment, however, the Church was called on the carpet by its adversaries and was obliged to take action.   At that time, Archbishop John Ireland, of St. Paul, assumed leadership of a temperance movement. Cf. JOHN IRELAND: *The Catholic Church and the Saloons*, North American Review (159), 1894. CALVIN, D.: *Prohibition in the United States: a History of the Prohibition Party and Movement,* New York, 1926; FISHER-BROUGHAM: *A Noble Experiment,* 1930; CATLIN, G. E. G.: *Liquor Control,* 1931; WARBURTON, CLARK: *The Economic Results of Prohibition,* 1932.

(4) Cf. BENIAMINO DE RITIS: *Impressioni e giudizi sugli Stati Uniti d'un giornalista colto,* Milan, 1934. To be frank to the point of self-accusation requires the courage to point out that much of this apparent paganism denounced by De Ritis is substantially anti-Puritanism of recent European importation. It is due to the immigrants, chiefly German and Italian, that the religious observance of the Sabbath day has been transformed from the « Puritan Sabbath » to the so-called « Continental Sabbath ». This scandalized, among others, a Baptist publisher, who described modern Chicago on Sunday as « a Berlin in the morning and a Paris in the afternoon ».

For other opinions in recent Italian works, cf. CECCHI, EMILIO: *America Amara,* Florence, Sansoni, 1940; SOLDATI, MARIO: *America, primo amore,* Turin, Einaudi, 1945; MAURO, FR.: *Gli Stati Uniti visti da un ingegnere,* Milan, Hoepli, 1945.

(5) Many have wondered to which denomination Abraham Lincoln subscribed. We shall see elsewhere that his home life during his youth was not, it appears, without Catholic contacts and influences. It is well known that he disapproved of the various Protestant denominations adhering to so many « isms ».

(6) Cf. EDWARDS, JONATHAN: *Works,* Vol. II, 337. Also DORNBLASER, T. F.: *Providence in Our History,* Lutheran Review (Gettysburg, Pa.), 1894, p. 386.

(7) Cf. WAGNER, CHARLES: *Vers le coeur de l'Amérique,* Paris, Fischbacher, 1907.

.(8) Literature on investigations into American idealism is extraordinarily rich in all languages. Some representative books: DE TOCQUEVILLE, A.: *De la Démocratie en Amérique,* Paris, 1835; JANNET, CL.: *Les Etats-Unis contemporains,* Paris, 1889; BRYCE J.: *The American Commonwealth,* New York, 1891; LEROY-BEAULIEU P.: *Les Etats-Unis au XX Siècle,* Paris, 1906; VAN DYKE H.: *The Spirit of America,* New York, 1910; ADAMS, EPHRAIM D.: *Power of Ideals in American History,* New Haven, 1913; HAMMOND, JOHN HAYS: *Great American Issues: Political, Social and Economic,* New York, 1921; QUINN A. HOBSON: *The Soul of America,* Philadelphia, 1932; CARNEGIE, ANDREW: *Triumphant Democracy,* Garden City, New York, 1933.

(9) Cf. WILL ALLEN SINCLAIR: *Life of Cardinal Gibbons,* 1922.

(10) Cf. Roz, Firmin: *L'énergie américaine, Evolution des Etats-Unis*, Paris, 1914.

(11) Cf. Alderson, A.: *Carnegie: The Man and His life*, New York, 1902.

(12) Cf. Sears J. Brundage: *Philanthropy in the History of American Higher Education*, Washington, 1922; Watson F. Dekker: *The Charity Organization Movement in the United States: A study in American philanthropy*, New York, 1922.

(13) De Tocqueville traveled in the United States (1831-32) with his friend Gustave de Beaumont, to prepare his major work « Democracy in America » (Paris, 1835). During their journey, the two struck up close friendships with a number of Catholic clergymen who helped them discover the true nature of the country. Their documents refer to about 200 such names. Cf. Caboara, L.: *Democrazia e libertà nel pensiero di Alexis de Tocqueville*, Milan, Hoepli, 1946; Denover, Pierre: *La Vie catholique aux Etats-Unis*, La Vie Intellectuelle, Paris, 1946, p. 277.

(14) Cf. Zollmann, C.: *American Civil Church Law*, St. Paul, 1917, pp. 9-23.

(15) Cf. Sanford Hunt: *Laws Relating to Religious Corporations*, New York, 1876; Klein, Abbé F.: *La Séparation aux Etats-Unis: Histoire, lois, coûtumes, documents*, Paris, 1908; Zollmann, Carl: *American Civil Church Law*, St. Paul, 1917 and 1933; Dudley G. Wooten: *Church and State in the United States*, Boston, 1923; Marshall, Ch. C.: *The Roman Catholic Church in the Modern State*, New York, 1928; *Grants of Lands and Gifts of Money to Catholic and Non-Catholic Institutions in New York, Compared*, Catholic Publishing Society; Dignan, Patrick J.: *A History of the Legal Incorporation of Catholic Church Property in the United States (1784-1933)*, Washington, 1933.

(16) Cf. Boutmy, M. E.: *Le Sentiment religieux aux Etats-Unis*, Revue Bleu, Paris, 1890, p. 744; Gourd, Alphred: *Les Chartes Coloniales et les Constitutions des Etats-Unis*, Paris, 1903; Rowe, H. K.: *History of Religion in the United States*, New York, 1924; Kistler C. E.: *This Nation Under God: A religious supplement to American history*, Boston, 1924; Hall, Thomas C.: *The Religious Background of American Culture*, Boston, 1930; Meysztowicz, Msgr. Valerian: *La Religion dans les Constitutions des Etats modernes*, Rome, 1938.

(17) Cf. Waring, G. J.: *United States Chaplains in the World War*, New York, 1924.

(18) Cf. Keyer, William C.: *American Trust in Providence*, Boston, 1925.

(19) Cf. A Discourse delivered at the Roman Catholic Church in Boston on May 9th, 1798, a Day recommended by the President for humiliation and prayer throughout the United States. By the Rev. John Thayer, Catholic Missioner, Boston, 1798; a Sermon preached on the 9th day of May, 1789, observed as a Day of fasting and prayer to implore Divine aid and protection in favor of the United States, By the Rev. S. F. O'Gallagher, Catholic priest of Charleston, Charleston (1798).

(20) HOUGH: *Proclamation for Thanksgiving*, Albany, 1858; LOVE: *The Fasts and Thanksgiving Day of New England*, New York, 1907; SCHAUFFER: *Thanksgiving*, New York, 1907.

(21) Cf. GUNTHER, JOHN: *Inside America*, New York, Harper, 1945.

(22) Cf. MITCHELL, A.: *The Bible and the Republic*, in Christian Thought, New York, 1893, p. 60; HAMPTON, VERNON B.: *Religious Background of the White House*, Boston, 1932. (Here the author points out that, of America's 32 Presidents, five were brought up in religious schools, as were seven « First Ladies », or wives of Presidents).

(23) « Si les habitants sont sages (cette Terre) doit étonner un jour le reste de l'Univers par sa puissance et peut-être lui imposer la loi d'être heureux comme lui ». Cf. MOREAU DE SAINT MÉRY: *Voyage aux Etats-Unis (1793-98)*, New Haven, 1913, p. 38.

NOTE FOR CHAPTER II

(1) For exclusively Protestant works, cf. BAIRD, *Religions in America*, New York, 1844; DANIEL J. RUPP, *History of the Religious Denominations in the United States*, Philadelphia, 1844; P. D. GORRIE, *History of the Churches and Sects of the United States*, Colpy, New York, 1850; HENRIOD, *Churches in America* (French), Neuchâtel, 1869; J. P. THOMPSON, *Church and State in the United States*, Boston, 1873; HARPER, *First Century of the Republic*, New York, 1876; D. DORCHESTER, *Christianity in the United States*, New York, 1888; H. K. CARROLL, *Religious Forces in the United States*, New York, 1893; BACON WOOLSEY, *A History of American Christianity*, New York, 1897; WILLIAM WARREN SWEET ,*The Story of Religion in America*, New York, 1930; W. E. GARRISON, *The March of Faith: The Story of Religion in America Since 1865*, New York, 1933; J. M. MECKLIN, *The Story of American Dissent*, New York, 1934; WILLIAM H. ALLISON, *Inventory of Unpublished Material of American Religious History in Protestant Church Archives and other Repositories*, Washington, D.C., 1910;

HENRY K. ROWE, *The History of Religion in the United States*, New York, 1924; THOMAS C. HALL, *The Religious Background of American Culture*, Boston, 1930; H. N. WIEMAN - B. E. MELAND, *American Philosophies of Religion*, Chicago, 1936; ERNEST SUTHERLAND BATES, *American Faith*, New York, 1940; G. SHERWOOD EDDY, *The Kingdom of God and the American Dream*, New York, 1941. For the generic bibliography of American Prot- estant church history, cf. S. M. JACKSON, *Bibliography of American Church History (1820-93)*, New York, 1894; J. F. HURST, *Literature of Theology* New York, 1896 (contains rich bibliography of heterodox church history in America); P. G. MODE, *Source Book and Bibliographical Guide for American Church History*, Menasha, Wis., 1921; S. I. CASE AND OTHERS, *A Bibliographical Guide for American Church History*, Chicago, 1931 (cf. *Christianity in America*, pp. 170-211, Chapter VIII).

(2) Cf. general bibliography of the history of Catholicism in North America in the Introduction.

(3) Cf. W. R. HARRIS, *The Mystery of a Land That Disappeared*, in the *Toronto Archaelogical Report*, 1918, pp. 54 et seq.

(4) Cf. PESCHEL-RUGE, *Geschichte der Erdkunde* (second edition), Mu- nich, 1877; PASTOR, *Storia dei Papi*, III, 493, Desclée, Rome, 1912.

(5) Cf. FATHER W. M. PEITZ, *Tolomeo e l'America*, in *L'Illustrazione Vaticana*, Oct. 1, 1933, p. 761.

(6) We are not entering into the subject of Apostolic evangelization in this part of the world. A scholar has noted that a « strange hypothesis, founded on an arbitrary interpretation of a passage in the Acts of the Apostles, contends that St. Thomas preached not only in India itself but in the lands Columbus discovered, similarly called Indies ' ». No authority lends the least reliability to such a bold thesis (cf. *American Ecclesiastical Review*, 1899, pp. 1-18. Nevertheless, one reads with interest, in *De Imperio Militantis Ecclesiae*, by Isidoro de Isolani (1513), that « ... *jussu regis Aragonum repertae sunt insulae mirae magnitudinis... ad quas insulas licet perveniret sonus predicationis Christi, etiam tempore Apostolorum ut a nobis creditur, de quibus dicitur ' in omnem terram exivit sonus eorum '*... » This is an individual opinion, founded on a convenient exegesis. It strikes the imagination. For a general pre-Columbian bibliography (it is under- stood that this is a presentation not of absolute facts but of present-day conjectures and research), cf. J. A. FABRICIUS, *Salutaris Lux Evangelii toto Orbi per Divinam Gratiam Exoriens*, Hamburg, 1731; RAFU, *American An- tiquity* (Latin), Copenhagen, 1837; E. H. HARRIS, *Bibliotheca Americana Vetustissima: A Description of Works Relating to America Published Be- tween the Years 1492-1551*, New York, 1866 (reprinted in Paris, 1922); BEAUVAIS, *Origine et Fondation du plus ancien Evêché du Nouveau Monde*,

Paris, 1878; J. WINSOR, *Narrative and Critical History of America*, Boston, 1886-89; GAFFAREL, *Etudes sur les Rapports de l'Amérique et de l'ancien Continent avant Christophe Colomb*, Paris, 1889; STORM, *Studies on Voyages to Vinland* (Danish), Copenhagen, 1889; JELIC, *L'Evangélisation de l'Amérique avant Colomb*, Paris, 1890; REEVES, *The Discovery of Vinland*, London, 1890; DE ROO, *America Before Columbus*, Philadelphia, 1890; ANDERSON, *America Was Not Discovered by Columbus* (fourth edition), Chicago, 1894; J. C. HEYWOOD, *The Mediaeval Church*, in *C. H. R.* (III), with documents discovered by the author in the Vatican Archives, Rome, 1893 (they are the same used by O'Gorman for his study, *Catholic Mediaeval Church* in the *Catholic University Bulletin*, I, 1895); J. FISCHER, *Die Entdeckungen der Normannen in Amerika*, Freiburg, 1902; FISKE, *The Discovery of America* (2 vols.), Boston, 1902; B. ANDERSON HAUCK-RASMUS, *The Flatey Book and Recently Discovered Vatican Mss. Concerning America As Early As the Tenth Century*, London-New York, 1906; M. DE MURROUGH, *Explorers in the New World Before and After Columbus*, London, 1909; W. A. CRAIGIE, *The Icelandic Sagas*, 1913; AMYAR EMBURY, *Early American Churches*, New York, 1914; H G. LEACH, *Scandinavia of the Scandinavians*, 1916; H. A. BELLOWS, *The Edda Sagas*, published by the American-Scandinavian Foundation, 1923; LELIO BASSO, *La scoperta dell'America prima di Colombo*, in the *Rivista Coloniale*, XIV, Rome, January 1924; LARSEN SOFUS, *The Discovery of North America Twenty Years Before Columbus*, Copenhagen-London, 1925 (in connection with this work, cf. the article by W. M. PEITZ, *Tolomeo e l'America* in *L'Illustrazione Vaticana*, Oct. 1, 1933, pp. 759-761); SATTEFOSSE-ROUX, *Bibliographie de l'Atlantide et des questions connexées*, Lyons, 1926; L. SPENCE, *The Preaching of the Crusades in America*, in *Discovery*, London, November 1926, pp. 386 et seq. (valuable Vatican documentation of the preaching of the Crusades in the Norwegian colony of Vinland), J. J. WALSH, *Catholic Background of the Discovery of America*, in *C. H. R.*, July 1927, pp. 175 et seq.; STETSON MERRILL, *The Catholic Contribution of the Norse Discovery of America*, in *C. H. R.*, January 1928, pp. 589 et seq.; LANGLOIS, *L'Amérique pre-colombienne et la conquête européenne*, Paris, 1928; HALLIDOR HERMANNS-SON, *The Northmen in America (982-1500)*; E. GRAY, *Leif Ericson, and the Sagas*, in *Open Court*, April-May 1930, pp. 193 et seq. and 272 et seq.; KOHT HALVDAM, *The Ancient Norse Sagas*, published by the American-Scandinavian Foundation, 1931. Cf. the following magazine articles: C. H. MEIMBERG, *The Norse Church and Mediaeval America* (XI), with bibliography, in *C. H. R.* (V. n. s.), 179-216; L. N. LARSON, *The Church in North America (Greenland) in the Middle Ages*, with bibliography, in *C. H. R.*, I, 175-194; STETSON MERRILL, *The Vinland Problem Through Four Centuries*, in *C. H. R.*, XXI, pp. 21-48; P. GUILDAY, *The Mediaeval American Church*, with bibliography, in *C. H. R.*, III, pp. 210-227.

374

(7) Upon his debarkation at Palos, Columbus wrote down the events of his extraordinary trip, with all their particulars, for the Treasurer General of Spain. It was in the happy spring of 1493, and only a few weeks later this exceptional document was circulated in several Latin editions published by two German printers in Rome, Plannck and Silber. On October 25 of the same year, in Florence, under the title, « This is the story of the discovery of the Canary Islands extracted from an epistle of Christopher Columbus », there appeared a little poem in octavo, which was actually a poetic Italian version of Columbus' letter. Its author was Giuliano De' Dati, a Florentine, then confessor-priest of the Vatican basilica and one of the founders in Rome of the Oratory of Divine Love. The rhythmic translation was commissioned by one Filippo La Lagname, or Del Lignamine, a native of Messina then in great favor at the court of Sixtus IV. For sources on the Columbian discoveries, cf. the official collections of Columbian manuscripts, published by Ponthenier in Genoa in 1823; *Cartas de Indias por primera vez por el Ministero del Fomento*, Madrid, 1877; *La Coleccion de documentos ineditos relativos al descumbrimento, conquista y organisacion de las antiguas posesiones españolas de ultra mar*, published by the Royal Academy of History; *Raccolta di Documenti e Studi*, published by the Royal Columbian Commission, Rome, 1894. Cf. also W. IRWING, *Viaggi e Scoperte dei Compagni di Cristoforo Colombo* (translation), Molina, Milan, 1842; PAOLO REVELLI, *Terre d'America e Archivi d'Italia*, Treves, Milan, 1926; RINALDO CADDEO, *C. Colombo, Giornale di Bordo (1492-93)*, Bompiani, Milan, 1939.

(8) Cf. LEO XIII, *Letter to Bishops and Clergy on Columbus*, in *Researches*, 1892, pp. 177 et seq.; F. FITA, *Quarto Centenario de Colon: Enciclica de Leon XIII*, published by the Royal Academy of History, Madrid, 1892, pp. 230 et seq.

(9) Cf. W. K. GILLET, *Religious Motives of Columbus*, American Society of Church History, New York, 1891, pp. 3 et seq.; F. J. HOLLY, *Ch. Columbus als Katholic*, in *Katholic*, Mainz, 1892, pp. 298 et seq.; J. BRUCKER, *Christophe Colomb, l'explorateur et le chrétien*, in *Etudes*, Paris, 1892, pp. 5 et seq.; WILLIAM STEPHEN PERRY, *Catholicism and Columbus*, in *Church Eclectic*, Milwaukee, 1893-94, pp. 812 et seq.; M. P. WILLAMIL, *Religious Character of the Discovery of America*, in *Catholic World*, 1893, pp. 244 et seq.; H. M. SCOTT, *Providential Preparation for the Discovery of America*, in *Our Day*, Boston, 1893, pp. 1-11.

(10) There survives, from Columbus' library, the work, *Coleccion de las profecias sobre la recuperacion de Jerusalem y el descubrimiento de las Indias*. Columbus' signature, affixed to a letter he wrote to Pope Innocent VIII, has been deduced to be a prayer to Christ. It is formed of the following letters: « S. - S.A.S. - X.M.I. - Xto Ferens », which were held

to mean: « *Servus supplex Altissimi Salvatoris Christus, Maria, Joseph, Christo Ferens* ». Cf. Fritz Streicher, *El Monograma de las Cartas de Colon*, in *Cultura Venezolana*, XIV, pp. 177 et seq.

(11) Cf. *Psalterium Quadrilinguae*: « *Psalterium hœbraeum, graecum, arabicum et chaldaeum, cum tribus latinis interpretationibus et glossis. Impressit Petrus Paulus Porrus, Genuae, in aedibus Nicolai Justiniani, 1516* ». This work is doubly precious, being the first polyglot edition of a Biblical work printed in type appropriate to each language, and for the above-mentioned note of Father Agostino Giustiniani   An original copy in the United States is at the famous Jesuit school at Woodstock, Maryland.

(12) For Columbus and his expedition, cf. Christopher Columbus, *Journal of the First Voyage to America*, New York, 1924; St. Grande, *La stampa missionaria nel periodo della scoperta ed esplorazione dell'America*, in the Bulletin of the Italian Royal Geographical Society, Rome, August 1926, pp. 658 et seq.; J. Walsh, *Century of Columbus*, Fordham University, New York; MacCarthy, *Columbus and his Predecessors*, Philadelphia; Prescott, *Ferdinand and Isabella*, 1892; J. Fiske, *The Discovery of America* (2 vols), Boston, 1892; Altolaguirre, *La Patria de D. Cristobal Colon segun las actas notoriales de Italia*, in *Real Ac. Hist. Bol.*, March 1918, pp. 200 et seq.; M. Beaufreton, *Aperçus nouveaux sur l'iconographie de Ch. Colomb*, in *Arch. Franc. Hist.*, July 1918, pp. 374 et seq.; Frank Owen Paine, *Our Memorials of Columbus*, in *Munsey's*, New York, October 1920, pp. 23 et seq.; Vignaud, *Le vrai Chr. Colomb et la légende*, Paris, 1921; W. T. Walsh, *Isabella of Spain*, New York, 1930, Bernard Duhr, S.J., *The Columbus Problem: A Study in Modern Historiography*, in *Stimmen der Zeit*, XX, pp. 195-207; Andre Marius, *Christophe Colomb sera-t-il canonisé?*, in *Revue de l'Amérique Latine*, Paris, April 1926, pp. 309 et seq., F. M. Paolini, *C. Colombo nella vita morale*, Leghorn, 1938; De Lollis, *C. Colombo nella leggenda e nella storia* (2nd edition), Rome, 1924; A. Mevil, *La Caravelle 'Santa Maria'*, in *Soc. Am. Paris Journal*, XXI, 1929, I, pp. 277 et seq.; *Columbus Codex* (work made about 1502 under the direction of the Discoverer himself, containing documents referring to his rights and privileges; a copy is in the manuscript collection of the Library of Congress in Washington); M. Serrano y Sanz, *El Archivo Colombino de la Cartuia de las Cuevas*, Madrid, 1930; F. Battistini, *L'Ancre de la Santa Maria' de Colomb*, in *Revue de la Corse*, Paris, XII, n. 71, pp. 235 et seq.; Emiliano Tejera, *Los restos de Colon en Santo Domingo*, San Domingo, 1926; R. Cronau, *The Last Resting Place of Columbus*, New York, 1928; D. Romulo Carbia, *La nueva historia del descubrimiento de America*, Buenos Aires, 1936; Idem, *La investigacion cientifica y el descubrimiento de America*, Buenos Aires, 1937; Piero Gribaudi, *Il Padre Gaspare Gorricio di Novara, amico e confidente di C. Colombo*, Turin, 1938; S. Madariaga, *Christopher Columbus; Being the Life of the Very Magnificent*

Lord Don Cristobal Colon, New York, 1940 (this author would actually make Columbus a Jew); D. SARGENT, *Christopher Columbus*, Milwaukee, 1941. A fertile field of research opens in relation to the direct influence of the Dominicans on the discovery of America. Cf. O. P. MANDONNET, *Les Dominicains et la Découverte de l'Amérique*, Paris, 1893; C. M. ANTHONY, *The Dominicans and the Discovery of America* in *Dominican Year Book*, 1915; JORDAN DILLON, *Dominican Influence in the Discovery of America*, in *Records*, Philadelphia, September 1930, pp. 193-299. These three authors mention Father Diego Deza, friend of Columbus, noted scientist and Spanish prelate. At the Rabida, the famous Franciscan convent a half-league from Palos, in Andalusia, Columbus in 1484-85, won the support of two illustrious Franciscans, Father Superior Juan Perez, confessor to the Queen, and Father Antonio de Marchena, a cartographer of note. In the latter Columbus found a person who understood him in a flash. Often historians have mistaken the two Franciscans for a single person. Directly in front of the Rabida is an imposing monument to Columbus, erected in May 1929, the work of the American sculptress, Miss Whitney. It was a gift from the people of the United States to Spain. It was in the church of the Rabida that the voyagers celebrated the Franciscan feast for Our Lady of the Angels, the day before they set forth on their epical journey. Cf. CASTILLO MARIANO, *El Convento de la Rabida: sa reedificacion, Huelva*, 1855; E. PALIZA-J. PEREZ, *La Rabida y C. Colon*, Huelva, 1855; J. COLL, *Colon y la Rabida* (2 editions), Madrid, 1892; VELAZQUEZ BOSCO, *El Monastero de N. S. la Rabida*, Madrid, 1914; ANGEL ORTEGA, *El Convento de la Rabida*, Madrid, 1914; V. FACCHINETTI, O.F.M. *C. Colombo e i figli del Poverello di Assisi*, in *Atti XXII Congresso Int. Americanisti in Roma* (Vol. II), Garroni, Rome, 1928. In New York alone there are three monuments to Columbus, the works of Gaetano Russo, J. Sunol and Emma Stebbins. Cf. also LÈON BLOY, *Le Révélateur du Globe*, Paris, 1882 (written to urge the beatification of Columbus); J. GRANT WILSON, *Memorials and Footprints of Columbus*, New York, 1888; *The Columbian Jubilee of Four Centuries of Catholicity in America*, Chicago, 1893.

(13) Cf. THEODORE DE BOOY, *On the Possibility of Determining the First Landfall by Columbus by Archaeological Research*, in *Hisp. Am. Hist. Review*, Baltimore-Washington, II, February 1919, pp. 55 et seq.

(14) For a biography of Father Boyl, cf. Fr. Fita, *Fray Bernard Boyl y Chr. Colon*, in *Bolet. de la R. Accademia de la Historia*, Madrid, 1891-1892, XIX-XX, pp. 173-233.

(15) Cf. A. LANNING, *The First Missionaries in the New World*, in *Records*, X, pp. 309-327.

(16) For the papal missionary decrees, cf. PEDRO DE LETURIA, S.J., *Las grandes Bulas misionales de Alejandro VI, 1493*, in *Bibl. Hispania Mis-*

sionum, 1930, I, pp. 209-251; Heywood, *Documenta selecta e Tabulario secreto Vaticano, quae Romanorum Pontificum erga Americae populos curam ac Studia tum ante tum paullo post Insulas a Chr. Columbo repertas testantur phototypia descripta;* Typis Vaticanis, 1893.

(17) Cf. Acosta, *De Natura Novi Orbis et de promulgatione Evangelii apud barbaros,* Salamanca, 1589. Cf. also recent studies by Father Imbillaga and Father Leturia.

(18) Cf. L. W. Bacon, *History of American Christianity,* New York, 1918, p. 3.

(19) For the absence of a priest on Columbus' first voyage, cf. Loughran E. Ward, *Did a Priest Accompany Columbus in 1492?,* in *C.H.R.,* 1930, XVI, pp. 164-174. For the presence of Father Boyl on the second expedition, cf. A. Ortega, *La Rabida: Historia documental Critica,* 1925-26.

(20) Cf. Fr. Fita, *La Primera Misa en America,* in *Bol. de la R. Acad. de la Historia,* Madrid, 1891, XVIII, pp. 551 et seq.

(21) Cf. Las Casas, *Historia de las Indias,* I, XI, p. 89, For D'Ailly, cf. Tschackert, *Peter von Ailly,* Gotha, 1877; L. *Salembier, Petrus de Alliaco,* Lille, 1886; Idem, *Le Découverte de l'Amérique et Pierre d'Ailly,* in *Revue de Lille,* 1892, V, pp. 622 et seq.; Idem, *Le Cardinal Pierre d'Ailly, Chancelier de l'Université de Paris,* Turcoing, Evêque, 1932; R. de Roquebrune, *Le Cardinal d'Ailly, inspirateur de Christophe Colomb,* in *Revue Am. Latine,* Paris, 1931, XXII, pp. 110 et seq.; Edmond Buron, *P. d'Ailly et la Découverte de l'Amérique,* in *Canada Français,* Quebec, XVIII, pp. 657 et seq.; G. E. Nunn, *The Imago Mundi and Columbus,* in *A. H. R.,* Washington, 40, 1935, pp. 646 et seq.

(22) Here is the salient passage of the famous Bull, *Inter Coetera,* of May 4, 1493: « *... fabricando et constituendo unam lineam a Polo Arctico, scilicet septentrione, ad Polum Antarcticum, scilicet meridiem, sive terrae firmae et insulae inventae et inveniendae sint versus Indiam ut versus aliam quamcumque partem, quae linea distet a qualibet insularum, quae vulgariter nuncupantur de los Azorez et Cabo Verde centum leucis versus Occidentem et Meridiem* ». Cf. R. Garnett, *The English Historical Review,* 1897, p. 571; M. Baum, *Die Demarcationslinie Papst Alexanders VI, und ihre Folgen,* Cologne, 1890. On the third and fourth of May, 1493, Pope Alexander signed not one but three acts of great consequence. With the first (May 3), the Pope gave Spain dominion over all the islands or lands Columbus had discovered or would discover, provided they were not already in the possession of another country. The second, of the same date, further clarified this privilege. And the third, of May 4, fixed

for Spain and Portugal the ‹ line of demarcation › we have described. In the Treaty of Tordesillas the line was defined with greater astronomical precision and transferred some 270 leagues to the west.

(23) Cf. CANTÙ, *Storia degli Italiani*, Vol. VIII, Turin, 1876, p. 586.

(24) Cf. EDWARD G. BOURNE, *The History and Determination of the Line of Demarcation Established by Pope Alexander VI, between the Spanish and Portuguese Fields of Discovery and Colonization*, in *American Report of American Historical Association*, Washington, 1891-92, pp. 103-130; JOHN CORDON, *The Bulls Distributing America*, in *American Society of Church History Papers*, New York, 1891, pp. 81 et seq.; J. BECKER, *Diario de la primera partida de la demarcacion de limites entre España y Portugal en America*, in *Real Soc. Geogr. Bul.*, Madrid (72), 1-4, 1920; PAUL GOTTSCHALK, *The Earliest Diplomatic Documents of America: The Papal Bulls of 1493 and the Treaty of Tordesillas Reproduced*, Berlin, 1927; E. STAEDLER, *Die Westindischen Investiture dikte Alexander VI*, in *Niemeyers Zeitschrift für Intern. Recht*, Leipzig, 50, 1935, pp. 315 et seq.

(25) Cf. UZIELLI, *Vita e tempi di Paolo dal Pozzo Toscanelli*, Rome, 1894; Idem, *Bibliografia della polemica concernente Paolo Toscanelli e C. Colombo*, Naples, 1905; VIGNAUD, *Lettre et carte de Toscanelli*, Paris, 1901.

(26) Cf. GALLOIS, *Les géographes allemands de la Renaissance*, Paris, 1900; Idem, *Americ Vespucci et les géographes de St. Dié*, in *Bul. Soc. Geogr. de l'Est*, Nancy, 1900; CAXTON FRAZIER, *The Christening of America*, in *Mentor*, New York, July 1925, pp. 54 et seq.; A. C. BAXTER, *How America Got Its Name*, in *Dalhousie Revue*, Halifax, October 1929, pp. 341 et seq.

(27) The Jesuit father, Joseph Fischer of Feldkirch, found in the library of Prince Waldburg, in Wolfegg Castle, the geographical map drawn by the scientist-priest, Waldseemüller, which had been considered lost.

(28) Cf. AMERICUS VESPUCCI, *Mundus Novus* (Florence, 1503), Boston, 1920; Fr. M. ESTEVES PEREIRA, editor, *Carta de Americo Vespucci*, in *Soc. Geogr. Lisboa Bol.*, October-December 1919, passim; F. W. P. LEHMAN, *A. Vespucci als Kosmograph und Nautiker*, in *Geogr. Zeits*, Leipzig, 1921, XXVII, pp. 145 et seq.; H. LUDIN, *The Naming of America*, in *Americana*, December 1911, VI pp. 1174-76; FRANK ALLABEN, *The Naming of America*, in *Journal American History*, V, III. pp. 335 et seq.; ENRIQUE J. ARCE, *A. Vespucci and America*, in *Inter America*, I, August 1918, pp. 323 et seq.; Idem, *A. Vespucio y el nombre de America*, in *Revue bim. Cubana*, Havana, May 1929, pp. 154 et seq.; Ch. G. HERMANN, *The First Map Bearing the Name America*, in *Records*, III, pp. 14-

23; JOSEPH FISCHER, S.J., *Claudius Clavus, the First Cartographer of America*, in *Records*, VI, pp. 73 et seq.; Idem, *The Four Voyages of Amerigo Vespucci* (transl. M. E. Cosenza); FISCHER-WIESER, *Die Erste Karte mit dem Namen America*; MARKHAM, *Vespucci*; HARISSE, *Americus Vespuccius*; ALBERTO MAGNAGHI, *A. Vespucci*, critical study, new evaluation of the sources and unedited documents of the Vaglienti Codex, Treves, Rome (2 vol.), 1924; THACKER, *The Continent of America: Its Discovery and Baptism; America, a Saint's Name*, in *Ave Maria*, March 21, 1925.

(29) John Cabot (Giovanni Caboto, 1450-98) was actually born in Genoa and from there went to Venice, where his son Sebastian was born. In Montreal, on the monument to the Cabots, there is a bas-relief depicting the landing at Nova Scotia. It shows a dignitary of the expedition, in priestly vestments, blessing the newly discovered country, while John Cabot stands next to him, sailor's cap in one hand, the other pressed to his heart. Cf. R. BIDDLE,, *Memoir of Sebastian Cabot*, London. 1831; H. HARISSE, *Jean et Sebastien Cabot, leur origine et leurs voyages*, Paris, 1882; Idem, *John Cabot, the Discoverer of North America, and Sebastian His Son*, London, 1896; WINSOR, *Cabot Controversies*, Cambridge, 1896; G. PARKER WINSHIP, *John Cabot and the Study of Sources*, in *Annual Report of the American Historical Association*, 1897, pp. 35 et seq.; Idem, *A Cabot Bibliography*, London, 1898; J. B. THACHER, *The Cabotian Discovery*; F. A. OBER, *John and Sebastian Cabot*; BEAZLEY, *John and Sebastian Cabot*, New York, 1898; J. A. WILLIAMSON, *The Voyages of the Cabots and the English Discovery of North America Under Henry VII and VIII*, London, 1929.

(30) Cf. J. DOURO, *Les aventures de Jacques Cartier*, Paris, 1933.

(31) Another monument has been erected to Verazzano in his native town of Greve del Chianti (1913). The manuscript record of Verazzano's voyages was discovered by G. W. Greene in the Magliabeccana of Florence. It contains the letter he wrote to Francis I of France on July 8, 1524. This manuscript was one of the few saved from the fire that destroyed the archives of the Verazzano family during the Siege of Florence. J. G. Gogswell has translated it into English. In this letter -- written so many years before the discovery of the Protestant Hudson -- he picturesquely describes the Hudson area as characterized by « the river flowing between high hills, through which one finds one's way with difficulty to the sea ». He also mentions the first religious service held in this region — one does not know whether by a priest or not — and notes that the savages « followed our acts of devotion with the keenest interest ». After Verazzano a Spanish expedition described the Hudson as « the river of the mountains » and named it after St. Anthony, having entered it on St. Anthony's Day. Eufrosino Ulpius' globe (1542), once the

property of Pope Marcellus II, is now in the Museum of the New York Historical Society. Cf. F. B. DA COSTA, *The Globe of Pope Marcellus II and Its Relation to the Voyage of Verazzano*, in *Records*, III, pp. 24-37. Verazzano's map is in the Museum of the Propaganda Fide in Rome. For Verazzano, cf. H. C. MURPHY, *The Voyage of Verazzano*, 1875; DA COSTA, *Verazzano the Explorer*; BREVOORT, *Verazzano the Navigator*; I. H. INNES, *The Lost Island of Luisa* (now Long Island), in the *New York Historical Association Journal* (I), April 1919, pp. 87 et seq.

(32) Cf. HARRIS, *History of the Early Mission in Western Canada*, Toronto, 1893; THWAITES (editor), *Early Western Travels*, Cleveland, 1906.

(33) Cf. M. KENNY, *America: A Land of Destiny*, in *C. H. R.*, VI (n.s.), p. 444.

(34) Cf. the most recent edition: *The Bay State Psalm Book, Being a Facsimile Reprint of the First Edition, Printed by Stephen Daye at Cambridge in New England in 1640*, Dodd, New York, 1903. (Of the original edition only ten copies are extant.)

(35) Key wanted his hymn sung to the air of *Anacreon in Heaven*, For studies of this question, cf. H. T. HENRY, *The Air of « The Star-Spangled Banner »*, in *Records*, XXIV, pp. 289-334; GRATTAN W. H. FLOOD, *The Air of « The Star-Spangled Banner »: A Reply*, in *Records*, XXV, pages 97-145.

(36) Cf. M. KENNY, *Loc. Cit.*

(37) That the Continental Congress took its inspiration from the Catholic Dryden, poet laureate and one of the most noted political thinkers of his day, may be inferred by the formula with which the assembly adopted the new flag, on June 14, 1777: « Resolved that the Flag of the United States be 13 stripes alternate red and white, that the Union be 13 stars white in a blue field representing a new Constellation ». Cf. also ROLAND M. J. DRIVER, *Old Glory: The True Story*, New York, 1918. Pape offers hypotheses of the possible relation between the American flag and Washington's coat of arms. Cf. T. PAPE, *Washington's Arms and 'Old Glory'*, in *Connoisseur*, London (89), 1932, pp. 179 et seq.; Idem, *The Washington Coat of Arms*, ibidem, pp. 100-107.

(38) C. CARL B. SWISHER, *Roger B. Taney*, New York, c. 1930; JOSEPH GURN, *After 75 Years: Chief Justice Taney*, in *Columbia*, February 1932. The memory of this Catholic magistrate is perpetuated in many monuments. We note the bronze statue (by William H. Rinehart) in front of the Colonial State House at Annapolis, erected by his native State of Maryland on December 10, 1872; another in Baltimore; and a bust of him in the grounds of the Court House at Frederick, Md., erected on Septem-

ber 26, 1931. He is buried at Frederick beside his mother. The preceding year his house was created a national monument — the Taney Home. His wife, Anna Phoebe Key, was the sister of the famous author of *The Star-Spangled Banner.*

(39) Cf. Chr. Colles, *Inland Navigable Communications,* 1808. For material on Colles, cf. RICHARD D. DOYLE, *Christopher Colles (1738-1821), Engineer and Philosopher,* in *Hist. Bul.,* IX, 1931, pp. 46 et seq.

(40) Cf. *I Corinthians,* XIII; 1-7, and *Fioretti di San. Francesco,* Chapter VIII.

(41) Cf. CARLTON J. H. HAYES, cited works: GILBERT J. GARRAGHAN, *Catholic First Things in the United States,* in *Mid-America,* 1939, pp. 110-136, in which the author sets down who was the first priest, where the first Mass was celebrated and who administered the first baptism in each of the 48 States of the Union and the Possessions. Cf. also Th. E. COAKLEY, *The Debt of America to Catholics,* Brooklyn. For Catholic contribution to American progress, cf. J. O'KANE MURRAY, *Leaves of the Catholic Heroes and Heroines of America,* New York, 1880; Idem, *Catholic Pioneers of America,* Philadelphia, 1882; Rev. J. HIGGINS, *Stories of Great Heroes, Discoverers, Explorers and Christianizers of America,* New York, 1919; *The American Catholic Who's Who,* 1911, etc., St. Louis; CHARLES MORRIS, *Heroes of Discovery in America* (2nd ed.), Philadelphia, 1919; H. MEHARD DAVIDSON, *Founders and Builders of Our Nation,* Chicago, 1920; M. F. VALLETTE, *States of Our Union Settled by Catholics,* in *American Catholic Quarterly Review,* July 1918, pp. 353 et seq.; THOMAS E. LAWLER, *Builders of America,* Boston, 1920; C. E. McGUIRE, *Catholic Builders of the Nation,* (5 vol.), Boston, 1923 (this is the arrangement of the five volumes: 1) Catholics in the Formation of the Nation; 2) Catholics in the Social Development of the Nation; 3) Catholics in Science, Industry and Public Service; 4) Catholics in the Liberal Professions; 5) Catholic Contribution to Religion and Education); W. FISH GORDY, *Leaders in Making America,* New York, 1923; Ph. I. FURLONG, *Pioneers and Patriots of America,* New York, 1926; J. A. WILLIAMSON, *Builders of the Empire,* New York, 1926; E. G. CATTERMALE, *Famous Frontiersmen, Pioneers and Scouts: The Romance of American History,* Tarrytown, N. Y., 1926; H. B. HUNTING, *Pioneers of Goodwill,* New York, 1929 (among these is Father Serra); J. WALKER MACSPADDEN, *Pioneer Heroes,* New York, 1929 (among them are La Salle, Iberville, Bienville and Father Juniper Serra); WILLIAM H. J. KENNEDY, *America's Founders and Leaders,* 1928; CLARENCE MANION, *Catholics in Our Country's Story,* 1929; P. W. BROWN, *A Forgotten Heritage: Catholic Beginnings in the United States,* in *Catholic World,* October 1935; E. S. KITE, *Catholic Part in the Making of America (1565-1850),* Philadelphia, 1936.

(1) For the « sun dance », cf. CATLIN, *A Religious Ceremony of the Mandans,* 1867. For the Lenape ceremony, cf. HOCKEWELDER, *Indian Nations of Pennsylvania,* 1867; BRINTON, *The Lenapes and Their Legends,* 1885.

(2) Cf. W. H. PRESCOTT, *History of Ferdinand and Isabella,* 1837; W. T. WALSH, *Isabella of Spain,* 1930, and *Isabella the Crusader,* 1935.

(3) Cf. MONTESINOS, *Informatio in Indorum defensionem.*

(4) Cf. MACNUTT, *Life of Las Casas;* DUTTON, *Bartolomé de Las Casas;* SIR ARTHUR HELPS, *Life of Las Casas,* London, 1883; L. HANKE, *First Social Experiments in America,* Harvard University Press, 1935; LAS CASAS, *Apologetica Historia de las Indias.*

(5) Cf. WILLIAM T. WALSH.

(6) Cf. J. B. BRENNER, *The Explorers of North America,* New York 1933.

(7) PADILLA A. DA VILLA, *Historia de la fundacion y discurso de la provincia de Santiago de Mejico de la Orden de Predicatores,* Madrid, 1596.

(8) Cf. PASTOR, *Storia dei Papi,* Rome, 1925.

(9) Cf. V. F. O'DANIEL, *The Friar Preachers,* 1917; ANNA C. MINOGUE, *Leaves of Dominican History.*

(10) Cf. H. E. BOLTON, *The Epic of Greater America,* in *The American Historical Review,* XXXVIII, p. 452.

(11) Cf. PAULA ALEGRIA, *La Educacion en Mexico,* 1936, p. 275.

(12) Cf. H. HASTINGS, ed., *Ecclesiastical Records of the State of New York,* Albany, 1901, Vol. 1, pp. 49-68.

(13) Cf. H. O'CALLAGHAN, *Colonial History of the State of New York,* Albany, 1856, Vol. 1, p. 340.

(14) Cf. J. T. ADAMS, *The Founding of New England,* p. 14.

(15) Cf. THOMSON, *Great Missionaries,* Edinburgh, 1862; G. CARNE, *Eminent Missionaries,* London, 1839. For other non-Catholic missionaries among the Indians, cf. J. EDWARD, *Life of David Brainerd,* 1749; G. H. LOSKIEL, *History of the Mission of the United Brethren Among the Indians,* 1593-1682, London, 1794; LATROP, *Life of Samuel Kirkland, Missionary to the Indians,* Boston, 1847; THOMAS SHEPARD, *The Clear Sunshine of the Gospel Breaking Forth Upon the Indians of New England,* New York, 1865; S. R. RIGGS, *Tah-Koo Wah-Kan or The Gospel Among the Dakotas,* 1869; E. L. YOUNG, *On the Indian Trail: Stories of Missionary Work Among the Cree and Salteaux Indians,* circa 1897; G. P. O'DWYER, *Puritan and Indian Missions in America,* 1922.

383

(16) Cf. WINSHIP G. PARKER, *The First American Bible*, Boston, 1929.

(17) Cf. SHEA, *The Early Franciscan Missions in This Country*, in *American Catholic Quarterly Review* (VII), 1882, p. 121.

(18) Cf. BEAUVAIS, *Origine et fondation du plus ancien évêché du Nouveau Monde*, Paris, 1878.

(19) Cf. J. G. ICAZBALCETA, *Don Fray Juan de Zumarraga*, Mexico, 1881.

(20) Cf. B. J. CODE, *Dictionary of the American Hierarchy*, New York, 1940, p. 347; DENT, *Perez and Columbus or The Franciscans in America*, Bilbao, 1935.

(21) Cf. FRANCIS BORGIA STECK, *The First School in the United States*, in *The Fortnightly Review*, St. Louis, 38, 1921, p. 3.

(22) Cf. RYAN, *The First Martyrs of North America*, in *The Illinois C. H. R.*, January, 1926, p. 250.

(23) Cf. JOSEPH LE CARON, *Au Roi sur la Nouvelle France*, Paris, 1626. A copy of this work is preserved in the National Library in Paris.

(24) Cf. P. HUGOLIN, *Notes Bibliographiques*. Father Le Clercq, in his *Premier Etablissement de la Foi* (pp. 321-4), tells us that nothing of Father Viel's possessions was salvaged except his hat and some « writings on notebooks of bark », including a journal of the Missions, a dictionary and a work entitled *Souvenirs of the Hurons in French Hands*. These manuscripts are unknown today, and it has never been determined whether or not they are forever lost.

(25) Shea, historian of the first Catholics in North America, translated this work into English and published it in New York in 1881.

(26) Cf. Ch. LE CLERCQ, *Premier Etablissement de la foi*; S. DIRKS, *Histoire littéraire et bibliographique des Pères Mineurs de l'Observance de Saint-François en Belgique et dans les Pays-Bas*, Antwerp, 1885; FREDERICK LANDON, *Lake Huron*, Indianapolis, 1945.

(27) Cf. MARION HABIG, O.F.M., *The Franciscan Père Marquette; A Critical Biography of Father Zenobe Membré, La Salle's Chaplain and Missionary Companion*, New York, 1934.

(28) It should be added that the French priest, Father A. S. Maillard, known as « the Apostle of the Micmacs », perfected this system and composed many works in ideographic manuscripts, published in 1886 by Father Kander, resident in a Capuchin monastery in Nova Scotia. The polyglot Capuchin, Father Pacifique Buisson, published numerous other works in Micmac, Au Pays d'Evangéline, Paris, 1890.

(1) For the Missions and activities of the Recollects in the New World, cf. T. G. SAGARD, *Histoire du Canada et voyages que les Frères Mineurs Recollets ont faits pour la conversion des infidèles*, Paris, 1691; SHEA *The Jesuits, Recollects and the Indians*, New York; ABBOT, *The Adventures of the Chevalier de La Salle and His Companions*, New York, 1875; BEAUBIEN, *Le Sault-au-Recollet*, Montreal, 1898; JONES, *Huronia*, Toronto, 1909; P. HUGOLIN, *Le Père Joseph Denis: Premier Recollet Canadien* (1657-1736), Montreal, 1926. For Father Louis Hennepin, greatest of the Recollects, cf. DIONNE, *Hennepin, ses voyages et oeuvres*, Quebec, 1897; SHEA, *Biography of Hennepin's Works*, New York, 1880.

(2) Cf. ROUVIER, *Trois apôtres de la Nouvelle France: Brebeuf, Jogues, Lallemant*, Lille, 1931; J. STEVENS, *A travers l'épopée Canadienne. Les trois Lallemant*, Louvain, 1931.

(3) Cf. PARKMAN, *Jesuits in North America*, 1862; H. KEPHART, *Captives Among the Indians*, 1862.

(4) It has been said that the narration of Father Bressani's imprisonment is one of the classic documents of the Jesuit *Reports*. Cf. THWAITES, *Jesuit Reports*, Cleveland, 1897.

(5) Cf. WALLACE E. LAMB, *Lake George: Facts and Anecdotes*, Glens Falls, N. Y., 1934. J. J. BIRCH, *The Saint of Wilderness*, New York, 1936.

(6) Cf. H. E. BOLTON, *Rim of Christendom*, New York, 1936, p. 4. For the missions in the Far West, cf. the same author's *The Spanish Borderlands*, New Haven, 1921, and *Spanish Exploration in the Southwest* (1542-1706), New York, 1930.

(7) Cf. J. F. X. O'CONNOR, *The Jesuit Missions in the United States*, New York, 1893; Father F. X. CHARLEVOIX, *Journal of a Voyage to North America*, translated by L. Phelps Kellog, Chicago, 1923; P. E. CHAPPEL, *A History of the Missouri River: Its Discovery by the Jesuit Explorers;* 1911; J. WALSH, *American Jesuits*, New York, 1934.

(8) Cf. T. M. OWEN, *A Bibliography of the Mississippi*, American History Association, Washington, 1899; I. G. SHEA, *Early Voyages Up and Down the Mississippi*, Albany, 1861. Basic reference is, of course, Father Marquette's *Journal*, translated into English by Shea. Dablon rendered a priceless service to his beloved colleague with his *Récit du second voyage et de la mort de Père J. Marquette*, published by R. G. Thwaites in his study, *Explorations of the Jesuit Missionaries in New France* (1619-1791), Cleveland, 1900; Cf. also F. B. STECK, O.F.M., *The Joliet-Marquette Expedition*, Washington, 1927; BRUCKER, *J. Marquette et la découverte de la*

Vallée du Mississippi, Lyon, 1880; C. RONCIÈRE, *Au fin du Mississippi avec le Père Marquette*, Paris 1935.

(9) For De Soto's discovery, cf. ADA MIXON, *De Soto's Route West of the Mississippi River*, in Americana, January, 1918, p. 70; THEODORE MAYNARD, *De Soto and the Conquistadores*, 1930.

(10) Cf. C. LE CLERCQ, *Etablissement de la Foi*, Vol. II, 128-157; HENNEPIN, *Description de la Louisiane*, Paris, 1683; MARION A. HABIG, *Gabriel de la Ribourde, O.F.M., The First Martyr in Illinois*, in Mid-America, October, 1930.

(11) Cf. REUBEN GOLD THWAITES, *The Jesuit « Relations » and Allied Documents*, Cleveland, 1896-1903; EDNA KENTON, *The Jesuit « Relations » and Allied Documents*, New York, 1925; LÉON POULIOT, S.J., *Etudes sur les « Relations » des Jesuites de la Nouvelle France*, (1632-1672). Montreal, 1940.

(12) Cf. *Pourquoi les Relations ont cessé d'être publiées*, in Etudes, 53, 1891, p. 511; W. CORRIGAN, *Propaganda and the Suppression of the Jesuit Relations* in Mid-America, April, 1930, p. 306-310.

(13) Cf. BARNES, *Two Thousand Years of Missions*, Chicago, 1900, p. 379.

(14) Cf. M. BATESON, in *Cambridge Modern History*, 1932, pp. 100-101.

(15) In 1939, out of an estimated 300,000 Indians in the United States, over one-third of them were Catholic. There were Indian missions in 33 dioceses in 21 States and the territory of Alaska, 207 priests and 45 schools with 7,714 pupils. In addition, 70 brothers assisted the priests and taught arts and professions to the Indians.

(16) Cf. WOOLSEY BACON, *The History of American Christianity*, New York, 1897.

(17) Cf. OAKLEY, *America's Debt to the Catholics*, p. 11; English, *Conquest of the Northwest*, Indianapolis, 1896; HOUGHTON L. SEYMOUR, *Our Debt to the Redman*, Boston, 1918.

(18) Cf. D. SARGENT, *Our Land and Our Lady*, New York, 1939, p. 107.

(19) Cf. PATTERSON FR. TAYLOR, *Whitewampum, the story of Kateri Tekakwitha*, New York, 1935; EVAN RICH X., *Bibliography for Kateri Tekakwitha*, in Le Bulletin des Recherches historiques, July-August, 1940; MARIA CECILIA BUEHRLE, *Kateri of the Mohawks*, Bruce Publishing Co., Milwaukee, 1953.

(20) Cf. *Summus Pontificatus*, Encyclical letter " *Function of the State in the Modern World* ", Wash., D. C., N.C.W.C., 1939, p. 34.

NOTE FOR CHAPTER V

(1) A curious book on Washington, written by an Ohio priest, may be seen in Rome at the Casanatense, with this title: Glass Franciscus A. M. OHIENSI, *G. Washingtonii Americae Septemtrionalis Civitatum Foederadatarum Praesidis Primi, Vita latina conscripta*, New York, 1835. Cf. These two works on Washington: RUPERT HUGHES, *George Washington*, New York, 1926; W. J. JOHNSTONE, *How Washington Prayed*, Arlington Press, New York, 1932 (for the counter-argument). For bibliography and for Washington's religion, cf. also J. MARSHALL, *Life of George Washington*, 1804-1807; C. FORD WORTHINGTON, *Writings of George Washington*, 14 vols., 1889-93; WILLIAM JACKSON JOHNSON, *George Washington the Christian*, New York, 1919; CARLTON D. HARRIS, *Was Washington a Christian, or Profane, Irreligious and Wordly-Minded?*, in *Minute Man*, Washington, June 1926, pp. 83 et seq.; G. ASHTON OLDHAM, *Washington, Christian Statesman*, in *Homilectic Review*, New York, February 1926, pp. 144 et seq.; A. J. E., *Washington's Religious Beliefs*, in *Pa. Mag. Hist.*, Philadelphia, July 1928, pp. 282 et seq.; J. C. FITZPATRICK, *George Washington and Religion* in *C. H. R.*, April 1929, pp. 23 et seq.; W. WILSON, *George Washington*; ROSCOE THAYER, *George Washington*, 1922; J. V. NASH, *The Religion and Philosophy of Washington* in *Open Court*, February 1932; J. BUFFINGTON, *An Overlooked Side of George Washington*, Philadelphia, 1933; G. A. KOCH, *Republican Religion: The American Revolution and the Cult of Reason*, New York, 1933; L. C. BARNES, *George Washington and Freedom of Conscience*, in *Journal of Religion*, October 1932; H. M. MORAIS, *Deism in XVIII Century America*, New York, 1934.

(2) Cf. J. H. TATSCH, *Freemasonry in the Thirteen Colonies*, New York, 1929; Idem, *The Facts About George Washington as a Freemason*, New York, 1931; SASCHE, *Washington's Masonic Correspondence*; HAYDEN, *Washington and His Masonic Compeers*; BROCKETT, *Lodge of Washington*.

(3) Cf. His Order of the Day issued in New York in July, 1776. For the public references to God made by Washington in his addresses to the Nation and his proclamations to the Army, cf. *Religious References in the Writings, Addresses and Military Orders of George Washington*, Washington, D. C., 1932.

(4) The complete title is: *Rules of Civility and Decent Behavior in Company and Conversation*. For the essential bibliography of this important subject, cf. J. M. TONER (ed.), *Washington's Rules of Civility and Decent Behavior in Company and Conversation, Copied from the Original*, Washington, 1888; MONCURE D. CONWAY, *George Washington's Rules of Civility Traced to Their Sources and Restored*, 1891; for the story of the original,

CHARLES MOORE, *George Washington's Rules of Civility and Decent Behavior in Company and Conversation*, Boston, 1926.

(5) Cf. Song for the Pope's Day, in William Tudor, *Life of James Otis*, Boston, 1823.

(6) For the so-called « Gunpowder Plot », cf. W. GERARD, *What Was the Gunpowder Plot?*, London, 1897; M. W. JONES, *The Gunpowder Plot*, London, 1909; HAY, *The Jesuits in the Papist Plot*, London. It seems that a survival of this anti-Papal rioting still exists in Portsmouth, New Hampshire, in the « Pope's Night », at least among the children of the town, who race through the streets blowing trumpets and waving pumpkin lanterns cut into fantastic faces. Cf. *Researches*, January 1892, p. 48.

(7) Cf. SPARK, *Washington*, IX, p. 137.

(8) Cf. CHARLES H. METZGER, *The Quebec Act: A Primary Cause of the American Revolution*, New York, 1936 (with rich bibliography of the argument, pp. 213-223); GRIFFIN, *The Anti-Catholic Spirit of the Revolution*, in *Researches*, October 1889, pp. 146-178.

(9) Cf. *American Museum*, I, p. 313.

(10) Cf. *Life and Works of John Adams*, X, p. 398. Here one reads his letter to Thomas Jefferson of July 16, 1814, describing Catholicism as « Platonic, Pythagoric, Hindoo and Cabalistic Christianity ».

(11) Cf. MOORE's *Diary*, Rev. II, p. 176.

(12) Cf. P. GUILDAY, *Life and Times*, etc., I, p. 172; F. J. ZWIERLEIN, *End of No Popery in Continental Congress*, in *Thought*, December 1936, pp. 357-377.

(13) Cf. A. H. YOUNG, *Dr. Charles Inglis in New York* (1766-83), in *Canad. Hist. Ass. Rep.*, Ottawa, 1932, pp. 87 et seq.; J. W. THORNTON, *The Pulpit of the American Revolution*, Boston, 1860; J. T. HEADLEY, *Chaplains and Clergy of the Revolution*, New York, 1864; ARTHUR L. CROSS, *The Anglican Episcopate and the American Revolution*, Durham, N. C., 1928; C. H. VAN TYNE, *Influence of the Clergy and of Religious and Sectarian Forces on the American Revolution*, in *Am. Hist. Review*, XIX, pp. 44-64.

(14) Cf. THOMAS NELSON PAGE, *Washington and Its Romance*, New York, 1923, pp. 148-152.

(15) Cf. T. E. KISSLING, *Charles Carroll, Friend and Supporter of Washington* in *Catholic Action*, February 1932; D. C. LAWLESS, *Catholics Were His (Washington's) Friends*, in *Columbia*, February 1936; M. J. O'BRIEN, *Hercules Mulligan: Confidential Correspondent of General Washington*, New York, 1937; Idem, *G. Washington's Associations With the Irish*, New York 1937; G. CHINARD, *G. Washington As the French Knew Him*, Princeton, 1940.

(¹⁶) Cf. O'BRIEN, *A Hidden Phase of American History*, New York, 1919, passim. Cf. the article, *Ann McCarthy: A Relative of the Mother of George Washington*, in the *Journal of the American Historical Society*, April 1, 1916, pp. 118-121.

(¹⁷) *An Address from the Roman Catholics of America to George Washington, Esq., President of the United States*, Coghland, London, 1790, republished in New York, 1865, in facsimile, with notes by Shea, in limited edition.

— (¹⁸) Cf. STANFORD H. COBB, *The Rise of Religious Liberty in America*, New York, 1902; HERMAN V. AMES, *The Proposed Amendments to the Constitution of the United States During the First Century of Its History*, Vol. II, Washington, 1896; P. LA CHESNAIS, *L'Eglise et les Etats: Trois exemples de Separation - Belgique, Etats Unis, Mexique*, Paris, 1904; AL-PHONSE GOURD, *Le Chartes Coloniales et les Constitutions des Etats-Unis de l'Amérique*, Paris, 1885-1903; L. CALL BARNES, *George Washington and Freedom of Conscience*, in *Journal of Religion*, Chicago, 1932, XII, pp. 493 et seq.; *Selections from Washington's Letters*, Washington, 1932, WILLIAM E. MCCLURE, *Washington and His Relation to the Constitution*, in *Sons of the American Revolution Magazine*, Washington, 1933, XXVII, pp. 224 et seq.; *The Code of the Laws of America*, in *Force*, January 3, 1935, Washington, 1935; WILLARD O'WATERS, *American Laws, Charters and Constitutions of XVII and XVIII Centuries*, San Marino, California, 1936.

(¹⁹) Cf. LEONARD, *Life of Charles Carroll of Carrollton*, 1918, pp. 256 et seq.

(²⁰) Cf. SEMPLE, *Virginia Baptists: Appendix*; GAILLAND HUNT, *James Madison and Religious Liberty*, in *Annual Report of the American Histor-ical Association*, 1901, I, pp. 165 et seq.; Idem, *Madison the Statesman*, in *Constitutional Review*, Washington, January, 1921, pp. 14 et seq. Mad-ison, fourth president of the United States, was baptized and brought up as an Episcopalian. His father was an influential vestryman of that denom-ination, and his cousin, also James Madison, was the first Episcopalian bishop of Virginia. As a boy he was deeply impressed by an incident in Orange, at which both he and his father were present, when he heard some Baptists preaching from the windows of the jail into which they had been thrown for their religious beliefs. From that time on, he hated and fought against religious intolerance, and in 1774 he stated with dis-gust: ‹ This diabolical principle of religious intolerance, which was born in Hell, makes my blood boil ›.

(²¹) Cf. JEFFERSON, *Works*, p. 45, where one finds his *Bill for Estab-lishing Religious Freedom*. Cf. also HOWLINSON, *History of Virginia*,

p. 298; N. Antrim Crawford, *Thomas Jefferson and Religious Freedom,* in *Virginia Journal Educ.,* Richmond, May 1926, pp. 355 et seq.; J. W. Price, *Thomas Jefferson's Statute of Religious Freedom,* in *Virginia State Bar Association Proceedings,* Richmond, 1931, (42), pp. 245 et seq.; Royden J. Mott, *Sources of Jefferson's Ecclesiastical Views,* in *Church History,* New York, 1934, III, pp. 267 et seq.

(22) Cf. Jared Spark, *The Writings of Washington,* XII, p. 202.

(23) John Cotton (1585-1652), the famous theologian and Puritan clergyman of theocratic Boston, who in a well-known controversy with Roger Williams, upheld the right of civil authorities to interfere in religious matters, also declared it was better to organize the State in a way to support the Church than to model the Church according to the needs of the State (*Letter to Lord Say*). It was on this premise, from 1631 onward, that the Puritan Congregationalists of Massachusetts added political rights to those they had as Church members, and they maintained this stand up till 1686. From this sprang the confusion of Church and State, with consequent intolerance toward those who thought differently from the Calvinist Congregationalists. That is why the patriots and legislators sought to a man to avoid falling into the error that set off an uninterrupted chain of religious persecutions in Massachusetts -- against Anne Hutchinson, Roger Williams, Catholics, Quakers, etc.

(24) Cf. *Researches,* October 1894, p. 176.

(25) Cf. *Church News,* Washington, July 29, 1888; T. E. Kissling, *The Pope's Stone for the Washington Monument,* in *Columbia,* February, 1933. Catholic reverence for Washington's tomb was not lessened by such an incident. On October 11, 1912, Msgr. Bonaventura Cerretti, then Auditor of the Apostolic Delegation in Washington, after visiting the President's tomb at Mt. Vernon, wrote in his diary: ‹ It was the first time I visited the house and tomb of the great man. Everyone spoke of the simplicity and austerity of the Father of the United States. The Apostolic Delegate deposited a crown of flowers. The Knights of Columbus did the honors of the house ›. Cf. E. Cerretti, *Il Cardinale Cerretti,* Rome, 1939, p. 155.

(26) Cf. *America Libera,* five odes by V. Alfieri, in *Opere di V. Alfieri,* Paravia, Turin, 1903, III, pp. 36-88.

(27) Cf. Gilbert Chinard, *Houdon in America,* Baltimore, 1930. (Besides the statue of Washington, Houdon also executed a design for an equestrian statue of the President and, by order of the State of Virginia, the bust of Lafayette). Cf. André Michel, *La Statue de Washington par J. A. Houdon,* in *Les Arts,* No. 172, pp. 7 et seq.; William A. Day, *Houdon's Washington,* Baltimore, 1922.

(28) Cf. CARLO BOTTA, *Storia dell'Indipendenza degli Stati Uniti d'A-merica*, 2 vols., Le Monnier, Florence, 1856.

(29) Canova's statue of Washington, ordered for 25,000 pounds by the State of North Carolina for its capital Raleigh, was delivered by the sculptor to American representatives at the beginning of 1820. Shipped from Civitavecchia, aboard the frigate Macedonia, it was unloaded at Wilmington, from where it was brought, in a wagon drawn by 12 pair of oxen, a distance of 50 miles to Raleigh, which welcomed it with great ceremony. Here it was decided to install the statue in the main hall of the State House. At the time a curious controversy arose, for the state architect wanted to protect it from fire by placing it on movable pedestals, so that it could easily be carried to safety. The idea was dismissed as eccentric, which was unfortunate, for 30 years later the roof of the building caught fire in a fierce blaze and collapsed upon the statue, shattering it under a weight of 12 tons. An English repairer, who for 502 pounds had agreed to piece together the fragments of the masterpiece, found the head almost intact, disappeared with it and was never heard of again. To make up as best it could for its loss, the State had another statue of Washington erected in the square outside. The citizens, nevertheless, always grieved for the lost Canova statue, and so in 1908 the Historical Commission of the State asked Italy through diplomatic channels for the right (which was granted) to make a plaster cast of the statue, whose only existing model was preserved in the museum at Possagno. Cf. R. CON-NOR, W. DIGGS, *Canova's Statue of Washington*, in *North Carolina Hist. Comm. Pub.*, Raleigh, 1910, No. 8; SHERMAN FAIRCHILDS, *The Portraits of Washington from Life*, in *Art in America*, New York, April 1930, XVIII, pp. 150 et seq.; MOORE R. WALTON, *General Washington and Houdon*, in *Virginia Hist. Mag.*, Richmond, 1933, (41), pp. 1 et seq.; DAVIS F. WITH-MORE, *George Washington in Sculpture*, Boston, 1933.

(30) Proofs of the admiration and affection felt by Catholics for Washington abound in all nations. Limiting ourselves only to Italy, we may mention the almost confidential esteem that bound Filippo Mazzei to the great man. The Tuscan, before leaving America, went to visit Washington at Mt. Vernon. Washington noted the visit in his diary (16-V-1785) with his usual terseness: « Mr. Mazzei came here to breakfast and went away afterwards ». Cesare Cantù has notably depicted a parallel with Mirabeau in *Vite parallele di Mirabeau e Washington*, Corona e Caimi, Milan, 1867. For documentation, cf. the work assembled and edited by G. Prezzolini, *Italy and the Italians in Washington's Times*, Columbia University Press, New York, 1932.

391

NOTES FOR CHAPTER VI

(1) This document is reproduced in the *Magazine of History* (extra number), n. 176 (Volume 44, n. 4), Tarrytown, N. Y.

(2) The minister was the Rev. Daniel Barber (1756-1834), a soldier of the Revolution, who in 1818 became a Catholic along with several of his sons. Cf. C. H. METZGER, *The Quebec Act: A Primary Cause of the American Revolution*, New York, 1937.

(3) Cf. P. GUILDAY, *Life and Times of John Carroll*, New York, 1922; JAMES WALSH, *Archbishop Carroll*; M. J. GRIFFIN, *Catholics in the American Revolution*, 3 volumes, Philadelphia, 1907-8; F. T. FUREY, *Catholics and the Revolution*, in *Catholic World*, 1897, pp. 495 et seq.; M. O'KANE, *Popular History of the Catholic Church in the United States*, New York, 1876; DURAND, *Documents on the American Revolution,* New York, 1889; FISHER, *The True Story of the American Revolution*, Philadelphia, 1902; McLAUGHLIN, *The Confederation and the Constitution* (1783-1789), New York, 1905; FISHER, *The Struggle for American Independence*, 2 volumes, Philadelphia, 1908; O'BRIEN, *A Hidden Phase of American History: Ireland's Part in America's Struggle for Liberty*, New York, 1919; A. NEVINS, *American States During and After the Revolution*, New York, 1924; J. HALTIGAN, *The Irish in the American Revolution and Their Early Influence in the Colonies*, Washington, 1908; A. BUSHNELL HART, *Race Elements in Washington's Time,* Boston, 1932.

(4) For literature on the hostility to the patriot cause, cf. SALINE, *Biographical Sketches of Loyalists in the American Revolution*, 2 volumes, Boston, 1864; EATON, *The New York Loyalists in Nova Scotia*, in *Grafton Magazine* (II), 1900, pp. 163 et seq.; STARK, *The Loyalists of Massachusetts and the Other Side of the American Revolution*, Boston, 1910; VAN TYNE, *The Loyalists in the American Revolution*, New York, 1902; JONES, *Orderly Book of the Maryland Loyalists Regiment, 1778*, Brooklyn, 1891; FLICK, *Loyalism in New York During the American Revolution*, New York, 1901; L. H. GILSON, *Jared Ingersoll: A Study of American Loyalism in Relation to British Colonial Government*, New Haven, 1920; J. T. VAUGH, *The United Empire Loyalists*, Buffalo, 1926; A. G. BRADLEY, *Colonial Americans in Exile: Founders of British Canada*, New York, 1932. For loyalism on the part of Catholics, cf. M. J. GRIFFIN, *Catholic Loyalists of the Revolution*, in *Researches*, April 1889, pp. 77-88; P. GUILDAY, *Father John McKenna, a Loyalist Catholic Priest*, in *Catholic World*, New York, pp. 21 et seq.

(5) Cf. CAMPBELL, *History of the Friendly Sons of St. Patrick*, Philadelphia, 1892.

(6) Cf. HERMANN J. NEUSER, *The Establishment of the First Vicariate in America*, in *Records* (1896), pp. 141 et seq.

(7) Signers of the Declaration of Independence who were of Irish origin were: Charles Carroll of Carrollton for Maryland; Matthew Thornton and William Whipple for New Hampshire; James Smith and George Taylor for Pennsylvania; Thomas Lynch Jr. and Edward Rutledge for South Carolina; George Meade and Thomas McKean for Delaware; Thomas Nelson Jr. for Virginia; William Hooper for North Carolina; and Philip Livingston for New York.

(8) Cf. THOMAS MAGINNIS, *Irish Contribution to America's Independence*, Philadelphia, 1913; J. E. HASBROUCK, *Some Irish Revolutionary Soldiers*, in *Recorder*, New York, May 1925, pp. 9 et seq.; L. R. FRANK, *Ireland's Important and Heroic Part in America's Revolution*, Chicago, 1924; T. P. PHELAN, *Catholics in Colonial Days*, New York, 1935.

(9) Cf. F. N. THORPE, *Constitutional History of the United States*, II, p. 249; W. F. OBERING, *Our Constitutional Origins*, in *Thought*, December 1937, pp. 587-618; D. C. LAWLESS, *Worthy of Immmortality: Daniel Carroll*, in *Columbia*, June 1934.

(10) Cf. DOWNING, *The American Capitoline Hill*; VARNUM, *Seat of Government of the United States*, Washington, 1854.

(11) Cf. H. J. BRENT, *Biographical Sketch of the Most Rev. John Carroll*, Baltimore, 1843; CAMPBELL, *Life and Times of Archbishop Carroll*, Baltimore, 1860; J. G. SHEA, *Life and Times of the Most Rev. John Carroll*, New York, 1888 (this is the second volume of his classic *History of the Catholic Church in the United States*); BRADLEY, *Life and Times of the Most Rev. John Carroll*; P. GUILDAY, *The Life and Times of John Carroll, Archbishop of Baltimore*, 1922.

(12) Charles Carroll of Carrollton was a great admirer of Franklin. When Franklin died, he proposed that the Senate go into mourning for a month—a motion that was, however, opposed and not passed. In regard to the Franklin-Carroll mission, cf. W. R. RIDELL, *Benjamin Franklin's Mission to Canada and the Causes of Its Failure*, in *Pa. Mag. Hist.*, Philadelphia, April 1924, pp. 111 et seq.; F. P. RENAULT, *La Politique de propagande des Américains durant la guerre de l'indépendence*, Paris, 1925.

(13) Father Farmer's letter is today in the archives of the Quebec archdiocese, Etats Unis, Diocès de Boston et de Philadephie, p. 124.

(14) Cf. GRIFFIN, *Father Lothinière*, in *Records*, XV, 1915, pp. 69-82.

(15) Cf. GRIFFIN, *The Priests of Canada and the American Revolution*, in *Researches* (XX), April 1903, pp. 64 et seq.; CARL WITTKE, *Canadian*

Refugees in the American Revolution, in *Canadian Historical Review*, Toronto, December 1922, pp. 320 et seq.; ABBE A. GOSSELIN, *L'Eglise du Canada après la Conquête*, Quebec, 1917.

([16]) Cf. M. P. KEHOE, *The Carroll Family in Maryland*, in *Am. Irish Hist. Assn. Journal* (IX), pp. 258 et seq.; WILLIAM I. GROVE, *History of Carrollton Manor*, Frederick Md., 1922; J. H. B. LATROBE, *Life of Charles Carroll of Carrollton*, Philadelphia, 1824; T. M. FIELD, *Unpublished Letters of Charles Carroll of Carrollton and of his Father*, New York, 1902; K. M. ROWLAND, *Life of Charles Carroll of Carrollton*, 2 volumes New York, 1897; L. A. LEONARD, *Life of Charles Carroll*, New York, 1918; BYRNE, *Charles Carroll of Carrollton*, Berkeley, Calif., 1919; JOSEPH GURNE, *Charles Carroll of Carrollton*, New York, 1932; W. S. HOLT, *Charles Carroll, Barrister: The Man*, in *Maryland Historical Magazine*, June 1936; C. W. HEATHCOTE, *The Signers of the Declaration of Independence*, Westchester, Pa., 1932. Several counties and towns in America are named after the two Carrolls, in Iowa, Illinois and Ohio. The city of Baltimore erected a monument to Charles Carroll in Carroll Park at the cost of $ 10,000.

([17]) For the education abroad of young Catholics of Colonial America, cf. GUILDAY, *English Catholic Refugees on the Continent*, London, 1914; RICHARD J. PURCELL, *The Education of the Carrolls of Maryland*, in *Cath. Educ. Review* (XXX), Washington, 1932, pp. 586 et seq.

([18]) For this daughter of Carroll's, cf. G. C. KEIDEL, *Mrs. Richard Caton (nee Mary Carroll)*, in *Maryland Historical Magazine*, March 1922, pp. 74 et seq.

([19]) Cf. C. A. BARKER, *The Background of the Revolution in Maryland*, New Haven, 1940.

([20]) Cf. *Leviticus*, XXV: 10.

([21]) Cf. S. HOOD, *Brief Account of the Friendly Sons of St. Patrick*, Philadelphia, 1844; J. CRIMMINS, *St. Patrick's Day*, New York, 1905; M. J. GRIFFIN, *General Stephen Moylan*, Philadelphia.

([22]) Cf. GRIFFIN, *Thomas Fitzsimons*, Philadelphia, 1887; HUNT, *Our American Merchants*, Boston, 1864; A. M. SCHLESINGER, *The Colonial Merchants and the American Revolution*, New York, 1918; T. P. PHELAN, *Thomas Fitzsimons: Patriot, Soldier, Statesman*, in *The Journal of the American-Irish Historical Society* (XXI), 1922, pp. 157-164.

([23]) Cf. ROWE, *Matthew Carey: A Study in American Economic Development*, Baltimore, 1933. The fact that Carey published 49 editions of the King James version of the Bible has led some to assume that he was a Protestant. This is not the case. At his death Carey was attended by the Augustinian Father Moriarty and the Rev. Dr. F. S. Gartland, future Archbishop of Savannah.

(24) Cf. McMASTER, *History of the United States*, II, p. 333. Lloyd is buried in the church of St. Augustine in Philadelphia.

(25) Cf. C. E. GODFREY, *Washington's March to Trenton*, Trenton, 1924; WILLIAM E. PEDRIE, *The Battles of Trenton and Philadelphia as Pictured by Artists*, Trenton, 1925.

(26) Cf. *Athenaeum Magazine*, May 1826.

(27) Cf. FROST, *History of the American Navy*, p. 86.

(28) Cf. M. J. GRIFFIN, *History of Commodore John Barry*, Philadelphia, 1903; WILLIAM B. MEANY, *Commodore John Barry, the Father of the American Navy*, New York, 1911; J. R. BOLANDER, *A Bibliography of Naval Literature in the United States Naval Academy Library*, 3 volumes, Annapolis, 1928; BRYAN HANNON, *Three American Commodores*, New York, 1935.

(29) Cf. F. R. HOLMES, *Battle of Monmouth*, in *Americana*, New York, July 1922, pp. 252 et seq.; H. W. SHOEMAKER, *Some Forgotten Pennsylvania Heroines*, Altoona, Pa., 1922; E. H. HALL, *Margaret Corbin*, New York, 1932.

(30) Cf. MOTT, *Due Process of Law*, p. 136. The precious parchment of the Magna Carta was brought from England to New York in 1939 to be shown at the World's Fair. During the war it was kept beside the Declaration of Independence in the Library of Congress. It was returned to England in 1946.

(31) For the indirect inspiration of St. Thomas Aquinas, cf. EDWARD MURPHY, *St. Thomas' Political Doctrine of Democracy*, Washington, 1920; O'REILLY, *Catholic Origin of Democracy*, in *Essay*, Dublin, VIII, pp. 17 et seq.; J. MOSS IVES, *St. Thomas Aquinas and the Constitution*, in *Thought*, December 1937, pp. 566-586.

(32) Cf. ZWIERLEIN, *Democracy and Bellarmino*, 1933; J. HUSSLEIN, *Democracy: A « Popish Innovation »*, in *America*, July 5, 1919; J. McNAMARA, *Catholicism: the Mother of American Democracy*, in *Truth*, February 1923; LUIS TEIXIDOR, S.J., in *Estudios Ecclesiasticos*, X, April 1931, pp. 161-243.

(33) Cf. JAMES SULLIVAN, *The Antecedents of the Declaration of Independence*, in *Annual Report of the American Historical Association* (1902), I, pp. 67 et seq. Sullivan traces the ideas behind the Declaration of Independence back to Pythagoras and Sophocles, Plato, Aristotle, the Cynics and Epicureans, Polybius and Cicero, passes to the early Christian fathers — St. Ambrose and St. Augustine — and Popes like Nicholas I and Gregory VII, and from them to the mediaeval scholars and theorists (Pier Lombardo, Alessandro d'Ales, St. Bonaventura, St. Thomas) and

later Popes such as Boniface VIII in his struggle against Philip IV. In Nicola Cusano's book, *Concordantia Catholica*, he finds an anticipation of the theory that « since all men are by nature free, it follows that government rests on the consent of the governed ».

(34) Cf. RICHARD W. WOODS, *The Study of the Bible, the Basis of the Declaration of Independence*, Carlisle, Pa., 1910; DAN GILBERT, *The Biblical Basis of the Constitution*, San Diego, 1936.

(35) Having sanctioned the law of 1606, James I defended it in a special book. Under the pseudonym of Matteo Torto, Bellarmino answered it with his *Responsio ad librum inscriptum: Triplici nodo, triplex cuneus*, Cologne, 1608. The royalist Paris Parliament condemned it. In 1609 Bellarmino wrote his *Apologia Bellarmini pro responsione sua ad librum Jacobi, Magnae Britanniae regis* and in 1610 his answer to Barclay on the power of the pope in temporal matters. Cf. DE LA SERVIERE, *De Jacobo I cum Card. R. Bellarmino, S.J., super potestate tum regia tum pontificia disputante (1607-1609)*, Paris, 1900.

(36) Cf. GAILLARD HUNT, *The Virginia Declaration of Rights and Cardinal Bellarmine*, in C.H.R. (1919), III, p. 289; JOHN C. RAGER, *The Bl. Card. Bellarmine's Defense of Popular Government in the Sixteenth Century*, in C.H.R. (1925), pp. 504-514; WILLIAM F. SANDS, *Phases of Relations Between Church and State*, in C.H.R., VIII (n. s.), pp. 143-148; D. S. SHAFF, *The Bellarmine-Jefferson Legend and the Declaration of Independence*, New York, 1927.

(37) The Jefferson collection in the Library of Congress was partially destroyed by fire and it is hence impossible to verify whether it is true that he made marginal notes in his copy of *De Laicis*.

(38) Cf. GAILLARD HUNT, work noted above in (36).

(39) Cf. WILLIAM B. McGROARTY, *The Family Register of Nicholas Tagliaferro* in *William and Mary Quarterly*, Williamsburg, Va., July 1921, pp. 145 et seq.

(40) Cf. CHARLES C. FARRINGTON, *Paul Revere and His Famous Ride*, Bedford, Mass., 1923; A. VAN LEE CARRICK, *The Revolutionary Home of Paul Revere*, in *Country Life*, Garden City, N. Y., December 1920, pp. 63 et seq.; F. S. PIPER, *Lexington, the Birthplace of American Liberty*, Lexington, 1920; ALLEN FRENCH, *The Day of Concord and Lexington*, Boston, 1925; H. E. O'BRIEN, *Paul Revere's Own Story*, Boston, 1929; EMERSON G. TAYLOR, *Paul Revere*, New York, 1930.

(41) Cf. *Works of Thomas Jefferson*, edited by Paul Leicester Ford, New York, 1905, Vol. XII, p. 21; RICHARD C. GARLICK Jr., *Philip Mazzei, Friend of Jefferson: His Life and Letters*, Baltimore, 1934.

(42) Cf. Bruno Roselli, *Vigo*, Stratford Press, New York, 1933.

(43) Published in 1928.

(44) Cf. Bancroft, *History of the United States*, Boston, 1875, X, p. 198. For bibliography of Vigo, in addition to the above-mentioned work by Roselli, cf. Schiavo, *The Italians in Missouri*, New York, 1929, pp. 34-41; H. W. Beckwith, *History of Vigo and Parke Counties*, Chicago, 1880; W. H. English, *The Conquest of the Country Northwest of the Ohio River*, Indianapolis, 1897; H. C. Bradsby, *History of Vigo Country*, Chicago, 1891; Dorothy Ricker, *Francis Vigo, A Member of Father Gibault's Congregation*, in *Indiana Magazine of History*, March 1930; J. Reynolds, *The Pioneer History of Illinois*, Chicago, 1887, p. 191; R. C. B. Thurston, *The Character and Achievement of G. R. Clark*, in *Indiana Historical Bulletin*, Vol. VI, p. 12; R. G. Thwaites, *How George Rogers Clark Won the Northwest*, 1903.

(45) For Father Gibault, cf. J. P. Dunn, *Documents Relating to the French Settlement of Vincennes*, Indianapolis, 1894, Charles and Henry Herbermann, *Very Rev. Pierre Gibault, V. G.*, in *Records*, VI, pp. 130-165.

(46) Father Marquette in his journal comes to the defense of the hard-working merchants who dealt with the Indians: « If the French have made some profit in this country, they deserved it, so difficult was the task of obtaining it ».

(47) About 40 names of Italian soldiers and sailors in the Revolutionary War are listed by A. F. Guidi in *Italy and the Italians in Washington's Time*, New York, 1933.

(48) Cf. Charles A. McCarthy, *The Attitude of Spain to the American Revolution*, 2 volumes, Philadelphia, 1908; J. Walton Caughey, *Bernardo de Galvez in Louisiana*, Berkeley, Calif., 1934; S. G. Coe, *The Mission of William Carmichael to Spain*, Baltimore, 1928.

(49) Cf. Falkenstein, *Kosciusko*, Leipzig, 1827; Chodzko, *Kosciusko*, Paris, 1837; Griffin, *History of Gen. Kosciusko and Gen. Count C. Pulaski*, Philadelphia; M. Haiman, *Poland and the American Revolutionary War*, Chicago, 1932; Monica Gardner, *Kosciusko, A Biography*, London, 1920; C. A. Manning, *Kosciusko et les Etats-Unis*, Paris, 1926.

(50) Cf. Richard H. Spencer, *Pulaski's Legion*, in *Maryland Hist. Mag.*, September 1918,, pp. 214 et seq.; William W. Gordon, *Count Casimir Pulaski*, in *Georgia Historical Quarterly*, Savannah, September 1929, pp. 167 et seq.; V. I. Alski, *Gen. C. Pulaski, the First Chief of American Cavalry*, in *Cavalry Journal*, Washington, May-June 1933, pp. 19 et seq.

(51) Cf. Philip Guedalla, *Fathers of the Revolution*, New York, 1926; Rene Pinon, *Louis XVI, Vergennes et la grande lutte contre l'Angleterre*, in *Rev. Hist. Dipl.*, Paris, January 1929, pp. 37 et seq.; B. Fay, *Bibliogra-*

phie critique des ouvrages français relatifs aux Etats-Unis, Champion, Paris, 1925.

(52) Cf. DE LA GORGE, *Histoire religieuse de la Révolution*, Paris, 1912; W. G. SUMMER, *Financiers and finances of the Revolution*, New York, 1925; A. FLINIAUX, *Quelques précisions sur les dettes des Etats-Unis envers la guerre de l'Indépendence et sur leur remboursement*, Toulouse, 1922.

(53) Cf. ELIZABETH S. KITE, *Extracts from the Diplomatic Correspondence of Conrad. A. Gerard, First Minister Plenipotentiary to the United States*, in *Records* (XXXI), pp. 215 et seq.; D'OMERSSON, *La première mission officielle de la France aux Etats-Unis*, Paris, 1924.

(54) Cf. WILLIAM E. O'DONNELL, *The Chevalier de la Luzerne*, Bruges, 1938; JAMES J. WALSH, *Sketch of the Chevalier de la Luzerne*, in *Records* (XVI), pp. 202-223; S. F. BEMIS, *The Diplomacy of the American Revolution*, New York, 1935.

(55) In the fleet of the Comte d'Estaings there were two Capuchin chaplains — Father Casimir, aboard the Magnifique, and Father Nicolas aboard the Fendant. Nine Capuchin chaplains were with De Grasse, seven with De Guichen, two with the Comte de Ternay. These chaplains, all members of the same Order, represented about a fifth of the total of chaplains in the French services aiding America.

(56) Cf. AURATUS EQUES, *La Chiesa Romana e l'Indipendenza d'America*, in *L'Illustrazione Vaticana*, January 16, 1933.

(57) Cf. C. TOWER, *The Marquis de Lafayette in the American Revolution*, 2 volumes, Philadelphia, 1895; LOUIS PONS, *Lafayette aux Etats-Unis*, Paris, 1918; L. DE ROYAUMONT, *Lafayette et Rochambeau au pays de Washington*, Grenoble, 1919; G. MORGAN, *The True Lafayette*, Philadelphia, 1919; O. ROBERT, *With Lafayette in America*, Boston, 1919; J. S. PENMAN, *Lafayette and Three Revolutions*, Boston, 1929; W. H. BURKE, *Valley Forge and the French Alliance*, Philadelphia, 1928. The renowned Alsatian sculptor Bartholdi, who designed the Statue of Liberty in New York, also designed Lafayette's statue in New York (1873) and the Lafayette-Washington group in Paris (1892). In 1917 the historic castle in which Lafayette was born was acquired by the French Heroes Fund, an American organization, to be restored and preserved as a museum dedicated to Franco-American amity.

(58) Cf. Rochambeau's own memoirs; also Wright, *Memories of Rochambeau Relative to the War of Independence*, 1938; J. E. WEELEN, *Rochambeau, Father and Son*, New York, 1936. In the manuscript collection of the Library of Congress are preserved Rochambeau's military correspondence, in five volumes; his letters in nine volumes, and an additional volume containing his *Histoire de l'origine et progrès de la guerre* (1763-1780) and his *Mémoire de la guerre en Amérique en* 1780.

(59) Cf. Correspondence of General Washington and Comte de Grasse, August 7 - November 4, 1781, in the manuscript section of the Library of Congress. Also, cf. M. CHARON, *L'Amiral de Grasse*, Tequi, Paris, 1919; T. BALCH, *The French in America During the War of Independence*, 2 volumes, Philadelphia, 1891-5; J. J. JUSSERAND, *The French and the American Independence*, New York, 1918; J. MERLANT, *La France et la guerre de l'Indépendence américaine*, Alcan, Paris, 1918; HENRY D'YVIGNAC, *Les Bretons et l'Indépendence américaine*, Paris, 1920; KITE, *Beaumarchais and the War of American Independence*, 2 volumes, Boston, 1918; J. B. PERKINS, *France in the American Revolution*, New York, 1911; E. S. CORWIN, *French Policy and the American Alliance of 1778*, Princeton, 1916; DE LA GORGE, *Histoire religieuse de la Révolution*, Paris, 1912; R. DE LOTURE, *Washington, nous voici! La France au cours de l'Indépendence américaine*, Hachette, Paris, 1934; A. LASSERAY, *Les Français sous les treize étoiles*, 2 volumes, Macon, 1935.

(60) Cf. CHARLES N. LINCOLN, *Naval Records of the American Revolution*, Washington, 1906; MERLANT-COLEMAN, *Soldiers and Sailors of France in the American War of Independence*, New York, 1920; SCOTT BROWN, *De Grasse and Yorktown*, Paris, 1931.

(61) Cf. M. B. DOWNING, *Washington's Associate at Yorktown (Rochambeau)*, in *Catholic World* (110), October 1919, pp. 99 et seq.; A. ANTHIAUME, *Le Comte de Grasse et la prise de Yorktown*, in *Mer et Colonies*, Paris, January 1924, pp. 2 et seq.; BARTON, *How Catholic Help Won Yorktown*, in *America*, October 17, 1931.

(62) The church where the Congressmen went was the Lutheran Church of Zion.

(63) Four Catholic ceremonies took place during the war in St. Mary's Church, Philadelphia at which Congressmen were officially present — (1) a Requiem Mass for the French engineer, General du Coudray; (2) a *Te Deum*, on July, 4, 1779, arranged by M. Gerard, first minister of France, to commemorate the anniversary of American independence, at which the preacher was the eloquent Father Seraphin Bandol; (3) a Requiem Mass for Don Juan de Miralles, Spanish diplomatic envoy who died at Morristown. N. J., during a visit to General Washington; and (4) the solemn Mass and *Te Deum* celebrating the victory of Yorktown.

(64) The Library of Congress preserves a copy of the royal instructions to the Bishop of Nancy for this *Te Deum*.

(65) Washington's letter is preserved in the archives of the Baltimore Cathedral.

(66) Cf. J. J. MENG, *Franco-American Diplomacy and the Treaty of Paris*, in *Records* (44), 1933, pp. 193 et seq.

399

NOTES FOR CHAPTER VII

(1) For the background of the triple line of ecclesiastical rule exercised in the New World by Spain, France and England, cf. WALSH, *The Origin of Ecclesiastical Jurisdiction in New Spain* (1492-1545), in *Records*, 1931, pp. 101 et seq.; J. A. ROBERTSON, *Notes on Early Church Government in Spanish Florida*, in *C.H.R.* (XVII), 1931, pp. 151 et seq.; DAVID W. PARKER, *Guide to the Materials for United States History in Canadian Archives*, Washington, D. C., 1913; WILLIAM RENWICK RIDDELL, *The First British Bishop of Quebec and the Catholics of Kaskaskia*, in *Ill. State Hist. Soc. Journal*, Springfield, XXIII, July 1930, pp. 205 et seq.; G. J. GARRIGAN, *The Ecclesiastical Rule of Old Quebec in Mid-America*, in *C.H.R.* (XIX), 1933, pp. 17 et seq. (researches for the years 1641-1794); IVANHOE CARON, *Msgr. Joseph Octave Plessis, Archevêque de Quebec, et les premiers evêques Catholiques des Etats-Unis*, in *Royal Soc. Canad. Proceed.*, Ottawa, third series, XXVIII, 1934, I, pp. 119 et seq.; W. M. BRADY, *Annals of the Catholic Hierarchy in England and Scotland*, London, 1885; BURTON, *Life and Times of Bishop Challoner* (2 vols.), London, 1909; W. R. CORRIGAN, *Die Kongregation der Propaganda Fide in ihre Tätigkeit in Nordamerika in XVII Jahr.*, Joergen, Munich, 1928; WILLIAM H. J. KENNEDY (co-author), *Old World Foundations of the United States*, 1927; LEGER, *Gifts of the Old World*, 1932.

(2) Cf. ABBÉ MAGNARD, *The Studies and Teachings of the Society of Jesus at the Time of its Suppression* (translation), Baltimore, 1885. The diary of Father Carroll's trip to Italy is contained in his biography by Daniel Brent (Baltimore, 1843).

(3) Cf. F. WAITE ARMSTRONG, *Historic Rock Creek Parish*, Washington, D. C. 1951.

(4) Cf. MENG, *Le Comte de Vergennes: European Phases of his American Diplomacy*, 1774-1780, Washington, D. C. 1932.

(5) Cf. the letters of Francois, Marquis de Barbé-Marbois, during his residence in the United States as secretary of the French Legation translated by E. P. Chase, New York, 1929.

(6) Cf. E. S. KITE, *Appointment of Bishop Carroll of Baltimore*, in *Records*, March, 1928 (XXXIX), pp. 45-51; idem, *The Establishment of the American Hierarchy: Diplomatic Sidelights*, in *Ecclesiastical Review*, November, 1932.

(7) Cf. JULES A. BAISNÉE, *France and the Establishment of the American Catholic Hierarchy: The Myth of French Interference*, Baltimore, 1934.

(8) Cardinal Antonelli wrote to Father Carroll that his nomination would be welcomed by many members of the Republic and « particularly by Mr. Franklin, the eminent personage who represents the Republic at the court of the Most Christian King ».

(9) For the interesting document referring to the establishment of the American hierarchy, found by Prof. Charles Russell Fish in the Vatican archives, cf. *Rivista Storica Americana* (XV), with the original French, Italian and Latin textes. Cf. also *A Short Account of the Establishment of the New See of Baltimore in Maryland, and of Consecrating R. R. Dr. J. Carroll First Bishop Thereof on the Feast of Assumption*, 1790, reprinted in Philadelphia in 1791 and published again in *Researches*, October 1890, pp. 161-175.

(10) Cf. JAMES WALSH in *The American*, VI, p. 71.

(11) Cf. NAGOT, *Mémoires pour servir à l'histoire de l'Eglise à la fin du XIX siècle*.

(12) Cf. W. J. HOWLETT, *The Very Rev. Stephen Th. Badin, Proto-Priest of the United States*, in *Records*, IX, pp. 101 et seq.

. (13) Cf. GOSSELIN, *Vie de Emery*, II, p. 104; J. W. RUANE, *The Beginning of the Society of St. Sulpice in the United States*, Washington, 1935.

(14) Cf. M. F. FOLEY, *Very Rev. A. L. Magnien, S. S., D. D.* in *Catholic World* (76), March 1903, pp. 814 et seq.

(15) The reestablishment of the Company of Jesus — after Pius VII with his Bull, *Catholicae Fidei* (1801), had annulled Clement XIV's Brief, *Dominus ac Redemptor noster* of July 21, 1773, suppressing it — took place with the Bull *Sollicitudo omnium Ecclesiarum* of Pius VII (August 7, 1814), 41 years after the suppression.

(16) Every year in January Catholic University honors the memory of Msgr. Carroll by celebrating « Founder's Day ».

(17) In the same year Carroll was made Administrator of the dioceses of Louisiana and the two Floridas.

(18) Cf. GUILDAY, *Life and Times of John Carroll, Archbishop of Baltimore*, 1922.

(19) In the third volume of the *Collectio Lacensis* is the text of all the North American Councils till the year 1869: *Acta et Decreta sacrorum Conciliorum quae ab Episcopis Americae Sept. et Imperii Britannici ab anno 1785 ad ann. 1865 celebrata sunt*. Cf. PETER GUILDAY, *A History of the Councils of Baltimore*, 1791-1884, New York, 1932; idem, *The National Pastorals of the American Hierarchy*, 1792-1919, Washington, 1923; J. D. M. BARRET, *Comparative Study of the Councils of Baltimore and the Code of Canon Law*, Washington, 1932.

(20) Cf. J. J. WALSH, *Our American Cardinals*, New York, 1926.

(21) Up until 1945 there were six papal delegates, all Italians and Archbishops: Francesco Satolli (1893-96), Sebastiano Martinelli (1896-1902), Diomede Falconi (1902-1911), G. V. Bonzano (1911-22), Pietro Fumasoni-Biondi (1922-33), and, in 1933, Amleto Cicognani.

(22) Cf. GUILDAY, *Four Early Ecclesiastical Observers in America*, in *Ecclesiastical Review*, September 1931.

(23) Cf. D. C. SHEARER, *Pontificia Americana: A Documentary History of the Catholic Church in the United States* (1784-1884) Washington, 1933; THOMAS NOLAN, *The Historical Geography of the Catholic Church in the United States* (1789-1931), Catholic University, Washington, 1932; S. M. BONIFACE, *Establishment of the Catholic Hierarchy in the United States*, in *Records*, December 1936; J. B. CODE, *Dictionary of the American Hierarchy*, New York, 1940 (with bibliography).

NOTES FOR CHAPTER VIII

(1) A large part of the diplomatic correspondence, most of it consular, between the Holy See and the United States is preserved in the Vatican archives.

(2) Robert Cushman, apart from securing the Mayflower for the Pilgrims' initial voyage to America, also preached the first sermon ever published in the New World. *On the Sin and Danger of Self-Love.*

(3) Cf. WADE H. MASON: *The Writings of Margaret Fuller*, 1941. This spiritual woman, prevented by sudden death from conversion to Catholicism, attempted to reconcile in her thinking the intellectualism of New England with her attraction for the true faith.

(4) Apart from his diplomatic duties, this Consul wrote a history of Amerigo Vespucci and an introduction to the Italian edition of Bancroft's history of the United States. Moreover, he translated Macchiavelli, D'Azeglio and Alfieri into English.

(5) His correspondence, of exceptional importance, is to be found in the archives in Washington. Cf. STOCK, L. F.: *United States Ministers to the Papal States*, Washington, 1933.

(6) During those turbulent times, the American Consular Agent in Rome, Nicholas Browne, was obliged to quit his post for having provoked

incidents against the French troops, for « having taken the part of the Republicans » and for « American anti-Catholic tendencies ». He was substituted by William Carroll Sanders on May 29, 1849.

(7) Rufus King served briefly, from April 16 to August 6, 1861, as Brigadier General of the Volunteer Corps in the Civil Guard.

(8) Cf. STOCK, L. N.: *United States Ministers to the Papal States.*

(9) Many rumors circulated to explain the abolition of the Legation. King was repeatedly obliged to deny the report that the Pope had given orders to the effect that the Legation chapel would be tolerated only beyond the walls of Rome, which in fact applied to the English and Scottish chapels, where Protestant rites were practised. The American diplomatic mission fully exonerated the Holy See. It was also said that the Legation was abolished for reasons of economy, also to pave the way for future American recognition of the New Kingdom of Italy. A more illuminating precedent, however, can be found in a letter written in 1862 at the dictation, it appears, of President Lincoln by Secretary of State W. H. Seward to Randall, United States Minister to the Holy See, when an initial attempt was made to break off diplomatic relations. « This Government », the letter ran, « does not have now nor has seldom had any special reason, either commercial or political, to attribute particular importance to a Minister to Rome. Let it be remembered that until recently, the United States never had a representative to that ancient and interesting Capital. The first colonists of this country were for the most part Protestants, who did not recognize the authority of the Pope. To the contrary, they were determined to do everything possible to prevent the Pope from using his political influence through some ecclesiastical authority in this Country, towards harming the liberty and autonomy of this Continent ». The American Minister wrote strongly-worded messages on the Pope to those in the United States who were thus badly misinformed.

(10) Cf. MARRARO, HOWARD R.: *American Opinion on the Unification of Italy,* New York, 1932; Feyertag, Sister Loretta Clare: *American Opinion on the Diplomatic Relations Between the United States and the Papal States* (1847-67), Washington, 1933.

(11) Some Civil War documents, the original manuscripts of which are kept in the Library of Congress, contain letters from Pius IX to Archbishop Hughes (1852); from President Davis to Pius IX (September 23, 1863); and from Piux IX to President Davis (December 3, 1863).

(12) Cf. SHEA: *Life and Pontificate of Pius IX,* New York; O'REILLY: *Life of Pius IX,* New York.

(13) In a letter dated February 2, 1904, to Bellamy Storer, Archbishop

Ireland wrote that Governor Taft « felt the keenest pleasure in recalling his trip to Rome » and that he was proud to be considered *persona grata* at the Vatican.

(14) Cf. FURREY: *Leo XIII*, New York.

(15) Cf. HOGAN, A.J.: *Economic Recovery in the Light of Catholic Principles*, New York, 1933.

(16) Cf. RYAN, J. H.: *The Encyclicals of Pius XI, 1927*; SHUSTER, G. N.: *Pope Pius XI and American Public Opinion.*

(17) Until 1930, Myron C. Taylor often vacationed in Florence at his Villa Schifanoia, which he subsequently donated to the Italian Government, and thus had many opportunities to meet Cardinal Pacelli personally. A lawyer and financier of wide renown, Mr. Taylor was named Chairman of the Board of the United States Steel Corporation in 1935. As patron of the arts and philanthropist, he has served as Vice-President of the New York Metropolitan Museum of Art; patron of the Metropolitan Opera of New York; administrator of the New York Public Library, the American Academy in Rome and Cornell University and President of American Relief for Italy, Inc. He also toiled intensively to provide relief for war-stricken Italians and to improve the living conditions of the poor. To cite an example, in October, 1944, when the destruction wrought by the German armies left the Pontina and Valle del Lirì sectors in grave danger of a malaria epidemic, Ambassador Taylor generously donated 1,250,000 units of atabrine to be distributed among the inhabitants. The benefits he bestowed in his civil and philanthropic capacities are incalculable.

NOTES FOR CHAPTER IX

(1) An acute theologian, Father Kolhmann, during the third centenary of Luther's « 95 Theses » in 1817, published a caustic booklet on the Reformation called *A Compatriot of Luther*. In 1821 he confuted the deism of Jared Sparks, Channing and other Unitarians with a two-volume work, *Unitarianism Philosophically and Theologically Examined*. In Rome, as instructor at the Gregoriana, he had as his pupils the future Leo XIII and Cardinal Cullen.

(2) The law inserted into the Statutes of New York on December 10, 1828 says explicitly: « No minister of the gospel or priest of any denomi-

nation whatsoever shall be allowed to disclose any confession made to him in his professional character in the course of discipline enjoined by the rules or practices of such denomination ».

(3) Cf. J. BRUCE, *A Collection of the Constitutions of Thirteen United States of North America*, Philadelphia, 1783.

(4) Cf. RAY ALLEN BILLINGTON, *Tentative Bibliography of Anti Catholic Propaganda in the United States* (1800-1860), in *C. H. R.* (XVIII), 1933, pp. 492-513.

(5) Cf. GEORGE LIVERMORE, *The Origin and Character of the New England Primer*, New York, 1915; PERRY MILLER, *The New England Mind: The Seventeenth Century*, New York, 1939; Sister LEONORE FELL, *The Foundations of Nativism in American Textbooks*, Washington, 1940.

(6) Cf. H. R. BRUCE, *American Parties and Politics*, New York, 1927; R. MAURY, *The Wars of the Godly*, New York, 1928; M. WILLIAMS, *The Shadow of the Pope*, New York, 1932; G. MYERS, *History of Bigotry in the United States*, New York, 1943; WARREN SIDNEY, *American Free Thought* (1860-1914), New York, 1943.

(7) Cf. MERTON COULTER, *William G. Brownlow: Fighting Parson of the Southern Highlands*, Chapel Hill, 1937. One of Brownlow's macabre fantasies was his estimate that 68,000,000 persons had been killed by the Catholics and if each of these contained four gallons of blood in his veins the amount of blood shed by these martyrs would be sufficient to flood the banks of the Mississippi and destroy the sugar and cotton plantations of Mississippi and Louisiana.

(8) Here are some typical titles of books influenced by the *Awful Disclosures* of Maria Monk; THEODORE DWIGHT, *Open Convents, Or Nunneries and Popish Seminaries Dangerous to the Morals and Degrading to the Character of a Republican Community*, New York, 1836; JOSEPHINE M. BUNKLEY, *The Testimony of an Escaped Novice from the Sisterhood of St. Joseph, Emmitsburg, Maryland*, Harper, New York, 1856; Rev. HIRAM MATTISON, *The Abduction of Mary Ann Smith by the Roman Catholics, and Her Imprisonment in a Nunnery for Becoming a Protestant*, Jersey City, 1868; ELIZA RICHARDSON, *Personal Experience of Roman Catholicism, with Incidents of Convent Life*, Philadelphia, 1869; EDITH O'GORMAN, *Convent Life Unveiled, or Six Years a Nun*, Hartford, Conn., 1871.

(9) Cf. Msgr. FENWICK, *Letter on the Destruction of the Ursulines' Convent of Charlestown, Mass.*, in *Records*, IX, pp. 187 et seq.

(10) Cf. RAY ALLEN BILLINGTON, *The Protestant Crusade: A Study*

of the Origins of American Nativism, Macmillan, New York, 1938; Sister MARY ST. HENRY, *Nativism in America,* Philadelphia, 1936.

(11) Cf. S. L. DAVIS, *Authentic History: Ku Klux Klan* (1865-1877), New York, 1924; BETHEL ROMINE, *A Story of the Original Ku Klux Klan,* Pulaski, Tenn., 1924.

(12) Cf. FRY, *Modern Ku Klux Klan,* Boston, 1922; J. H. GILLIS, *The Ku Klux Klan,* New York, 1922; J. M. MACKLIN, *The Ku Klux Klan: A Study in the American Mind,* New York, 1924; L. A. CURRY, *The Ku Klux Klan Under the Searchlight,* 1924.

NOTES FOR CHAPTER X

(1) Cf. I Peter, III, 15.

(2) Cf. BOWERS, CLAUDE E.: *Jefferson and Hamilton,* p. 264.

(3) Cf. TRACY, I. J.: *Tributes of Protestant Writers to the Truth and Beauty of Catholicity.*

(4) Sf. SHEA: *Defenders of Our Faith;* GORMAN, R.: *Catholic Apologetical Literature in the United States,* Washington, Catholic Univ., 1940.

(5) This periodical changed titles many times. After four months, Msgr. Fenwick called it *The Catholic Intelligencer,* but shortly afterwards reverted to the original title. On December 27, 1834, it was renamed *The Irish and Catholic Sentinel,* in 1835 *The Catholic Literary Sentinel,* in 1836 *The Boston Pilot* and finally in 1837 *The Pilot.*

(6) McGILL, JOHN: *The True Church Indicated to the Inquirer* (1862); *Our Faith, Our Victory: or a Comprehensive View of the Principal Doctrines of the Christian Religion* (1865).

(7) Cf. BROWNSON: *Native Americanism* (1845-46).

(8) Cf. HALL, CHARLES D.: *Patriotism and National Defense,* New York, 1885; RICHARDS: *A Loyal Life: The Catholic Movement in the United States,* St. Louis, 1913.

(9) Cf. DE TOCQUEVILLE: *Democracy in America,* New York, 1900, I., p. 304.

(10) On January 27, 1832, he was made Cavalier of the Holy Roman Empire by Pope Gregory XVI for his literary output and *Eques auratae Lateranensis Comes Palatinus.*

(11) Cf. SPALDING: *Dissertation on the American Civil War,* 1863.

(^{12}) Cf. MACARTENEY, C. E.: *Lincoln and His Generals*, Phila., 1925.

(^{13}) Cf. BACHE, R. M.: *Life of General G. C. Meade*, Philadelphia, 1897; PENNY-PACKER, J. R.: *General Meade*, New York, 1901; MEADE, GORDON G.: *With Meade at Gettysburg*, Philadelphia, 1930. Four statues commemorate the heroism of General Meade: on the battlefield at Gettysburg, Pa.; in Fairmount Park, Philadelphia; at the Soldier's Memorial; and in Botanical Gardens in Washington, D. C.

(^{14}) Cf. FORCE, M. E.: *General Sherman*, 1899; LIDDEL HART, B. H.: *Sherman, The Genius of the Civil War*, London, 1929.

(^{15}) General Sherman's correspondence is kept in the manuscript collection of the Library of Congress. There are 54 portfolios of sketches of his letters (1853-88) in addition to 69 volumes of his letters (1862-86). Much of his Civil War correspondence has been destroyed by fire. Cf. *Personal Memoirs of P. Sheridan, General of the United States Army* (two vols), New York, 1888; NEWHALL: *With General Sheridan in Lee's Last Campaign*, 1866; DAVIES, H. E.: *General Sheridan*, New York, 1895; SHOTWELL, W. G.: *The Civil War in America* (two vols.), 1923; WILSON R. E.: *Lee, An Interpretation*, 1924; WOODWARD, W. E.: *Meet General Grant*, 1928; HERGESHEIMER, J.: *Sheridan: A Military Narrative*, New York, 1931.

(^{16}) Cf. MOHR, E. A.: *Peace Organization During the Civil War*, in « *Social Studies* », December, 1940.

(^{17}) Cf. ADAMS, C. F.: *The Trent Affair: An Historical Retrospect*, Boston, 1912; ANDREWS, R. M.: *Archbishop Hughes and the Civil War*, Chicago, 1935.

(^{18}) Cf. HOLBROOK, F. F.: *Minnesota in the Spanish-American War and the Philippine Insurrection*, St. Paul, 1923, pp. 3-4.

(^{19}) Cf. CHADWICK, F. E.: *Relations of the United States and Spain*, New York, 1911; LODGE, H. C.: *The War with Spain*, 1899; MILLIS, WALTER: *The Martial Spirit*, 1931.

(^{20}) Cf. Handbook of the National Catholic War Council, published by the authority of the Administrative Committee of Bishops, Washington, 1918; WILLIAM, M.: *American Catholics in the War*, New York, Macmillan, 1921.

(^{21}) Cf. EGAN-KENNEDY: *Knights of Columbus in Peace and War*, New York, 1920.

(^{22}) Cf. WARING, G. J.: *United States Catholic Chaplains in the World*

War, New York, 1924; GERMAIN, A. H.: *Catholic Military and Naval Chaplains* (1776-1917), Washington, 1929.

(23) Cf. FLICK, ELLA M. E.: *Chaplain Duffy of the 69th Regiment*, New York, 1935.

NOTE FOR CHAPTER XI

(1) Cf. I. J. LAUX, in the « Nat. Encyclop. » (Collier), New York, 1934, VIII, 518.

(2) Cf. FARRAND MAX, *The Development of the United States from Colonies to a World Power*, Boston, 1918; Th. M. Marshall. BOLTON H. E., *The Colonization of North America* (1492-1783), New York, 1920; HARLOW R. V., *The Growth of the United States*, New York, 1925; SAVAGE SISTER M. LUCIDA: *A Statistical Survey of the Church in the United States* (1841), in « Records », September 1927, pp. 193 ss.

(3) Cf. *The Catholic Mind.*, vol. XXII, 9, May, 6, 1924.

Cf. ALLEN SINCLAIR WILL: *Vie du Card. Gibbons*, Paris, 1925, page 14.

(5) Cf. M. WILLIAMS, *American Catholics in the War*, p. 50.

(6) Cf. DUVAL, *Le Catholicisme en Amerique. Le caractère religieux de l'Amerique*, in « Le Correspondant » (Paris), 75, August 10, 1868, p. 547.

(7) Cf. F. BRUNETIÈRE, *Le Catholicisme aux Etats-Unis*, in « Revue des deux Mondes », November 1, 1898.

(8) Cf. U. S. Census of Religious, I, p. 123.

(9) Cf. I. J. LAUX., in « Nat Encyclop. » (Collier). New York, 1934, VIII, 517.